COLLECTING ACROSS CULTURES

THE EARLY MODERN AMERICAS
Peter C. Mancall, Series Editor

Volumes in the series explore neglected aspects of early
modern history in the western hemisphere.
Interdisciplinary in character, and with a special emphasis
on the Atlantic World from 1450 to 1850, the series is
published in partnership with the USC-Huntington Early
Modern Studies Institute.

COLLECTING ACROSS CULTURES

—⚭—

MATERIAL EXCHANGES
IN THE EARLY MODERN ATLANTIC WORLD

EDITED BY

Daniela Bleichmar AND Peter C. Mancall

PENN

University of Pennsylvania Press

Philadelphia

The editors thank the USC College of Letters, Arts, and Sciences and the Mellon Foundation for financial support for this volume.

Published by
University of Pennsylvania Press
Philadelphia, Pennsylvania 19104-4112
www.upenn.edu/pennpress

Printed in the United States of America on acid-free paper

1 3 5 7 9 10 8 6 4 2

Library of Congress Cataloging-in-Publication Data
Collecting across cultures : material exchanges in the early Atlantic world / edited by Daniela Bleichmar and Peter C. Mancall.
   p. cm.
  Includes bibliographical references and index.
  ISBN 978-0-8122-4305-5 (hardcover : alk. paper)
  1. Material culture—Collectors and collecting. 2. Antiquities—Collectors and collecting. 3. Preservation of materials. 4. First contact of aboriginal peoples with Westerners—History. 5. Commerce—History—Atlantic Ocean. 6. Atlantic Ocean Region—Exchange—History. I. Bleichmar, Daniela, 1973– II. Mancall, Peter C.
GN406.C65 2011
930.1—dc22
                                              2010023073

COLLECTING ACROSS CULTURES

CONTENTS

—ɷ—

III. COLLECTING PEOPLE

IV. EUROPEAN COLLECTIONS OF AMERICANA IN
THE EIGHTEENTH AND NINETEENTH CENTURIES

ILLUSTRATIONS

Color Plates (follow p. 174)

FOREWORD

—⁓—

Malcolm Baker

The publication of *Collecting Across Cultures* marks a significant moment within the history of collecting as it has developed as a distinctive discipline over the previous quarter century. But what of its lineage? The generally acknowledged starting point for this area of study was Julius von Schlosser's *Die Kunst- und Wunderkammern der Spätrenaisssance*, published in 1908, with its analysis of that astonishing range of material that made up the "Cabinet of Curiosity." After that, however, the most innovative work on collecting was concerned largely with art collecting, led by Francis Haskell with his *Patrons and Painters: A Study in the Relations Between Italian Art and Society in the Age of the Baroque* (1963) and *Rediscoveries in Art: Some Aspects of Taste, Fashion, and Collecting in England and France* (1976). In 1983, however, a groundbreaking conference was organized at the Ashmolean Museum in Oxford to commemorate the tercentenary of the institution's foundation. As a member of that audience, I remember vividly how, through a succession of papers about the amassing in many different places of objects as diverse as shells, *Kleinplastik*, scientific instruments, and fossils, the collection was once more revealed to be made up of much more than works of art. Of course, these papers did not grow out of nothing and pioneering work on the breadth of specific collections had already been done by, among others, Lina Bolzoni on Francesco de Medici's *studiolo*, Krzystof Pomian's studies of Parisian and Venetian collectors, and Thomas DaCosta Kaufmann on Rudolf II's *Kunstkammer*. Around the same time, Stephen Bann's influential book, *The Clothing of Clio: A Study of the Representation of History in Nineteenth-Century Britain and France* (1984), exploring the rhetorical models employed by early public museums, opened other interpretative possibilities, while the research for Paula Findlen's equally important *Possessing Nature: Museums, Collecting, and Scientific Culture in Early Modern Italy* (1994) was already well advanced. But the Ashmolean conference was a turning point. Out of this event came not only the proceedings, edited by Arthur MacGregor and Oliver Impey as *The Origin of Museums* (1985), but also the first issue of the new *Journal of the History of Collections* (1989), which gave this emergent discipline a periodical that established its identity and legitimacy.

Since then, the history of collecting has moved center stage, as it were. Collecting and the collection have become prisms through which we perceive the shifting valencies of meaning, the social life of things, and the gendering of the material world, to mention but a few of the preoccupations of those working within the humanities and the historical disciplines. Already implicit in the 1983 Oxford conference, the history of collecting has been understood to be, above all else, an interdisciplinary activity. An important part of its appeal and a prime reason for its centrality are the way it not only requires but also provides a structure for the crossing of customary disciplinary boundaries.

So far, so familiar. But what of *Collecting Across Cultures* and what of the future of the history of collecting? If the most striking feature of the 1983 Oxford conference was its reestablishment of a sense of the totality of collections, the present volume takes this further by going global. By making the movement of objects across continents and cultures its principal theme, *Collecting Across Cultures* reorients the subject and allows us to recognize a new dynamic at work. If *The Origin of Museums* established the history of collecting as a major field of study, *Collecting Across Cultures* registers how, twenty-five years or so later, it has come of age.

MALCOLM BAKER

COLLECTING ACROSS CULTURES

Introduction

Soon after Hernán Cortés arrived in Mexico in 1519, he recognized that he had entered a world very different from the one he had known in Spain. Like Christopher Columbus and other Europeans who had arrived in the Americas after 1492, Cortés knew it was important to record what he saw. In his case, he wrote a series of letters to King Charles V, the sponsor of his mission. In the course of that report, he mentioned that he had had a tour of some of Emperor Moctezuma's many properties in the great city of Tenochtitlan. One in particular struck him: a menagerie filled with birds and mammals, one more incredible than the next. The conquistador might not have realized it, but back in Europe, Pope Leo X had also assembled a group of beasts, which he housed at the Vatican. One of his most treasured creatures was an elephant, whose entry into Rome had been such a sensation that thousands of people flocked to see its transit into the home of the Church.[1]

The Holy See and the man who would soon fall victim to the unholy conqueror of Mexico shared more than a love of animals. The creatures in their dwellings were not pets in the modern sense of the word. They were specimens in living collections, brought together in an age when peoples across the Atlantic basin—and far beyond—avidly tried to amass and display physical objects or their visual representations. Well aware of the importance of collections and of the special interest that New World objects held for European viewers, Cortés sent gold and silver artifacts, gems, and striking featherwork back to Spain. These American collectibles, which impressed Charles and audiences throughout Europe, served as material evidence to demonstrate the Spanish king's authority, as well as Cortés's work on behalf of his patron. Soon, New World objects stood or hung side by side with artifacts from Asia, Africa, and the Old World in European cabinets of curiosities. Those who spent endless energies and vast fortunes to bring exotica into rooms or cages acted out the acquisitive impulses that lay at the heart of what one historian aptly called "the age of mutual discovery."[2] They also initiated a process that would permanently alter global cultures.

The modern museum has its roots in the early modern era. Between the sixteenth and the eighteenth century, it grew from its origins as the *Wunderkammer* or "cabinet of curiosities," the private possession of an individual (most often a wealthy elite owner), toward a public institution. The rise of the collection in the early modern age reflected some of the central developments of the period: the rediscovery of classical antiquity and the discovery of the New World; European exploration and colonial expansion; global exchanges through trade, colonization, and missionary activity; the political and religious reorganization of Europe; and the redefinition and reinvention of the identity of both science and art, as well as the relationship between the two. To study the history of early modern collecting is to engage with the larger historical questions and narratives of the period.

Early modern collecting was closely related to the cross-cultural travels of people and things. Since the mid-fourteenth century, more people had traveled farther than ever before, and they typically returned home with stories to tell about distant lands and at least some of the wares they acquired there. Elites eagerly tried to gain possession of the most dramatic or remarkable goods. Yet as the passion for collecting rippled across many lands, there was no single individual or group who determined what all collections might contain. Many Europeans played crucial roles, especially those who sponsored collecting missions. But there were Native American collectors too, and Asian and African, and all of them sought to acquire and often display the rarities that their power or wealth enabled them to acquire. African princes traded captured members of other African groups so they could get the newest kinds of cloth produced in Europe. Goods from the Old World changed hands repeatedly in the Western Hemisphere when one group after another tried to gain access to novel items. Chinese porcelain had a prized place in European palaces as well as humbler homes, and its arrival led not only to the birth of the European porcelain industry in the eighteenth century but also to the development of new types of blue-and-white ceramics in Europe and the Americas. The court in Java marveled at the goods brought through its halls. The Siamese greeted the arrival of European material objects with joy. Native Americans sought colored glass beads made in Europe, often trading them to other groups. Items crossed cultures, gaining new value and meanings in the process. Human beings—living Africans, the skeletons of Americans—found their way into collections too, suggesting that their bodies were as worthy of contemplation and study as the alligator suspended in the Portal of the Lizard in the cathedral in Seville or the Brazilian capybaras featured so prominently in Dutch paintings. Exoticism and its many meanings collided with the scholarly and religious impulses of the European Renaissance and the Enlightenment.

The act of collecting could have aesthetic, religious, scientific, political, and social resonances. The birth and rapid expansion of print made it possible for collectors to explain the value and meaning of exotic goods to a wide audience. In the eighteenth century, European naturalists often used the language of Linnaean systematics to communicate their findings in a standardized fashion. Collectors thus played a crucial role in the development of science because they provided the raw materials to allow those in cabinets, libraries, pharmacies, and courts to create both specimens and categories of meaning, which could be used to compare different specimens of *naturalia*. Artists used new techniques to communicate visually what they and their audiences had not seen before. Many also endowed the act of collecting with religious significance: every new object found for a collection was yet further proof of the infinite diversity of God's creation. Collectors gathered the world around them and also helped shape it.

Early modern collectors responded to the cultural impulses of their time. So have modern scholars. The study of collecting, collectors, and collections was for generations a minor and less glamorous subdivision of the study of art, concerned primarily with questions of connoisseurship and authenticity. But for the past twenty-five years, art historians and historians have taken more seriously the importance of studying not only *what* was in a collection but *how* and *why* a collection came into existence in the first place. When Oliver Impey and Arthur MacGregor published their landmark anthology *The Origins of Museums* in 1985, they helped establish a new field of study, solidified four years later with the creation of the *Journal of the History of Collections*.[3] Since then, innovative scholarship has demonstrated the importance and interpretive richness of collections in the early modern period.

The history of early modern collections has focused, to a large extent, on the cabinets of curiosities as the earliest incarnations of what later became institutionalized museums; on the practices of collecting in their social and political context; and on the participation of a wide cast of characters, from princes to apothecaries and merchants, in the cultures of collecting.[4] These studies have alerted readers to the seemingly limitless acquisitive practices of early modern Europeans, who sought to collect the Earth's products in a room. They gathered artworks, antiquities, maps, books and prints, relics, shells, desiccated plants and reptiles, unusual inventions, preserved animals, curious stones, and much else, transforming their cabinets into models of the larger world. The uses of collections were as rich as their holdings. Princes used their cabinets to demonstrate their wealth, connections, and might. Apothecaries, physicians, and naturalists viewed collecting as a way of making knowledge and creating social relationships in the republic of letters, establishing networks to exchange both things and facts.

To date, the scholarship on early modern collecting has focused almost exclusively on European spaces and figures. Historians have for the most part paid scant attention to collectors outside Europe, to the circulation of goods across cultures and vast geographical spaces, or to the ways in which collecting and collections helped shape conceptions of other cultures in the first truly global era. The chapters in this volume attempt to push the analytical framework farther through a focus on collecting across cultures in the early modern period, considering evolving collecting practices across the Atlantic basin—even across the entire world. The practices and experiences of collecting in the early modern age were diverse and varied. This volume reveals the myriad ways that the desire to acquire, display, and study new objects can be best understood through a cross-cultural lens. Contributors here make clear that the desire to acquire and display wares was not a European passion alone and that it often involved cross-cultural contact. While not all peoples developed equivalents of the cabinet of curiosity, many nonetheless thought about the expanded range of goods that the increase in long-distance travel made possible. Here the peoples of the non-European parts of the world often acted just as acquisitively as Europeans. Curiosity about other places, peoples, and their objects and the desire to display the rare or the remarkable reached around the world.

The chapters contained here suggest the range of collections and collecting practices that could be found across the Atlantic basin—and in places where Europeans traveled in Asia. Daniela Bleichmar's chapter focuses on the meaning of exotica in early modern collections, emphasizing the imprecision and mutability of definitions and understanding from one locale to the next. As she reveals, a single object could be considered "Indian," "Chinese," "Mexican," or Japanese" at different times. She draws on case studies from the seventeenth century, including a little-known collection belonging to Vincencio Juan de Lastanosa—a Spanish collector, scholar, editor, and patron—as well as very well-known depictions of cabinets belonging to Ferdinando Cospi, Ferrante Imperato, Ole Worm, Manfredo Settala, and Francesco Calzolari. As she argues, meaning resided not in the objects themselves but in their interpretations. A visit to a cabinet meant coming into contact with the collector (or perhaps his or her heir), who provided guidance to the objects on display and a narrative that infused them with particular meanings. The visit itself became part of the process of understanding the contents, especially when the visitor, as was common, told others about what they had seen.

Benjamin Schmidt takes up the theme of exoticism at greater length in his chapter on the parasol. As he reveals, from 1670 to 1730, Europeans became fascinated with the huge increase of exotic materials within their reach. Dutch

printers capitalized on the commercial opportunities afforded by this new interest, flooding the market with a torrent of literary, cartographic, and visual
depictions of the wider world. The abundance of materials, avidly collected and
broadly circulated, encouraged what might be called a "transmedia effect": the
liberal recycling, strategic borrowing, and subtle replication of images and
motifs, which distilled the non-European world into a form that has come to
be associated with the catch-all category of "exoticism." Exotica could be found
in printed images, ceramics, wallpaper, and theater stage sets and costumes.
Schmidt argues that close examination of these materials demonstrates how
European representations of the world and its goods could become clichéd or
stereotyped and ultimately codified as exotic icons. Yet such representations
could also shift in meaning as they moved across media and from one part of
the world to another. Some symbols of the exotic became icons. Allegories of
America, for example, could be found in multiple media and moved from one
audience to another; specific images traveled in what he calls "iconic circuits."
Hence, representations of the parasol appeared on paper and on porcelain, in
two and three dimensions, as symbols for seemingly every culture in the world.
It was ubiquitous, which should have undermined its exotic value. But wherever
it appeared, it always came packaged as a kind of exotica loaded with specific
cultural interpretations. The parasol did not have a single meaning; what it
meant shifted from place to place and over time. The instability of its meanings
becomes the essence of the story. The parasol became to Europeans a symbol
of Asia, Africa, or America—an early global commodity whose essence
depended on the proclivities not of the object itself but on those who collected
and displayed it.

The value of studying the parasol derives from observing it in different contexts and tracing its specific meanings. But collecting practices can also be
understood as manifestations of particular cultures. Juan Pimentel and José
Ramón Marcaida examine still life paintings from seventeenth-century Spain in
an effort to understand the relationship between art and science. As they reveal,
Spaniards embraced both the emerging discipline of experimental science and
the cross-European aesthetic movement known as the baroque, which intended
to dazzle the eye through often lavish display, notably in painting and architecture. Earlier scholars have suggested that the goals of the naturalist and of the
artist were often in conflict in Spain at the time. Yet Pimentel and Marcaida
offer a very different argument. Artists, they contend, often did the work necessary for the advancement of science. Still life paintings, which flourished in this
era, enabled naturalists to further their pursuits. The collector played a pivotal
role here, serving as the intermediary between the artist and the naturalist. The
obsession that still life painters had for common objects such as insects and

bones assisted naturalists who studied them—in large part by preserving them and thus giving them objects (the physical paintings) to which they could return time and again. When painters turned their attention to flowers, they brought naturalists directly into the botanical garden, one of the early modern era's most important kinds of collection. By examining how still life paintings could be collected and displayed, then, we can understand that science and art were not antagonistic foes but rather tools to be used by the curious to explain nature.

European painters and naturalists worked on common ground when they were dealing with familiar objects. But the boom in acquiring meant confronting new kinds of objects, all needing to be interpreted when they entered collections. The issues could be especially vexing when travelers returned home with products made from precious materials. Soon after the conquest of Mexico, Hernán Cortés shipped the first cargos of gold, silver, gems, and feather treasure to Europe. They were a gift from the conquistador to Charles V, and they had the desired effect: once the haul reached Spain, the king and his court marveled at the Mexican goods. Their reception reflected then-prevailing ideas not only about treasure but also about royal regalia. Carina Johnson's chapter explores the twinned fates that awaited these transported treasures. Spaniards saved some objects as exemplars of royal Mexican regalia; displaying them symbolized the Spanish conquest over a distant ruler. Charles V recognized their value and distributed some of the objects to his Habsburg relatives to show them the significance of his efforts in the Western Hemisphere. His was an act of boasting and celebration by a Christian king whose triumphs had become known across Europe. But at the same time that Cortés vanquished Moctezuma, the Protestant Reformation had begun to spread across much of central and northern Europe. By the 1530s, the development of this alternative kind of Christianity posed a threat to the Iberian ruler. To respond to the challenge, he looked again at his Mexican treasure. Cortés, Charles, and his brother Ferdinand had once understood that the Aztec regalia served as a symbol of the Christian triumph over an idolatrous king and human-sacrificing priests. Now that ideologies of reformed Christianity condemned the notion that even once-sacred regalia should be preserved, Catholic leaders saw the Aztec horde in a more utilitarian way. They melted the idols because they wanted gold, thereby destroying the meaning they once conveyed. But they did not consign all the Aztec treasure into the flames. The Habsburgs kept the intricate featherwork that Cortés had sent. These marvels dazzled Europeans, who realized that there was nothing to be gained from destroying them like a golden idol. They understood too that they could continue to import featherwork once Mexican craftsman had been converted to Christianity because their feather images would be cleansed of idolatrous imagery. Spanish bishops employed Aztec featherwork in devotional

DANIELA BLEICHMAR AND PETER C. MANCALL

ceremonies for the Virgin Mary and all the saints alike. As Johnson tellingly reveals, feather objects once again became inalienable for the Catholic clerics and princes who possessed them, admired as Christian rather than Aztec sacral material objects.

Featherwork fit into European categories of the "exotic," but an object did not need to be so unusual to be prized. Among the goods that could be found in collections were manuscripts, many of them intended to provide visual clues about distant places. At times, travelers or missionaries created the manuscripts, as was the case with the Capuchin friars who went to central Africa from the mid-seventeenth to the mid-eighteenth century. As Cécile Fromont reveals in her analysis here, the Capuchins who took up residence in the Portuguese colony of Angola and in the Kingdom of Kongo described natural phenomena, such as flora and fauna, as well as local customs (and even the challenges facing the missionaries themselves). Like European missionaries in the Americas and Asia, they wrote home to provide other clerics with information to facilitate later encounters on the mission field. They were especially careful to depict central African idols, which often looked abstract to European eyes and thus could fail to be recognized as sacrilegious religious artifacts. They did so not out of some sense that later missionaries should appreciate the aesthetics of indigenous cultures but instead to facilitate the eradication of local religious practices. But not all manuscripts arriving in early modern Europe had the same function. As Robert Batchelor notes in his chapter, Javanese palm-leaf manuscripts entered British collections in the seventeenth century. Taken together, they provide insights into Malay, Sundanese, and Javanese societies. They too depicted objects and peoples, though in a less obviously evangelical context. His chapter serves as a stark reminder that collecting practices in the early modern world were global; cultural impulses that proliferated in the Atlantic basin resonated far away.

Sarah Benson too focuses on wide areas of exchange, though she inverts the dominant geographical paradigm in the history of collecting by describing collecting practices in Southeast Asia. Near the end of the reign of Phra Narai, who served as king from 1656 to 1688, the Siamese sent a diplomatic mission to the court of Louis XIV, king of France. It turns out that the Siamese monarch, like members of royal families in Europe, became an eager collector. His interests focused on European technology, especially scientific and optical instruments. His collection included telescopes, spyglasses, spectacles, mirrors, orreries, and globes representing both the earth and the heavens.

There is no doubt that collecting was a global phenomenon in the early modern era. The obsessions of collectors were most evident in the encounter between the Old World and the New. After the first voyage of Columbus, many

Europeans in particular became fascinated with obtaining all things American. At times, that meant indigenous peoples. Peter Mancall's chapter here traces an arc in the European collection of American bodies, beginning with late fifteenth- and sixteenth-century efforts to bring live specimens across the Atlantic, part of the desire to understand indigenous peoples and cultures in order to facilitate their conversion to European ways (notably Christianity). The human body needed to be known so that the human residing in it could be civilized. Over time, Europeans and Euro-Americans focused on creating visual depictions of Indians—especially in the nineteenth century, when many Euro-Americans believed they were about to vanish from the earth. But painting pictures of indigenous peoples did not end the desire to collect their bodies, as the experience of the naturalist Samuel George Morton (1799–1851) revealed when he collected thousands of skulls, excavated from indigenous graves. Trevor Burnard's contribution also focuses on American bodies, though in a more abstract sense. He uses Jamaican inventories produced between 1674 and 1784 to reveal that slaveholders looked on their bound African and Afro-Caribbean laborers much in the way that Europeans gazed on physical objects in their cabinets. His reading of journals, letters, and inventories suggests that these documents served like written corollaries to *Wunderkammer*. Markings on these pages reveal an entire value system, including the fact that African slaves, like exotic goods, were commodities in a trans-Atlantic market. Slave lists served functions similar to manuscripts written on palm leaves or illustrations from central Africa: they became objects conveying meaning of distant places and peoples.

The remaining chapters focus on European interest in collecting Americana. The diversity to be found in this section mirrors the cross-continental drive to understand the Western Hemisphere. Europeans, it should be noted, had interests in the world beyond their continent long before 1492. At least 200 manuscript copies of the *Travels* of the fourteenth-century English knight John Mandeville have survived in a dozen languages, and the extensive *Natural History* written by Pliny the Elder in the first century C.E. was enormously influential. Each of these works, like others, testified to earlier European interest in what and who could be found elsewhere.

The growth of regular shipping across the Atlantic in the generations following 1492 made it possible for new reports to come into Europe. Soon enough, printers sensed a wide audience for them and began to produce accounts in ever larger numbers of editions. Returning travelers also brought objects with them, as well as tales of distant populations. They brought pictures too, or imaginative artists created illustrations based on what they read. Books, objects, and pictures all went into collections, usually with the goal of edifying the owner. As Alain Schnapp reveals in his contribution here, the arriving catalog of landscapes encouraged European antiquarians to compare the pasts of the Old World and the New. There was no single response to the novel materials. Some British antiquarians, for example, saw parallels between Native Americans and ancient Britons and Picts, an association reinforced in such vital works as the Flemish engraver Theodor de Bry's edition of the English traveler Thomas Harriot's *Briefe and True Report of the New Found Land of Virginia*, published in Frankfurt in 1590. Britons thought about their own conquest of Wales, Scotland, and Ireland and drew on information about Americans to make judgments about more local situations. In Spain and New Spain alike, antiquarians looked at the mounting evidence very differently. They came to understand that the Western scriptural tradition could no longer stand as the sole means of establishing history. Fascination with lessons extracted from America survived for generations. By the early eighteenth century, history on both sides of the Atlantic could be written by taking new paths in the collection of material, nonclassical texts, hieroglyphs, drawings, monuments, and oral traditions.

In the final section, Paz Cabello Carro's chapter turns attention away from antiquarians and back toward collectors, specifically the people who acquired materials from New Spain. Her survey of late eighteenth-century Spanish collections has two purposes. On the one hand, she matches extant objects in modern museums to inventories and textual descriptions that survive from when artifacts arrived. On the other hand, her research emphasizes the importance of the Royal Cabinet of Natural History, established in Madrid in 1771. As she demonstrates, monarchical authorities provided instructions to Spaniards in the field specifying what and how to collect and also funded multiple expeditions throughout the empire. Explorers brought back crucial evidence and artifacts from archaeological excavations in Peru and in the Mayan city of Palenque, as well as objects gathered during scientific expeditions to South America, the Pacific Northwest, Alaska, and the Pacific.

Throughout the Hispanic world, collectors sought to fulfill Madrid's request for information and goods from every corner of the empire. Baltasar Jaime Martínez Compañón, bishop of the Peruvian intendancy of Trujillo from 1779 to 1791, assembled during the 1780s an extensive collection that included pre-Columbian art and artifacts. Lisa Trever and Joanne Pillsbury reveal how the cleric sent thousands of objects to Madrid for Charles III's recently inaugurated Natural History Cabinet; he also oversaw the creation of a paper museum, a series of over 1,400 watercolor illustrations by local artists who systematically depicted nearly every aspect of the natural and social worlds of Trujillo.

Pascal Riviale extends our analysis of cross-cultural collecting into the nineteenth century, revealing how the practices of collectors played a central role in the development of the disciplines of anthropology and archaeology. At the time, scholars argued that the acquisition of information and objects meant the entire world could be studied and classified. Many focused their attention on the Americas because they realized that artifacts and images that had arrived in Europe from earlier collectors revealed cultures very different from Europe itself. Riviale uses anthropologists' and archaeologists' inquiries into Spanish America in order to draw conclusions about larger cultural phenomena.

Megan O'Neil also shows how early modern collecting practices had an afterlife in the nineteenth century. Her chapter discusses two nineteenth-century photographic albums assembled by Frenchmen in Mexico between the 1860s and the 1880s. Just like the printing press proved central to the depiction and collection of the wider world in the early modern period, the new medium of photography allowed these two French travelers to capture Mexico in albums, another type of paper museum. But the process was not simple. As she reveals, collectors' memories had as much of an impact on their albums as the materials they had at hand. The artifact that survives in the archive can tell as much about the collector as about the collection.

As the chapters in this volume attest, early modern collecting meant much more than the accumulation and display of unusual or rare items. Naturalists assembled and visited cabinets to gather basic knowledge about the world. Painters crafted careful images of *naturalia* to show off their talents and contribute to the spread of information. Objects in collections taught cultural lessons—about the unfamiliar ways of a distant people and their crafts, for example, or the possible profits to be made from establishing trade in new areas.

Objects taught religious lessons too. In 1607, the English naturalist Edward Topsell published a massive volume entitled *The Historie of Foure-Footed Beastes*. It was, and remains, an extraordinary book, totaling more than 750 folio pages. Topsell was not responsible for compiling all the details that the reader could find there. He was very aware that he was following in the intellectual footsteps of the Swiss polymath Conrad Gesner, who in the mid-sixteenth century had put together his own large book on the world's nonhuman creatures. (That project succeeded, unlike Gesner's planned bibliography of every book ever written.) Topsell's main task was to translate the work into English and to incorporate any information that had come to Europe, primarily as a result of increased long-distance travel and trade with the Americas and East Asia. One mark of the transnational dimension of the work could be found in a series of lists at the end of the book "of all the Beastes contained in this Hystory, in divers

Languages." He presented species names—and the pages where information on them could be found—in Greek, Latin, Italian, Spanish, French, German, and Illyrian. These lists did not in fact contain the names of every creature in the book but nonetheless testified to the expanse of his (or Gesner's) abilities. Knowledge, obtainable via observation, crossed boundaries.

At the start of the volume, Topsell laid out his reasons for constructing what was, in a very real sense, a collection—in this case, a collection of documents and testimonies, including illustrations, bound into a single book. The book was needed, he informed his patron Richard Neile, the dean of Westminster, because God had recognized that learning was as important as life itself. "As an Interpretor in a strange Country is necessary for a traveler that is ignorant of Language (or else he should perish)," he wrote, "so is knowledge and learning to [us] poore Pilgrims in this our Perigrination, out of Paradice, unto Para-dice[.]" Life itself was a journey in search for fulfillment, intellectual and spiritual, but it was necessary to know how to interpret what one experienced. Only through the accumulation of knowledge would people be able to break away from the confusion of "BABELS tongues"—the world's many dialects, which prevented peoples from understanding one another—so that they could together build the new Jerusalem.[5]

Topsell believed he could advance this grand dream by presenting knowl-edge about all the "beasts" of the world. He included long chapters on animals familiar to Europeans, such as horses, pigs, and deer and also less common creatures that had special attributes, such as the beaver, the satyr, and the sphinx. Everything had meaning, but every bit of nature needed to be collected and displayed before it could be understood.

PART I

━ⅲ━

COLLECTING AND THE CONSTRUCTION
OF KNOWLEDGE IN THE
EARLY MODERN WORLD

—⚏—

CHAPTER 1

Seeing the World in a Room: Looking at Exotica in Early Modern Collections

Daniela Bleichmar

The Elusive Object

The large collection compiled by Vincencio Juan de Lastanosa (1607–81) in his residence in Huesca, a city in the Spanish region of Aragon, included an impressive range of objects.[1] Lastanosa, a minor nobleman interested in antiquities, coins, and the arts, is best remembered today for his patronage of the celebrated writer Baltazar Gracián (1601–58). Lastanosa's collection attests to his interest in fashioning a cultivated identity and in presenting his palace as a site of civility and sociability. A visitor to the palace would encounter the collection distributed among many rooms. It included *naturalia* and *artificialia* and all sorts of objects prized as wonders, curiosities, and rarities. Lastanosa owned antiquities such as bronzes, marbles, and coins and medals (on which he authored a treatise); a significant collection of books; mathematical and optical instruments; works of fine craftsmanship such as maps, prints, paintings, fine tapestries and decorative hangings, sculptures, and carvings; exotic objects from distant lands; and rich furnishings, from the cabinets used to house the collection to luxurious chairs, tables, and beds (a major status-signifier in early modern homes).[2] The sense of plenty and luxury was amplified by the large number of mirrors—flat, convex, concave—that hung throughout the house reflecting and repeating the collection, turning each room into a spectacular kaleidoscope.

We know about the items in this collection through several accounts from the mid-1600s, written in various genres. An exaltation in verse by the Aragonese lawyer and writer Juan Francisco Andrés de Uztarroz, published in Zaragoza in 1647, provides a description of Lastanosa's collection of antiquities and gardens. A manuscript inventory in prose by the same author, dated ca. 1650, covers much of the same ground, describing the Lastanosa residence room by room, as well as the garden. An anonymous manuscript from around 1662 provides the account (*relación*) of an encounter—real or imaginary—between Lastanosa and a visitor to the palace, taking the reader on a virtual tour of the collection. Finally, an unsigned manuscript inventory of the library, dated ca. 1640–62, lists not only the books that Lastanosa owned but also many other objects that were kept in that same room.[3] The existence of four different accounts of the same collection is rather uncommon and allows us to examine the various ways in which objects could be described at the time.

These documents attest to the presence in the collection of many objects characterized as "exotica," that is, marked by their distant origin in non-European lands.[4] Lastanosa owned exquisite stones used by "Indians" as medical remedies; a shell in the shape of a boat (probably a Nautilus shell), which was carved with "men, birds, and plants from China"; a sculpture of a black man's head in jet—like the shell, exotic both in terms of the material and the subject; two Chinese chests with mother-of-pearl and gilt inlay; and three New World "idols," among other items.[5] It is not particularly surprising that Lastanosa owned exotica, nor that he owned these specific objects. Collectors at the time held such items in high regard, as their presence in inventories, catalogues, and still life painting attests. Indeed, it would have been a surprise *not* to find them in such a magnificent collection. However, it is far from obvious what role these objects played for Lastanosa, for other collectors, and for contemporary viewers of this or other collections. Much has been made of the early modern cabinet as "a world of wonders in one's closet shut."[6] However, this rather general sentiment has not been investigated to parse out the ways in which collections expressed and constructed ideas about the larger world in the early modern period, during which the known world expanded and became increasingly interconnected through global trade and colonialism. What did seventeenth-century collectors and viewers in Europe make of objects from distant lands?

This essay examines the framing of exotic objects in Lastanosa's and other contemporary collections as a launching pad for exploring questions about display, viewing practices, and the notion of collections as both spaces and narratives. I also reflect on questions of methodology, examining the historical questions we can ask of objects, texts, and images. I argue that objects in early modern collections cannot be understood in isolation from one another, although this is precisely the approach encouraged by the two textual genres associated with collections, the catalogue and the inventory. Instead, I argue for the need of thinking of collections as spaces that constructed narratives through strategies of display and the protocols of the visit, guiding visitors into highly specific viewings.[7] Rather than thinking of collections as accumulations of objects, I suggest that we view them as spaces for displaying and looking at objects.

While, as far as I know, no exotic objects from Lastanosa's collection have come down to us, we do have a drawing of one of them that was created at the time (Figure 1.1). It depicts a carved ivory olifant, seen in profile. The image is accompanied by two inscriptions providing information about the object, written in different hands. At the top of the page, a legend identifies the item as an "ivory horn that is in the antiquities of Vincencio Lastanosa in the year 1635." Curving alongside the image, a second inscription notes, "Ivory horn measures in length a *resma* less than a *vara* it is in one piece." This double inscription identifies the artifact as a horn, as well as its size (roughly 80 cm. or 33 in.) and the material out of which it is made. It also tells us something about its craftsmanship, the fact that it was carved out of a single piece of ivory rather than assembled from multiple smaller pieces. More important to my discussion, the text frames the object as a collectible, indicating who owned it, a moment in time when it formed part of that collection, and the category to which it belonged: that of antiquities—not, as we might think, exotica.

The issue of categories is significant for the historian trying to establish what this object was understood to be in the seventeenth century. The question turns out to be harder to answer than one might initially think, and the more information we have to inscribe the object within the collection, paradoxically, the more elusive it gets. Uztarroz described this artifact ca. 1650 as: "Another [horn] in ivory almost a *vara* in length, from a Japanese King, two thirds striated and the last [third] covered in scales; it ends with a caiman head that grabs with its mouth the head of a king."[8] He identifies two kings, one depicted in the object, the other its former owner. The item is similarly, if more succinctly, explained in the *Relación* of 1662: "An ivory horn almost a *vara* in length from a Japanese King."[9] These two statements confirm the function, material, and size of the artifact and introduce a new and very interesting piece of information, one that does not have to do with the physical aspect of the artifact or with its present existence within Lastanosa's collection: the object came from Japan, where it belonged to a king. With this additional information, an object considered an antiquity becomes instead, or rather additionally, exotica. For the two are not mutually exclusive categories. Seventeenth-century antiquarians and collectors extended their interest in classical antiquity to a comparative evaluation of artifacts from different cultures, so that the spectrum of human cultural variability accommodated distance in time as well as distance in space. Perhaps the best-known example of this type of approach is the Jesuit polymath Athanasius Kircher, with his interests in Greco-Roman, Egyptian, Chinese, and New World cultures, but other collectors shared this attitude.[10]

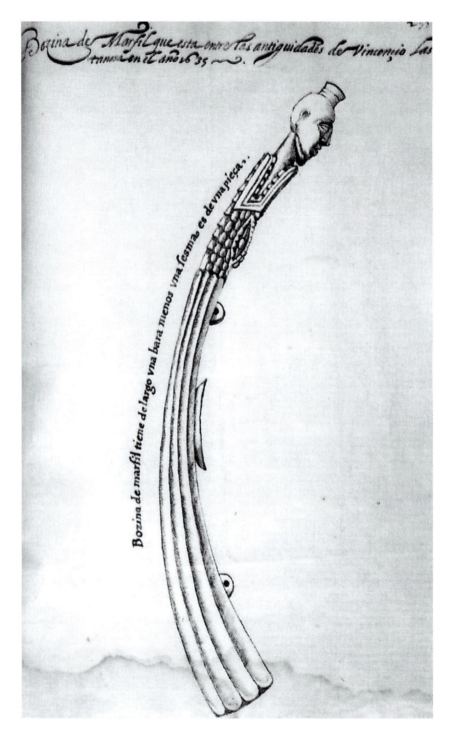

1.1. Unsigned drawing of an ivory oliphant in the collection of Vincencio Juan de Lastanosa in Huesca, Spain, ca. 1635. Private collection.

Additional information makes the olifant even more slippery. The very same piece is itemized in the catalogue of Lastanosa's library (ca. 1640–66) as "An ivory horn almost a *vara* in length, in one piece. The [bottom] two-thirds very finely striated, the last [third] spurts a caiman head with many scales, and from its mouth comes out the head of a crowned Indian. It belonged to an Indian king."[11] This account introduces new variations: the craftsmanship is assessed and pronounced "very fine," the human form depicted is that of a crowned Indian (insisting, as the previous two sources, on the figure's royal identity), and the king who owned the object before it entered Lastanosa's collection was not Japanese but from "India," though whether this word denotes the New World or a region in Asia is unclear.

This geographical instability, the fact that the horn is pronounced Japanese in one statement and Indian in another, is not particular to this item or to Lastanosa's collection. Early modern man-made and natural objects, texts, and images were often said to come from regions far from where they originated. Vague and imprecisely used terms such as "India" or "China" did not stand for specific geographic locations but for an exotic origin that was hard to pin down, remained unspecific, and could mutate unexpectedly. For instance, Lastanosa's contemporary Ferdinando Cospi (1606–86) received in 1665 an Aztec codex as a gift for his celebrated Bologna collection. The codex, now known as the "Codex Cospi," was identified not as an American object but rather as a "Libro della China." Another New World codex entered the collection of Holy Roman Emperor Leopold I in 1677 or 1678. While this Mixtec manuscript now known as the "Vienna Codex" was recognized as coming from New Spain, in the Habsburg Imperial Library, it formed part of a section labeled "Oriental Manuscripts."[12] Geographical imprecision seems to have been the norm rather than the exception.[13]

And geography was not the only slippery category. Was the ivory horn in Lastanosa's collection considered an antiquity or an exotic object? Or both, and if so, did it belong to both categories simultaneously, or did it move from one to the other depending on context? What do we make of the fact that the *Descripción* places it in the room in Lastanosa's palace dedicated to arms, while the 1662 catalogue includes it in the section on "Medals or coins and other antiquities" within the library? How would the object signify, for seventeenth-century audiences, if it were not simply a rare horn but a rare horn that had once belonged to a king, somewhere far from Europe? Would it mean something different if this king were Japanese or Indian? Geography might have been imprecise and uncertain, but it was not meaningless: in the sixteenth century, the Vienna Codex was said to come from "South India," while in the seventeenth century the attribution was revised to "Mexican." The inscription "Libro della China" on the Codex Cospi was revised to "Libro del Messico," and it is as such that the item is described in the published catalogue (1677) and inventory (1680) of the collection.[14] Origin was important enough to merit debate and revision.

For the historian, the issue is not one of precision, of whether "they got it right." My intention is not to bring into question the veracity of early modern descriptions, even less to pin down the identity of a particular object—to figure out exactly where the horn was from (it is almost certainly African). Rather, I want to make both a methodological point about the ways in which we read early modern accounts of collections and an interpretive one, by suggesting that the slipperiness of early modern collectibles originated not in their descriptions but in the objects themselves, or rather in the possible responses available to viewers. If early modern sources provide inconsistent accounts of objects like Lastanosa's ivory horn, it is precisely because these artifacts could be understood and described in many different ways. I am not referring to the ways in which objects in early modern cabinets constantly blurred the line between the natural and the artificial, the scientific and the artistic, the antique and the exotic, a phenomenon amply studied by historians.[15] This multivalence and categorical fluidity can be exemplified, to give but one example, by the rhinoceros cups so highly prized by European collectors in the sixteenth and seventeenth centuries. The material out of which these objects were crafted, rhinoceros horn, made the cups both *naturalia* and rarities; they were also objects of wonder since rhinoceros horn purportedly had magical properties, as well as exotic ones since the material came from outside Europe, most probably from Goa after the Portuguese conquest of 1540. In addition, rhinoceros cups often included elaborate gilt silver mounts and lids, again made of a material both natural and precious but one crafted by man. These mounts would often refer to the natural through floral or zoological decorative patterns but also served as evidence of *artificialia* and of fine craftsmanship.

Going beyond the hybridity inherent in this type of object, I want to highlight not the multiple categories in which an object could fit but rather the multiple ways in which the same types of objects, or even a single object, could be interpreted. As Martin Kemp has argued, early modern collectibles were fundamentally multivalent and variable not only in their corporality but also in their interpretability.[16] Artifacts would have yielded various interpretations and associations according to the specific settings in which they were embedded, that is, the contexts in which they were displayed, whether religious, courtly, civic, professional, institutional, and so on. Early modern collections show remarkable consistency in the types of objects they included—as inventories and catalogues show, the repertoire of collectibles is fairly standardized, something I would attribute both to exchange networks, whether of trade or gift giving, and to the referentiality created by print culture: the fact that a collector mentioned a particular object in publication made it more desirable to other collectors. It is worth noting the level of consensus necessary for Lastanosa's collection in Huesca to be so similar in spirit and in contents to those of his contemporaries throughout Europe. However, the possible interpretations of objects were strongly context dependent. A feather cape from the New World, for instance, could signify differently according to multiple political, artistic, historical, religious, and sociological factors depending on who owned it, what that person made of it in his or her collection, who viewed it, and the location of the collection itself. These symbols were overdetermined, making automatic or transparent iconographic readings impossible.[17] For Kemp, "much of the life and sustained fascination of the collections for highly sophisticated viewers lay in the refusal of many of the individual objects to submit docilely to precise categorization."[18] The issue, then, is to explore what seventeenth-century collectors, viewers, or readers would have made of particular objects within the specific contexts in which they encountered them. The history of collecting, collections, and collectors needs to be, to some degree, a history of display and of reception.

Questions of meaning and interpretation have been central to the history of collecting, such as Paula Findlen's study of sixteenth- and seventeenth-century Italian naturalists and their collections as spaces for the production of knowledge and the construction of social networks; Thomas DaCosta Kaufmann's analysis of the spectacular collections of Holy Roman Emperor Rudolph II in Prague according to the notion of *representatio*, which implied a symbolic mastery of the world connected to political power; Kryzstoff Pomian's study of the changes in the cultural and social history of collecting and the persona of the collector in France and Italy between 1500 to 1800; or Joy Kenseth's framing of sixteenth- and seventeenth-century cabinets within a culture of curiosity and wonder, a topic richly expanded by Lorraine Daston and Katharine Park's magnificent study on wonder, wonders, and the ordering of nature from the Middle Ages through the early modern period.[19] But studies of early modern cabinets have paid scant attention to issues of display and viewership—to the questions of looking and of the type of looking that the collection as a space required.[20] This is in stark contrast, it bears mentioning, with the literature on contemporary museum studies, which tends to focus on exhibition techniques and visitor's experiences.[21]

Trying to trace a history of displaying and seeing collections in early modern Europe, however, is far from easy. Viewers are no less elusive than objects. For all their fascination with cabinets, early modern writers left precious little testimony of what collections actually looked like and what viewers made of them. Collectors emphasized the interest their cabinets arose but mentioned almost nothing about display or viewers' responses. While Neapolitan apothecary Ferrante Imperato (1550–1625) owned one of the most renowned cabinets of his age, his son Francesco barely mentioned visitors' reactions in his account of the famed collection: "There is not a Signor or great person who comes to Naples from far and remote parts who does not wish to see [the cabinet] out of curiosity and who is not overcome with amazement, after having seen it."[22] Accounts from viewers are rare; those we have tend to be similarly vague. A visitor to the collection of Ole Worm (1588–1655) in Denmark stated in 1654 that in it are "found and can be examined with wonder, odd and curious rarities and things among which a large part has not been seen before, and many royal persons and envoys visiting Copenhagen ask to see the museum on account of its great fame and what it relates from foreign lands, and they wonder and marvel at what they see."[23] As with Imperato, we know little beyond a register of characters of notable standing and the tropes of curiosity, rarity, marvel, and wonder. There is no mention of display arrangements or techniques or of the collection as a space—even though that is what might be most striking to a modern viewer of the prints that depict both cabinets, most likely in highly idealized ways (Figures 1.2 and 1.4).

We get more insight from Thomas Platter (ca. 1574–1628), a native of Basel who wrote about seeing Sir Walter Cope's renowned collection of curiosities in London in 1599. Platter's account of the visit begins: "This same Mr. Cope inhabits a fine house in the Snecgas; he led us into an apartment, stuffed with queer foreign objects in every corner, and amongst other things I saw there, the following seemed of interest."[24] Several things are noteworthy about this opening. First, the collection occupied a discrete space within Cope's residence, constituting a cabinet as such rather than spilling out throughout the entire residence, as was the case with Lastanosa's palace. Second, the collector personally took visitors into this space and led them through his collection, as Lastanosa's *Relación* also suggests. Third, Platter immediately remarks on rarity and exotic origin as the significant attributes of the objects. Finally, Platter's brief account does address the cabinet's mode of display: the space is crowded, with a prevailing aesthetic of plenty and accumulation—"queer foreign objects in every corner." It is worth noting that, at the very moment in the travel narrative

1.2. Francesco Imperato, *Historia naturale di Ferrante Imperato napolitano* (Venice, 1672). Research Library, The Getty Research Institute, Los Angeles.

in which Platter enters the cabinet, as he walks through the door into the room, he immediately abandons narrative and switches to an inventory format, as if this were the genre best suited to writing about collections. He tells us, "Amongst other things I saw there, the following seemed of interest" and then proceeds to list fifty numbered items: "1. An African charm made of teeth. 2. Many weapons, arrows and other things made of fishbone. 3. Beautiful Indian plumes, ornaments and clothes from China" (note that India and China are uttered in the same breath). He goes on to mention such notable items as "9. Beautiful coats from Arabia. . . . 12. The horn and tail of a rhinoceros, is a large animal like an elephant. . . . 16. A round horn which had grown on an English woman's forehead. . . . 19. The bauble and bells of Henry VIII's fool; 20. A unicorn's tail [not its horn]. . . . 33. Porcelain from China; 34. A Madonna made of Indian feathers. . . . 41. A mirror which both reflects and multiplies objects;" ending with "50. A long narrow Indian canoe, with the oars and sliding planks, hung from the ceiling of this room." After this inventory, Platter returns to narrative, noting that Cope also "possesses besides many old heathen coins, fine pictures, all kinds of corals and sea-plants in abundance."[25]

The list focuses on those items that Platter found most noteworthy. This process of selection does not give any indication of the total scope of the cabinet—we do not know whether Platter lists fifty items out of a total of dozens, hundreds, or thousands. It is clear that Platter as a viewer was interested in the curious rather than in antiquities, paintings, or *naturalia*; he dispatches the latter rather quickly at the end of the list, not showing much interest. The objects he itemizes evidence the characteristic attributes of the culture of curiosity: rarity, uniqueness, geographic origin, provenance from a famous person, beauty, medium, material, craftsmanship, and scale. Themes reappear throughout the list, mostly in terms of shape or material: feathers, teeth, stones. Objects across the collection resonate with one another; visual motifs are repeated as if reflected in multiple mirrors: there is a horn from a rhinoceros, another from a bull seal, yet another from a woman's forehead.

However, Platter does not detail how items were stored or displayed, nor does he indicate what was placed next to what, whether arrangement was based on typology, size, material, some other principle, or a combination of factors.[26] We do not know the relationship between the order in which items appear in the list and their spatial arrangement within the cabinet. Did Platter number entries in the order he saw objects, moving down the list as his gaze moved from one part of the room to another? Though it is impossible to know, it seems highly unlikely that he would have been putting pen to paper while Cope led him on a visit through the cabinet; and if we assume he wrote the list post-facto, then he most probably would have been deploying strategies based on the theater of memory tradition—that is, putting into practice the idea of the cabinet as both a theater of the world and a theater of memory as expressed in Samuel Quiccheberg's 1565 treatise on collecting, which in turn drew heavily on Giulio Camilo's work on memory.[27] This would imply that there is at least some relation between the order in which items appear in the list and the way in which objects were displayed in the cabinet.

Platter provides only two pieces of information about display: item 44 lists, "Saddles from many strange lands; they were placed round the top on stands." This suggests that there was some sort of cabinetry or shelving, perhaps high, so that stands could be placed on top of it. It also reveals that certain items were not contained within specific sections of the cabinet but spread around it in a horizontal stratum. This is reminiscent of what we see in the depiction of Cospi's cabinet (Figure 1.3), in which a bust of Dante and four taxidermical preparations appear on top of the cabinet, in the far wall and in the center of the image, and various sets of shields and arrows are mounted all around the room on the

DANIELA BLEICHMAR

1.3. Lorenzo Legati, *Museo Cospiano* (Bologna, 1677). Research Library, The Getty Research Institute, Los Angeles.

1.4. Ole Worm, *Museum Wormianum* (Leyden, 1655). Research Library, The Getty Research Institute, Los Angeles.

wall space immediately above the shelving. The same exhibitionary principle applies to medals, which form a distinct bottom layer around the room. Item 50 in Platter's list, the "Indian canoe," hung from the ceiling—not unlike the kayak in Ole Worm's cabinet (Figure 1.4). I should make clear that these depictions of Cospi's and Worm's collections cannot be taken at face value as literal renditions of what their cabinets actually looked like. As all prints of early modern cabinets, they must be understood as an idealized rendition of a collection in a state in which it most probably never existed. However, they do provide a sense of the display aesthetic that was also at work in Cope's and Lastanosa's cabinets and of practices of looking that resonate with Platter's list.

Today, contemporary practices for display and viewing art are interconnected, with protocols of spatial arrangement for both art objects and their visitors and with practices of seeing that require specific body positions and movements, a silent and concentrated looking, and a spatial relationship between thing and person. Similarly, early modern spaces called for specific

DANIELA BLEICHMAR

viewing practices. Platter's list conveys a particular type of viewing, one that is also in evidence in the texts documenting Lastanosa's collection and in seventeenth-century images of cabinets. This is a way of seeing in which the eye is in constant motion from object to object, zooming in and out. A viewer would first look around the room to get a sense of the cabinet as a whole, as a space or as a composite artwork that brings together multiple parts (*Gesamtkunstwerk*); then focus on a specific portion, a group of objects—the animals hanging from the ceiling, the group of small items in one box or shelf; then focus on one single object, perhaps a medal, a shell, or a stone that can be held in one's hand, brought toward the body for close inspection; only to sprint back to another object, near or far in space, that resonates with the first one; and so on. Early modern cabinets demanded an agile and darting eye, one that constantly shifted focus from wide to narrow and speed from slow to fast.

Like Platter's list, Andrés de Uztarroz's *Descripción* suggests a display strategy based on plenty, with "queer foreign objects in every corner." But Lastanosa's collection far exceeded Cope's rather compact cabinet. Belongings did not occupy a single room but spilled over the entire palace in a cornucopia of luxury that extended from room to room, from wall to wall, from floor to ceiling. The aesthetic is a baroque one of ornamentation and *horror vacui*, and, though no representations of Lastanosa's collection exist, it is clear that it had much in common with contemporary cabinets such as those of Francesco Calzolari (1521–1600) or Manfredo Settala (1600–1680), as evidenced in the prints depicting these two Italian collections (Figures 1.5 and 1.6).[28] The aesthetic is maximalist: more is more. The arrangement is strongly symmetrical, and there is a delight in the richness of materials—marble floors, finely and richly crafted shelves (in Calzolari) or smaller cabinets (in Settala). There is a predilection for variety by alternating shapes, media, types of objects. We can also see a hint of groupings, of collections within the collection: Calzolari's line-up of birds, perched atop the shelves that run along either side of the room, or the classical structure at the end of the room, with niches to hold small figurines; Settala's own line-up of paintings (most probably, though they could be wall hangings) and of the cabinets that hold items. There is so much information that the viewer needs to look bit by bit to be able to see the birds that appear to be about to fight with the animals, the furious movement, almost the noise produced by the creatures hanging from the ceiling; the way in which shapes and materials echo, with the curving scroll motifs that decorate the sides of the furnishing suggesting the shapes of the shells on a shelf or the fluted ridges of a shell repeating the shape of an urn or the spines of books; the fact that drawers burst open to reveal neatly lined up series of minimally varying objects or, somewhat terrifyingly, the neatly ordered rows of cabinet after cabinet, each of which

1.5. Benedetto Ceruti, *Musaeum Francisci Calceolarii* (Verona, 1622). Research Library, The Getty Research Institute, Los Angeles.

would open up, like a Russian doll, to reveal yet more collections, so that what appeared like excess turns out to be restraint, and the unrestricted outpouring of so many things onto the page, which seemed to imply that nothing was being held back, actually reminds the viewer that there is still more (and more!), that the cabinet does not show it all as much as reveal through careful looking.

With this in mind we can return to Lastanosa's ivory horn (Figure 1.1). The blank page that isolates the item so it appears like an island floating on a sea of white space now looks incongruous. How can we reinscribe the horn within a display space in which viewers would have encountered it and within a type of looking? We have a hint in its entry in the *Descripción*: the first adjective connected to the olifant is "another." The horn was never meant to stand alone but was part of a larger group of objects and would have been seen in relation to them. Andrés de Uztarroz mentions the horn within his description of the room in Lastanosa's palace that he calls the armory. He writes:

DANIELA BLEICHMAR

1.6. Paolo Maria Terzago, *Museo, ò Galeria, adunata dal sapere e dallo studio del sig. canonico Manfredo Settala nobile milanese* (Tortona, 1666). Research Library, The Getty Research Institute, Los Angeles.

There are in this same room three shelves with harquebuses and muskets with all their trimmings, some of them rare due to the shape of the barrels and boxes, and a variety of exquisitely manufactured pistols . . . arms of great antiquity, war instruments, hunting crossbows, quivers with *madrazos*, war crossbows with quivers with arrows and darts with little lances, and steel heads. Hunting and fighting bows, the former with turquoise projectiles, the [latter] war ones with quivers and arrows. Ivory [shooting] rings. A bronze horn. *Another [horn] in ivory almost a vara in length, from a Japanese King, two thirds striated and the last [third] covered in scales; it is crowned with a caiman head, which grabs with its mouth the head of a king.* A historic weapon of the Queen of the Amazons, mentioned by Father Acuña in the memoir already cited. Two sabers, one from the King of the Tatars, garnished with tortoiseshell and gilded bronze, with most exquisite relief work; given to don Vincencio Juan de Lastanosa by his Excellency don Fernando de Gurrea Aragón y Borja, Duke of Villa Hermosa. The other saber is from China, the blade like a ray, entirely engraved with waves, it ends with a little devil used as the hilt.

A dagger of King Don Pedro the III of Aragon [1239–85], with which he cut his fingers when he cut the Privileges of Union. There is a copious variety of most antique arms, such as bibs, breastplates, a steel shield from Milan, another made of wood from Salamanca, many other items such as are used in war as well as in jousting and tournaments.[29]

Thus, while catalogues and inventories present us with lists of individual objects, collections were experienced spatially as aggregates of multiple objects. The experience of the collection was a narrative, constructed by the collector and by the visitor, which pinned down the meaning of objects. The gaze operative in the collection, traveling from object to object, was a way of seeing that constructed narratives. The collector who guided a visitor through his cabinet directed the experience by telling stories about the objects on display—that is precisely the function of the prose account of a visit to Lastanosa's collection or of the guides depicted in the engravings of Imperato's and Cospi's cabinets (Figures 1.2 and 1.3). The collection functioned not only as an accumulation of objects but also as a narrated social experience. The guide, with his pointing stick, invites us not so much to see objects as to see them in a certain way and as part of a certain story. Andrés de Uztarroz's *Descripción* of Lastanosa's collection allows the reader to wander the palace room by room and in this way to attempt to reconstruct the collection as a space, as an experience, and as a narrative.

CHAPTER 2

—ᴟᴟ—

Collecting Global Icons:
The Case of the Exotic Parasol

Benjamin Schmidt

Prologue: Palm Trees in New England

Do palm trees grow in New England? Fanciful and incongruous as this horticul-
tural proposition may seem, it was seriously contemplated by early modern
Europeans, particularly those who amassed materials depicting the exotic
world—those who "collected across cultures." Such materials were produced
abundantly in the late seventeenth and early eighteenth century, and they circulated widely—New England palm trees, in various forms, seemed to spring up
across much of early Enlightenment Europe. Among the many sources showcas-
ing this remarkable phenomenon was Johannes van Keulen's enormously popular *Paskaart van Niew Engeland*, which was printed as a single-sheet map,
included in the many editions of van Keulen's maritime atlas, and copied freely
by other cartographers far into the eighteenth century (Figure 2.1).[1] Van Keulen
was among the preeminent mapmakers of his day, and he specialized in what
might be called cross-cultural cartography: maps that displayed the expanding
European world and its global encounters. His New England chart shows the
lately well-trafficked waters of the North Atlantic, lapping the coastlines of New
England and Nova Scotia (here labeled "Acadia"); and he embellishes this maritime image with a terrestrial vignette of what we might call globalization. A
gesticulating European and a pair of indigenous Americans—merchants all, one
assumes—gather beneath a palm tree and engage in what appears to be a commercial transaction, bartering over tobacco rolls in the neighborhood of Penob-
scot Bay. Another American Indian, crowned with a feather headdress and

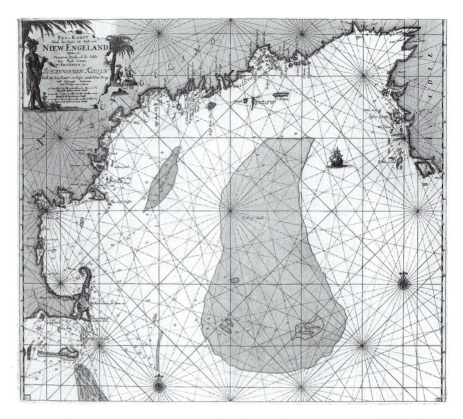

2.1. Johannes van Keulen, *Niew Engeland* (Amsterdam, 1688). Universiteitsbiblio-theek Amsterdam, Bijzondere Collecties.

bearing a standard-issue bow and arrow, stands guard over the map's cartouche, which is gracefully shaded by the fronds of a second palm tree, this one only partially visible. The message, in any case, is clear: the tropical sun shines brightly in this northern outpost of New England—at least to a European collector of circa 1700.[2]

To make sense of this global conceit, we need not so much suspend our disbelief as adjust our notions of collecting across cultures. Two critical modifications may help. First, the category of collecting should be expanded to encompass more than the mere amassing of foreign artifacts and global curiosities, as were gathered in early modern *Wunderkammern*.[3] Collecting took place in multiple forms, across many media, and at various economic levels. Recent research points to a broader social and professional range of collectors (along with the princes and merchants, we now know more about the physicians and apothecaries, the innkeepers and beachcombers, and the travelers and artists who collected); to the richness of the items collected (among the bric-a-brac of natural and artificial objects, we also find ethnographic and religious paraphernalia,

BENJAMIN SCHMIDT

floral and entomological specimens, medical simples and foreign weaponry: the list is truly endless); and to the many variations on the practice of collecting in this period.⁴ It is the last expansion that seems most vital. Collecting took place in specially designated cabinets and purpose-built treasure rooms, carefully arranged by their curators. Yet collecting took place as well in printed volumes—literary *Wunderkammern*, as it were—designed to invoke the ethos of collecting; in personally assembled albums, or "atlases," comprising visual and textual exotica idiosyncratically compiled over many years; in commonplace sets of ceramics, of both high (porcelain) and low (delftware) value, decorated with exotic motifs and used in domestic settings; in medical gardens and taxidermy collections intended for scientific study; in painters' and engravers' ateliers, where foreign objects served as models for still lifes and other compositions with global motifs; in the theatrical world, where exotic dramas were all the rage; and much more. Indeed, the final decades of the seventeenth century and the first few of the eighteenth saw an absolute explosion of exotica on the European market—maps, books, paintings, engravings, decorative arts, and artifacts related to the non-European world—and this created an unusually impressive body of materials suitable for collecting across cultures.⁵

This plenitude of exotic consumables and their intensive manufacture and collection at this time lead to a second important modification. The period around 1700 marks a distinct highpoint in Europe's engagement with the non-European world: a period of thickening overseas commerce and colonialism; of increasing interest in geography and other forms of cross-cultural knowledge; and, not unrelated, of vigorous production of texts, maps, pictures, and objects depicting Europe's expanding world. In truth, exotica were consumed across several media: collecting across cultures was an inherently multimedia enterprise. Collecting exotic materials had a *transmedia* quality, as well, in the sense that images, forms, and motifs relating to exotic subjects could (and commonly did) cross from medium to medium—from travel books to maritime atlases to decorative arts and so on—in a way that might evoke what modern media analysts would term "synergy." This manner of media transfer is implicit, of course, in the numerous instances where textual materials were poached, pirated, and otherwise pilfered by competing printers for republication in other genres or editions, not to mention translation into other languages. It is also evident in the many cases where textual descriptions served as the basis for visual productions—as when prose depictions of a foreign landscape induced stay-at-home artists to render words into pictures. It occurs in less obvious ways, however, when a visual form crossed generic lines—when graphic work designed for a book turns up in cartographic sources—or when a two-dimensional image, such as an engraving, served as the basis for three-dimensional objects, such as tapestry, delftware, furniture, and the like.[6] To cite a quick example, the engraved frontispiece to a book on religious practices in Malabar reappeared as a decorative cartouche to a nautical map of trading ports in South Asia.[7]

What is more, the exotic motif in question, even while retaining its basic form, could become transformed in its various iterations: religious messages could morph into commercial ones (as occurs in the Malabar vignette), even though the image itself does not substantially change. Those items carefully assembled in the wide-ranging, cross-cultural collections of early modern Europeans—artifacts, texts, and icons of the exotic world—spoke to each other in subtle, formal ways. Moreover, they were ultimately less static than we often assume. Collectors played a role in assigning meaning to the materials that they accumulated, to be sure. Yet exotic objects, images, and motifs could themselves borrow meanings and, in this way, take an active part in the process of cultural diffusion. Exotic imagery, or what might loosely be called exotic icons—the tropical palm tree, for example—circulated across media and among cultures, and they were transformed by their journey. By dint of their collective production and their cross-cultural collection, exotic icons could influence one another. In this sense, exotic icons were performative.

This raises an important theme for the study of collecting across cultures. Icons like the palm tree are taken to stand for a vaguely situated, generically tropical culture. The same can be said for several other iconic renditions of the non-European world: the colorful parrots that populate so many paintings and engravings of this period; the feathered skirts and headdresses in which all manner of "natives" are clothed; the ubiquitous parasol (more on that later); and the many other serially summoned images intended to denote the exotic world. These are stereotypes, to use a technical term from the argot of printing, in that they get reused, again and again, in more or less the same form. Yet as they circulate, icons can and do change. Sometimes a palm tree is not quite a palm tree—as when it figures in a New England landscape. Paradoxically, then, while purveyors of exotica certainly may have traded in stereotypes, the oft-repeated images and motifs they favored could also shift in meaning. A stereotype could be solid in terms of its basic form—this, after all, explains its value to printers and engravers, who relied on a "set piece" to save production costs—yet it could also demonstrate, ironically enough, a fair degree of malleability. The very process of collecting across cultures, furthermore, could contribute to these geographically indiscriminate shifts of meaning.

How does the solid turn supple, the iconic become indeterminate, the palm tree grow in New England? This essay looks for answers in a single, and in many ways singular, moment in the history of European collecting, exoticism, and global expansion: the final third of the seventeenth century and first third of the eighteenth, when attention to the non-European world greatly intensified, especially in descriptive materials. The output of exotic materials in this period was stupendous—a torrent of literary, cartographic, and visual sources flooded the market with European-made or amassed images of the world—and the process of their production and consumption is highly significant. The abundance of materials, avidly collected and broadly circulated, encouraged what might be called a "transmedia effect": the liberal recycling, strategic borrowing, and subtle replication of images and motifs, which distilled the non-European world into a form that has come to be associated with the catchall category of "exoticism." I would like to consider these many crossovers, confluences, and simple copying, not so much to enumerate their substantial quantity but to remark on their particularly innovative quality. Looking at transmediated exotica demonstrates how European images and ideas called on to represent the world could become, on the one hand, clichéd or stereotyped and ultimately codified as exotic icons, while, on the other hand, they could also shift in meaning as they moved across media and global space. They reveal some of the dynamics of collecting across cultures.

Making (and Collecting) Global Icons

Hardy New England palm trees hardly stand alone in the landscape of global icons. The energetic borrowing of images and topoi and the ease with which these migrated among various representational forms is, of course, scarcely new or even exceptional to this moment (1670–1730) of European geography. Such habits of cross-fertilization have long been the process by which icons are created, after all; and the very earliest projects of Renaissance geography provide one of the most basic examples of this phenomenon: the depiction of the "continents" as reconceived following Europe's encounter with the Americas. Consider, for example, the approach of Cesare Ripa in the *Iconologia*, a catalogue of icons that greatly shaped early modern draftsmanship from the late sixteenth through the eighteenth century. Printed originally (and somewhat paradoxically) without any images, Ripa's much-referenced *Iconologia* first appeared with woodcuts in 1603 and then in a revised, picture-rich edition of 1611, which had a profound impact on the symbolic representation of the globe. Broadly speaking, the volume consisted of simple images covering a wide range of topics, including a series of allegories of the "parts" of the world, which now numbered four: Europe, Asia, Africa, and, America (Figure 2.2).[8] Ripa's working method followed a proven formula. He depicted each global landmass (or continent, as they came to be called) allegorically; he presented each allegory in the form of

2.2. "America," woodblock print in Cesare Ripa, *Iconologia* (Rome, 1603). University of Washington Libraries, Special Collections, UW28591z.

a woman (following classical sources); and he dressed, accessorized, and surrounded each woman with the garb, accoutrements, and products of her geographic home. Again, this approach was not in and of itself novel (medieval cartography is rife with visual allegories). Yet it had been lately revived and keenly explored in the wake of European voyages overseas, and Ripa's approach

BENJAMIN SCHMIDT

had the effect of "iconizing" earlier projects of geographic representation. His allegory of America, more particularly, borrowed from a series of Flemish prints and drawings done in the late sixteenth century and from decorative elements appearing in early atlases—for example, the frontispiece to Abraham Ortelius's *Theatrum orbis terrarum* (1570).[9] The resulting image, in turn, formed the basis for various decorative arts: designs for ceramics, cartouches for maps, cartoons for tapestries, and the like. Ripa's allegory, in this way, distilled and codified the most distinctive features of "America" and furnished artists working throughout Europe and across media a model of the newest continent and its imagined attributes. These attributes would be invoked and imitated for years to come: the partial nudity of America for lack of "civil" dress; her unusual headdress made of exotic feathers; her iconic bow and arrow (which endure in the popular media even today); the not-too-subtle intimation of cannibalism, as suggested by the severed head; the strange *naturalia*, here taking the form of a tropical alligator (which has mutated from a bizarre lizard in the 1603 woodcut and, before that, a grinning armadillo in the 1589 engraving by Maarten de Vos that likely inspired Ripa). Well into the eighteenth century, these qualities and guises appeared regularly in pictorial renditions of the "new" continent—if sometimes with telling twists and variations. Thus, in certain later versions of this "iconic" form, an artist might blend attributes that point to other continents: Gottfried Bernhard Goetz's engraving of *America* (ca. 1750) features a dark-skinned (African?) queen bearing a prominent cornucopia—an accessory typically affiliated with the wheat-rich continent of Africa (Color Plate 1).[10] And a porcelain figurine made in Spain's Alcora factory displays another dark-skinned "America" with distinctively African features—quite deliberate coloring and modeling, considering the medium of porcelain—which, like the Goetz engraving, produced a composite, catchall, non-European "native."[11] Such geographic mixing notwithstanding, the iconicity of "America" prevailed: it endured for decades, if not centuries, following Ripa's durable design.[12]

Icons of continents could be capriciously presented, since they were presented so commonly. Part of the habit of reformulating and riffing on a standard image had to do with its repeated usage; repetition instigated revision. Sheer quantity is part of this process. Yet also important are the shifts that occur across genres and the adjustments made to accommodate varying media—what I have called media transfers. Moving from paper to porcelain, from two dimensions to three, can induce not merely formal variations but also functional meanings. Early modern Europeans consumed and collected exotica in myriad forms. We take for granted the primacy of textual sources, yet this can often mean neglecting other less accessible (and therefore less apparent) media—and the trajectories of iconic transfer. The move to other media, moreover, typically took place in the context of "collecting"—of gathering materials in an artisan's atelier, in a scholar's *Wunderkammer*, in a prince's *studiolo*—which allowed media to mingle. And while very few of these sites of production can be fully recovered, texts offer clues of their inherent materiality. Along with relatively straightforward examples of "transmediation"—the movement of motifs (most commonly) from text to picture or object—other, less direct cases of mediation can thus be inferred by reading between the printed lines. Volumes describing early modern *Wunderkammern*, for example—the numerous printed catalogues advertising the sale or extolling the virtues of well-known cabinets of curiosities—imply the presence and widespread habit of collecting exotic artifacts, even if these collections have long been dispersed or lost.[13] In some cases, texts do not invoke a specific collection but hint, all the same, at a cast of mind that organized materials in collectors' terms. Pieter van der Aa's *La Galerie agreable du monde*, as its title implies, assembled the world's wonders in the form of a textual museum.[14] The titles of Simon de Vries's omnibus volumes—"Great Cabinet of Curiosities" and "Warehouse of Wonders," for example—likewise suggest a rich world of material culture.[15] So do the many "theaters" of exotica, which, in the language and style they employ, indicate a performance or staging, in material form, of the exotic world: Petrus Nylandt's *Theater* [schouwtoneel] *of All the World's Creatures*; Levinus Vincent's *Marvelous Theater* [wonder-tooneel] *of Nature*; and, the granddaddy of the genre—the volume that arguably first suggested geography's performative nature—Abraham Ortelius's *Theatrum orbis terrarum* or "Theater of the Terrestrial Globe."[16] In each case, recourse to the metaphor of collecting, displaying, and staging implied that, even as global objects and images were reproduced in print, there existed elsewhere collections, displays, and performances of the real thing.

One further example, in this case taken from the actual world of theater, suggests the way the textual can reveal the material or even the performative qualities of exotica. Actual staged performances that addressed global themes also proliferated in this period—think of John Dryden's *Indian Emperour* and *Indian Queen*, Thomas Southerne's *Oroonoko*, Molière's *Le Bourgeois gentilhomme*, and the many plays of Félix Lope de Vega set in America—and these events would have entailed exotic props. We know this to be the case from specific theatrical directions and staging notes. This implies the routine production, in the theatrical workshops of London, Paris, and Madrid alike, of ersatz exotica: of material objects replicating the exotic world, which would have been taken by the theatergoing public to stand for non-European landscapes and to embody the exotic motifs associated with foreign lands. A particular case of this exotic staging is described by the theater historian Joseph Roach, who studied the career of Thomas Betterton, considered "the greatest actor on the Restoration stage and the producer of some of its most opulent scenic extravaganzas."[17] Roach draws attention to Betterton's involvement in the production of Americana, including what Roach refers to as the manufacture of New World "ethnoscapes" (invoking the anthropologist Arjun Appadurai).[18] These ethnoscapes would have comprised scenic props, stage decor, and foreign-looking artifacts—perhaps bona fide imports, yet more likely artful replications—which were designed not only to suggest exotic locales but further to essentialize these locales by creating a theatrical synecdoche. Theatrical ethnoscapes—theatrical exotica—reveal what Roach terms, more prosaically, "mental atlases," citing the dramatist Henry Fielding (1730): "My head is a map, a map of the whole world."[19] We might think of them, more simply, as geographies of the imagination, exotic landscapes erected from scattered texts, miscellaneous images, and disparate artifacts; and we might look for them, not least, in the world of Baroque theater. This was a world that took its cue from printed geographies, to be sure, but also from the material bric-a-brac collected abroad. Early modern theatrical productions, in all cases, offer superb evidence for the migration of exotica to sites of production that have long gone understudied.

The production and consumption of these theatrical "exotiscapes" (to tweak Appadurai's critical vocabulary) have much to teach us. The world of the stage, particularly in seventeenth-century London, operated on principles of profit, and this points to the commercial imperatives of collecting, crafting, and circulating exotica. The improvisational qualities of theater also show, in very tangible ways, the processes by which artifacts, images, and tropes become transformed through their transfer from medium to medium—through the elaborate forms of cultural "telephone" that occur in the assimilation of exotic spaces. When these transformations take place, moreover, new icons or stereotypes are formed, and these novel forms have the perverse effect of stripping "icons" of their original meaning. The textual description and graphic reproduction of the non-European world, the process of visualizing and replicating foreign "ethnoscapes," the habit of collecting and reproducing exotica: all encouraged a certain improvisational looseness in terms of geography, a casual approach to spatial specificity, which is the opposite of what we intuitively expect from the so-called science of geography. Icons of exotica, as produced by Europeans circa 1700, do not represent a particular place or landscape but come to stand for an entire and somewhat arbitrarily defined exotic world.

Spinning an Exotic Parasol

I would like to explore this point by investigating one of the most ubiquitous icons of the early modern world, a close cousin in this regard to the pervasive palm tree and, as it happens, a common prop of the Baroque stage: the exotic parasol. The parasol appears repeatedly and revealingly in Europe's exotic ethnoscapes, not so much as an innocuous scene-filler placed in the distant background of an exotic vignette but rather as an easy-to-spot, formal device, which found its place front and center in scene after scene of the exotic world. The exotic parasol was literally universal, and its very omnipresence points to the core paradox of the exotic icon: the imprecision of geographic signs related to the exotic world. The parasol's iconicity and ubiquity pose a dilemma: how can a distinctly Asian accouterment flourish equally well in the wilds of America, in the heart of Africa, and, not least, on the stages of Europe?

Of all its iterations, the "American" passage of the parasol makes for an especially compelling case study, since the parasol, closely associated since antiquity with the East, had become transformed by the late-seventeenth century into a veritable symbol of the New World. It came to be included even in allegories of America—as in William Vincent's famous engraving of "The Indian Queen" (Figure 2.3). First printed in the 1680s by John Smith after Vincent's design and republished several times over the coming decades, this elegant mezzotint served as an advertisement for the theater.[20] It features the actress Anne Bracegirdle in a well-known stage role, playing the character of Semernia in Aphra Behn's *The Widow Ranter* (not to be confused with the eponymous heroine of Dryden's *The Indian Queen*). An utterly Baroque drama produced posthumously in the year of Behn's death (1689), *The Widow Ranter* is a tragicomedy set in Virginia around the time of Bacon's Rebellion (1676). Semernia, the fictional love interest of Nathaniel Bacon, is an Indian "queen" who possesses all the honor and dignity absent from the colonial English government. In this regard, she embodies those heroic qualities celebrated in another pair of colonial protagonists, Oroonoko and Imoinda, the African lovers featured in Behn's tropical novella *Oroonoko*, set in West Africa and Suriname.[21] Semernia is a "tropical" heroine, and this point is made tangibly by the central prop of the scene: a parasol, which is held above Semernia by a cherubic "Indian" lackey. The parasol is no mere accessory. Its placement in the center of the print, framing the heroine's delicate head, gives it a plainly theatrical function. The parasol marks the scene as tropical and indicates, more particularly, the character's inherent Americanness. This "Indian" queen, to be sure, cannot so readily be identified as an indigenous American from the forests of "Virginia." Her dress is distinctly Old World, its rich fabric and exquisite drapery contrasting sharply with the feathered attire of the mostly nude, dusky-toned, somewhat African-looking boys. Semernia wears a feathered headdress, in this case matching the boys', and she also holds a bouquet of feathers. Indeed, feathers are another essential prop for this scene, and iconic Indian feathers

BENJAMIN SCHMIDT

The Indian Queen

J. Smith ex.   *W. Vincent fe.*

2.3. William Vincent (published by John Smith), *The Indian Queen* [Anne Bracegirdle as "Semernia"], ca.1700, mezzotint, 19.4 x 14.5 cm. Harvard Theater Collection, Houghton Library.

prompt another interesting story—which will have to be left untold for the time being.[22] The parasol, in all events, is the key formal device in the print. Along with the feathers and perhaps also the pearls—two consumer items closely associated with America and the rich West Indies trade—it announces the Indian Queen's exoticism, not to mention her high social standing.[23] She is an "Indian" "queen," inappropriate though that ranking may be in the context of the Powhatan polity from which her character putatively derives.

How did the parasol, of all things, an object that otherwise bore no relation to Virginia Algonquian material culture—or, for that matter, relation to any Native American culture more generally—become associated with America in the imagination of Restoration audiences? How, in other words, did the parasol become part of the American ethnoscape? There are few obvious precedents in early sources on America (not to mention, early English theatrical productions) for this iconographic strategy. What traces that exist of the American parasol are both uncommon and far-fetched. The Incan emperor Atahualpa is sporadically shown under a feather sunshade—not quite a parasol per se—although this formula is relatively obscure. No parasol appears in the most widely circulated prints of Atahualpa, those in Theodor de Bry's "Americae" series; one surfaces in a crude woodcut made for a minor Spanish history from the mid-sixteenth century.[24] This "royal" treatment could also be accorded to Atahulapa's Aztec colleague, the emperor Moctezuma—as in a mid seventeenth-century painting of *The Meeting of Cortés and Montezuma*, now in the Library of Congress.[25] Yet this configuration was fairly infrequent, and most of these anonymously made images circulated narrowly. They would, in all events, have had a comparatively limited impact on early modern viewers.

While these imperial affiliations of the "American" parasol admittedly do follow a certain political logic, they make very little geographic sense. For while Incan and Aztec rulers would surely have required some shading from the hot tropical sun of the Americas, their putative parasols, at least in their iconic forms, derived from other places. They came indubitably from representations of *Eastern* rulers, the all-powerful Oriental potentates of Western imagination, which were deeply embedded in European memory since classical times. "From time immemorial," explains one antiquarian history of the parasol, "the umbrella has been among Oriental peoples a symbol of dominion," a sign of high political rank and luxurious power.[26] In this vein (which is not inaccurate: the East is the birthplace of the parasol), images of the "oriental" parasol abound, and they would have been the prevailing form of the icon for centuries. Stylized umbrellas figure as emblems of dominion on Assyrian reliefs, for example, and on Egyptian wall-paintings. One relief from Nineveh (now in the British Museum) shows a conquering monarch, shaded by a parasol, receiving the homage of a vanquished prince; on another, a king sits under a parasol while he directs a military siege.[27] The parasol has long been associated with South Asian royalty as well, who commonly styled themselves "Brother of the Sun and Moon, and Lord of the Umbrella"; and the parasol appears regularly in Indian royal iconography—as in the ancient banner of Sri Lanka. To cite the OED gloss: "The parasol or sunshade was originally used by persons of high rank in

South and South-East Asian countries, and was later adopted in Western countries where it became fashionable as a woman's accessory, especially in the nineteenth century." Parasols also appear on Greek vases and in Roman literature—a parasol is made to embody the quality of gallantry in Ovid's *Ars Amatoria*—and, once again, they tend to be associated with power, splendor, and, by extension, the ways of the Orient.[28]

In many regards, these long-standing Eastern associations persist in the early modern period. A parasol turns up, for instance, in a theatrical ballet of 1673, Elkanah Settle's *The Empress of Morocco*.[29] (And in the shrewd world of London theater, it is not unlikely that this was the same prop used a decade and a half later in Behn's *Widow Ranter*.) Yet these affiliations are not at all stable, and it is fascinating to watch the parasol migrate over the course of the century across oceans and continents. This trend can in truth be "watched," since the parasol, only infrequently described in texts, appears regularly in engraved prints and other visual media, where it established itself, by the second half of the seventeenth century, as an icon of global exoticism. This period and this process coincides with the profusion of exotic production in late Baroque Europe, when a deluge of books, maps, plays, and artifacts, derived from and pertaining to the non-European world, streamed onto the market and thereby established the look of the newly expanded, rapidly colonized world. And the parasol gets especially prominent billing in this emerging exotic ethnoscape.

While there is no distinct, original point of departure for this iconographic journey, there is a signal image that in many ways launched the exotic parasol, establishing its visual form and allegorical value for years to come. This image springs from the most pure of geographic sources—a map—and it was manufactured in the epicenter of early modern European exoticism: the ateliers of Amsterdam, where Nicolaes Visscher's serially copied map of the Americas was first printed around 1650 (Figure 2.4). Visscher's *Totius Americae*, a cartographgic product impressive enough to challenge Willem Blaeu's bestselling yet mildly outdated American map of the early seventeenth century, contains dual cartouches designed by the well-known painter Nicolaes Berchem; the upper cartouche provides patronage details, while the lower one serves as a more traditional title plate.[30] These vignettes combine to offer one of the most sophisticated and dynamic allegories to date of the American continent. Their principal message is plainly religious, albeit with a commercial addendum—and with a centrally placed parasol that complicates any easy reading of the whole. In the upper cartouche, a cross-wielding woman, meant to stand for the Christian faith, expels diabolism (in the form of a falling figure with talons) and ushers the true religion into the "newest" world. Meanwhile, the allegorical figure of "America" standing below points across the map's title to the vast mineral

2.4. Nicolaes Visscher, *Novissima et Accuratissima Totius Americae Descriptio*, (Amsterdam, ca. 1650). Universiteitsbibliotheek Amsterdam, Bijzondere Collecties.

wealth spilling literally at her feet, which accounts for her/the continent's super-fluous riches. The connection? The two allegories, of Christian faith and American riches, pun subtly on the relation between "god" and "gold"; they visualize an oft-cited proverb that held that the two (*god* and *goud* in the original Dutch) flourished naturally in inverse proportion to each other.[31] Berchem's "America," not surprisingly, also borrows from Ripa's allegory and from late sixteenth-century Flemish designs—America remains a mostly nude figure, clad in a flimsy feathered skirt and matching headdress, and clasps an arrow-like weapon. Yet she is now shaded by a parasol. In fact, the parasol plays a key formal role in the Berchem composition, as it will later in Vincent's "Indian Queen," by guiding the viewer's eye from the lower cartouche to the upper image and signaling the unity of the two. It is both central and essential to the map's design.

It is important to underscore the religious message of the composition, a fact further attested to by Berchem's original drawings and notes (preserved in

Windsor Castle), which plainly emphasize America's predilection to heathenism and its affiliation with mineral wealth (not much god, yet superabundant gold).[32] This clarifies a basic, yet vital, point. The parasol here does *not* function as a symbol of Oriental power, since the allegorical figure of America, like the indigenous peoples of America, occupied a position largely of deference and sometimes even servitude to Europeans: both were subjects of European colonial rule. As the Old World audience for Berchem's allegory surely understood, Europeans not only delivered the Christian god to America, but they also collected abundant gold from America in the form of tribute payment—this, at least, was the understood order of things. The parasol, rather than a signifier of Occidental luxury and political might, somehow alludes to the New World's *dependency* on the Old. It adds an element of exoticism to the image, yet in a form oddly disconnected from its original context.

Geographically and historically accurate or not, the image took off, first in maps and later in a range of sources bearing exotic iconography. Visscher's *Totius Americae* was itself reprinted copiously and copied brazenly, and Berchem's cartouche and allegory were imitated in ways that crossed both genres and media. The parasol, particularly, was a hit—as theater producers of Restoration London instinctively understood. Most immediately, the image circulated in cartographic sources, sometimes even stripped of its geographic specificity. In the first place, the Visscher atelier (run by Nicolaes II on his father's death in 1679) printed several editions of the maps, both as a single sheet and for inclusion in atlases.[33] The map was also picked up, largely unchanged, by competing Dutch cartographers, generally through some form of legal arrangement: Petrus Schenk's atlases carried it well into the eighteenth century. It was appropriated illicitly, as well, copied for the international market. John Ogilby, the royal cosmographer under Charles II, used a variant of the Visscher map for his *English Atlas*, simply engraving a new dedication; and Justus Danckerts and Frederick de Wit adapted it for their new maps of America, in which they ditched the allegory of faith while preserving the wholly secular figure of "America"—and, naturally, her parasol. "America" appears on the frontispiece to an early (1719) printed volume of Russian geography—in fact, one of the first substantial geography texts set in Cyrillic type—in which she retains most of her attributes and, in addition, gains the company of two beavers, who serve as a sly allusion to the Russian pelt trade (Figure 2.5). The engraving and the book were commissioned by Peter the Great—an "Oriental potentate," if there ever was one—and furnished imperial-minded Russians with what would become the most enduring image, up until the nineteenth century, of the by now not-so-new continent.[34]

2.5. "Ameriki opisanie" (Description of America), engraving, 24 x 15.2 cm, in Johann Hübner, *Zemnovodnago kruga kratkoe* opisanie [Short description of the terraqueous globe] (Moscow, 1719). Courtesy of the John Carter Brown Library at Brown University.

The allegory and the parasol branched out further to other regions and other sources. Hendrik Donker brought the ensemble to the "dark" continent of Africa in his nautical chart of *Guinea* (circa 1689), which incorporates a near-identical image of the Berchem cartouche, simply in reverse.[35] "America" has now decamped to West Africa, her gold, feathers, and parasol having effortlessly bridged the Atlantic. A slightly more convoluted variant of this geographic mélange appears in Johann Wolfgang Baumgartner's allegory of *America*, painted in the mid-eighteenth century (Color Plate 2). Here a more voluptuous figure of the continent holds the parasol herself for a dark-skinned, masculine partner, who grips the emblematic bow and arrow of the Western continent and wears golden jewelry draped across his lap. The male figure's *African* features, however, and the elephant tusk (to his right) suggest that the process of mixing and matching allegorical attributes is well under way. The iconic parasol, in any event, has regained some of its original purpose as a shade for a princely warrior, even while it retains its broader meaning as a symbol of generic exoticism.

Where did the exotic parasol now reside? In the wake of Berchem's popular allegory of "America" and its widespread distribution by Visscher and others, it is easy enough to locate the parasol popping up all over the American landscape. Yet there is simultaneously another stream of images that flooded the market for consumable exotica; and in these instances, the parasol has relocated to the East. Despite this homecoming, however, the parasol's form, utterly reminiscent of the Berchem design, harks back to "America" rather than "Asia"—to the West Indies of Visscher's map rather than the East Indies of its birth. Form, in other words, has shifted meaning, insofar as the Occidental parasol does not carry the same message of power and majesty that had once characterized the Oriental parasol. This peripatetic quality of the iconic parasol is evident already in the shaded, feathered "Indian" decorating Doncker's map of West Africa. That generically tropical figure, as it turns out, joined a crowd of parasoled non-Europeans, who turned up routinely in print media and material objects in Eastern no less than Western locales. Indeed, the indiscriminate nature of its appearance becomes part of the parasol's meaning: it develops into an icon for tropical indolence, implied servitude (it must be borne by a lackey), extravagant luxury, and so on. By dint of these images and objects, the parasol comes to signify, in essence, global exoticism.

Once established, the parasol was launched on what the art historian Craig Clunas calls an "iconic circuit": "an economy of representations in which images of a certain kind circulated between different media in which pictures were involved."[36] In the case of the iconic parasol, moreover, this circuit was emphatically global. One could take a virtual tour of Europe's exotic world,

2.6. Jacob van Meurs and atelier, "Habit of a Floridian King," engraving in Arnoldus Montanus, *America* (Amsterdam, 1671). Huntington Library.

through the media of geography circa 1700, under the shade of a parasol. A parasol can be seen shielding the Mughal Shah Jahan from the hot Indian sun in a widely printed volume on Persia and South Asia, authored by Olfert Dapper and published in English by John Ogilby. A samurai (or "chevalier" as he is fashioned in French editions) receives respite from the Japanese sun under a parasol in a popular book on Japan and also in Pieter van der Aa's *Galerie agreable*. (And note, in this case, that the Oriental association is inaccurate: umbrellas were uncommon in Japan until the arrival of Admiral Perry and the opening of the country in the late nineteenth century.) A parasol protects a richly dressed Chinese woman—although the same handsomely illustrated volume also includes engraved peasant women under the shade of parasols. And, to bring us full circle, the so-called Floridians of Arnoldus Montanus's *America* receive the royal treatment in the form of princely pearls, an elaborate cloth train borne by a lackey, and—to complete the scene—a parasol held aloft by a young boy (Figure 2.6). With this image, which was published as well in the many translations of Montanus's book, we land back in the New World. And with the English edition done under the name of John Ogilby, we also land in London, where an American parasol, pearls, and train, as assembled by the theater impresario Thomas Betterton, mark Anne Bracegirdle as an "Indian" queen.[37]

The theatrical connection can hardly be accidental. The catalogue of Betterton's library, auctioned after his death in 1710, lists several volumes of geography, along with prints and maps of the exotic world. (The catalogue went by the name *Pinacotheca Bettertonaeana*, a title that, by invoking an art gallery, emphasized the visual quality of its contents.)[38] Betterton likely owned the volumes from which these images derived (although it is difficult to verify this, since many titles are listed without much bibliographic precision), and he certainly owned numerous works by the royal geographer, John Ogilby. A former dance master and a man of the theater himself, Ogilby might seem an unlikely figure to be elevated to reigning geographer of England. Yet the staging of the globe, whether in print or performance, clearly required some of the same devices and props. This is another way of pointing to the considerable overlap between the fields of geography and drama, the happy borrowing from one another, and the way objects and images moved across media to form the sort of exotic icons epitomized by the parasol. What is more, just as Behn's production borrowed props from Dryden's—the feathers used originally in *The Indian Queen* were later used in *The Widow Ranter*—Ogilby borrowed the images in his books. In this, he lifted them wholesale from Amsterdam printer extraordinaire Jacob van Meurs, who oversaw the publication of scores of parasol engravings made in this period—and for that matter, who manufactured much of the textual and graphic exotica of the 1670s and 1680s, which appeared in the many volumes of geography that rolled off van Meurs's press.[39]

Rather than see these as direct borrowings (which they certainly could be), it is perhaps more productive to appreciate the shifts in meaning that took place when images "transmediated." For if tropes, images, and objects moved from graphic to theatrical form and across linguistic and national lines, they also migrated to painting, tapestry, ceramics, and a whole range of decorative arts. In each of these transfers, moreover, icons both lost and gained signification; the further they traveled from their point of origin, the less of their original meaning they retained and the more they came to stand for a new and generic exoticism. If Visscher's map begat ample "American" parasols, it launched scores of "Oriental" parasols, too. And if the correlation between the two genera is not quite exact, links between East and West are easily detectable—for example, in the person of Jacob van Meurs, who was responsible for so many of the prints exhibiting exotic imagery. The indispensable image for the late seventeenth-century Oriental parasol is a van Meurs product: the frontispiece to Johannes Nieuhof's *L'Ambassade . . . vers L'Emperour de la Chine, ou Grand Cham de Tartarie* published (and perhaps also engraved) by van Meurs in 1665.

The French title appeared concurrently with a Dutch edition and one year before a German translation (1666); these were followed by Latin (1668) and English (1669) editions, the latter done under the name of Ogilby (Figure 2.7).[40] It was a mega-bestseller. The parasol on the frontispiece, which prominently crowns "the Grand Cham," once again plays a crucial formal role in the composition. It centers the image, and it counterbalances the massive globe, whose spherical shape it replicates. The tilt of the "Oriental" umbrella mirrors almost exactly that of the "American" parasol (and, looking ahead, Anne Bracegirdle's prop: compare Figure 2.3). Both Berchem's allegorical American and van Meurs's Chinese emperor hold one arm akimbo while stretching the other arm out. These languidly regal gestures, it seems, traveled as easily as the parasol itself.

The Chinese parasol traveled, too. Not only was it repeated in the several editions of van Meurs's book, but it also appeared in prints, maps, decorative arts, and more. It showed up several years later—at roughly the same time as the Bracegirdle image—on a cabinet-cum-writing desk painted with exotic scenery (Figure 2.8). The central panel of the cabinet lifts the parasol image more or less directly from van Meurs's design, even as the parasol itself has become extraneous for an "emperor" who now stands under a baldachin. No matter: it lends the pastiche an air of exoticism. The splendid duke of Arenberg's tapestries, woven by the Flemish workshop of Jodocus de Vos around 1700 (and now in the Seattle Art Museum), offer a variation on the same scene, at once more simplified and fantastic than the painted cabinet: emperor, lackey, and parasol, set in a world of pagodas, parrots, and palm trees. We have now arrived in the territory of chinoiserie, yet it may be ultimately unhelpful to lump these images under a catchall "Oriental" rubric, since some of them may well have originated in Occidental ethnoscapes: to wit, the "American" parasol. These sorts of sources and categories of representation could be amplified with copious examples.[41] Yet one more suffices to show just how far and wide—and how incongruously—the exotic parasol could voyage. Standing on a bronze and gilded clock decorated with tropical scenes from the novel *Robinson Crusoe*, the eponymous hero of that story holds a parasol, somewhat improbably, for his servant Man Friday, who has been notably Africanized (not unlike the allegorical figure in Baumgartner's painting).[42] The exotic parasol has landed literally in no man's land, an island in the Caribbean (where Defoe's story was set), or perhaps the South Pacific (where the events on which it was based took place), or perhaps the North Atlantic—Europe, and particularly imperial Britain and France— where the story was widely popular. In all cases, the parasol now shades all the world's continents. It is an icon of global exoticism.

BENJAMIN SCHMIDT

2.7. Wenceslaus Hollar after Jacob van Meurs, engraved frontispiece to Johan Nieuhof, *An embassy from the East-India Company of the United Provinces, to the Grand
Tartar Cham Emperour of China*. Translation of *Gezantschap der Neerlandtsche Oost-
Indische Compagnie aan den grooten Tartarischen Cham, den tegenwoordigen keizer
van China*, 1655 (London, 1669). Huntington Library.

2.8. "Oriental scene with parasol" (detail of Leipzig cabinet), in Otto Pelka, *Ostasia-tische reisebilder im kunstgewerbe des 18. Jahrhunderts* (Leipzig: K.W. Hiersemann, 1924): plate 192. Courtesy of the University of Southern California, on behalf of USC Libraries.

Epilogue: Tyranny in the (Exotic) Bedroom

An iconic object reproduced by printers, painters, ceramicists, enamelists, and weavers with workmanlike regularity, the parasol showed remarkable variability and plasticity in its representational form. The parasol was no doubt collected in some original, authentic type, a souvenir of Asian voyages. Yet it soon became a visual cliché across several media, broadly represented and widely reproduced, shifting from map to book to stage to decorative arts. In a sense, this final category is an apt descriptor of the way geographic icons functioned in this period: in an almost decorative, aesthetically compelling, loosely defined form. For while the parasol had traditionally served as a signifier of Oriental royalty and power, it became in the Berchem vignette, by contrast, an almost ironic prop for the indigenous American: a sunshade for an enslaved Indian, who must labor miserably in Western mines to feed the gold-starved empires of Europe. The parasol may revert to form in certain depictions of Asia and America; yet in other images it does not. In its wide iterations, moreover, and its seemingly random zigzags between east and west, the parasol loses any trace of geographic specificity. It becomes simply exotic.

It is worth considering, by way of conclusion, how the mobility of exotic icons shaped their meaning: how the geographic range of these symbols and the process of their transmediation may have affected their implicit message. To a degree, the migration of pictures inexorably produces a slackness of form; the process of transferring images across space and media leads to a softening of original shapes and meanings. When parasols move from Asian contexts to American ones, that is to say, they lose something in the process: a symbol of royal status can become a prop for colonial subjects. The more they are handled, in other words, the more malleable exotic icons become. Yet, more than just their mobility, the direction icons travel can also make a difference. By this is meant not simply their traffic between east and west, but the voyages they take from collected object to engraved vignette to decorative design. As exotic icons progress from geography to decorative arts—from maps to books to paintings to cabinets and even to stage props—they take on new and often significantly altered meaning.

Consider one final exotic trope, not so much an icon as a recurring motif, which made its way from literary to visual sources: "tyranny," which in the context of early modern Europe implied the excessive exercise of political power and which had been associated since antiquity with rulers of Asia (sometimes also Africa). Early modern Europeans had inherited from classical sources a cautionary vision of "Oriental despotism": of omnipotent princes renowned for their power and even brutality in matters of governance. Those sitting under the exotic parasols might well be "tyrants," too—as is the case with the shaded "Cham" on Nieuhof's frontispiece, who sits in justice over four victims, one of whom is harshly encased in a pillory. Oriental "tyranny" has, of course, an extensive history. It had been embodied, first, by the mighty potentates of Persia, who threatened the Greek polities; later, by the invading Asian chieftains of late antiquity and the early Middle Ages; next, by the fiercely sadistic (it was widely presumed) Ottoman sultans, who menaced Europe from the early Renaissance. By the seventeenth century, however, the trope of tyranny had turned again, this time westward. It was now the Habsburg overlords of America who were fashioned "tyrants" and represented as such by scores of authors and draftsmen, especially in northern Europe where colonial rivalry drove this attack—above all in editions of Bartholomé de Las Casas' *Brevíssima relación*, which offered a stunning catalogue of Spanish "tyranny" in America. Once more, however, this trope remains unstable. It migrates across global space and consumer media, and it transforms in the process into a scarcely fixed emblem of the exotic world, where "tyranny" and torture are made to seem veritably commonplace. It is, moreover, particularly in the decorative arts that images of global violence show up. Decorative arts, at first blush, would hardly seem the best forum for this sort of fare. Yet scenes of exotic cruelty appear regularly and haphazardly on decorative objects, and merely by replicating these motifs in the context of consumable luxuries, their signification necessarily shifts. Thus, an image of Chinese "caning," originally engraved for a volume of Asian geography and meant to attest to the puissance of the emperor, resurfaces in an English pattern book on the art of lacquering ("japanning"), reformulated as a model for a chest of drawers (Figure 2.9). (One shudders to contemplate the Enlightened English gentlemen pulling out his hosiery in the morning, casually taking in this scene of "soft" torture. Although the decorative and aesthetic impulse behind these designs may be obvious, no less apparent are the dangerous implications of normalizing torture in the colonial world.) In a slightly later iteration, the caning scene combines with a second depiction of corporal punishment to form a design for bedroom wallpaper (Figure 2.10). Note that a central palm tree fills the background of the caning vignette (on the bottom), perhaps to remind a drowsy viewer of his or her exotic locale.[43]

Thus, we have arrived back at palm trees, be they on a map of New England or in a Baroque bedroom. Palm trees could flourish in northerly climes, just as Oriental parasols could shade Indian queens and torture scenes could spruce up early modern bedrooms, since exotic geography allowed them to do so. Sources of geography, produced and collected by Europeans as never before in

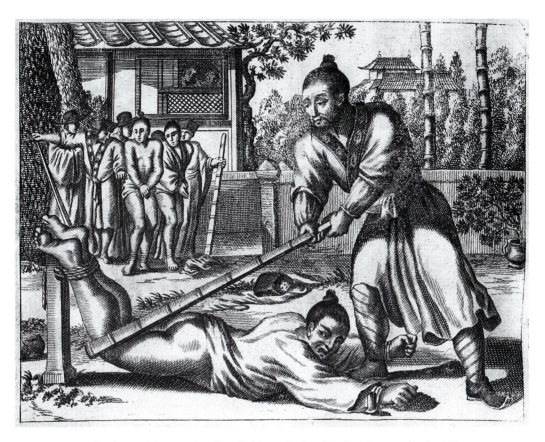

2.9. Jacob van Meurs and atelier, "Chinese Justice (Caning)," engraving in Olfert Dapper, *Gedenckwaerdig bedryf der Nederlansche Oost-Indische Maetschappye, op de kuste en in het keizerrijk van Taising of Sina* (Amsterdam, 1670). Huntington Library.

the late seventeenth and early eighteenth centuries, exhibited a remarkable fluidity in terms of content and meaning. They created durable and recognizable forms—stereotypes in the parlance of printing or icons in the vocabulary of visual reproduction—yet these could change their sense and significance as they passed from region to region and medium to medium. A science meant to delineate spatial and cultural difference, geography often did precisely the opposite by collapsing distinctions and producing symbols of imprecise provenance and indeterminate meaning. Geography could thus segue into decorative arts—two realms of representation that may not be as far apart as one might imagine. The space of collecting around 1700 was indeed global in its dimensions. Yet it was not particularly finicky when it came to its global clichés. Objects and motifs that might be considered "American" could surface in Asian or African ethnoscapes, while typical Asiana might turn out to have followed American

2.10. "Chinoiserie Caning Scenes," wallpaper for bedroom, South German, ca. 1700–1725, in Otto Pelka, *Ostasiatische Reisebilder im Kunstgewerbe des 18. Jahrhunderts* (Leipzig: Hiersemann, 1924), plate 177. Courtesy of the University of Southern California, on behalf of USC Libraries.

pathways. Exotic icons were fixed in their exoticism yet indeterminate in their place and purpose: thus the global icon. This led to misplaced palm trees and peripatetic parasols—which make perfect sense in the context of early modern geography. It also makes sense in the context of early modern collecting, as the two processes could work in tandem. Collecting across cultures brought together disparate exotica from multiple media. These combinations could be productive. Rather than sorting out the world, early modern collectors may have been complicit in collapsing global differences. Or rather, they may have been part of a process of creating a new form of globalism, which did not so much establish stereotypes of this or that exotic meaning as it established icons of exoticism writ large.

—ᴧᴧ—

Ancient Europe and Native Americans: A Comparative Reflection on the Roots of Antiquarianism

ALAIN SCHNAPP

Antiquity embodied a horizon of thought that obsessed European curiosity from the Renaissance through the Enlightenment. The Greeks, the Romans, and even the Egyptians were omnipresent in the discourses of philologists, in the scholarly research of antiquarians, and in the obsession of men of state and even sovereigns. We owe the discovery of Herculaneum and Pompei to Bernardo Tanucci and his king, Charles of Naples, Charles III of Spain. For the king and his first minister, the buried cities of the area around Vesuvius were not just a simple field of ruins, an open mine of the antique; they were the means of revealing to the men of the Enlightenment an antiquity consisting of entire towns waiting to be uncovered.

The scale of research into the life of ancient times changed with the excavation of Vesuvius's buried cities. After the uncovering of Herculaneum and Pompeii in1738 and 1748, such research could no longer consist merely of collecting rare objects or excavating a few prestigious monuments: Herculaneum and Pompeii revealed groups of objects, ways of life—in short, a past that that could be observed in a nearly intact state. Of course, to see the past in this fashion required excavation, restoration, and conservation on an industrial rather than an artisanal scale.

The most dogged, most inquisitive, and most learned of Europe's thinkers criticized the excavation techniques employed at Herculaneum and Pompeii, such as the galleries dug by the military engineer Roque Joachim de Alcubierre.

Charles de Brosses, Denis Diderot, Scipione Maffei, and Johann JoachimWinck-elmann used their conception of history and exercised their critical sense to scrutinize the work carried out by the engineers and scholars working for the king of Naples. Their words did not fall on deaf ears; men of the Enlightenment soon took up these arguments, leading to the definition of a strategy for explor-ing the past that prefigured archaeology in its modern sense.[1]

In Naples itself, objections were raised not only to the methods but also to the objectives of this gigantic cultural enterprise. The social and economic situa-tion that the city was facing led many critics to suggest that the money being spent to expand the royal collections would be more wisely invested elsewhere. As an affair of state, the exploration of the past became the subject of economic debate. Those Neapolitans who felt that priorities such as building schools, enhancing commercial development, and supporting growing industries out-weighed archaeological expeditions denounced a court caught in improvident antiquarian folly. The king and the court were accused of neglecting the present for the sake of an expensive cult that worshiped the past.

The most ferocious criticism of antiquarianism in general was expressed by John Douglas, an explorer and companion of Captain James Cook:

> It is a favorite study with the scholar to trace remains of Grecian or Roman workmanship, he turns over his Montfaucon with learned satis-faction; and he gazes with rapture on the noble collection of Sir William Hamilton . . . but . . . will he not find even more real matter for impor-tant reflection, by passing a hour in surveying the numerous specimens of the ingenuity of our newly-discovered friends? The expense of his [Captain Cook's] three voyages did not, perhaps, exceed that of digging out the buried contents of Herculaneum. And we may ask that the novel-ties of the Society of Sandwich Islands, seem better calculated to engage the attention of the studious in our Times, than the antiquities, which exhibit proof of Roman magnificence.[2]

Douglas not only lashes out against antiquarians and their "conspicuous con-sumption" of the sumptuous folios of Bernard de Montfaucon and the luxuri-ous prints of Sir William Hamilton's collection of Greek vases, but he also questions the generous financing of the digs around Naples that revealed old, already well-documented facts in contrast to the extraordinary discoveries being made by travelers in the Pacific and in the Americas. In a way, these considera-tions revisit Francis Bacon's argument for ethnography made more than a cen-tury earlier:

We must also take in consideration that many objects in Nature fit to throw light upon Philosophy have been exposed to our view and discovered by means of long voyages and travels in which our times have abounded. It would indeed be dishonorable to mankind, if the regions of the material globe, the Earth, the Sea and Stars should be so prodigiously developed and illustrated in our age, and yet the boundaries of the intellectual globe should be confined to the narrow discoveries of the ancients.[3]

Bacon had pleaded for continuity between the discovery of the material world and the laws of human intelligence; he had tried to emancipate intellectual tradition from the dogmatic reverence paid to ancient sources. He took care not to question the exploration of the past itself, but he openly criticized the authority of the ancients. Douglas implicitly echoes this position, though where Bacon had employed the metaphor of discovery, Douglas uses his own experience of long travels; they both express the desire for resonance between the ongoing discovery of the planet and the exploration of the human mind. For Douglas, the ethnographical adventure embodies both these dimensions and reveals a new world. A universe rich in symbols provides new resources for a curiosity dependent on conventional images of ancient times.

Diderot expresses the same idea in his preface to Nicolas Antoine Boulanger's *Antiquity Revealed*, a study in direct opposition to Montfaucon's *Antiquity Explained*. Boulanger, contrary to Montfaucon, uses objects, monuments, and ruins as his starting point before referring to texts and tries to explain prehistory through the tales of primitive men considered to be witnesses to earth's natural and original history. As an engineer, Boulanger had studied history while constructing roads by observing the sky and the ground, as well as the seasons and customs of men. According to Diderot, Boulanger turned to nature as a source for history:

Having considered in all aspects the catastrophes of the earth, he sought their effects on its former inhabitants; thence his conjectures on societies, governments and religions. But he acted to verify his conjectures by comparing them with tradition and stories; and he says: "I have seen, I have sought to interpret; let us now see what has been said and what is."[4]

Southern Versus Northern European Traditions

In the southern European antiquarian tradition, the observation of monuments and landscapes is the consequence of the study of ancient texts: antiquarians

ALAIN SCHNAPP

imagined an ancient landscape and then tried to put it in the context of classical texts. But in northern Europe, antiquarians discovered monuments of a kind not described by classical authors. To interpret them, antiquarians had to develop methods different from those of their southern contemporaries. The antiquarian model invented in Italy could not be applied to runic writing, which did not resemble Latin texts. Likewise, when the seventeenth-century English architect Inigo Jones tried to prove that Stonehenge was a Roman temple, his contradictor Walter Charleton did not hesitate in attributing this strangely built monument to the Danish civilization. Although Charleton was wrong, his colorfully described principle of interpretation is the very basis of the antiquarian method:

> So true it is, that Monuments themselves are subject to Forgetfulness, even while they remain: and that when neither the Writings of Men living in the same Age, or not long after their Erection, nor uncorrupted Tradition hath concurr'd to give them Life, they usually stand rather as dead Objects of popular Wonder, and Occasions of Fables, than as certain Records of Antiquity.[5]

Thus, northern European antiquarians used a very different approach from their southern counterparts: in the absence of texts, they regrouped individual monuments together to form intelligible sets. British antiquarian John Aubrey expressed this new approach in nearly mathematical terms: "these antiquities are so exceeding old, that no bookes doe reach them: so that there is no way to retrieve them but by comparative antiquitie, which I have writt upon the spott form the Monuments themselves."[6]

How might one combat the wear of memory, the corruption of traditions, the erosion of monuments? By looking at living traces of the past, by trying to rediscover intelligible vestiges of history in the present. Douglas accused antiquarians of fossilizing the past, of preferring it to the rich and varied lives of the inhabitants of Oceania. During the first periods of colonization in the Americas, some of Douglas's predecessors observed that new ways could be found to the past by studying the customs of the savages, paths until then unexplored for examining what Charleton coined as "uncorrupted tradition."

The Discovery of Florida and Virginia

The importance of Virginia's discovery by Thomas Hariot and Walter Raleigh lies more in the accounts that they gave of their journeys to America than in the perpetuation of their colonies.[7] A publication by Theodor de Bry, brought out in Frankfurt in 1590, some five years after the expedition, examines the customs of the indigenous inhabitants of Virginia using all the contemporary rules of ethnographic enquiry. The quality of de Bry's book is as much due to Hariot's descriptions as to the plates that illustrate the book, done after the drawings of John White, one of the first governors of the colony.[8]

White was a talented sketcher who captained the second English expedition to Virginia in 1587 before returning to England to bring back more equipment and subsidies.[9] (He unfortunately failed to rejoin his companions on his return because they had moved to another location in 1590.) His original drawings no longer exist, though some copies survive, including aquarelles and prints made by de Bry. With those of his contemporary, the Frenchman Jacques Le Moyne de Morgues, these are the first Western images depicting Native Americans.

Le Moyne accompanied René de Laudonnière to Florida in 1564 on an expedition organized by Admiral Gaspard de Coligny. In the context of the Wars of Religion being waged in Europe, the presence of the French and the English in an area under Spanish control was not without significance. Laudonnière, Le Moyne, and others escaped a Spanish retaliatory assault on a French colony led by the Spanish governor Menéndez de Avilés, who ordered all the survivors of the fighting, with the exception of women and Catholics, executed. Not only were these expeditions risky, but more often than not they came to a bloody ending.

The work of Theodor de Bry and others must be understood in a larger context than that of the colonization of the Americas. It was a response to the philosophy of power and territorial expansion practiced by Portuguese and Spanish theologians and writers. The exploration of the Americas by the English and the French can be understood not only from the point of view of national interests and conflicts but also in the religious and political context of the Reformation (Coligny, for instance, was, of course, a Huguenot). Marcel Bataillon has underlined the existence of Protestant writings that led to the creation of the "black legend" surrounding the exactions of Portuguese and Spanish settlers. All this is well known; what strikes me is that, in the ideological quarrel that pitted Protestants against Catholics, the Protestants undertook to illustrate and collect precise information concerning the customs of the Native American populations. The conquistadores did not fail to show interest in the Mexican and Peruvian populations, but, at least in the beginning, they did not dispatch illustrators as talented or observers as curious as Le Moyne, White, and Harriot. They lacked editors and engravers like de Bry who could interpret the observations and reports made by the first explorers.

For English and German humanists, the discovery of Indian Americans was not just a chronological or ethnographic question but, as the younger Richard Hakluyt and Michel de Montaigne understood it, also a philosophical one. The existence of Indian Americans demanded that one reconceive the relationship between the classical, Greco-Roman world and the barbarians who were the predecessors of the populations of northern Europe. If Renaissance scholars relinquished the fantastic genealogies established during the Middle Ages, how then, without the Trojans and the Egyptians, could one defend the cultural singularity of non-Romanized people? At the time of James Stuart VI's accession to the throne of England in 1603 (when he became James I), the Scottish poet James Maxwell asserted that "against the Romaine Doctores by scripture and nature, bye theologie and astrologie, by philosophie and history, that the north is absolutely the most divine and excellent, the very seate of God and not Sathan, and the chief receptacle of his Church."[10]

For the North to claim theological and humanist equality with the South, a comparative history of cultures and races had to be attempted. To these ends, the Indian Americans provided scholars with a mirror that would allow them to use the present to reflect on the past. This process of ethnohistoric reflection had been evolving since at least the middle of the fifteenth century. In 1457, Sigismond Meisterlin wrote in Augsburg the first chronicles of Germany's towns. In the tradition of Lucretius and Latin authors, Meisterlin compared the Germanic hunter-gatherer tribes with the Romanized populations who had discovered agriculture and founded towns:

> This population [the Swabians] possessed a great part of the German land / and passed its time in hunting animals / and lived on their meat / and on plants and fruit / and on acorns. . . . There (Between the Lech and the Wertach) they began to build houses to live in / while before, naked and weaponless, they had shelter in neither castle nor in any house / againt the frost and heat / and neither they secure among themselves.[11]

Meisterlin revisited the Greek and Roman tradition by underlining the virtues of the savages. At the Diet of Frankfurt in 1453, Enea Silvio Piccolomini had called on the warrior skills of the old Germanic tribes to confront the insolence of Turkish victories.[12] The identity of the North was thus twofold: warrior and civilian values developed alongside the barbarous.

The discovery of the Americas presented an opportunity to compare faraway barbarians with those closer to home, to establish a link between the modern and the ancient world through a study of customs that appeared to be similar. As T. D. Kendrick and Stuart Piggott describe, the political situation in Elizabethan England forced scholars to rethink the complex relationships between Scotland, Wales, Ireland, and England by means of a comparative model that gave weight to the analysis of customs and the "degree of civilization."[13] An anonymous seventeenth-century author wrote, "We have Indians at home— Indians in Cornwall, Indians in Wales, Indians in Ireland."[14]

The Scotsman John Mair, who made a brilliant career at the University of Paris and in his own country, was one of the first theoreticians to justify the slavery of American Indians,[15] which brought him immediate recognition from Spanish theologians as well as from Scottish scholars, who convinced him to try to distinguish between the good and the bad savages of his Scottish homeland. Mair concluded that the Lowlanders were opposed to the Highlanders because their customs were governed by reason; Highlanders could be divided into those who owned large herds and "yield more willing obedience to the courts of law and the king" and the others, who made up a very different category:

> The other part of these people delight in the chase and a life of indolence; their chiefs eagerly follow bad men if only they may not have the need to labor; taking no pains to earn their own livelihood, they live upon others, and follow their own worthless and savage chief in all evil courses sooner than they will pursue an honest industry.[16]

It is remarkable how much this kind of description is based on medieval tradition, especially the writings of fourteenth-century author Johannes de Fordun, who compared the populations of the South with the Highlanders.[17] Mair, however, goes beyond a strictly cultural point of view, embracing the issues of customs and economics. In so doing, he returns (as did Meisterlin) to a kind of evolutionary model more akin to Lucretius than to the medieval description of "savages." Yet Mair is hardly in accordance with his predecessor from Augsburg on the idea of the "good savage": the animal herders represent a stage in human history, and by observing savage behavior in modern man, one could better understand that of the ancients.

This background allows us better to imagine the context in which John White and Jacques Le Moyne made their drawings and aquarelles. When the Flemish painter Lucas de Heere represented the "ancient Bretons going to war" in a watercolor sketch, he displayed nude, toned, and tattooed warriors clearly modeled after the bodies of the natives of Florida and Virginia depicted in drawings by White and Le Moyne (Figure 3.1). As a painter who was also one

3.1. "Les premiers anglais comme ils allaient en Guerre au temps de Jules César," in Lucas de Heere, *Théâtre de tous les peuples et nations de la terre avec leurs habits et ornemens divers, tant anciens que modernes, diligemment depeints au naturel par Luc Dheere peintre et sculpteur Gantois*, sixteenth-century manuscript. Ghent University Library.

of the first to execute precise aquarelles of Stonehenge, de Heere depicted the Picts with an ethnographic vision.

When White made aquarelles of the ancient Picts, it was, as de Bry stated, as "fownd as he did assured my in a old English chronicle." The explorer had turned historian; his travels were the guarantee of the precision and quality of his drawings. Although unable to observe the ancient Picts directly, White asserted that his models for them were taken from an ancient manuscript.

As suggested by Charleton, the monuments of the past cannot speak for themselves, and if tradition is absent, then it must be compensated for by some other means. To Renaissance thought, the attentive painter could evoke and even reconstitute the past. Le Moyne and White used their experience of portraying Native Indians to draw the Picts, and so the Picts appeared to be the brothers of the Natives of Virginia and Florida.

Were Le Moyne and White antiquarians? They were certainly the products of Elizabethan curiosity, and, although they did not draw monuments (North Indian culture having none), they became the first to attempt a systematic iconographical study of the customs of the populations they observed. Thanks to their pen and brush, indigenous populations no longer appeared as deformed monsters. Like animals, plants, and landscapes, indigenous people became the motifs of images that obeyed certain rules of visual objectivity. The work that had been carried out by Italian antiquarians on classical monuments was taken up by their English, German, French, and Scandinavian counterparts in the second half of the sixteenth century and the Italians' method applied to previously neglected monuments such as megaliths, tumuli, thunderstones, and funerary urns. Ethnographers made man's body, attitude to work and war, and ceremonies new themes of observation. They traveled far to unknown countries inhabited by people with strange customs and unfamiliar bodies. At the same time, they participated in a kind of exploration that brought up new formulations of old questions. Were Americans a different type of man than Europeans? Were their customs radically different from those of Westerners? European theologians, philosophers, and jurists had asked similar questions with regard to their own "Indians," the Lapss and Eskimos of the Great North, nomadic populations at the edge of European frontiers, and animal herders in Scotland and elsewhere who refused to conform to the laws of modern states.

These new images delivered a message: certain societies did not use monuments, and they defined memory by procedures other than those used by modern Western cultures. By studying these procedures and related artifacts, researchers could expose elements until then hidden, as well as demonstrate

ALAIN SCHNAPP

3.2. "H" shows an excavation in Patagonia during the Schouten expedition (1615). In Theodor de Bry, *America oder die neue Welt*. Willem Schouten, Diarium vel Descriptio laboriossissimi & molestissimi (Amsterdam, 1619). Huntington Library.

improbable similarities. If the Native Virginians were so similar to the ancient Picts, then how could modern inhabitants of the British Isles be considered the free citizens of a civilized kingdom? Montaigne, who was confronted in Rouen with Indians from Brazil, understood the philosophical consequences that a discovery of this otherness would have. Antiquarians lost some of their innocence; the past was no longer what it had been. Proof of this change is provided by an image that we owe to the Dutch explorer Wilhelm Schouten.[18] While anchoring their ship during a 1615 journey to Patagonia, Schouten and his men discovered the "tombs holding the remains of bodies over ten to twelve foot long, whose heads were large enough for them to be used as helmets by the Dutch" (Figure 3.2).[19] In the print from this excavation, one can distinctly make out the men digging up bones. It echoes the oldest surviving images that we have of a dig, the cover page to the 1600 edition of William

A. Saxa quæ vocantur *Corseslones pondere, i...(unai...*
astitudine 24. pedes, latitudine pedes 7. ambitu. 16.
B. Saxa quæ vocantur Cronecf. 6. vel 7. toniarum.
C. Locus ubi ossa humana effodiuntur.

3.3. View of Stonehenge, in William Camden, *Britannia, sive florentissimorum regnorum, Angliae, Scotia, Hiberniae, et insularum adiacentium ex intima antiquitate chorographica descriptio* (London, 1600). Private Collection, Paris.

Camden's *Britannia*: with Stonehenge in the background, bones and an enormous calvarium are being uncovered (Figure 3.3). The caption beneath reads, "Locus ubi ossa humana effodiuntur."[20]

Sketchers and etchers were establishing links between the antiquities of the Americas and the antiquities of Britain that justified a comparative lesson, as

ALAIN SCHNAPP

later conceived by John Aubrey.[21] The lesson was clear: antiquity was not an exclusively Western experience but something that came to light wherever one examined the ground for its traces.

The Conquistadors and the Monuments
of Mexico and Peru

In Europe, the Limes formed a cultural limit that weighed on the historical conscience of scholars more than it defined the actual landscape. The juxtaposition of North and South America with Europe revealed a phenomenon of a similar kind. In Mexico and Peru, colonizers confronted states with their own administrations, their own armies, and their own social traditions and urban centers. J. Alcina Franch established the difference between American and European antiquarian approaches:

> Archaeology was in Renaissance Europe an archaeology of dead relics; evidence of a vanished, utopia like imaginary world, that one dreams of reviving and resuscitating but only through what can be revealed from those relics.[22] On the other hand the archaeology that was developed in the Americas is ethnographic archaeology, an archaeology of the living because its monuments were still inhabited, the objects still used by those that produced them, the statues and divinities still being adored by those that believed in them.[23]

A break between the past and the present had been the basis of Western antiquarian thought since Petrarch. This detachment was the stamp of Renaissance antiquarianism. For French and English explorers in the Americas, the moderns—the Indians that they observed—were actually the ancients in terms of their customs, their habits, and the techniques they used. Those who had had the opportunity to observe them could better understand the original inhabitants of non-Romanized areas of Europe. In other words, Native Virginians were more similar to the Picts than Western man was.

This distance between the past and the present was obliterated in Mexico and Peru, where the conquistadores met people with armed and administered states and monuments rather than hunter-gather tribes. The first Spanish reports speak of Hernán Cortés visiting the Templo Mayor de Tenochtitlan in the company of Moctezuma, and Francisco Pizarro discovering the temple of Pachamac on the Peruvian coast: a kind of archaeological outing that recalls Mehmet's visit to the ruins of Troy after conquering Constantinople—a Troy whose monuments were still in use.[24]

The conquistadores' shock at seeing the exceptional stone constructions was enormous. The Spanish capital of the Yucatan, founded on the Mayan site of T-ho, was named Merida in 1579 because when the Spaniards arrived, "they found well-constructed buildings of rough stone and mortar with many moldings similar to those that the Romans had made in Mérida in Spain."[25] Admiration of American Indian architecture was expressed in the writings of Francisco Pizarro's secretary, Pedro Sancho, when he described the fortifications and the houses of Cuzco:

> The Spaniards who see them say that neither the bridge of Segovia nor any other edifices which Hercules or the Romans made is so worthy of being seen as this. The city of Tarragona has some stonework in its walls made in this style, but neither so strong nor of such large stones.[26]

The ideology that led to the conquest of the Western Indies was in some ways a continuation of the Reconquista—the reconquest of Spain from the Moors. Thus, writers nourished by Greek and Roman literature could not help but compare the monuments of New Spain with those of Old Spain, and the idea could not escape them that the architecture that they came across showed similarities to that of former Roman Spain so eloquently discussed by Renaissance antiquarians.

In Mexico and in Peru, the invaders discovered inhabited monuments that contained unimaginable—and quickly coveted—treasures. Bernardo Diaz del Castillo tells of how Cortés and his followers forced open the doors of the Moctezuma palace to get their hands on the royal treasure of the Aztecs.[27] The diversity, the quantity, and the quality of the objects they plundered were so great that the collection was exhibited in Seville, Toledo, and Valladolid and then sent on to Brussels, where Albrecht Dürer admired it. Dürer praised the rarity of the objects as much as the ingenuity of their execution.[28]

The societies of Central and South America also offered colonizers the spectacle of a complex social system. The Mexicans, like the Peruvians, had traditions and a history expressed in works of art and impressive monuments. The Spanish quickly realized that the indigenous elites had mastered specialized knowledge: they were capable of constructing imposing temples and palaces and of collecting enormous amounts of rare objects and precious metals. Their historical traditions had been formed independently from Western written traditions.

The Europeans were astounded by the Mexican codices and Incan quipus. The Mexicans used a sophisticated alphabet with logograms and pictograms that rapidly became the subject of fascination for the Spanish, who realized that

ALAIN SCHNAPP

the codices were reliable tools for studying the history and the customs of these people. During the first decades after conquest, the curiosity and the conversion politics of missionaries led to the translation and adaptation of indigenous traditions. For Spanish clerics, the Mexican codices were at once objects of fascination and of loathing. The same men who—with the help of Indian informers—exerted infinite patience in collecting and copying texts did not hesitate to confiscate and burn them if it seemed likely that they might serve in the rituals of indigenous religions. Not all Europeans appreciated the culture of American Indian societies in the same way that Dürer did.

Whether they admired or detested Hispanic American culture, the conquistadores were aware that they were not dealing with man in his "natural" state. Each society was marked by its own very long history. Mexican sources were not simply legends; they bore witness to historical events that historians had to take into account. Diego Duran was part of a group of clerics who made the effort to study Nahuatl, the local language, in order to communicate with informers. A Dominican living and working in the second half of the sixteenth century, Duran wrote one of the first books dedicated to Aztec history.[29] Jorge Cañizares-Esguerra proposes that the originality of Duran's work lies in the way he juxtaposed Spanish sources with indigenous ones, similar to how Herodotus contrasted Greek with non-Greek sources.[30] Take the tale of Moctezuma as an example. Although the Spanish attributed Moctezuma's death to the action of his own subjects, Duran writes that indigenous witnesses gave a very different explanation:

> Had the history not said it, had the paintings that I have seen not certified it, it would have been difficult for me to believe [the account of Moctezuma's death]. However I am obliged to put what the [indigenous] authors I have followed in this history tell me, in writing and painting.[31]

Those who showed interest in indigenous populations and studied their language were capable of understanding the pertinence of their historical traditions and the precision of their reports. It was not enough to limit contact with such a culture to an ethnographic approach—a historical and scholarly approach was necessary to reveal the traditions and the intellectual and material context of what was, even though the term was not applied, an indigenous civilization.

To perfect their program for systematic conversion, clerics, particularly the Franciscans, set out to study indigenous cultures through local informers and by learning the local languages. Faced with the profusion of documents produced by the indigenous cultures, the converters had to make some choices.

Toribio de Benavente Motolinia was one of the first Franciscans to arrive in Mexico and to show an interest in indigenous cultures. He classified Aztec books into five categories—ritual calendars, books of dreams, predictions, horoscopes, and historic annals—and concluded that only historic annals should be preserved; objects belonging to the other categories could be destroyed.[32]

The paradox of Franciscan erudition is obvious. By combining linguistic inquiry, ethnographic observation, and antiquarian method, the Franciscans were able to make more progress in deciphering indigenous texts than European philologists from the Renaissance to the Enlightenment had in their efforts to decipher ancient Egyptian texts. Diego de Landa, a Franciscan who became superior of the provincial order and an antiquarian of the Mayan world, tried to interpret the Mayan glyphs and traveled the country to gather inscriptions and draw up plans of the most important sites. He recounts his progress in *Relación*.[33] De Landa's ability to interpret Mayan sources was well known, and modern specialists consider him an early pioneer in the effort to decipher the Mayan script.

Like other contemporaries such as Diego Duran, de Landa was passionate about the history of the ancient Americans, and he approached it with the same curiosity and classical sensibility as his Italian, English, and French contemporaries. (Duran's depiction of the founders of Tenochtitlan is remarkable: they are dressed in a kind of white toga decorated with a red stripe recalling the clothing of Roman citizens.)[34] De Landa's method was similar to that of great antiquarians in the Italian tradition such as Pirro Ligorio or Fabio Calvo. He studied landscapes and drew what were to him the most striking monuments. Chapter 8 of *Relación*, "Los edificios de Yucatán," is devoted entirely to architecture. De Landa mentions Izamal, T-ho or Mérida, Tikoh, and Chichen-Iza. Like Ligorio, de Landa carefully describes the edifices and accompanies his text with drawings (Figures 3.4 and 3.5).[35] In the course of his research, he went as far as to carry out digs to find tombs, relating their discovery with precision.[36]

In their role as ethnographers and antiquarians, the Franciscans, as well as other orders, pursued religious and political ends. In order to convert the native Indians to Christianity as rapidly and efficiently as possible, priests needed knowledge of Indian culture as well as the help of Indians. This required an intense effort of acculturation that aimed to distinguish between those aspects of local tradition that could be conserved and those that could be irrevocably destroyed. With the goal of creating a mixed culture that prefigured the French monarchy's *jeunes des langues,* the Franciscans founded the Colegio de Santa Cruz de Tlatelolco in 1534.[37] It was designed to provide a Christian education to an elite group of Indians through the language and traditions of the Nahuatl.

ALAIN SCHNAPP

de cora, y muy de mayores cuerpos, y fuerças y aun vee se esto
mas aqui en Yzmal que en otra parte en los bultos de medio talla
que algo estan oy en dia de argamasa en los bestiones que son
de hombres crecidos, y los estremos de los braços y piernas del hombre cuyas eran las ceniças del cantaro que hallamos en el edificio que estavan a maravilla por quemar, y muy genessos.
Vee se tambien en las escaleras de los edificios que son mas de
dos buenos palmos de alto, y esto aqui solo en Yzamal y en Merida.
Ay aqui en Yzmal un edificio entre los otros de tanta altura y her-
mosura que espanta, el qual se vera en esta figura y en esta
razon della. Tiene

[figura]
capilla
escalera
quiere la plaça

Plaça muy grande y hermosa

Escaleras muy agras pa subir

XX gradas de a mas
mos de alto, y au
y ternam mas
de largo, son estas
muy grandes
das, aunque co
tienpo, y estar
estan ya feas
Tiene despues labra
senala esta raya de
canteria una muy
a la qual como esta
alto sale una ceja

de dos buenos pal-
mos cada una
de cien pies
gradas de
piedras labra
el mueso
al agua
y mal tratadas,
lo en torno como
donde labrado de
fuerte pared
do y medio en
de hermosas piedras todo ala redonda, y desde ellas se
torna despues a seguir la obra hasta ygualar con el altura de la plaça que se hage despues de la primera escalera
Despues de la qual plaça se hage otra escalera como la
primera aunq no tan larga ni de tantos escalones siguien-
do se siempre la obra de la pared redonda de la redonda.
Encima destos escalones se hage otra buena plaçeta, y en
ella algo pegado ala pared esta hecho un cerro bien alto con
su escalera al medio dia, donde donde caen las escaleras
grandes, y encima esta una hermosa capilla de canteria bien labrada. Yo subi en lo alto desta capilla, y como
Yucatan es tierra llana se vee desde ella tierra quanto pue-
de la vista alcançar a maravilla, y se vee la mar. Estos
edificios de Izamal eran por todos XI o XII aunq es esta el
mayor, y estan muy cerca unos de otros. No ay memoria de los fundadores y parecen aver sido los primeros.
Estan VIII leguas de la mar en muy hermoso sitio, y buena tierra, y comarca de gente por lo qual nos hizieron
los

3.4. "Templo de Izamal," in Diego de Landa, *Relación de las cosas de Yucatán* (1586), ms. 9/5153, f. 46v. Real Academia de la Historia, Spain.

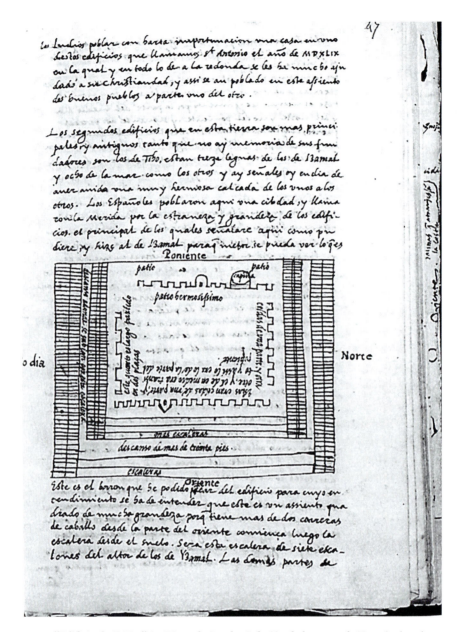

3.5. "Edificio de T-Ho," in Diego de Landa, *Relación de las cosas de Yucatán* (1586), ms. 9/5153, f. 47r. Real Academia de la Historia, Spain.

In just a few years, thanks to professors such as Bernardino de Sahagùn, the most gifted students were able to express themselves in such elegant Latin that they could in turn teach newly arrived priests from Spain.[38] A notary and landowner from Tula in a North Mexican valley, Jeronimo Lopez, believed that it was his duty to warn the Council of the Indies of the risks that such educational

ALAIN SCHNAPP

practices could entail, especially the effects that the knowledge of Latin might have on the future behavior of the Indians:

> The elegance of the Latin language, making them read various kinds of exact knowledge from which they have come to know the whole beginning of our history and where we come from and how we were subjugated by the Romans and converted from paganism to the faith and everything else that has been written about this, all of which inspires them to say that we too came from the pagans and were subjects and defeated and subjugated and were subjects to the Romans and revolted and rebelled and were converted to baptism so very many years ago and are not even yet good Christians, we who demand that they convert in so short a time.[39]

Lopez and others feared that, if the Indians were given access to classical history, then they might apply the same historical methods to their own condition, a measure that could have very obvious and very alarming political consequences. The speculations of the astute notary were to prove judicious. One of the main caciques of Texcoco, don Carlos Ometochtzin, declared before being burned at the stake: "Christian doctrine? It is nothing at all, and there is nothing sound in what the Brother says."[40] His was a rational criticism of a religion enforced through violence and slavery.

The colonizers were threatened by a potential reversal of the positions of the colonizer and the colonized. Lopez also reported on secret meetings of Mexican noblemen held in 1545 during which they stated that they had learned "all the techniques of the Spanish, their way of fighting, their strengths, their horsemanship and all the rest that we were ignorant of and did not know."[41] Fear of an indigenous elite as familiar with Hispanic culture as with their own traditions developed into the specter of anticolonial revolt in which the indigenous people would use the colonizers' arms against them. The cultural relationship between the Spanish and the Indians went beyond simple curiosity; it was part of a power struggle.

It soon became clear that the Spanish were not alone in developing a passion for antiquarianism. The Indian nobles who had been to the school of the brothers became as curious about local traditions as the Castilian clerics. Two Nahua chroniclers educated by the Franciscans, Francisco de San Anton Munon Chimalpahin Cuauhtlehuanitzin (1579–1660) and Fernando de Alva Ixtlilxochitl (1578–1650), set about to explore Mexican history using the erudite methods of their masters. They collected codices and transcribed them into the Roman alphabet.[42]

Ixtlilxochitl was a descendant of one of the last sovereigns of Texcoco and Tenochtitlan. Governor of Texcoco and then of Tlalmanalco, he dedicated himself to the transcription of texts and to the lengthy task of reclaiming territories that had once been owned by his family. *Relación histórica de la nación tulteca* and *Historia chichimeca* are the bases of our knowledge of the history of Mexico before its conquest.[43] Ixtlilxochitl was the prototype of the mestizo: he combined both cultures in a sometimes hazardous historiographic construction that allowed for an intercultural dialogue that was to have a role in the historiographical debates of the Renaissance.

The crossbreed culture that was a product of colonialism was not limited to central Mexico. The Augustinians founded a bilingual college in Tiripio where Tarasque elites could study Latin, Greek, and Hebrew. A large number of mestizos, including the scholar and future governor of Michoacan Antonio Huitzimengari, were thus introduced to classical culture.[44] In Peru, Juan de Betanzos, a Spaniard from Cuzco, married an Inca princess, writing in 1551 a *Suma y narracion de los Incas* that (according to its author) was superior to its predecessors because it proceeded directly from indigenous sources: "I have been informed not only by one but by many [scribes; among them] those [who kept annals] of the greatest antiquity and credit."[45]

But in the wake of the Council of Trent and the establishment of the Inquisition in the Vice-Kingdom of Peru in 1571, the mingling of cultures ended. Colleges were closed, and a new kind of relationship was established between the colonizers and the colonized.

The antiquarians of New Spain, whether of Hispanic or indigenous origin, were conscious that they were dealing with a historical tradition very different from that in western Europe, built on its own traditions and techniques. The Western scriptural tradition could no longer claim to be as the sole means of establishing true history. Just as European antiquarians had collected manuscripts in Europe's vernacular languages, learning from runic inscriptions and Celtic coins and digging up monuments, so American antiquarians tried to employ all the means available to them to understand the strange tales and the evidence concerning American Indian populations.

But how reliable were the Amerindians sources? José de Acosta classified the sources of written history into three groups: alphabetic writing; symbolic writing (akin to Chinese ideograms); and paintings, which might be primitive but were common to nearly all people. According to de Acosta, this last group offered pertinent historic information; even the quipus of the Incas could open new perspectives for historians, "for astonishingly quipus can store history, law, customs, and business transaction as accurately as books."[46]

ALAIN SCHNAPP

In Europe, antiquarians at the end of the sixteenth century investigated objects such as urns, polished stone tools, and megaliths. They attempted to establish links between the languages spoken in ancient and modern Europe—Old Norse, Saxon, Welsh, Breton—with observations made in digs. They gathered runic inscriptions with the same passion as they collected Roman inscriptions and discovered the virtues of site excavation and methods of cartography. The similarity to what happened in Latin America is obvious. But the shock induced by the sight of Mexican and Peruvian monuments and the discovery of strange customs was far greater than that experienced by European antiquarians, as evidenced in the writings of a Olaus Magnus describing ancient Scandinavia or a William Camden in *Britannia* or a Philipp Clüver in *Germania*.[47]

Antiquarian science in fifteenth-century Italy paralleled Greek and Roman literary tradition. By going beyond the Limes, antiquarians took into account other monuments, interpreted other languages, and discovered new methods. Just like the discoverers of Mexico and Peru, they realized that the frontiers between the past and the present are permeable because the customs of the present and the past are indissolubly linked. In the sixteenth century, the Atlantic played the same role that the Limes had a century before: it was a frontier. Antiquarians realized anew that they had to be attentive to spoken languages, oral traditions, and landscapes, in short, to be in contact with the present. They realized that the past is—as suggested by Charleton's "forgetfulness" and expressed by Alcina Franch—made of wreckage, of debris that present-day man observes.[48] In the terms of Francis Bacon, the past is a present that is not tributary (to anyone) from the sole scriptural tradition:

> With regards to authority, it is the greatest weakness to attribute infinite credit to particular authors, and to refuse his own prerogative to Time, the author of all authors, and, therefore, of all authority. For truth is rightly named the daughter of time, not of Authority.[49]

Carlos de Sigüenza y Góngora (1645–1700) was the most famous seventeenth-century Mexican antiquarian.[50] Son of a functionary in the vice-kingdom, he became a professor of mathematics at the University of Mexico after studying with the Jesuits and being named royal cosmographer. He embodied the typical seventeenth-century scholar, as well versed in science as in history. His friendship with the son of Fernando de Alva Ixtlilxochitl gave him access to rare codices and collections and explains his interest in Teotihuacan where, according to some sources, he undertook the first excavations of the Pyramid of the Moon.[51] Sigüenza's work as an author of annals and in compiling texts was considerable; he was one of the first to include a history of the people of the

Americas in a general history of the Spanish Empire. (A man of varied accomplishments and action, Sigüenza also came up with a remedy for a disease that had struck maize crops and caused famine.)

In 1680, Sigüenza and Sister Ines de la Cruz (another emblematic figure of seventeenth-century Mexico and a fervent reader and translator of Athanasius Kircher) were commissioned to build a triumphal arch erected to celebrate the entry of the new vice king, the Count of Paredes. The wooden monument was decorated with Corinthian columns and niches for statues, which Sigüenza filled not with portraits of Roman emperors, as was customary, but with images of the Aztec god Huitzilopochtli and the eleven sovereigns of the Aztec Empire. By combining the images of the vice king with images of Aztec gods and emperors, Sigüenza proposed a kind of equivalence between the classical West and the historical and political tradition of the indigenous states. The governor of Mexico defended the decision: "The love of our country is the reason that has led us to leave aside the legends [of classical mythology] to seek out a more plausible concept for the decoration of the triumphal portal."[52]

The triumphal arch embodied a new cultural and historical awareness. The art of representing ancient European populations initiated by Le Moyne, White, and de Heere gave way to depictions of populations until then unspoken of. The frontispiece of Ole Worm's *Danicorum Monumentorum libri sex*, published in Copenhagen in 1643, features the effigy of the Denmark's first royal couple (Gormon and his wife, Tyra) amid a classicist decor of cherubs bending over the holy tetragram in Hebrew characters and holding a portrait of the current king of Denmark; at the feet of the former sovereigns lie some runic tomb stones.[53] This imagery, combining the theme of biblical revelation and classical tradition, could be found in a number of other contemporary images. To take the yet more explicit example of J. H. Nünningh's *Sepulchretum gentile* of 1714: In front of a Corinthian colonnade, Time armed with a scythe holds a parchment reading *memento mori* (Figure 3.6).[54] Above Time, a crowned History holds a quill, while Mercury turns the pages of the great epochs of history. In front of this group, a cherubim sits over an open coin cabinet. In the forefront of the scene, a *putto* plays with protohistoric vases; spread out on the ground are a mixture of stone and bronze axes, lamps, medals, and Roman statuettes. Just as in Sigüenza's project, classical and nonclassical antiquity are joined in a unified universal history.

By the early eighteenth century, history on both sides of the Atlantic could be written by taking new paths in the collection of material, nonclassical texts, hieroglyphs, drawings, monuments, and oral traditions. The antiquarians of the Americas laid the foundation for the comparative method that is still one of the tools of universal history today.

ALAIN SCHNAPP

3.6. Frontispice to J. H. Nünningh , Jodoci Hermanni Nunningh, *Sepulcretum West-phalico-Mimigardico-Gentile* (Frankfurt and Leipzig, 1714). Private Collection, Paris.

PART II

COLLECTING AND THE FORMATION
OF GLOBAL NETWORKS

CHAPTER 4

—ʍ—

Aztec Regalia and the Reformation of Display

CARINA L. JOHNSON

After Hernán Cortés shipped the first cargos of gold, silver, gems, and feather treasure from Mexico to Europe, they were viewed with marvel and admiration. The treasure was a gift from the conquistador to Charles V, king of Castile and elected Holy Roman Emperor. Albrecht Dürer's delighted view of these objects, at Charles's court in Brussels in August 1520, is often quoted:

> I have seen these things, which have been brought to the King [Charles] from the new golden land. . . . They are so splendid, that one would treasure them at a hundred thousand guldens' worth. And I have not seen anything, in all my living days, that delights my heart as these objects do. I have seen marvelously artistic things and I am amazed at the subtle craftsmanship of the people in the foreign land.[1]

Fifteen years later, in May 1535, the ambassador Martín de Salinas reported on the fate of some of this gold and silver treasure from the Americas: "[Charles] has ordered all the moneyers of his kingdom to come to this city [the port of Barcelona], so that they may melt down all the gold and silver of the Indies into coins."[2] Much of the gold and silver treasure from the Americas was liquidated by the end of the 1530s, while other objects disappeared for decades before reappearing in the new collections of curiosities. What happened in Europe during the fifteen years between 1520 and 1535, between early reception and later destruction of precious Mexican objects? Dürer's admiration has often been held up as a sign that he was an exceptional artist, one who transcended a dominant rejection of a "pagan" aesthetic.[3] If, however, this treasure's reception in the 1520s is examined in the context of European attitudes toward materiality, sacrality, and rulership, a more complex story unfolds. Precious and valuable objects were transferred across the Atlantic Ocean in a series of exchanges, from Moctezuma as ruler of the Aztec Empire to Hernán Cortés, from Cortés to his own sovereign Charles as king of Castile, and then from Charles as elected Holy Roman Emperor to several Habsburg family members. From the treasure's entry into Cortés's possession, the exchanges illuminate treasure's shifting cultural significance during its first fifteen years in Europe. Mexican treasure's received value and its subsequent revaluation in the 1520s and 1530s reflect broader cultural transformations of treasure during the early Reformation era.

At the beginning of the sixteenth century, treasure was a vitally important tool for ambitious rulers. In the prehistory of collecting, European treasuries had not yet become cabinets of collection or *Kunstkammern*.[4] A ruler's material and symbolic worth could be expanded through the possession of treasure and, thus, princes engaged in competitive accumulation of such splendid and marvelous objects.[5] Mere wealth was inadequate for the acquisition of treasure, particularly treasure with great symbolic significance; only princes, whether secular or ecclesiastic, legitimately possessed such objects. The values of treasure ran the gamut between the more material and the more symbolic. The distinction between the two types was illustrated in two of Holy Roman Emperor Maximilian I's monumental print projects, the Triumphal Arch (*Ehrenpforte*) and the Triumphal Procession (*Triumphzug*). Maximilian, Charles V's grandfather, had planned a series of print projects to valorize his life and dynasty. Each print in a project could be viewed as a scene, while the set of prints formed a larger spectacle when assembled as a whole. Thus, in the Triumphal Arch, the small captioned vignettes from Maximilian's reign fit together to create a two-dimensional, paper triumphal arch. One of the Triumphal Arch's woodcuts, created ca. 1515 by Albrecht Altdorfer, described Maximilian's treasury (*Schatzkammer*). The woodcut depicted a secure room, with treasure stored in chests on the floor and displayed on separate platforms or tables set against walls to the left, center, and right of the viewer. The room's organization mapped out a typology of treasure. Even the table covers suggested a hierarchy of value, from left to right: the table to the left was covered with a plain cloth, the center and right tables with fringed textiles signaling their greater value. The contents of the right-hand table were further elevated in importance by a canopy that sheltered this table and its treasures. The lesser-value table on the left wall held plate and other metalwork, while the center table held ecclesiastical treasure: reliquaries, a crucifix, a monstrance, and other liturgical items. On the table to the right, Maximilian's regalia, including crowns and collars, were arranged under the canopy. The caption announced the contents of the *Schatzkammer*,

CARINA L. JOHNSON

noting the objects' two-fold values: material wealth and attendant spiritual authority. The verse touted Maximilian as the possessor of an unparalleled treasury of silver, gold, gems, and robes that was greater than that of any other prince. The verse concluded by noting, as a sign of this greatness, Maximilian's generous donations to the Church.[6]

The Triumphal Procession, the second print project to illustrate Maximilian's treasure, represented the peripatetic emperor's processional train. Two of the work's miniatures separated this treasure explicitly into two categories of a ruler's authority, secular and sacral. One image represented objects intended for "*Gebrauch*" (use) and the other for "*Andacht*" (devotion). The *Gebrauch* treasure of jewels, gold, and silver plate was material and alienable. Because the pieces demonstrated grandeur and wealth primarily through sumptuous display rather than the symbolic value of any individual item, these treasures could be pawned or converted into specie with relative ease.[7] In the other Triumphal Procession miniature, sacral treasures (*Andacht*) of reliquaries, gold liturgical vessels, crosses, and other sacred objects were carried in a canopied wagon, and accompanied by an eternal flame.[8] *Andacht*, the second form of treasure, contributed to the authority of a ruler not simply through the objects' material values based on cost and artistry, but more importantly by enhancing his prestige as the possessor of such sacral objects and relics. Relics were among the most valued symbolic gifts sent from one ruler to another, and they, along with other sacral treasures, were valued for their associations with the divine.[9] Notwithstanding theological distinctions about the relationship between the divine and material objects, early sixteenth-century practices of viewing relics and other sacral objects emphasized their beneficent power over all who came within sight of them.[10]

In the Holy Roman Empire, another subset of highly inalienable treasure was regalia, closely connected with the sacral treasure used in religious worship. Regalia, even more than the treasury itself, contained a dual symbolism of holy and political authorization for rule.[11] Just as theories of rule understood sovereign authority to be twofold, derived from divine and secular sources, regalia spanned religious and temporal meanings, symbolizing sacral power and sumptuous possession. Several pieces of regalia were common to kings and emperors throughout Europe: crown, orb, and scepter. The crown of the Holy Roman Emperors was doubly sacred at the beginning of the sixteenth century: it not only contained relics, it was itself a relic of the sainted emperors Charlemagne and Henry II, who were believed to have worn it. Other imperial regalia, silk ceremonial robes, were also held to be relics of St. Charlemagne.[12] As regalia acquired more symbolic significance, it became less alienable, since to alienate such a piece would signal a failure to retain the authorization of rule. Regalia played a role in the ceremonies of ordered succession, symbolizing authority and kingship passing from one ruler to another. The coronation of an emperor or king of the Romans included the investiture of the imperial regalia as part of his ceremonial acquisition of secular and sacral authority.[13] The emperor- or king-elect only assumed the imperial ceremonial garments after taking the coronation oath. He then received the sword, scepter, orb, and the crown, displaying his invested regalia to the assembled dignitaries and other witnesses. The coronation and its display of sacral objects were a visual spectacle: sacral treasure overall, including regalia, was rarely seen by the public and its usual seclusion lent force to its rare viewings. Underscoring the visual impact of Charles's coronation, Dürer described the spectacle as "never seen in his lifetime" soon after using the same phrase to characterize the Aztec treasure exhibited at court.[14]

Important sacral treasuries were displayed in annual relic viewings (*Heiltumweisungen*). By the beginning of the sixteenth century, these ceremonies of sacred display were widely popular: Maximilian I even sought credit for initiating a viewing at Trier, by claiming to discover a previously hidden robe of Christ during the 1512 Imperial Diet.[15] In contrast, an important set of relics at Nuremberg, known as the imperial relics (*Reichskleinodien*), had long been publicly treasured. The imperial relics included the imperial regalia and several instruments of the Passion, most importantly the Holy Lance used to wound Christ and a piece of the Holy Cross. Reflecting their role in coronations and their histories, the imperial relics were closely associated with the Holy Roman Emperors. They had been relocated in Nuremberg from Bohemia permanently during the early fifteenth century by Emperor Sigismund, in recognition of the imperial city's wealth and security. There they became linked not only to coronations but also to the first ceremonial entrance of a new Holy Roman Emperor into Nuremberg. For people who wished to see the imperial relics at other times and years, the annual public viewings were held on the second Friday after Good Friday. Pamphlets were sold to commemorate these events, detailing the sacred treasures and the number of days or years of remission from purgatory that the viewer could receive for each object seen. Participating in the relic viewing could result in a gain of almost forty years' indulgences. The pamphlets provided a hierarchy of importance for the relics: the lesser relics of Christ's life, family, and of other saints and martyrs were shown first, followed by the imperial regalia: the imperial crown "with many relics and precious decorations upon it," the array of magnificent garments believed to have been Charlemagne's, and the other ceremonial insignia (orb, scepter, and lastly sword).[16] The viewing culminated in the exhibition of the most valuable sacred objects, the instruments of the Passion.[17]

At the beginning of the sixteenth century, then, treasure and treasuries in the Holy Roman Empire fell into a spectrum ranging from the material and more mutable to the inalienable and more sacred. Objects imbued with sacrality, whether of religious worship or regalian ceremony, were more valuable and inalienable than other treasure. According to Annette Weiner's definition of material objects and gift exchange, inalienability is a mark of great value. While all treasured material objects possess aesthetic and economic value, treasure that is more inalienable departs further from a strictly economic value, by acquiring additional symbolic or cultural density.[18] In the case of regalia and relics, this symbolic value was gained through associations with particular former owners and sacred purposes. Weiner argues that a spectrum of material goods, ranging from those whose cultural or symbolic density results in their becoming highly inalienable to those that are highly exchangeable, is a fundamental component of valuables such as treasure. These different types of treasure depend on each other for their meaning; the highly interchangeable objects allow those more symbolically precious goods to remain out of circulation and thus to maintain their value as inalienable.

As both Weiner and Arjun Appadurai have emphasized, such material possessions have fluid values: their cultural or symbolic valence can and does shift at any given time, along with their relative alienability. Within an exchange, an object might possess symbolic value that is not completely agreed on by all parties to an exchange. In such cases, a successful exchange is still possible if the "regime of value" is broad enough to encompass a meaningful exchange based on the valuation that is shared. Dürer's use of the same language to describe the splendors of Charles's sacral coronation, his treasure from Mexico, and a remarkable church suggests that for him, at least, some of these Aztec treasures could be ranged amid other spectacles, both regalian and religious. For other European observers, the late medieval treasury categories of inalienability and alienability framed the Aztec treasure's initial transfer and translation into European treasuries. For Cortés and Charles V, their evaluation of treasure was sufficiently expansive to include Aztec and Mexican precious objects as part of Charles's princely accumulation of splendid princely treasure of both alienable and inalienable types. From 1519 to 1522, Hernán Cortés continued to send further shipments of splendid gifts along with reports of his actions; both practice and rhetoric promoted an understanding of the Mexican treasure as commensurable for his European audience.

Cortés followed preexisting practices toward sacral spaces and objects when presuming the translatability of sacral space and regalian treasures. During the previous centuries, sacral spaces had been triumphally co-opted in Europe for use by rival religions. Latin Christians appropriated Muslim and Jewish sacred spaces in Iberia and the Germanies, and Ottomans appropriated Orthodox Christian spaces in Constantinople.[19] In Mexico, conquistadores continued this strategy. When the conquistadores recognized indigenous temples, they established Christian churches within those religious structures. They replaced images of Aztec divinities with those of Mary and the saints, leaving the formerly idolatrous priests to tend the purified sites.[20] Material symbols of sovereignty were important in the rivalries of rulers. Throughout Europe and Asia Minor, political competitors asserted power and authority through the appropriation or possession of regalia, symbolizing their political domination over former or future holders. Thus, the Habsburgs parlayed their possession of electoral crowns or miters into political advantages when maneuvering with secular and ecclesiastic electors.[21] Regalia might also be newly fashioned for these competitions of material possession; Sultan Süleyman I commissioned new regalia from Venetian artisans, designed to make his claims of world empire more intelligible to Latin Christian viewers.[22]

Cortés began sending Aztec treasure back to Iberia in an effort to gain Charles V's approval for his unauthorized conquest. Initially, Cortés presented the precious objects as gifts from a newly encountered, potential client kingdom. The evidence from 1519 argues that their symbolism as regal treasure survived the trans-Atlantic voyage for observers at Charles's court. Emphasizing the wonderful craftsmanship of the objects, the court historiographer Peter Martyr Anglerius identified the gifts as regal: he reported on a jeweled scepter, several gold collars, and two great discs, one of gold and one of silver, that depicted enthroned figures. The figures, he noted, appeared to be sovereigns but were, in fact, divinities.[23] Ambassadors at Charles's court were summoned for a viewing of the treasures and spread word that the accompanying Indians were envoys from a prince who sought a treaty with the Habsburgs. The papal nuncio, the archbishop of Cosenza, described Moctezuma's major gifts as regalia or otherwise religious in content: wheels of gold and silver containing images of their enthroned gods, a jeweled scepter, feather crown, and other ornaments.[24] In his public, printed *Carta de relacion* of 1522 (referred to as Cortés's Second Letter), Cortés described the worked gold, silver, jewels, and featherwork in language similar to Dürer's. Cortés wrote, "in addition to their intrinsic worth, they are so marvelous that considering their novelty and strangeness they are priceless; nor can it be believed that any of the princes of the world, of whom we know, possess any things of such high quality."[25] As news of Mexico spread, the symbolism of the treasure in princely rivalries was an explicit part of the discussion. A 1522 French translation of Cortés's letter detailed the princes with whom Charles was competing worldwide: Charles's new treasure was more

CARINA L. JOHNSON

exquisite than that held any other European or African prince, whether Christian, Saracen, "Turk," or pagan.[26]

In his public letters, Cortés emphasized the regalian symbolic meanings of the gifts. By reading the account of Moctezuma's speech acknowledging vassalage, Charles and the wider European readership could interpret the regalia proprietarily. In the Second Letter, Cortés also identified the Aztec territories as an empire and accorded Moctezuma the status of an emperor who actively performed ceremonial and diplomatic gestures just as European rulers did. To underline the commensurability of this new empire and its ruler with European cultural values, Cortés also described Moctezuma's status through familiar material symbols of rule. Along with his treasury and collections, Moctezuma possessed a scepter and throne, and his attendants were exceedingly courtly.[27] The extent of treasure collection and court ceremony at the Aztec court exceeded that of the Castilian court.

The subsequent gifting of treasure from Cortés to Charles, and from Charles to his Habsburg relatives, revealed that the variegated Aztec treasure fit into the spectrum of values for treasure in Europe. Some objects were esteemed as regalian symbols, while others, like plate in the imperial treasury of the early sixteenth century, could be and were melted down. In Cortés's 1522 shipment of treasure, mostly intercepted by French pirates off the Azores, a hierarchy of treasure was offered in his catalogue of gifts. He divided the objects into three categories.[28] Two of the lists describe treasure to be gifted from Cortés to Charles: the one list itemized objects already weighed and melted into bullion and the second, ornaments evaluated in terms of artistic and symbolic value rather than weight. This second list consisted of objects adorned with feathers, precious stones, or gold. A third list designated the jeweled and feather ornaments that Cortés had intended to gift to religious foundations in the kingdom of Castile and/or to members of Charles's court. Cortés reserved certain types of valuable gold and jeweled ornaments for his king. Only Charles was to be given items identified as miters and scepters, as well as the great wheels in 1519 that were figured with divinities. Only the king and the shrine of Guadalupe were offered ceremonial items identified with priestly ritual sacrifice in Mexico, while the king and several important Castilian religious sites[29] received plumed crowns. In contrast to these reserved treasures, every grantee, whether church, religious, or secular official, received a symbol of military triumph, an ornamental shield or buckler (*rodela*). Cortés had described the military use of these feathered shields in the *Carta de relacion*, and their gifting echoed the longstanding Castilian practice of displaying trophy shields in churches.[30] The wide disbursal of shields as trophies of victory would ensure that news spread throughout Castile about this military conquest.

Although much of the 1522 treasure instead became trophies of French victory over Castile, Charles received other news and treasure from Cortés during the years after 1519. After visiting the Low Countries and the Germanies for his coronation as King of the Romans and presiding over the 1521 Diet of Worms, Charles had returned to Iberia in 1522. He remained there despite repeated requests that he return to the Holy Roman Empire and preside over imperial diets held at Nuremberg in 1522, 1522/23, and 1524. Charles chose to appoint his Habsburg relatives as his regents and representatives. His aunt Margaret served as his regent in the Low Countries and his brother Ferdinand as his archducal representative in Austria and, eventually, in the Holy Roman Empire more broadly. By spring of 1523, Charles received the report of Moctezuma's capitulation to Habsburg authority and then the conquest of Tenochtitlan in more detail through Cortés's *Carta tercero de relacion* (Third Letter).[31] In the summer and fall of 1523, Charles sent treasures from his empire of New Spain to Margaret and Ferdinand. Such rare treasures would remind viewers, through these objects' very display, of Margaret and Ferdinand's connections to Charles and the emerging Habsburg world empire.

Margaret of Austria received Charles's gifts at her court in Mechelen in August 1523. She placed the gifts in the most intimate of her public spaces, her library. Margaret's library contained other precious ornaments and information about the world, including Peter Martyr's report of the 1519 treasure, in a display of her princely possessions and erudition.[32] The displayed treasures from Charles included a silver wheel, most likely that described by observers in 1519–20, a mirror, and jeweled collars, all objects that Cortés had reserved for his sovereign. Charles also sent more commonplace weapons, shields, cloaks, and other clothing. Margaret would allow these last objects to circulate outside the Habsburg family, as gifts to two important dignitaries. In 1528, she gave the duke of Lorraine's envoy a sword, helmet, shield, fan, and two animal heads to deliver to his lord, perhaps to secure support for Margaret's proposed peace treaty between the Habsburgs and France. Another set of gifts—a shield, fan, and banneret—was presented to Archbishop Albrecht of Mainz sometime before 1530, when Margaret died. Although the exact date of her gifts to Albrecht is unknown, Albrecht figured importantly in Holy Roman electoral politics through 1530, particularly in negotiations for the election of the next king of the Romans. Albrecht's vote had been promised to a Wittelsbach prince as late as 1529, before he finally cast a vote for Ferdinand, Margaret's candidate, in 1530.[33] Margaret's selections of political gifts maintained Cortés's ranking and avoided gifting objects that might have a regalian or sacred significance. The feather helmets, weapons, and shields could be easily read as military and sumptuary by their non-Habsburg recipients. Along with the trophy status of weapons from conquered Mexico, the feather helmets approximated European feather plumes decorating the hats and helmets of lords, soldiers, and elite commoners in the early sixteenth-century sumptuary display.[34]

Charles's gifts to Ferdinand also reinforced links between Charles's realms, expanding awareness of the new Habsburg territories in central Europe. Ferdinand had been sent by Charles from Castile to central Europe after the death of their grandfather King Ferdinand of Aragon (1516) and gradually was becoming Charles's key representative there. For the occasion of the third imperial diet of 1524 at Nuremberg, Charles sent Ferdinand a set of gifts that symbolized imperial or regnal authority, eleven pieces of treasure from his vassal Aztec Empire. They increased Ferdinand's personal collection of treasure significantly; before 1524, Ferdinand's treasure had primarily contained modest *Gebrauch* objects, pawnable and usable plate and medals. Ferdinand's treasury inventory detailed some of the cultural categories through which the Mexican treasure was understood in 1524.[35] The inventory included categories of usable treasure and sumptuous clothing. The habit of the English order of St. George was entered into the category of sumptuous clothing after Ferdinand received it as a gift from an English embassy in December 1523.[36] The Aztec treasures, however, were defined and placed into a more restricted category, distinct from the sumptuous costumes of other nonallied states. They were placed with Ferdinand's few other *ornamentos* (adornments), a term used primarily for ceremonial adornment and regalia.[37] The other items in Ferdinand's ornament category had been used to support Ferdinand's previous appearances at the imperial diets. The first, brocade robes embroidered with eagles and imperial crowns, had been prepared for the beginning of the 1522 diet; the second set of robes and jewels was purchased during the 1522/23 diet; and the third, a square of black velvet perhaps to be used for display (Margaret's display of Aztec treasures used a similar piece), had been acquired before the start of the 1524 diet.[38]

The inventory descriptions emphasized a triumphal reading of the treasure. The treasure's origin was identified as that newly encountered kingdom of the Indies, renamed in light of its conquered status. Mexico was the kingdom "that was lord Montezuma's and now is named New Spain."[39] Charles sent Ferdinand items of treasure that Cortés had reserved for Charles himself or for the most important religious foundations in Castile, the ceremonial robes and feathered crowns of the Aztec Empire. Ferdinand's inventory clearly identifies four of these ornaments in terms of their sacred, ceremonial functions. The first four ornaments listed—a cape, two tunics, and a ritual instrument—were described as used in Aztec priests' ceremonies when they made "sacrifice to the gods and idols."[40] Five of Ferdinand's other Aztec ornaments were plumed crowns or helmets, acknowledged throughout the sixteenth-century Mediterranean world to symbolize rule, while the last two, a tunic and a feathered shield, were also intelligible.[41] These gifts, with their regalian and ceremonial symbolism, soon became entangled with the onset of the early Reformation's attack against relics and empty ceremony, as well as the imperial estates' frustration with Habsburg and papal intransigence on these matters of religious reform. Cortés and Charles, as gift givers, could not have anticipated that, in this new context, even Christian relics and sumptuous religious robes would come under attack as failing to possess the religiously correct significance.

The imperial diet of 1524 was called under politically charged circumstances. The previous diet had ended in a recess that left an array of issues unresolved: legal and institutional reform in the empire, monopolies, taxes for the war against the Turks, and, thorniest of all, Martin Luther. The Pfalzgraf Frederick refused to continue serving in the office of Statthalter (vicar), despite having acted as a needed compromise figure between Habsburg and princely interests. Charles turned to his brother Ferdinand to fill the important position. Becoming Statthalter expanded Ferdinand's authority as a representative of Habsburg concerns and publicly signaled Charles's increasing willingness to depend on his brother. For Ferdinand's own goal of election as the next king of the Romans, these were significant improvements in his political stature. Ferdinand and other members of the diet spent November, December, and early January waiting for Charles's orator Jean Hannart and several important princes, including the duke of Bavaria and the ecclesiastical electors of Köln and Trier, to arrive. In early January, Ferdinand's courier arrived with personal instructions from Charles to Ferdinand and also the Moctezuman treasure. On January 12, the same day that the treasure was added to Ferdinand's treasury, Ferdinand stopped waiting for absent dignitaries and called for the diet to open two days later, which it did in apparent harmony with the customary ceremony of a mass at St. Sebald's.[42]

Ferdinand was still very much an outsider in central European politics in 1524, and his political limits were evident at the imperial diet. Ferdinand's advisors and backers, particularly Gabriel Salamanca and the Fuggers, were disliked in the Holy Roman Empire; by the beginning of March, Ferdinand's reliance on them was anonymously lampooned on a wall of the imperial castle. Along with growing resistance to Ferdinand, reform sentiments began to build in the city of Nuremberg during February and March. When Jean Hannart had finally arrived at the end of January, he announced that Charles expected the Edict of Worms, with its condemnations of Luther's teaching and writing, to be reinforced by all imperial authorities. Ferdinand attempted to check critiques of unreformed religion, asking the Nuremberg city council to meet with him and discuss its compliance. Only a fraction of the council attended this meeting, during which Ferdinand exhorted the council members to obey Charles and the Edict of Worms and halt the inflammatory preaching of the popular Diepold Peringer.[43] Peringer followed Andreas Bodenstein von Karlstadt's position, assaulting the veneration of saints and the use of images and especially images decorated with luxurious objects such as rich fabrics, gold, and jewels as idolatry that diverted devotion away from Christ and the scriptures.[44] The city and city council upheld their support of religious reform, and in subsequent days, religious tensions escalated in the diet and city. The papal legate Lorenzo Campeggio was snubbed on his arrival to the city and, on the following Sunday, Andreas Osiander openly preached that the pope was the anti-Christ. Traditional rituals associated with the beginning of Easter week were not celebrated due to their nonscriptural superstitious basis; instead, communion in both kinds began to be offered. On March 26, in the face of demands by papal and Habsburg representatives that the Edict of Worms be enforced and Luther's teachings curtailed, the city council declared that there would be no ritualized public display of the imperial relics that year. Perhaps reflecting a concern over future controversy, the decision was recorded, unusually, as a majority vote without any councilor's name mentioned in the council minutes. On April 8, the annual *Heiltumweisung* date arrived, with no public viewing ceremony of imperial regalia or other relics. The associated commercial fair, however, continued to take place.[45]

The Nuremberg city council's decision to ban the annual viewing of the imperial relics had both direct and indirect consequences. Explicitly, the ban acted on the council's religious convictions that rituals involving the veneration of material objects or the use of sumptuous display in religion were problematic. In an iconoclastic Reformation, thus, multiple aspects of the *Heilthumweisung* were condemnable. The veneration of relics (part of the idolatrous veneration of images) and the use of indulgences were signs of the church's superstition, corruption, and avidity. Halting the annual public viewing allowed the council to demonstrate its respect for Reformation critiques and implicitly chide Habsburg and papal authorities. The viewing also contravened papal authority through the rejection of a papal bull that had established the annual display in 1452.

The cancellation, and the imperial regalia's removal from public veneration, promoted not only a redefinition of these inalienable treasures but also a redefinition of imperial ceremonial authority. In the eyes of reformers, relics were an inappropriate basis of imperial authority. By no longer participating in the production and reinforcement of one aspect of imperial sacral authority, the Nuremberg city council moved to reframe imperial authority away from the sacrality of material display. This move was not without cost. By rejecting imperial religious spectacle as inappropriate, the council rejected a previous significant source of city identity and reputation and a popular draw for the city's commercial fair. The annual viewing of relics was not renewed after 1524. The imperial regalia were stored away, the relics of Christ's Passion mostly forgotten, and the imperial ornaments kept for the next coronation.[46] The rejection of relics as idolatrous became so widespread in the next few years that even a Habsburg propagandist, Alfonso de Valdés, declared relics "a trap of idolatry." He argued that the church's willingness to allow such idolatry justified the sack of Rome.[47] On the part of the Habsburgs, Ferdinand's treasure inventory reveals no further additions of ornament or splendid garments to his possessions during the next few years. Ferdinand's austerity, while in part perhaps reflecting monetary concerns, might also acknowledge the broader impacts of the Reformation's call to reject the "idolatry" of sumptuary material culture.

Even the print representation of the Aztec Empire changed subtly in 1524, reflecting the concerns over idolatry in the early Reformation. The first Latin translation of Cortés's Second and Third Letters appeared in Nuremberg during the diet. The Second Letter's translation had been completed by Peter Savorgnano, secretary to the bishop of Vienna, by the beginning of March and was typeset by March 4, in time to be read during the escalation of religious and political tension during that month.[48] The translation was printed with an imperial privilege by the reform-minded printer Friedrich Peypus, whose 1524 production otherwise consisted primarily of texts supporting religious reform, including Luther's vernacular Bible.[49] The Latin account allowed the assembled dignitaries at Nuremberg who might have seen the treasures to interpret them as regalian and religious treasure. Cortés's description of the sovereign Moctezuma, his court, and his magnificent treasure were all included in the Latin translation. The new summary "Argument of the Book" narrated Moctezuma's offer of vassalage and identified the sumptuous treasure of gold, silver, robes, plate, and feather art as gifts given by "Lord Muctezuma" to Cortés, then sent to Charles, his Sacred Catholic Majesty.[50] For the reform-minded reader, however, the edition subtly undercut the value of the new treasure by underscoring the idolatrous aspects of Aztec religious practice. As in the original, the body of the Latin text described temples magnificently decorated and filled with idols and images that the Aztecs worshiped. Paratextual additions in this edition foregrounded idolatry and, in particular, child sacrifice, further creating a focus on these subjects which was greater than in the original edition. The subtitle promised that the book would describe "the sacrifice of children" along with cities, customs, and priests. The "Argument of the Book," whose authorship is unspecified, listed as one of the book's topics religious practices, particularly

CARINA L. JOHNSON

idolatry and the sacrifice of both children and older people, in between Moctez-uma's court ceremony and his political submission.[51] This Latin edition also added a visual representation of these problematic religious practices, in an image often considered the first European map of the capital city Tenochtitlan. The center of the map depicts the main plaza of Tenochtitlan, with several structures and figures on the plaza labeled for the viewer: a central figure prominently captioned "stone idol," a two-towered structure identified as the "temple where they sacrifice," and two racks with the "heads of the sacrificed."[52] Despite other elements of the map such as impressive buildings, marketplaces, bridges, and canals, the material evidence of a condemnably superstitious and idolatrous Aztec religion was the focus of attention. If the idolatry of papal luxury and superstitious practice was evident through the extravagant material objects and images found in unreformed church spaces, idolatry was no less problematic in other settings. Whatever imperial symbolism Cortés, Charles, or Ferdinand had understood or intended by the gift of Aztec regalia, this treasure from what had been branded an idolatrous king and human-sacrificing priests could not retain a positive value in the face of the Reformation's general condemnation of superstitious and false religious practice. Arguably, the map assaults not just Mexican people but also Christian Europeans who allow similarly idolatrous practices to flourish elsewhere. While this comparison would be implicit, using a parallel critique of non-Christian culture and religion to attack "papal" religion was a strategy that Luther and the Wittenberg circle would certainly employ explicitly later in the decade.[53]

The symbolism of Habsburg sovereignty in Nuremberg had relied on the material projection of sacral splendor that was no longer universally accepted in Europe. Resistance to sacral display in relation to Habsburg sovereignty persisted past the initial iconoclastic phase of the Reformation. Nuremberg hoped that Charles would finally formally grace the city with an entry in 1532, but he avoided the now "Lutheran" imperial city. The city tried to lure Charles to Nuremberg with *Gebrauch* treasure and proposed festivities, agreeing to hold a procession and a welcoming mass at the church of St. Sebald. Yet even in its plans to demonstrate loyalty to Charles, the city council did not soften its stance on symbolic matters of religious reform: no monks would form part of the assembled clerics who would greet Charles, and St. Sebald's would be decorated with fine altarcloths and tapestries for a mass but not with the imperial sacred relics. Although the pragmatic conflicts of 1532 were the political negotiations over military and financial support of troops for the Ottoman front, contention over the appropriate symbolic or sacral components of imperial authority was not set aside. Charles would not make a first entry into reformed Nuremberg until 1541. By then, the city council and Charles engaged in a new classical idiom for the imperial entry; the viewing of sacred relics was replaced with tableaux referring to classical Rome or to victories over the Ottoman enemy.[54]

The early Reformation caused one area of inalienable possessions, the religious, to lose its symbolic value. The imperial regalia survived to be used in future coronations, but with a different signification. In 1623, the Protestant Johannes Müllner described the shift to a more correct use of the "insignium imperii," freed from the misuses of idolatry. These treasures were no longer seen as relics, along with the relics of Christ's Passion; instead the objects were treasured for their historical value and as a special charge for Nuremberg to protect. They were now even further removed from public view, appearing in public only once a generation rather than once a year.[55] Other religious and regalian treasure did not survive as sacred or unalienable. Cities that had embraced the Reformation might melt down reliquaries for their metal content in times of civic need. In Nuremberg, this action was not taken until 1552 when, with the exception of several important shrines and some of the instruments of Christ's Passion, many of the city's reliquaries and extraneous religious treasure were inventoried, weighed, and melted down for military defense.[56] Charles himself never condoned the reclassification of Christian sacral treasure, and his 1532 Carolina, the criminal code of the Holy Roman Empire, mandated harsh punishment for the theft of relics or other sacred objects from churches.[57] A transformation in the cultural value of treasure emerged elsewhere in a mid-century era of increased warfare and military threats. Costs in this era of militarization were high; for example, Ferdinand ordered gold and silver objects from the Hungarian treasury to be melted down to cover his costs as one of two rival elected kings of Hungary.[58] Similarly, Philip II melted down the crown of Charles V and Maximilian I when it became clear that his cousin Maximilian II would become Holy Roman Emperor rather than himself.[59] Melting down treasure from the Americas, then, should be understood in this context of a sixteenth-century reevaluation and reuse of treasure. With forms of beneficent sacrality dismissed as malevolent superstition, some treasure would become alienable and other treasure retired from active display.

The example of the first treasure and the events recorded by Martín de Salinas from the Inca Empire underscores the transition. The new treasure arrived in Castile during the last weeks of 1533. News of this gold- and silver-rich Inca Empire and its reported conquest circulated widely (both in print and within the Habsburg family) and quickly, just as news from Mexico had. [60] Descriptive accounts of the Inca Empire followed the triumphal strategies developed by Cortés. The Castilian conquistadores reported on the political structure of Peru: an organized polity ruled by a sovereign and "natural lord" Atahualpa, who was quickly subordinated, and subject peoples who would become willing

CARINA L. JOHNSON

vassals of Emperor Charles V. The conquistadores described their gold, silver, and feather treasures as marvelous.[61]

Initially, the Crown did not express interest in displaying the new treasure of gold and silver plate and other objects. Hernando Pizarro sought to present Charles with some of the treasure by emphasizing its never-before-seen and unique qualities.[62] Charles agreed to view "some pieces which are most unusual and of little weight," eventually authorizing Pizarro to exhibit whichever pieces were "estrañas," or unusual and foreign, regardless of their size or monetary value.[63] Traveling to the court at Toledo, Pizarro presented Charles with two gold and one silver vessels, a retable, a gold cornstalk, and a small gilded tambour.[64] The extant descriptions do not suggest that the victorious Castilians ascribed a symbolism of sovereignty to the objects. Instead, descriptions identified them as plate (vessels, platters, goblets) and, with the exception of the retable, convertible secular treasure. After viewing his new treasure, Charles sent it to his stronghold at Medina del Campo rather than to Ferdinand or the new Low Countries regent, his sister Mary, the widowed queen of Hungary.[65] In the 1530s, Charles's ambitions were focused not on the Americas but rather on his most dangerous rival to world empire, the Ottoman Sultan Süleyman. Planning to attack the advancing Ottoman Empire in North Africa, Charles mustered all his available financial recourses to fund an assault on Tunis in 1535. Within months of receiving his Inca treasure, Charles sent out the orders, recorded by Salinas, to melt down all the gold and silver treasure from the Indies to finance his upcoming military confrontation. With even Christian regalia stripped of its ability to signify sacral lordship for large numbers of Charles's subjects, treasure from the empires of New Spain and Peru was more valuable as metal, needed to pay for the military costs of empire.

In the initial reception of Aztec treasure at the Habsburg courts, these precious objects could be perceived as commensurable in their dense cultural value, as the treasure passed through gift exchanges across the Atlantic, from Mexico to Iberia, and then from Iberia to the Low Countries and Central Europe. Even as the sacred garments, feather crowns, and instruments of sacrifice arrived in the Holy Roman Empire, the early Reformation's attack on material display in sacral contexts as insidious idolatry began to shatter commonly held valuations of treasure and treasuries. Sacral and inalienable objects were transformed into desacralized and alienable items through the actions of many in the Holy Roman Empire. Preconquest nonmetal objects, particularly feather and stonework, could gain new desacralized roles as *Kunstkammern* exemplars of Mexican craftsmanship. Feather craftsmanship had been a marvel to Europeans from the time that the first gifts arrived from Mexico, and featherwork continued to be held in high estimation by Catholic writers. Venetian ambassador Gasparo

Contarini lauded the splendid qualities of featherwork in 1525, as did Dominican bishop Bartolomé de Las Casas in the 1550s, when he praised the artisans for their deft ability to approximate natural forms and to create a brilliant play of light and shadow that animated the featherwork.[66] Feather objects possessed another important quality in the mid-sixteenth century: they were not dissoluble into specie. They could be alienated by gift, purchase, or exchange, but they could not be melted down and exchanged for munitions or food in times of military or demographic pressure. Once Mexican craftsman had been converted to Christianity, their feather images would be cleansed of idolatrous imagery. Featherwork in the form of bishops' regalia was used to celebrate mass and in the form of religious images inspired devotion to the Virgin Mary or the other saints that they depicted. Feather objects once again became inalienable for the Catholic clerics and princes who possessed them, admired as Christian rather than as Aztec sacral material objects.

—ᴍ—

Dead Natures or Still Lifes? Science, Art, and Collecting in the Spanish Baroque

José Ramón Marcaida and Juan Pimentel

Introduction: Early Modern Science and Baroque Culture

This work arises from an inquiry concerning two of the most influential intellectual enterprises of the seventeenth century: the new sciences and baroque culture. Equally imprecise in terms of definition and historiographical characterization, both projects shared a somewhat similar social, political, and cultural background. Historians of science, however, seem to have overlooked many of these connections. Since Heinrich Wölfflin and Werner Weisbach introduced "baroque" as a category in the history of art, the term has been widely used in numerous areas: architecture, painting, literature, drama, and so forth. This category, however, has not succeeded in entering the field of natural knowledge in general and the history of science in particular. To us, this absence seems to be related to a particular historiographical school, whose explanation of the "scientific revolution" was dominant in the Anglo-American context from the 1940s to the 1960s. This explanation, inherited from the Enlightenment, not only contrasted rationality, objectivity, and utilitarianism with such typically baroque values as ostentation, excess, and irrationality but also emphasized that the social codes of Puritanism and the ideals of the Counter-Reformation were profoundly antagonistic.

From this perspective, it made sense to argue that, in certain cultural spaces—imperial Spain, for instance—baroque culture flourished at the expense of science. But did such an inverse relationship really exist? How, in fact, were the two projects related? These questions may have permeated discussions on cultural expansion during the early modern period, but the idea of "baroque science" has elicited only moderate attention from historians of science.[1] This essay traces the connections between the new sciences and baroque culture, arguing that they were by no means separate entities. While we focus on one particular subject, still life painting in the Spanish Golden Age, we locate it within the broad framework of the relationship between art, science, and collecting in the context of baroque culture.

Still Life Painting

The case of still life painting illustrates the complex interplay between natural knowledge and visual representation, which pervaded the practice of both art and science during the baroque period. Indeed, the subject resonates strongly with recent interest among historians of modern science in exploring the relationships between science and other disciplines during this period.[2]

Most art historians seem to agree that still life painting made its appearance during the Renaissance, in connection with the rediscovery of decorative paintings in ancient Roman villas: frescoes representing fruits, flowers, and household artifacts such as jars or baskets. These were the so-called *xenia*, a genre described in several ancient texts, particularly in Philostratus's *Imagines* and Pliny's *Natural History*.[3] It is interesting to note that in both texts we find not only some of the central themes of this genre (food and domestic life, illusionism, and simulation) but also the double affiliation of these paintings with a zeal for collecting and an interest in natural knowledge. Philostratus described the villa of a wealthy noble who had his possessions represented in fresco as both a symbol of opulence and a sign of hospitality for his guests (the term *xenia* can be translated as "hospitality"). Pliny wrote down what is probably the most-quoted anecdote in the history of still life painting. In a competition to determine the more skilled of two artists, Zeuxis's fresco of grapes was so successfully naturalistic that birds mistakenly took the representation for the real thing, attempting to eat the painted grapes; Parrhasius, in turn, managed to fool his rival Zeuxis with a fresco featuring a curtain painted with such a degree of realism that the latter asked the former to please remove it so he could have a look at his work. Pliny's anecdote appears in the context of a much wider intellectual project: his highly influential *Natural History*.[4] Nevertheless, despite the frescoes at Campania, the references from the classical world, and the precedents of the Italian Trecento and the so-called "grotesques," it was not until the seventeenth century that the genre became prominent and truly independent. In fact, it is then that the term "still life" was adopted to refer to paintings featuring such objects as fruits, flowers, vegetables, game, fish, and utensils.[5]

The relevance of this genre in places such as the Low Countries and Spain, two cultural spaces where the religious divide between Protestantism and Catholicism was particularly conspicuous, is noteworthy. The Northern Provinces saw the rise of Puritanism and a buoyant bourgeoisie, two factors that greatly influenced the development of artistic and scientific practices during this period.[6] Spain, in sharp contrast, was dominated by the ideals of the Counter-Reformation and occupied a peripheral position in terms of scientific and technological progress.[7] But despite the evident signs of imperial decadence, Spanish culture flourished. Both countries contributed significantly to what Jonathan Brown has termed the "triumph of painting": the success of art collecting over other forms of collecting.[8] In a European setting dominated by global trade as well as cultural and commercial expansion, collecting had become one of the trendiest activities in courtly circles. The Renaissance affinity for novelties, together with a revalorization of curiosity and connoisseurship, had given rise to a form of courtly taste fascinated with the gathering and display of rare and exotic objects: gems, fossils, shells, mechanical devices, and so forth. In the seventeenth century, as the category of the marvelous expanded, this affinity for the rare and unusual turned curiosity into wonder, and collecting became synonymous with spectacle and display.[9] By the middle decades of the seventeenth century, with King Philip IV of Spain championing the trend, painting had become the most fashionable of all collecting subjects.[10]

As a direct consequence of this, the cabinet of curiosities—the kind of collection Ferdinand II of Tyrol had in Ambras and to which he referred with a term that remains in use today, the *Kunst- und Wunderkammer*—gradually yielded to specialization. Many seemingly indiscriminate compilations of relics, ethnographic objects, natural specimens, furniture, and antiques remained common into the eighteenth century because of the interest of individual patrons, scholars, and apothecaries. Powerful kings and princes, however, began to favor painting and to pay much less attention to other items, whose accumulation, classification, and study were assigned to learned men, physicians, and naturalists working at the university or associated with the newly created scientific academies. To a great extent, baroque collectors chose to have their possessions replaced by pictorial representations and lived surrounded by them. In Madrid, the Buen Retiro Palace, the grand project that Count Duke of Olivares dedicated to the magnificence of King Philip IV, was mainly intended to accommodate the royal collection of paintings.[11] Nature was certainly not absent from the Buen Retiro: the palace contained a huge cage with a remarkably diverse collections of birds, a menagerie that inspired citizens of Madrid to call the imposing building the "hencoop." Nevertheless, the Room of Kingdoms (the

Salón de los Reinos) and other areas of the palace were decorated with paintings, and more particularly with paintings that praised the monarchy and celebrated the military victories of the Spanish army.[12]

The dominance of painting over other forms of collecting in the Spanish case should be considered in the light of two factors. First, the mercantile bourgeoisie and commercial activities associated with the traffic of goods were weaker in Madrid and Seville than in Amsterdam, London, and Paris. Second, the scientific institutions of the Renaissance had not been replaced by more modern ones, and most resources, including royal patronage, were devoted to the arts rather than to the sciences. These factors remained true in Spain throughout the early modern period. The dominance of painting prevailed into the nineteenth century: in 1818, a new important building located next to the botanical garden and astronomical observatory in Madrid, which had been originally intended to house the Academy of Sciences, the natural history museum, and a chemical laboratory, became instead the venue for one of the most important art collections in the world, today's Prado Museum. Thus, the supremacy of painting not only managed to conquer the past but also to project itself into the future, forging an image with which Spain and other European nations could identify themselves. In the Spanish case, according to Fernando Rodríguez de la Flor, this image was that of a "metaphysical peninsula" devoted to the arts, poetry, or asceticism; in other words, an antimodern space.[13]

The triumph of painting was not an exclusively Spanish phenomenon. Let us briefly mention, for instance, the case of Flanders, which is interesting for three reasons. First, it was located at the frontier separating the Protestant United Provinces and the lands of the Catholic monarchy—the two regions of Europe where still life painting was most popular. Second, the city of Antwerp housed one of the most important art markets in Europe. And third, it was in Antwerp that a singular subgenre, gallery painting or cabinet painting, flourished. This subgenre presented noblemen and courtiers from Antwerp surrounded by their most treasured objects: paintings.[14] Besides praising the trading and collecting of pictorial works, many of these compositions indirectly alluded to the decline in interest in miscellaneous collections. For example, works by Frans Francken the Younger and Adriaen van Stalbemt feature an allegory of Ignorance in the form of human beings with the heads of asses destroying objects such as books, armillary spheres, musical and scientific instruments, and antiques—familiar elements in any *Wunderkammer*. Generally interpreted as a reference to the iconoclastic movements of the sixteenth century, these allegories, according to Jonathan Brown, may also suggest a connection between ignorance and old-fashioned collecting practices (the gathering of no-longer valuable objects) and present a contrast to the collection of paintings, which was inherently valuable.[15] This negative judgment on the value of *Wunderkammern* and the type of knowledge they generated was shared by many of the leading intellectuals of the modern period. The Enlightenment would endorse this reprobation. Denis Diderot, in his entry on natural history cabinets in the *Encyclopédie*, mocked the heterogeneous and disordered knowledge gained from cabinets of curiosities assembled by amateurs. Georges-Louis Leclerc, Count of Buffon, and Jean-Baptiste Lamarck, among many others, also condemned the cabinets as outdated and associated them with collectors inspired not, as the age of Enlightenment demanded, by reason but by idle curiosity.

Let us go back to still life painting. Art historians devoted to this genre, from Charles Sterling in the 1950s to the present, have emphasized its relation to trompe l'oeil. Ornamental, decorative deceit had been its precedent: since the Renaissance, numerous examples of this type of representation had been produced and included in cabinets, libraries, and *studiolos*. The first still life paintings, therefore, were representations of both natural products and artificial objects, grouped together in private spaces such as cabinets or in domestic places such as larders, cellars, or kitchens. Thus, as Ernst Gombrich has pointed out, it may be argued that still life paintings were originally created for the admirer of the trompe l'oeil, the *kunstschrank*-oriented type of collector.[16] The use of this genre to decorate dining halls and other rooms dedicated to food, either in the houses of the nobility or in the royal palaces, is well documented.[17] At the Alcázar in Madrid, for instance, still life paintings adorned the rooms where Philip III and Philip IV lunched and dined.[18] In these and other places, there was an interchange and deliberate interplay between two presences: one real, the other simulated; one referring to the things themselves, the other referring to the painted objects. Comparing one to the other reveals an intended confrontation between the natural and the artificial, which then motivates a characteristically baroque reflection on the limits of reality and the rivalry between divine and human creations. Illusion and disillusion, familiar subjects in the literature of the Spanish Golden Age and which also permeate the epistemology of early modern science, are the very essence of still life paintings. This quintessence is captured in the phrase *Lo fingido verdadero* ("the feigned true"), an expression used in a comedy by the Spanish playwright Lope de Vega.[19]

Doubt and delusion are also present in the linguistic ambiguity of the name given to this artistic genre in modern European languages. While in Spanish, French, and Italian this genre is termed "dead nature," in Dutch, German, and English they are "still lifes." Dead or alive? That is exactly the point. Wilma George begins an essay on seventeenth-century zoological collections with the same question.[20] In these collections, a coral or a fossil, organic and inorganic at the same time, problematically called for their place in the chain of being and were regarded as wonders. Likewise, still life paintings reproduced the same uncertainty, calling into question the dead/alive status of their content. Stuffed animals and herbariums posed the same problem. Obviously, nobody put into question the *painted* nature of these natural beings and products; audiences attending to a comedy by Calderón de la Barca or a drama by Shakespeare knew it was nothing but a representation. Nevertheless, to expand, not to limit, the possibilities of artifice and illusionism was part of the intended aim. In these paintings the "dead natures" appear silent.[21] But is this so? Strictly speaking, in these works nature is completely inanimate, bereft of life. And yet these paintings also grant nature a permanency, an immortality. To a certain extent, nature remains "still alive"—fossilized in time, preserved from corruption and death. In short, these paintings refer to appearance and reality but also to decadence and decay.

This leads us to another aspect of the relationship between the content of this art and the practice of collecting. Jean Baudrillard, in his well-known study on the system of objects, distinguishes between the property of being used and the property of being possessed.[22] In his view, objects become part of a collection when they are no longer in use, that is, when they are stripped away from their ordinary function and turn into mere possessions. In other words, their functional aspects, according to Baudrillard, yield to the subjectivity of the collection, which not only modifies their meaning but also adds new dimensions to it, an idea that suits our object of study very well. The different varieties of food depicted in still life paintings, for example, seem to have lost their edible character. Objects in a collection, Baudrillard adds, tend to abolish time.[23] As a cultural practice, collecting has been strongly associated with the idea of, the need for, preservation. In the case of still life paintings, the nutritional need has been substituted somehow by another one, also related to survival, but from a symbolic perspective: the need to last, the need to remain. Observing a still life painting or a vanitas, therefore, we observe an elusion of death: that of the "natures" in the painting, which echoing their particular *memento mori*, are depicted before timely corruption leaves them unrecognizable.

Still life painting is also related to the history of modern science and modern collecting through its choice of motifs. In contrast to biblical and mythological themes, royal portraits, and epic battles, the attention is focused on ordinary objects. Art historians use the term *rhopography* to describe the representation of trivial objects. *Megalography*, in turn, applies to the depiction of grand themes.[24] The cool calmness of a larder, a brass jar that is about to lose its luster, the quiet endeavors of a fly on a bunch of grapes: it is hardly surprising that still life painting was regarded as a minor genre by Vicente Carducho and most seventeenth-century treatise writers.[25]

This interest in looking at mundane objects parallels an interest in ordinary natural phenomena advocated by the "new science" of the seventeenth century. The early articles in the *Philosophical Transactions*, for example, feature many references to seemingly trivial recordings of mundane events. A long list of apparently insignificant issues related to notions (and realities) such as air, water, heat, and attraction also mattered. Seventeenth-century scientists discovered, to their astonishment, that commonplace facts, when observed meticulously revealed not only glimpses of the structure of reality but also its most prodigious aspects.

In order to learn about natural philosophy, Descartes advised, one should visit a butcher's shop. Still life paintings, like the work of the first mechanicists and experimentalists, placed mundane objects at the center of everyone's attention. There is a kind of anatomy, a dissection taking place in these paintings. On many occasions, the insides of fruits and vegetables are revealed to us like a human body in the hands of a surgeon or the world itself in the hands of a geographer. Some of these paintings, in contrast, feature geometrical compositions, which evoke the symmetries and equilibrium of contemporary cosmography. Commenting on a still life by Juan Sanchez Cotán, *Still Life with Quince, Cabbage, Melon and Cucumber*, Charles Sterling wrote that the quince and the cabbage "turn and glow like planets in a boundless night" (Color Plate 3).[26] The inclusion of a Mexican chayote in a similar composition by Sánchez Cotán (*Still Life with Game*, held at the Art Institute of Chicago) evokes the domestication of the exotic and is directly related to the idea of global cultural transfer, to which we refer later.[27] Or take a less obvious example: Galileo's drawings of the phases of the moon. Compared with many depictions of fruits, particularly apples and oranges, these studies of shaded spherical volumes display remarkable similarities.

In both contexts, artistic and scientific, material facts gain a new status and, as a consequence, not only gods, kings, and heroes but humanity itself disappears from these representations. A lot of scholarly work has been done on the first images produced by such early scientific instruments as the microscope and the telescope. These images capture new realities below or beyond the human scale. The human element somehow vanishes. A new step is taken toward the loss of humanity's centrality as the measure of everything; these images reveal a devastating materiality. We need to recall only the engravings by the Spanish microscopist Crisóstomo Martínez or the famous illustrations in Robert Hooke's *Micrographia*: the point of a needle, the eyes of a fly—micrography as a form of astonishing rhopography. Mundane objects studied from a new perspective turn into marvels. Similarly, still life paintings somehow preserve the ephemeral and exalt the prosaic. On the canvas, ordinary objects manage to survive, turned, through artifice, into facts worthy of attention: natures as dead and wonderful as those that filled any *Wunderkammer*.

Dazzling Flowers, Dem Dry Bones

Time and caducity, on the one hand, and transformation of the ordinary into the extraordinary, on the other: two common themes in still life painting. In this section, we focus on two elements that poignantly illustrate these topics: bones and flowers. Bones and flowers, it is not a fanciful choice. There is a tension between them, a powerful dialectic between the hardest and least perishable part of the human body and the most delicate and ephemeral part of vegetal species.

The representation of the human skeleton, and of the skull in particular, is a central theme in vanitas paintings, those moral allegories whose chief aim was to invite the observer to reflect on the brevity of life and the caducity of earthly glories.[28] The skulls in these paintings are naked, discarnate bones. They hardly turn their gaze to the viewer, claiming his or her stare instead. As in an anatomical study, these craniums let themselves be observed from multiple angles, some of them almost unsuspected, such as those featured in many vanitas paintings by Antonio de Pereda (Figure 5.1). Their gaps are revealed, their voids exposed; the light they reflect is not very different from the glint and shine of weapons, coins, and jewels lying next to them.

Very often, these skulls are represented in a pile. Vanitas paintings remind us that among the perishable goods from this worldly existence one should not fail to include the particularities of each individual self. For this reason, the skulls in these paintings, either by themselves or in a heap, look unbearably the same. The case of ossuaries in many cemeteries and churches illustrates this point. For many centuries, it was a relatively common practice in sacred places to accumulate skeletal remains; in these charnel houses, surrounded by the crowd of dead, the absurd anonymity of the deceased is demonstrated.

Relics were somehow an exception. Bearing a deep religious meaning, imperceptible but with enough symbolic opacity as to cover, to mask, their nakedness, these bones were coveted objects both in chapels and vestries and in royal collections, where they were often exhibited as part of a complex display of craftsmanship in gold, silver, and glass. Apart from their evident spiritual value, relics (not only bones but also limbs, hair) were credited with miraculous, curative powers. In this sense, the parallelism between these sacred objects and some elements in the *Wunderkammer* is clear. Mummies or, more specifically,

JOSÉ RAMÓN MARCAIDA AND JUAN PIMENTEL

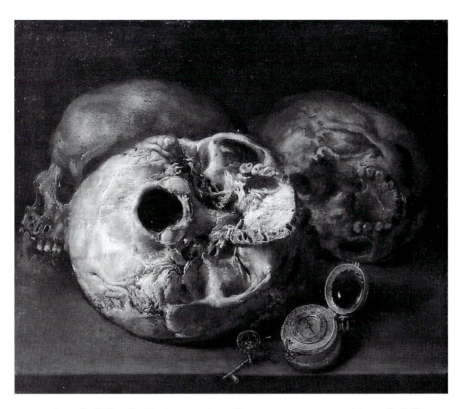

5.1. Antonio de Pereda, *Vanitas*, ca. 1640, oil on canvas, 31 x 37 cm. Museo de Bellas Artes, Zaragoza.

mumia (a kind of dust obtained from them that was used in all sort of remedies) is a good example of objects with curative powers held in *Wunderkammern*.[29] This appreciation and valorization of bones and relics were in full accordance with the Counter-Reformation values in force during this period, and it is through the arts that the most elaborate expression of these values was achieved. In baroque art indeed, skeletons and skulls, and in a more general sense vanitas and still life paintings, bring forth a *meditatio mortis*, where the macabre and the ephemeral, the sinister and the sublime, are summoned and represented.[30]

As far as seventeenth-century natural philosophy is concerned, bones seemed to be loaded with a wide range of meanings. The renovated interest in anatomy greatly contributed to the revalorization of the study of bones, a part of the human body that, when compared to certain organs or humors, had been regarded as minor, mundane, prosaic. Andreas Vesalius, in his famous treatise *De humani corporis fabrica* (Basel, 1543), had dared to deal with this subject in the first book, quite a novelty given that, in medical faculties, bones were considered at the end of term. Anatomical illustrations featuring vanitas-like poses are not rare in his work.

The physical proximity between the first anatomical theaters and many cabinets of curiosities, and the fact that these places were sometimes managed and visited by the same learned men, turned the human skeleton into a familiar item in both spaces; bones were gathered, conserved, exhibited, and studied in both knowledge-producing locations. Whatever happened in these places, its visual materialization in the form of engravings definitely had an impact on the pictorial ambitions of those artists interested in this theme. We need only to compare examples of vanitas painting and certain anatomical images of the same period to appreciate the extent to which they all belong to the same knowledge program, a program that focuses both on the formal and the symbolic, producing results whose artistic value is not less captivating than its scientific content. *Still Life with Walnuts*, by Pereda, reveals, for instance, the striking resemblance between a painted representation of walnuts and an anatomical study of the skull and its inner parts (Figure 5.2). And to take an example from the anatomical side, Govard Bidloo's anatomical atlas, *Anatomia Humani Corporis*, in particular its illustrations by Gerard de Lairesse, is clearly influenced by the representational norms of still life painting and trompe l'oeil.[31]

On the subject of the representation of the skull, Rodríguez de la Flor has brought attention to its implications in relation with religious asceticism, but more importantly to its connection with "the seat of the soul" problem, a problem of great religious and scientific relevance during the modern period.[32] Deeply connected with this question, the preservation of life was another central issue for many experimentalists, mechanical philosophers, and physicians. Both concerns inspired, among other innovations, dissecting methods aimed at preventing the putrefaction of inner parts of the body. As a consequence, new taxidermist techniques intended to achieve a better resemblance to life were developed, and interest in ancient skills and processes intended to preserve a lifelike body, Egyptian mummification, for instance, increased enormously.[33]

All these efforts to prolong life contrast with the message of caducity and decay expressed by vanitas and still life paintings, also discernible when observing the quiet objects in a collection. The representation of these "dead natures" in a painting, or their careful arrangement as silent objects in a cabinet, provokes the suspension of life but also the objectivization, the fixation, of death. The extinguished, smoking flame of a candle, a soap bubble that is about to explode: these elements in Juan de Valdés Leal's *Vanitas* (Color Plate 4), together with a reference to Father Juan Eusebio Nieremberg's treatise *On the Difference Between the Temporal and Eternal and Crucible of Disillusionments* (*De la diferencia entre lo temporal y lo eterno y Crisol de desengaños*), contribute to define a moment captured (deliberately designed, in fact) by the artist.[34] The

JOSÉ RAMÓN MARCAIDA AND JUAN PIMENTEL

5.2. Antonio de Pereda, *Still Life with Walnuts*, 1634, oil on canvas, 20.7 cm diameter. Private collection.

result is the singular, almost impossible, portraiture of an instant.[35] It is a typically baroque motif: examples range from Caravaggio's early *Boy Bitten by Lizard* (which features a still life) to Bernini's *Ecstasy of St. Theresa*. Time is abolished, but instants remain—instants that reveal a gesture, detail an expression, and deliver a warning.

Conveniently displayed, bones could also perform their own tribute to temporality. Frederik Ruysch, for instance, one of the most original anatomists of the late seventeenth century, designed a set of dioramas, consisting of small human skeletons arranged in different poses, standing on a stage featuring hardened arteries and veins as plants, and bladder stones as rocks.[36] The moral was the same: to warn about the brevity of life and the caducity of worldly goods. Interestingly enough, his daughter, Rachel Ruysch, was a renowned painter who specialized in flowers. Bones and flowers: hard, dry, inert remains; delicate, colorful, captivating specimens. Both featured prominently in many vanitas and still life paintings, bearers of the same truth: caducity. And flowers alone became the sole theme of yet another subgenre within this style of painting, also devoted to the representation of "still" lives.[37] Flower painting, indeed, constitutes another example of the uses of artificiality and realism in order to achieve a perfect, and yet fictional, imitation of nature. Similar to a cabinet of curiosities, which, as we have seen, may be regarded as a remarkable gathering of extremely diverse objects, a flower painting depicts the impossible coincidence of a large number of floral species arranged artificially. These works, like still life paintings, are deliberately designed constructions: not the product of a fortuitous encounter between the artist and reality, but the result, naturalistic in appearance, of careful combinations of different elements.

These paintings depict plants and flowers that not only belonged to different geographical locations, originally but also to different seasons, given the differences in flowering periods. When painting *ad vivum* was no longer possible, flower-painting artists resorted to models, illustrations, taken from botanical studies and herbaria.[38] The play here between the natural and the artificial is certainly noteworthy: What do these *flower* paintings represent? To what extent may be regarded as naturalistic the mimetic zeal that seems to inspire them? These questions directly relate to the analysis of certain aesthetic ideals characteristic of the baroque period and also fit with a present reflection on the incipient visual culture that emerged at the time and its connections with the difficulties in observing and representing nature that natural philosophers had to face.[39]

Focusing on the aesthetic issue first, let us recall the early modern tendency to categorize still life and flower paintings as minor genre. Facing the challenge of recreating nature and its attributes on a canvas with the highest realism, painters such as Caravaggio rebelled against the dominant pictorial hierarchy, which advocated an artistic superiority of figural painting over those works featuring subjects as mundane and banal as fruits and flowers.[40] Through their talent, their *ingenio*, to capture the natural world, artists were able not only to obtain a vivid representation of their subjects but also to improve, and perfect— that is, idealize—them, knowing full well that, as in the case of many illustrations in botanical compendiums or natural history treatises, a sort of model, a prototype, was being created out of those images. As Lissa Roberts has pointed out, "representation of nature—be they in the form of still life paintings, anatomy sheets whose flaps could be raised to reveal bodily organs, natural histories or maps—helped to standardize portrayals of natural phenomena by adopting a naturalist style that made them, in all their uniqueness, amenable to surface comparison and categorization."[41]

While bones were usually associated with cabinets and anatomical theaters, flower painting was related to another key site for collecting: the botanic garden. This is the period when the transoceanic interchange of seeds began and the first experimental hybridizations took place. The impact caused by the arrival of tulips in Holland, for example, is well known both in terms of experimental hybridization and of its financial implications.[42] Like experimentalism or microscopy, these botanical exercises referred to the same issue: the manipulation of nature, the way science and art, through their various techniques, change and perfect the natural world.

Although gardening was a long-running, well-established practice (in monasteries, for instance), the process of cultivating a wide range of vegetal species could be costly and discouraging. In particular, many exotic plants, brought from distant parts of the globe, simply could not become acclimatized to European settings. The standard method of conserving plants and flowers for taxonomical purposes was to press them between sheets of paper as they dried, so that their shape and, for some time, their color, could remain imprinted on the paper.[43] Herbariums were, thus, collections of dried plants, catalogs with hardly any color or smell. Paradoxically, compilations of floral illustrations derived from herbariums were a main source for the flower-painting imagery. In this respect, it may be worth recalling the "floreros" by Tomás Hiepes, which typically depict more than twenty different types of flowers and form what we might describe as a colorful microgarden (Figure 5.3).[44] Moreover, Hiepes's paintings, like many others belonging to this genre, deliberately express the contrast between the natural beauty of flowers and the "created" beauty of objects such as the china vase or the decorative motifs that adorn it—another manifestation of the never-ending dialogue between nature and art. At the same time, one is forced to conclude that the natural beauty of these flowers is as artificial as that of the objects themselves. Is this part of the deliberate confusion instigated by this seemingly naturalistic illusionism? Paula Findlen has written on how Girolamo Cardano encouraged his readers to examine carefully the exotic and rare specimens in their collections, in particular their joints and sutures, in order to check whether they were true *naturalia* or fraudulent *artificialia*. She concludes: "One of the less well-studied aspects of the cabinets of curiosities regards the significance of objects that purported to be natural while actually being artificial."[45] As far as flower painting is concerned, her conclusion seems to be equally valid.

It was not unusual for these paintings to feature expensive, rare vessels, made up of Italian cut glass, Chinese porcelain, or elaborate bronze from the New World, exotic materials that matched the exotic origins of certain specimens.[46] On the one hand, this was clearly a demonstration, for the painting's

5.3. Tomás Hiepes, *Flower Painting with a Quadriga in Profile*, 1643, oil on canvas, 115 x 86 cm. Museo del Prado, Madrid.

contemporary viewers, and a reminder, for us, of the global scale of European commerce. On the other hand, the presence of these items—which somehow represented power, luxury, and ostentation—echoed the rivalry between grandiose subjects in figural painting and prosaic motifs such as fruits and vegetables.[47]

Interpretative disquisitions apart, the decorative purpose of this genre is beyond question. During the 1630s, for instance, King Philip IV of Spain had the Buen Retiro Palace and the Torre de la Parada filled with an enormous number of paintings featuring flowers, animals, and hunting scenes. Even at the Alcázar, the famous work by Diego Velázquez, *Las Meninas*, was surrounded by flower paintings. It was a merry setting designed to celebrate the success of the king's own majesty and of painting itself.[48]

Commerce, Science, and Visual Culture

The presence of still life, vanitas, and flower paintings in palaces and private residences, or the gathering of bones, tusks, horns, and fossils in many *Wunderkammern*, marked the end of a long and sometimes intricate process involving many agents and many geographical locations. Enmeshed in political and religious conflicts at home, seventeenth-century European nations competed abroad in the domains of global commerce and cultural expansion. As a result of these international networks, the already complex circulation of objects— articles and commodities of all kinds, including relics and wonders from exotic locations—within and between continents was reinvigorated. A wooden idol carved in Africa could be sold to an Asian merchant and then exchanged for other goods in a Dutch-controlled port. Later on, the idol could be presented as a gift to a diplomat or taken as an ethnographical object by a missionary. Once in Europe, it could be sold by a dealer to a wealthy collector, enter the studio of a courtly artist, or rest in a sacristy with other religious items. The circulation of botanical specimens—indeed, of all kinds of specimens—had equally colorful and varied possibilities.[49]

The rise of collecting as one of the most fashionable activities in courtly circles was a direct consequence of this frantic trend of exchange and expansion. Collecting brought patronage and commerce together: kings, princes, and noblemen joined forces with travelers, merchants, and brokers who specialized in dealing with this complex transit of worldly goods. One group aimed at satisfying its collecting urge, motivated by genuine curiosity in most cases and a desire to materialize and exhibit power. The other group, apart from seeking commercial benefit from the transactions, took advantage of their privileged position to obtain protection, establish contacts, and expand their networks. This interest in displaying unique (or at least rare) and marvelous goods gradually transformed the culture of collecting into a form of business, as Paula Findlen has pointed out.[50] *Naturalia* and *artificialia* became exchange currency among collectors and dealers. Even whole collections could become the object of financial transactions, valued as they were not only as intellectual fancies, caprices devoted to private enjoyment and public ostentation, but also as economic resources, potential capital to invest and negotiate.

Natural products, without doubt, were favorite subjects in trading activities. As Findlen writes, "nature was for sale in many marketplaces throughout Europe," since it "had always been a commodity."[51] But many other types of objects also inspired the commercial interests of patrons and traders alike: instruments for navigation or surveying, ethnographical objects, antiques, and works of art. Paintings, in particular, became highly valuable objects, especially after the "triumph of painting." The rise of commerce in painting, historians of art agree, had important consequences not just for the spread of workshops, the creation of refined styles and novel genres, and the improvement of certain techniques, but also for the tastes and affinities of those social sectors investing and trading in these works and supporting their makers.[52]

The stimulation of a visual culture interests us here because of its strong connections with the development of natural knowledge in this period. With new types of audiences fascinated by the vivid spectacle of nature, knowledge claims entered the realm of the visual. Words were still regarded as powerful and influential, but images, naturalistic images in particular, came to be in high demand. This novel visual language, based on the premises of *imitatio naturae* in vogue during the sixteenth century, would eventually turn into one of the decisive factors in the development of new cognitive tools for modern scientific culture. Images, like the objects featured in them, began to circulate rapidly, widely, and in large numbers.[53]

Painting and collecting traditions contributed to the development of innovative approaches to nature as part of this emerging visual culture, which would eventually lead to the configuration of the new *science*.[54] The arrangement of objects in a cabinet with the aim of recreating the world in a single, closed space; the depiction, in flower paintings, of numerous floral specimens in one impossible and yet naturalistic bouquet; the visual description of the inner parts of a walnut or the morphology of a skull in a still life painting: all these examples refer to the same issue—how the natural world was understood and represented in this period. For this reason, we can reasonably argue that, among the cast of actors who contributed to the development of modern scientific practices—a cast traditionally dominated by natural philosophers, mathematicians, medical practitioners, botanists, and apothecaries—a place must be found for patrons of the arts, artists, collectors, merchants, and dealers.[55]

Possessing nature, *representing* nature. To try to reduce the world to a manageable scale and reproduce it in a limited, private space, whether in the form of a cabinet or a garden, not only demonstrated social and political ambitions but also revealed an implicit conception of those aspects of reality that were

JOSÉ RAMÓN MARCAIDA AND JUAN PIMENTEL

meant to be recreated, that is, a set of theoretical assumptions about the world, its composition, and its limits—in other words, a natural philosophical account of reality. Once the *order of nature* was established, the assemblage of items followed the collector's preferences. Some collectors aimed at exhausting the possibilities of reality within the natural order, as in the case of encyclopedic collections. Some others chose to collect those objects that challenged somehow the established order: monsters, preternatural objects, and other wonders. Both styles of collecting approached nature in some way, and both ended up producing a representational account of it. Similarly, still life and flower paintings, apart from their potential to define a purely aesthetical space, as Norman Bryson has pointed out, could be interpreted as sophisticated attempts to represent nature, their deceptive realism being overshadowed by other prevailing aspects such as their moral content and their religious message.[56]

In conclusion, further study of the connections between such a typical baroque artistic genre as still life painting and the culture of collecting may shed some light on several issues concerning modern culture in general, and modern science in particular. At one level, we may end up knowing more about the world that caused the hustle and bustle of ports and squares in many important cities of Europe; more about the issues that encouraged some of the most powerful men of this age to invest large amounts of money, mobilize personnel and resources, and spend much time: their intellectual, political, religious, and even recreational motivations; more about the type of realities they surrounded themselves with: the world that filled their homes, their private rooms, and stirred their wildest ambitions or inspired their innermost fears. At another level, we may learn more about the emergence of a visual culture that, when combined with experimentalism and induction, would form the basis of the new empiricist approach to nature, one of the pillars of modern science. Botanists and painters, anatomists and engravers, polymaths and patrons, dealers and collectors: the inclusion of new characters to the story would undoubtedly enrich the already complex, and still captivating, narrative regarding the origins and development of modern science.

CHAPTER 6

Crying a Muck: Collecting, Domesticity,
and Anomie in Seventeenth-Century
Banten and England

ROBERT BATCHELOR

The devilish Java perceiving the Master to be absent . . .
arose from the place where he sate, which was on the
starboard side, and when about the Table next the
Mizzen Mast (where *Roberts*, *Rawlings* and *Perks* were
walking) with his Target about his Neck for defence
against Pikes, or the like; and his 2 Crests in his hand,
and upon a sudden cryes a *Muck*, which in that language
is, I hazzard or run my death: Then first he stabd *Roberts*,
secondly he stabd *Rawlinson*, thirdly *Perks*; all three at an
instant.

—Anon., *A Most Execrable and Barbarous
Murder done by an East-Indian Devil.*

Saur sang mahapandita: The wise man said:
"Kumaha girita ini?"   What commotion is this?
Mana sinarieun teuing   Why so unexpectedly
Teka ceudeum ceukreum   This gloom and depression?
teuing?
Mo hateu nu kabékéngan."   No doubt there are people in
                                distress."

Saur sang mahapandita: The wise man said:
"Di mana éta geusanna?   "Where is this taking place?"
                                    —*Bujangga Manik*, old Sundanese palm-leaf
                                    manuscript, western Java.

According to Bernard Bailyn, we owe our concept of the Atlantic world to an article by Walter Lippmann in the *New Republic* from February 1917, encouraging the United States to enter the Great War and defend the integrity of this early modern construction. Compared with that piece, "Some Jacobean Links Between America and the Orient" by Boise Penrose, appearing in *Virginia Magazine of History and Biography* in October 1940 and January 1941, seems quite obscure, albeit also in its own way prescient. Penrose contended that "of the leading figures in the early history of the East India Company and of the Virginia colony, a very large number took part in the activities of both enterprises; which fact indicates that neither venture was wholly bulkheaded off from the other, nor from the general life and thought of the time, but rather that Virginia and the Indies were closely related."[1] Penrose described people like Christopher Newport and Sir Thomas Dale—veterans of Elizabethan wars with Spain and in Ireland and founding figures in the Virginia enterprise who subsequently died in Banten and Masulipatam, respectively. Much recent early modern scholarship follows the lead of Penrose, writing biographies of "global" rather than "Atlantic" lives. The best of this work still shows not "bulkheads" but increasing contrasts between Atlantic, Indian Ocean, and West Pacific economies by the eighteenth century, in part because of slavery and the mass migrations associated with plantation economies.[2] But if this second Atlantic world drew much of its energy from English, French, Dutch, and Portuguese plantations, its predecessor in the sixteenth and seventeenth centuries focused more on the collecting and exchange of silver demanded by Ming China and other Asian commodity producers.[3] In this earlier "world," practices of collecting not only illuminate its uncertain limits, but they also provide a sense of where and how concepts of both collecting and Atlantic exchange break down—in the case of the "Muck" described above on the Banten Road on the northwestern coast of Java.

The story in question appeared in print in London on July 18, 1642, the first story and image of "a *Muck*" or an *amuk* in Java. A group of English sailors on the ship *Coster* in the harbor of Banten failed to recognize the value and collectability of a Javanese *keris* or ceremonial knife offered in exchange for a silver Spanish *real*. The Bantenese trader of foodstuffs, whose offer of a more complex exchange than simple supplies had been refused by the sailors, took the *keris* he had tried to sell along with one other, which had not been offered for purchase, and killed eight men before himself dying at the hands of a vigilante mob of sailors from a second ship, the *Royal Mary* (Figure 6.1).

While hardly at the level of the Protestant and Catholic massacres going on in Ireland at the same time, events making news pamphlets like this common in early 1640s London, this pamphlet did similarly advertise the murders as a religious story in which justice and order suppressed darkness, disorder, and death.[4] Coping with a remarkable number of overlapping languages and practices, the pamphlet claims on the title page to take place at two very precise points in space and moments in time relative to each other—the Banten Road on October 22, 1641, and the bookseller's shop of Thomas Banks along London's western wall on July 18, 1642.[5] Banks pioneered the newssheet—his *Diurnall occurrances in Parliament* (1641–42) and the "revived" *Mercurius Britanicus* (1648) published at the front and tail ends of the Parliamentary attempt to seize the process of newsmaking were among the earliest examples of the genre. The pamphlet is precisely a technique developed in relation to collecting gone "muck," an effort on the eve of civil war to assert the possibility of a coherent cosmology and language in the face of threats by "Pagans, Heathens and Infidels" to the coherence of the body of an "undeserving Nation" like England.

The image freezes the moment of death in an emblematic collection of dead and dying bodies along with two sets of the same "Crests (or dangerous waving Daggers)," one in action and a second collected and laid out as evidence in the upper left corner.[6] The *keris* on the cover would have been familiar to many Londoners. Almost immediately, Edmund Scott, along with other members of the first English factory including a mulatto servant, acquired *keris* that they wore around Banten. Others brought them home as souvenirs. Four *keris* could be seen on display at John Tradescant's museum in Lambeth in the 1640s, while the pangéran of Banten regularly sent them to Charles I as gifts.[7] In this woodcut, they become souvenirs or a *memento mori* of the recollection or remembrance of sacrifice (Luke 22:19), alluding to both Protestant martyrs in Catholic murder pamphlets as well as the emblematic language of the *arma christi*.[8] Plato conceptualized such recollection under the term ἀναμνήσις (*anamnesis*) as the recovery of lost knowledge (*Meno* 86b) and the cathartic purge of the distractions of the body that allowed for such knowledge to be reclaimed (*Phaedo* 65b–67b). Yet, it is not at all clear that this kind of "proper" collecting occurred. Exchange had broken down dramatically, while the title's claim that the *amuk* had been "justly requited" was not borne out by the story of "a strange sort of justice" in the pamphlet itself.

Was collecting in Java really a problem for Londoners with their guns and shiploads of Spanish silver? Although objects from Java began to arrive in

A MOST
EXECRABLE
AND BARBAROVS MVRDER,
done by an *East-Indian* Devil, or a Native of *Java-Major*, in the Road of *Bantam*, Aboard an *English* Ship called the *Coster*, on the 22. of *October* laſt, 1641.

Wherein is ſhewed how the wicked Villain came to the ſaid Ship and hid himſelf till it was very dark, and then he mudrdered all the men that were a Board, except the Cooke, and three Boyes.

And Laſtly, how the murderer himſelfe was juſtly requited.

Captain *William Minor* being an eye-witneſſe of this bloudy Maſſacre.

LONDON, Printed for T. Banks, Iuly the 18, 1642.

6.1. Titlepage, Anon., *A Most Execrable and Barbarous Murder done by an East-Indian Devil, or a Native of Java-Major in the Road of Bantam, Aboard an English Ship called the Coster, on the 22 of October last, 1641. Wherein is shewed how the wicked Villain came to the same Ship and hid himself till it was very dark, and then he murdered all the men that were a Board, except the Cooke, and three Boyes. And Lastly, how the murderer himselfe was justly requited. Captain William Minor being an eye-witness of this bloudy Massacre* (London, 1642). British Library.

England with Francis Drake in 1579 and Walter Cope had a set of Javanese clothes in his collection of "strange objects" in 1599, remarkably few appear in seventeenth-century collections. By contrast, when the British temporarily ruled Java from 1811 to 1815, vast amounts of both texts and objects poured into British archives.[9] One explanation of the absence of seventeenth-century collections of Javanese objects, the internal one, has to do with early seventeenth-century Europe itself where, in the words of Paula Findlen, "the structures through which collectors viewed their world turned in on themselves, dissolving the patterns that they have created." Under this interpretation, the Algonquian canoe, the Spanish holy relics, the Javanese clothes, the Chinese lacquerware box, and other items Cope or later the Tradescants collected became obsolete as their aura of curiosity faded. The internal thesis comes in two versions—an older approach about the advance of European subjectivities, knowledge practices, and self-interest (the Cartesian/Gallilean "revolution" of the 1630s) and a newer one, also European, describing discursive shifts concerning the nature of "order," "truth," "evidence," and "certainty."[10]

An alternative approach would be to consider collecting as a much more diverse phenomenon not only within Europe but also globally. Recognizing this also requires a historical acknowledgment of collecting as more often than not a transcultural practice tied into complex questions about global exchange in the sixteenth and seventeenth centuries.[11] Collecting became a problem in the early seventeenth century in relation to global processes, which C. A. Bayly has neatly summarized as the "Great Domestication." This involved, as John Richards explains, both an "unprecedented intensity" of expansion of exchange relations and the simultaneous development of highly "efficient state and private organizations," or to borrow a phrase, collection agencies.[12] Differing languages and valuations of collections (state and private) related directly to practices of collecting on maritime and territorial frontiers that were simultaneously expanding and devolving or fragmenting.

Historians trying to grapple with this complex process have resorted to sociological types—emphasizing either the "feudal" aspects of Banten in this period and its failure to develop as a modern state or its "cosmopolitan" character as a precursor to the global cities of later eras.[13] This ignores the particularly dynamic role of Java and Sumatra in linking up and redefining global processes of domestication in the early seventeenth century. The Straits of Sunda, which open onto the Indian Ocean between the two islands, enabled sixteenth-century Banten, which controlled them, to compete with Portuguese Malacca and to become the major center of English trade with eastern Asia for almost the entire seventeenth century (1602–82, with the exception of 1619–28). The large overseas

Chinese community made Banten a key node in the "silver cycle" for the transfer of Spanish silver onto Chinese ships after England had made peace with Spain in 1604. Especially in Banten, gaps and failures in the process of exchange, translation, and collecting emerged because of the intensification of such processes across linguistic and political lines during the early seventeenth century. New practices and languages of domestication and domesticity developed to resolve those issues but often only partially.

That "running amuck," or "crying a *muck*" as the 1642 pamphlet and later poets phrased it, entered into common English usage in the early seventeenth century should not be merely regarded as an old exotic curiosity or Orientalist slur. Soon after the first East India Company factor (in general and at Banten) Edmund Scott in his *Exact Discourse of the Subtilties, Fashions, Pollicies, Religion, and Ceremonies of the East Indians, as well Chyneses as Javans, there abyding and dweling* (1606) had introduced "amucke" in a printed publication in English, the word had already become common in London. In 1609, aldermen worried the grass planted in new walks in Moorfields would "growe amock." It was a word that spoke to a rapidly growing city obsessed with domestication and fearing dissolution into disorder.[14] But in Scott's text, "*amucke*" was a foreign concept. Despite the appearance that "every thing hath been ordered and performed," Scott and his fellow employees nevertheless seem traumatized by their experience in Banten. Flaming arrows shot at their house kept them up nights, and periodically large sections of the town burned. When impoverished Chinese tunneled into the English warehouse from an adjacent dwelling, Scott had some captured and relished in long descriptions of torture, especially of one who was also a counterfeiter of Spanish *reales*. Orderly rhetorical distance in part allowed the Calvinist Scott to have few qualms about pulling fingernails, breaking bones, and letting ants eat his Chinese prisoner. Perhaps this is also why his Javanese transliterations remained for him Javanese.[15]

But the 1640s were no longer the heady Elizabethan days of circumnavigation and looting of the Spanish Atlantic. Trade required continuity, translation, and diplomacy. After 1604, the English in the face of Dutch competition needed to maintain their connection with Banten, which, because of its location, history, and linkage with Chinese and other trading networks, allowed for collecting of pepper and other spices. Even Scott acknowledged that Banten was "the chief mart towne" where pepper "hath been brought in times past from all places" from "divers other countreys" whose trade "doth farre exceed Achin or any towne or citie thereabouts."[16] Unlike the Portuguese fortress at Melaka or the Dutch one at Batavia, which combined military rule with commercial control, the English had to cooperate at Banten not only with the pangéran or Sultan and his administrators but also with Chinese and Portuguese merchant communities to supply credit. The Ming dependence on silver imports for stabilizing its internal economy pulled exchange relations in Banten from a different direction. Collecting and keeping at the warehouses and the ships in Banten were important to a wide variety of peoples—Chinese, Javanese, European, and others—for reasons simultaneously more mundane and more complex than the threat of flaming arrows, siege tunnels, and shipboard massacres.[17]

Collecting Houses

Aside from their respective access to commodity silver and pepper, England and Western Java held a great deal in common in the early seventeenth century. Both still depended heavily on single commodities for their economic vitality (wool and pepper), although their labor and ownership practices and languages remained quite distinct. Both centered on an emporium port (London and Banten), which needed to extend and consolidate territorial influence to secure food and trade commodities (in Ireland and Scotland and in south Sumatra and central Java) and looked to derive more revenue from customs. Both thrived on the margins of larger economic systems (Iberian, Dutch, and Ming Chinese). Finally, both were what Claude Lévi-Strauss in his late work called "house societies" (*sociétés à maison*) for which entities like the ship, the court or *kraton*, and in the English case, the company ("the East India House" and the houses of its factors) were a kind of extended metaphor. Such houses subverted languages of kinship by "transcending" and "naturalizing" rank differences in the absence of a distinct language for politics and economics, with interlinkages counting for more than continuity of lineages.[18] The collecting practices of the sixteenth- and seventeenth-century west Javanese house, *pasren* in Javanese or *bumi* in Sundanese, formed the initial basis for assembling all the diverse houses of English, Dutch, Chinese, Gujarati, and Malay merchants together on the Bantam Road.[19] Palm-leaf manuscripts in Javanese and old Sundanese obtained in northwestern Java in the early seventeenth century and collected in the Bodleian Library help show the development of this house society during the preceding two centuries. Two donated by the merchant Andrew James in 1627 relate to the encounter between the Sundanese and Javanese languages and traditions in western Java. The Javanese *Rosa Crita* (*Carita*) (Figure 6.2) about the seven spheres of the cosmos borrows words from old Sundanese. The old Sundanese *Bujangga Manik* tells the story a pilgrim who goes east to learn Javanese (Figure 6.3). A third manuscript donated by the Earl of Pembroke in 1629 (Color Plate 5) was a Javanese *Ménak* story about the Islamic hero Amir Hamzah, a popular Persian tale frequently depicted in *wayang golék* drama in Java about the uncle of the Prophet Mohammed. All three are contained by lacquerware, boxes (described as a "capsula") in the case of the James donation and end-pieces on Pembroke's gift. Such palm-leaf books were "heirlooms" or objects of "inheritance" (*kaliliran*, an old Javanese word) as well as power objects (*pusaka*) and jewels (*manik*) of truth.[20] If loot, they at least give a window onto the region in the early seventeenth century. If gifts, arguably they were meant to provide the English (or Portuguese or Dutch) an introduction to modes of translation and exchange in that same region—unread manuals on heroism, domesticity and the cosmos.

The James donation is of particular interest both for the content of the manuscripts and their manner of acquisition. When he donated them, he had no idea what they were or where they were from (aside from the "East Indies").[21] It would be easy to attribute this to Orientalist *zeitgeist*, mere curiosities from the East, but a more plausible story has to do with sibling rivalries. His older brother, Richard James, who died a debtor in 1613, was a well-traveled merchant, mayor of Newport, an MP, and most likely the prior owner of the manuscripts. Richard's son Richard (d. 1638), later a famous linguist and antiquarian, went to Russia to seek his fortune and in the 1620s worked for three of the great manuscript collectors of the era—John Selden; Thomas Howard, earl of Arundel; and Sir Robert Cotton. In 1618 while he was in Russia, Andrew seized the father's house and in the process evicted Richard's siblings.[22] Most likely this was when the manuscripts came into Andrew's possession. He presumably had no idea as to their content when he donated them to the Bodleian through his younger brother, Thomas James (d. 1629). Thomas, who served as the librarian at the Bodleian until falling ill in 1620 believed that through proper research into unknown languages, Catholic forgeries, and prohibited texts the Babel problem and the hostile principles of a fragmented religion could ultimately be reconciled. In keeping with general strategies at the Bodleian in this period as defined by Bodley and Archbishop William Laud, the Javanese manuscripts were literally kept in cages for both their antiquarian value and, more important, with the future hope of reestablishing the textual unity of Christianity through philology rather than evangelism.

Of these manuscripts, the *Bujangga Manik* in particular concerns collecting and the house. It is a kind of anti-*Odyssey* in the ultimate refusal of its protagonist both to return home and to set up an opposition between the *oikos* and the world. It is the most austere of the three manuscripts—in a black lacquer case, on *nipah* palm, incised with a *pangot* knife but uninked.[23] The name of the pilgrim Bujangga Manik, used as the title only by scholarly convention, makes a double reference to writing as the ultimate act of collecting. The text is itself a jewel (*manik*) while the process of retelling of the pilgrim Manik's story is also a kind of journey to mastery of writing and poetry (*bujangga* or *pujangga*).

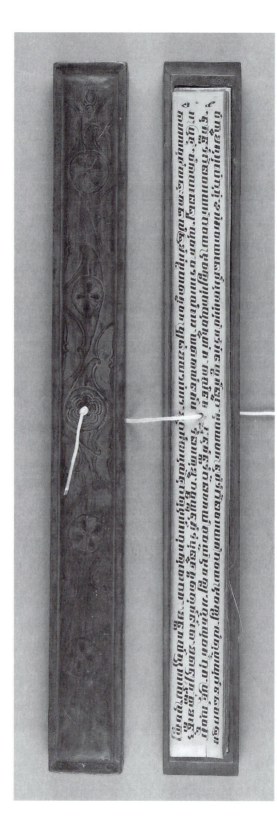

6.2. *Rasa Carita mwang Kalpa rakwa manawatsa*, West Java ca. 1500, red lacquer case & f.1, ink Old Javanese quadratic script on nipah palm, given by Andrew James, 1627. Bodleian Library MS. Java b.1(R).

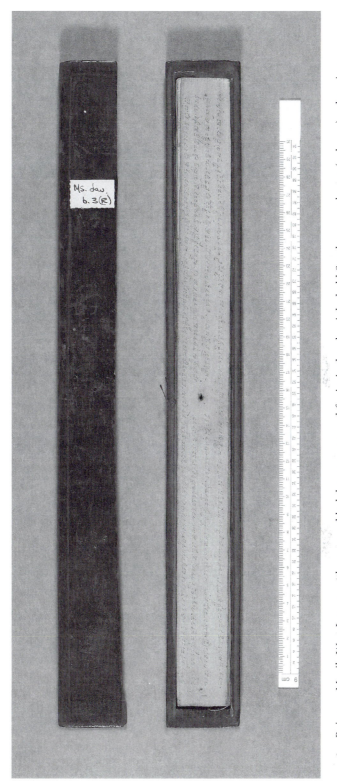

6.3. *Bujangga Manik*, West Java ca. 16th century, black lacquer case and f.1, incised and uninked old Sundanese on lontar (palmyra) palm, given by Andrew James 1627. Bodleian Library MS Java b.3(R).

Bujangga Manik's first journey into eastern Java into the rump of the old fourteenth-century Majapahit Empire and the newer late fifteenth-and early sixteenth-century kingdom of Demak dramatizes the opening of Sundanese to Javanese language, texts, and trade practices. Afterward, he speaks Javanese (*carek Jawa*) and has learnt the sacred texts (*tangtu*) and law (*darma*) (ll. 327–31). Even though the manuscript is in old Sundanese, it clearly values the introduction of Javanese words and concepts to revive religious practice at home. Upon returning, the princely pilgrim decides to reject an offer of marriage with all the domestic trappings of the betel tray, Chinese luxuries, fine clothing (including a *wayang* figure belt), and the *keris* knife that come with it. Sundanese, Javanese, Malay, and indeed Chinese fashions were all collected and domesticated through the house itself. But Bujangga Manik reads these collections and gifts as "word riddles" (*carék cangkrim*, l. 564). They suggest the princess is lovesick, not only infirm but also an improper object of love compared with that love acquired through worship and study (*Héman ku beunanging bakti*, 575). Such lovesickness inverts the typical trope of the vital household and the temporal rhythms of the Javanese *slametan* feast.[24]

The ships on which the pilgrim travels, both on his first journey and on the second that takes him to Bali, are also another kind of vital and mobile collection—of wood, of people, and of commodities. Detailed descriptions—for example, of the varieties of teak, bamboo, rattan, and other woods making up the ship—echo the attention given to building woods in Javanese houses, drawing attention to the performative space in which the manuscript would have been read.[25] Even the crew is a collection:

Bogoh ku nu mawa inya,	I was attracted by the crew,
Bibijilan para nusa	They came from all the regions
Nu badayung urang Marus	The oarsmen people from Marus
Nu babose urang Angke	the paddlers people from Angke
Nu balayar urang Bangka	the sailors people from Bangka,
Juru batu urang Lampung	the boatswains people from Lampung
Juru mudi urang Jambri	the helmsmen people from Jambi,
Juru wedil urang Bali,	the gunmen people from Bali,
Juru panah urang Cina,	the archers people from China,
Juru tulup ti Malayu,	the blow-pipers from Malayu,
Juru amuk ti Salebu	the amuk people from Salembu
Pamerang urang Makasar	the soldiers from Makassar
Juru kilat urang Pasay,	the boatswains people from Pasai (ll. 917–30)

Sixteenth- and seventeenth-century Javanese, Sundanese, and Malay texts tend to mention *amuk* in this kind of context, as part of a larger and highly differentiated group of people who, when collected or gathered together, in turn make the boat work. The best armies and traders deploy collections, importing different skills from different regions while maintaining a distinct relation to the place from whence they came.[26]

Bujangga Manik participated in the basic collection strategies of house and ship, but for him, truth meant leaving both the earthly household and the ship behind, dying as an ascetic hermit. He continues on to the "golden house" (*bumi kancana*), a common trope in writings emerging from Sundanese religious houses (*mandala*) and hermitages in West Java. Only here can true immateriality (*jati niskala*) be achieved and the essential jewel (*manik premana*) of truth and light be found. Even that occurs through a vision of the house as a vast global collection. As Teeuw has suggested in relation to another old Sundanese manuscript, *The Ascension of Sri Ajnyana*, the golden house seems to be a kind of way between Buddhist suffering and the void—the complex and layered heaven of the heirloom and divided space.[27]

Texts like the *Bujangga Manik* were designed to be translatable and portable. This one in particular promised a kind of general economy of the house. Yet, before it got to the Bodleian, as it traveled between ships and houses, its economy had been restricted through various processes of domestication—at least once by Andrew James when he seized it from his relatives by force of law and then reintroduced it into a new gift economy. Perhaps, as the pilgrim might tell us, this was an inevitable consequence of a certain violence or "sickness" that lay at the very basis of exchange, collecting, and the collection.[28] But that does not explain why texts like this, unlike others in Turkish, Arabic, Persian, Malay, Japanese, and Chinese, largely cease to be collected objects in England after the 1620s.

The Space of Flows: Pepper and Silver

In 1635, William Laud donated a fourth Javanese palm-leaf manuscript to the Bodleian. This donation only involved two palm leaves, one a protective cover and the other folded in half showing a debt or bill of exchange in Javanese used for the purchase of pepper (Figure 6.4).[29] At the time, Laud was actively using the Levant Company to gather manuscripts from the Ottoman Empire, sponsoring professorships in Arabic and Hebrew and commissioning fonts in the same at the university's press with the goal of producing a polyglot Bible to rival the recent Parisian one. The pepper receipt represented a part of this kind of sacred recollecting, but it additionally alluded to the larger problem of non-biblical languages like Javanese increasingly entangling England in patterns of

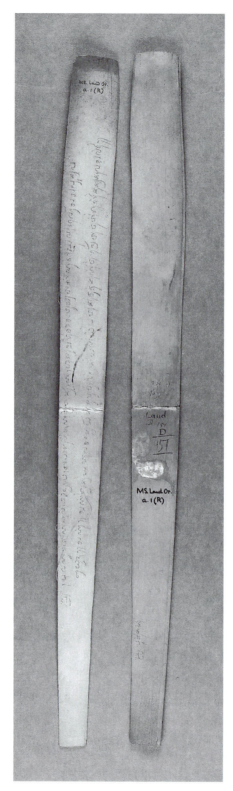

6.4. Palm leaf pepper receipt and cover, early seventeenth century, n.d., palm leaf cover and incised and uninked Javanese carakan script, given by Archbishop William Laud 1635. Bodleian Library MS. Laud Or. Rolls a.1.

global exchange and credit. In fact, flows of pepper and silver appear to be one element disrupting household modes of collecting in both England and Banten in this period, encouraging reevaluations of sovereignty, law, and religion.

Laud was committed to peace with Spain (and its silver) during his service in 1635 on the treasury, trade and foreign affairs committees as well as to church and university conformity in his roles as Chancellor of Oxford (1630–41) and Archbishop of Canterbury (1633–45). Like Charles I, he also wanted to maintain a certain intellectual and financial openness to concepts and practices that could secure the time needed to build such stability and conformity. Bantenese pepper was one such support. Unlike Algonquian tobacco, so troubling to James I, pepper had a long history in England as a kind of money, notably as the most micro of economic symbols, establishing the difference between leases ("peppercorn rents") and freeholds. The pepper receipt, like the more extensive palm-leaf books donated by Andrew James and the Earl of Pembroke, marked a debt in terms of the background of English valuations (the long history of the Pepperers/Grocers who controlled the "Great Beam" and tonnage) that the silver of the Spanish Americas and the ships of the English East India Company had now dramatically intensified.

Because of pepper and silver, in the 1620s and 1630s a number of efforts to establish state-oriented exchange between England and Banten emerged, but these consistently stayed at the level of symbolic gifts. For a short time between 1619 and 1622, the English Company had cooperated with the Dutch to try and overthrow Banten. This proved unsuccessful, and the Amboyna Massacre of 1623 chilled Anglo-Dutch relations. After negotiating terms with the new Pangéran Ratu (r. 1624–51), the English Company returned to Banten in 1628. Ratu sent a letter to Charles I along with as "presents" a "'crest' or dagger with a gold handle," a gold-plated "lance," and 500 *pikul* (ca. 30 metric tons) of pepper to London. While the *keris* and lance were clearly symbolic, the pangéran expected in return for the pepper forty snaphance rifles with shot and powder that could be used to defend Banten in case the war between the Dutch and the Mataram sultan spilled over.[30] The *Morris* on which the gift was sent to London wrecked off the Dutch coast, and Charles saw no need to send a "present" (guns) in return. As a result when the presidency and council officially returned to Banten under George Willoughby after 1634, attempts to formalize relations failed. Pangéran Ratu told Willoughby that he "had neither perused the King's [Charles I] last letter nor the said Articles [a draft treaty] because he had turned over the Government unto his Sonne [Pangéran Anom, later Sultan Ageng, 1651–1682/3]" and that he simply wanted the English to abide by traditional arrangements according to the "the customs and manner of Bantam." In 1635, Anom promised the Dutch factory in Jakarta to the English if they helped in the war with shipments of powder and ammunition. He sent no gifts of pepper but only "two cassowary birds, a jewel-encrusted keris and one lance." The company's desire for something more formal went nowhere.[31]

Without a formal alliance or tribute in weapons from England, Banten entered into a long war with Dutch (1635–45). In this context, Anom and Ratu sent an embassy to Mecca in 1637. Anom in particular sought advice at this point about how he should behave generally as a ruler, especially the status of gifts and the question of mysticism in Sufi Islam. The questions reached the famous Muhammed Ali Ibn Alan (996–1057/1588–1647), whom the embassy tried to convince to travel to Java. He responded instead by sending two treatises, probably in addition to other books, the impact of which as objects was significant enough to have Alan included in the court history known as the *Sajarah Banten* (ca. 1660).[32] Ibn Alan's treatise, the *al-Mawahib al-Rabbaniyyah an al-As'ilat al Jâwiyyah* or "Gifts and Grace: On the Questions from Java," was a commentary on the great Sufi scholar al-Ghazali's (450–505/1058–1111) Persian work *Nasihat al-Muluk* ("Counseling Kings").[33] It dealt with questions of how to be a sultan, and in particular the role of the exchange of gifts in defining sovereignty. With these new texts and supposed permission from the sharif of Mecca, Ratu became in 1638 Sultan Abu al-Mafakhir Mahmud Abd al-Qadir. This happened at the same time Charles I was insisting on the use of the Book of Common Prayer in Scotland and going to war over the expulsion of his bishops. In both "Britain" and Banten, there seem to have been simultaneous attempts to redefine the sources of religious and legal legitimacy in order to expand sovereign authority.

At the same time, the English East India Company began to think of London as less of a consumer destination and more of an emporium like Banten. A small home market along with Dutch competition in whose shadow the English economy operated—overcollection—formed the core of the Company's early problem. The solution was to make London into an emporium, reexporting pepper back out to the Baltic by Eastland merchants and to the Mediterranean on Levant Company ships to Venice, Livorno, and the Ottoman Empire. Due to a host of factors, prices once again began to rise in 1637, and with the backing of the Lord Mayor of London, the East India Company agreed to directly sponsor reexport to the Levant in 1639 and 1640, funded by its joint stock and cooperative basis with the latter company (the "Levant-East India combine").[34] This system of emporial reexports—first to Europe and later to Africa and the Americas, subsequently codified for the American colonies in the Navigation Acts (1651, 1660, 1663)—marks one of the clearest moments in the early definition of the "Atlantic World."

The revival of pepper led to one of the more bizarre incidents in the final years before the English Civil War, Charles I's 1640 loan and sale of pepper to shore up his finances. After trying in September 1640 to obtain £120,000 in credit from the Company for all pepper brought in that year, Charles ordered 2,310 bags of pepper (valued at over £63,000) seized in November, for which the sellers received tallies in customs revenue to be repaid without interest in five installments between March 1641 and December 1642. This was one of five expedients—along with the request of a loan from the City, seizure of bullion from the mint, the threat to coin brass money, and ultimately calling Parliament—brought on by the financial crisis related to the war in Scotland.[35] Because of this, calls for a new (fourth) joint stock for the Company went out in April 1640, and starting in April of 1641, the English, utilizing funds from both the third and fourth joint stocks, tried to draw all the Chinese junk trade to Banten by offering to buy large amounts of pepper with equally large amounts of silver and gold. This made both Ratu and Anom quite happy, as the president of the factory noted, "ye Sultan and Pengran hath promised us that not any men whatsoever, shall buy it but ourselves." The factors also borrowed large amounts of silver locally, on credit from the Portuguese and Chinese, no doubt increasing the number of palm-leaf receipts in circulation.[36] Finally, the Company began to sell arms to the sultan in September 1641 to help the sultan suppress a rebellion in Sundanese-speaking Lampung on the Sumatran side of the Straits. Just as the Lampung revolt ended on October 2, two big East India Company ships arrived in Banten, the large 800-ton *Royal Mary* and the smaller but still substantial 400-ton *Coster*.

Anomie, or the Death of a Salesman

The incident on the *Coster* took place twenty days after the end of the Lampung rebellion, on October 22, 1641.[37] Early in the evening, a small flatboat came alongside the *Coster*. Aboard, in the words of the pamphleteer, was a "proper young man," "a Java," "a man born or native of the territory of Java." He traded six hens for half a Spanish *real* of eight. When another small boat arrived, the trader gave the silver to its occupant who went back for more hens and even a goat. As darkness fell, the first trader remained on board and taking out a *keris*, he carefully wrapped the hilt in fine linen and tried to sell it. The English sailors expressed no interest in buying it, although this was not the kind of exchange—*mas kawin*, literally marriage gold—to be refused lightly. Nor was he invited to dinner, outrageously rude according to the traditions of the Javanese *slametan* feast in which the neighbor (although not the servant) is invited, indeed collected. According to a Javanese proverb, "Mangan ora mangan asal ngumpul" ["food or no food it is important to gather together"]. *Ngumpul* here means to gather together in a group, and the derivative *ngumpulaké* means to gather together or collect.[38] When the ship's master retired to his cabin, something snapped as the gatherning fell apart.

To the survivors, the *amuk* did not seem driven by some primitive code of honor, what Durkheim in his famous study *Suicide* referred to as altruistic, in which suicide is a kind of social duty provoked by the joy of sacrifice. The story circulating among the "King and the Natives" was that "it was upon discontent, that he could not obtain a woman in marriage (after their fashion) and had vowed therefore he would be revenged on any whom soever, he cared not who, and that affront was the period of his revenge."[39] And although the pamphlet blames barbarism and the devil, the description focuses on the details of the exchange. In this regard, the *amuk* was closer to what Durkheim called "anomic" suicide, resulting from a "disturbance of equilibrium" or "serious readjustment" in the social order, "chronic" according to Durkheim in the world of trade.[40] All this might have been postponed if someone had bought the *keris* or invited the man to dinner—the equivalent of extending him a line of credit. Money can serve to cover over a fundamental gap in the relationship between buyer and seller, paralleling the gap between Plato's teacher and learner that gets resolved through the myth of recollection.[41] Anomie results when symbols are no longer exchangeable, the threat of which makes the *amuk* so terrifying. As Sir Thomas Browne wrote when he coined the word "suicide" in 1642, "'Tis not only the mischief of diseases and the villany of poisons that make an end of us; we vainly accuse the fury of guns and the new inventions of death: 'tis in the power of every hand to destroy us, and we are beholding unto every one we meet he doth not kill us."[42]

The inability to claim justice in relation to individually anomic as opposed to socially altruistic suicide opened the door to another alternative—conspiracy. Some claimed that one "Keyradding, who is in that Cuntrey a Noble man (one that is in good esteem with our nation)," had been on board the ship the previous day and saw some gold he wanted to purchase, sending the trader to steal it. Given the possible conspiracy and confusing signs, the president of the East India Company Council in Banten requested justice ("Howkame") from the sultan. The *shari'a* practice of *hukuman* (translated by our pamphleteer as "howkame") meant paying a fine for wounds not described in the Qu'ran or hadith, and it could also mean a court that had the power to impose such a fine. That the pamphleteer translated *hukuman* along with *amuk* not only shows increasing visible, collective, and performative attempts by the sultan to use *shari'a* frameworks for decision making but also reveals the ways in which comprehending the *amuk* required the use of open-ended institutions within Islamic law to adapt to Javanese circumstances. The sultan offered *shari'a* as a symbolic and collective gift of justice (not to mention a novel technique of translation) to restore proper collecting and the relation between Keyradding and the English factors. To achieve this, the sultan decreed that no conspiracy existed. The event had occurred because of the failure to marry (the man was a loner). The pamphlet refers to this circuitous attempt to resolve the unresolvable as "a strange sort of justice." Here the gap is between emerging assumptions about the universality and international character of both law and divinity, coming out of languages that are increasingly being seen as radically different (English and Arabic, Anglican and Islamic) despite efforts by Laud and others at Oxford to put them on a common ground.

The problem with collecting in the 1630s and 1640s came out of growing gaps between the particularity of domestic collections of both symbols and things and the proliferation of collecting languages and practices. From October 1641 (the same month as the events in the Banten Road) and into 1642 as the Catholic gentry revolted, massacres and countermassacres racked Ireland with tens of thousands slaughtered (London pamphlets claimed far more), and Charles I desperately continued his search for more money. Events in Banten might seem to literally be a distraction from the well-studied terrain of the "Wars of the Three Kingdoms" and the early formation of the American Colonies. In fact, when the historical relations embodied in exchange and collecting are examined closely, that "distraction"—in the sense of the Latin *distractus*, to draw in different directions—away from the main narrative might actually reveal the process of world formation, Atlantic and otherwise. Stories like that of the *Coster* in serial publications, ancestors of the newspaper and what Benedict Anderson has called the "imagined community," addressed not only the creeping antinomialism of the domestic disintegration into the Civil War but also the analogous yet distant and apparently unrelated problem of the globalization of collecting—of objects, people, exchange practices—and the emerging legal frameworks designed to classify such objects. By focusing on collecting and collections rather than the more limited conception of "property," a perspective opened up through the circuitous route of the Straits of Sunda, we might come to understand better how and why the Atlantic World emerged as it did.

—ɯ—

Collecting and Translating Knowledge Across Cultures: Capuchin Missionary Images of Early Modern Central Africa, 1650–1750

Cécile Fromont

This essay analyzes the role played by images in the collection and communication of knowledge across cultures in the context of seventeenth- and eighteenth-century Central Africa. It is based on the study of a set of illustrated manuscripts created between approximately 1650 and 1750 by Capuchin friar missionaries to the West Central African Kingdom of Kongo and Portuguese colony of Angola. These documents vary in size from a single page ink-on-paper panel to longer, richly illustrated manuscripts ranging between fifteen and over one hundred folios. Yet they form a cohesive group united by a common mode of operation that centers on the strategic use of images as descriptive, didactic, and prescriptive tools. The manuscripts tackled a variety of themes from the presentation of Central African fauna and flora to the description of local customs and the practice of missionary work. In this regard, they resembled other early modern genres approaching similar issues, such as botanical treatises, travelogues, or illustrated catechisms, but also differed from them in crucial ways. They were primarily visual documents that aimed at communicating practical knowledge of the mission field to future missionaries in Europe. They presented knowledge about the natural, social, and religious environment of Central Africa visually in carefully constructed images using representation as a strategic tool to bridge the gap between the visible and unseen, to shape viewers' understanding of elusive forms of knowledge, and to translate ideas across cultural lines.

As objects, these manuscripts were the product of the commercial, diplomatic, and religious networks that defined the early modern Atlantic World but also participated in their making. The Atlantic World was as much molded by the intellectual encounters that took place between the peoples along its shores as it was by the more visible and to some extant quantifiable movements of merchandise and people—and of people *as* merchandise. Knowledge, images, religious thought, and worldviews met and clashed as commerce and empires marched their paths. The documents analyzed here were created in an attempt to capture and manage the intellectual and visual encounters that took place in the seventeenth and eighteenth centuries between several Central African peoples and the friars of the Capuchin order. The authors of the documents used the commercial routes of the Atlantic and traveled on merchant and slave ships from Europe to Africa, via Brazil, bringing with them the paper, ink, and paint that they would transform into their illustrated volumes. The manuscripts, in turn, would travel back to Europe to inspire, educate, and warn the next generations of missionaries.

The Capuchins were members of a strictly mendicant order that forbade the accumulation of property, so its members did not collect artifacts. The manuscripts they created, however, formed a connection between distant points of the Atlantic, materially as physical objects sent to libraries and intellectually as compilations of knowledge and experiences. In this regard, they functioned in a similar manner as that intended by the collections of natural and artificial curiosities in the *Wunderkammern* of the time. From their creation to their use, the manuscripts contributed to the shaping of the intellectual and imaginary realm of the early modern Atlantic. Their authors molded images able to bring Central African reality to European eyes and to elucidate Central African concepts for European intellects. The friars also played on the paradoxical nature of their images as both artificial constructions and visual objects with the agency to create a form of observable reality in order to use them as efficient didactic tools and powerful apparatus of cross-cultural translation.

Historical Context of the Capuchin Central African Missions

The context in which the manuscripts were created was that of the cross-cultural artistic and religious encounters between Christianity and Central African worldviews in the early modern period. Christianity entered into the political, religious, and social realm of the historical Kingdom of Kongo at the end of the fifteenth century with the arrival on its coast of Portuguese explorers and their following of priests. Yet, when the kingdom officially embraced Catholicism under the patronage of Portugal in 1491, it was at the command of the Kongo crown itself. The Kingdom of Kongo extended over a large region south of the Congo River, on the Atlantic shore of Central Africa. The kingdom was a highly centralized polity organized around the person of the king, who ruled his provinces from the capital city through governors he chose among the court nobles. Once Christian, the kingdom established and maintained diplomatic relations through correspondence and ambassadors with Rome and several European powers in addition to Portugal.

By adopting Christianity, the Central African monarchy benefited from the powerful support of the papacy against the territorial claims and colonial ambitions of Portugal. Portugal, in turn, hoped to find in the development of the Catholic Church in Central Africa under its patronage a means to exercise control over the great kingdom and to gain access to its real and putative riches. From the baptism of the king in 1491 to the 1620s, a first phase of development of the Church took place in Central Africa, on the basis of the good relationship between Kongo and Portugal. The Iberian Crown controlled, by right of Tordesillas and related treaties, the bishop and clergy of the region and, therefore, hoped to hold sway over the spiritual and secular affairs of the African kingdom. However, in reality, the Kongo crown maintained throughout the period financial responsibility and de facto authority over the priests active in the region.

In the 1620s, the already strained relationship between the Kongo and Portugal unraveled. In 1622, Portugal invaded the south of the kingdom from its nearby colony of Angola founded fifty years earlier; and in 1624, it permanently called back the bishop of Kongo to Angola, which prevented further ordination of local clergy. From this date, a new phase opened for the Kongo Church, marked by its independence from Portuguese clerical hierarchy. In direct response to the departure of the bishop, the king of Kongo obtained from the papacy the dispatch of Capuchin missionaries from nations outside Portugal, who would work in the capital as well as in the provinces under the direct control of the Kongo Crown and nobility. The Capuchin missionaries, thus, arrived in Central Africa as guests of the Kongo elite and with the lukewarm approval of Portugal. They worked in the already Christian kingdom as well as in neighboring unconverted lands, mostly in the territories in and around Portuguese Angola.

A handful of manuscripts describe visually the environment of early modern Central Africa. The first illustrated document of the period is the Araldi Manuscript, a complex work made of three codices composed in the 1660s by the Capuchin Giovanni Antonio Cavazzi that described in twenty-seven bold and disorderly images a mix of historical and everyday scenes.[1] The second was a three-volume military chronicle written around 1680 by António Oliveira de Cadornega, a Portuguese soldier, which related the first century of the history of Angola and depicted with sixteen images a selection of animals and scenes of local civilian and military life.[2] The images of these two manuscripts provide invaluable information about early modern Central Africa but function mostly as illustrations of the texts with which they are associated. In contrast, this essay focuses on a third group of manuscripts that form a definite genre and have the particularity of not being simple illustrations to a written account but rather documents intended to function on their own as collections of natural, social, and religious knowledge as well as tools of cross-cultural translation. These images were authored over several decades by Capuchin friars veteran of the Central African missions with the stated purpose of educating future missionaries before their departure from Europe to the African field.

Capuchin Central African Didactic Manuscripts

The Capuchin missionaries produced a range of written accounts documenting their work in Central Africa. Alongside administrative reports to their order's hierarchy and personal correspondence to their family and friends in Europe, the friars composed a particular set of illustrated manuscripts with a format and a content specific to the historical and cultural context of their Central African mission. Bernardino Ignazio da Vezza d'Asti's *Missione in prattica: Padri cappuccini ne' Regni di Congo, Angola, et adiacenti*, written around 1750 and now in the Turin Civic Library, is the best known and the only of these Capuchin Central African illustrated didactic manuscripts that has been fully published to this day.[3] It is a set of full-page images glossed by a few lines of text (Color Plate 6). The vignettes of the guide, all in a format similar to that in Color Plate 6, presented scenes of missionary activity, examples of local customs, and elements of the natural environment. This exceptional work has been mostly considered an idiosyncratic opus and used by modern editors as illustration for other written accounts about Central Africa, seemingly in an attempt to palliate its lack of text.

In fact, that characteristic primacy of the visual over the written hints to its belonging to a larger set of works that I propose to group together as a single genre. The corpus would include not only the several versions of the Turin manuscript but also at least two other unpublished works. Chronologically, the first manifestation of the genre is a single-page ink-on-paper drawing, measuring 73 by 40 centimeters from the Museo Francescano in Rome (Figure 7.1). The drawing, which was bought on the art market a few decades ago, does not

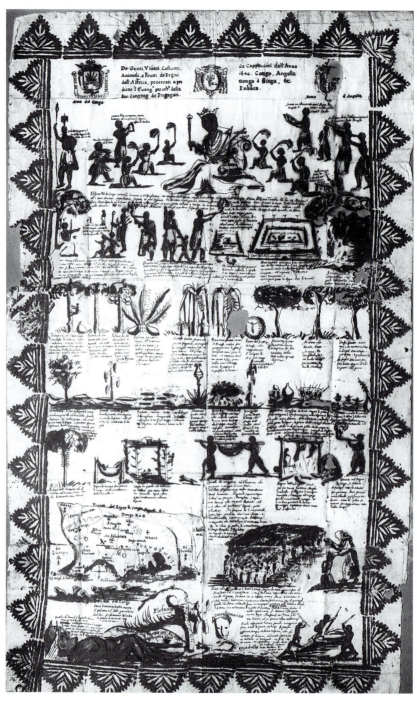

7.1. Anonymous, *People, victuals, customs, animals, and fruits of the Kingdoms of Africa penetrated to predicate the Gospel by order of the Sacred Congregation of the Propaganda by the Capuchins since the year 1644: Congo, Angola, Dongo or Singa [Njinga] and Embaca*, ca. 1652–63, 73 x 40 cm. Museo Francescano of the Capuchin Historical Institute, Rome, MF1370.

contain a date or a signature in its text. It was probably composed after the death, considered martyrdom by the friars, of the Flemish Capuchin George de Gheel in 1652, depicted on the page, and during the reign of the Angolan Queen Njinga who died in 1663, referred to in the text of the page in the present tense.[4] These landmarks place its production in the early years of the Capuchin presence in Central Africa. The poster, according to its title, is a presentation of the "People, victuals, customs, animals, and fruits of the Kingdoms of Africa penetrated to predicate the Gospel by order of the Sacred Congregation of the Propaganda by the Capuchins since the year 1644: Congo, Angola, Dongo or Singa [Njinga] and Embaca."[5] Rows of individual drawings, each commented on in a short paragraph, proceed to achieve the task described in the title. The king of the Kongo is enthroned at the top of the poster, presiding to a courtly ceremony. A Christian king, he is represented with a European-style crown and scepter and holds in his left hand two arrows and a cross, as the protector of the Church. He also wears regalia of local significance, such as the many strings of necklaces around his neck and the iron bracelets at his wrists.[6] Six courtesans kneel around him waving flywhisks to the sound of musicians gathered at either side, playing accurately represented Central African instruments: ivory horns, marimba, harp, bells, and tambourine.[7] The next register down is a collection of scenes of local customs and architecture. The two following strips are concerned with the "victuals" or edible plants and modes of food preparation of the region. Below, the author describes the particularities of distant areas of the Kongo and Angola and provides information on the modes of travel in the wilderness. The last third of the page is occupied by a map, images of animals, and scenes of Capuchin missionary work, including the description of the death of George de Gheel. Alongside the animals, the friar included a depiction of one of "these little men who come from a kingdom neighboring the Congo," reclining on a neck rest, perhaps an early description of a man from the Mbuti people.

Overall, the drawing touched on three themes: the flora and fauna of the region, the specificities of local customs, and the practice of missionary work. Each of the topics is treated in a similar manner, with an image commented by a few lines of text at its foot. The author of the drawing chose to communicate his message and organize information primarily visually. The texts merely provide a commentary on what was first exposed in the pictures. The sometimes awkwardly shaped paragraphs in fact occupy the blank spaces left between the drawings; they were clearly added to the page after the images had been drawn.

This arrangement of drawings complemented by short texts in the one-page poster is similar to that found in another significantly longer and more ambitious Capuchin manuscript, an anonymous work of which remains today sixty-two loose folios measuring 24 by 34 centimeters (Figures 7.2, 7.3, and Color

7.2. Unknown artist, *Fruit of Banana*, ca. 1663–87, watercolor on paper, 24 x 34 cm. Private collection, f. 35. Photograph by the author.

Plate 7). The individual pages are full-page images in landscape format and were once bound together by the left side, as indicated by the remaining stitching marks. They were numbered at the top with successive even and uneven Arabic numerals from number 2 to number 104, with lacunae, indicating that the extant pages represent slightly more than half of the original codex. I refer to this manuscript as the *Parma Watercolors* after the region where it is kept today. The eyewitness images of this manuscript are not clearly dated or signed. They were composed, to the best of my knowledge, between 1663, the year in which a historical scene depicted in one of them took place, and 1687 when several engravings based on the watercolors were used as the basis for the printed as illustrations for Cavazzi's *Istorica Descrizione*, the most influential and almost universally quoted work on seventeenth-century Kongo.[8] The keen eye of the author and the accuracy of the watercolors in their depiction of Central African flora, fauna, customs, and religious life, as well as of the methods of Capuchin missionary work, place their creation in the hands of a Capuchin friar with firsthand knowledge of the Kongo and Angolan mission field. The textual and pictorial description of other little-known tropical fruits, such as the purple mombin (*Spondias purpurea* L.) on folio 39 of the *Parma Watercolors*, confirms

7.3. Unknown artist, *Unicorn*, ca. 1663–87, watercolor on paper, 24 x 34 cm. Private collection, f. 56. Photograph by the author.

the observing eye of the unknown artist and his precise knowledge of the Central African environment.[9]

The affinity between the single page drawing and the *Parma Watercolors* resides not only in their primarily visual format and their content centered on the three themes of natural life, local customs, and Capuchin missionary life in Central Africa, but also in a more direct manner in the similarities between several of their illustrations. Both works included a map, although that announced in the text of the *Parma Watercolors* is today missing. In both manuscripts, animals, plants, and artifacts are rendered in a simple, intuitive style but with great detail and accuracy, as is demonstrated, for instance, in the depiction of the banana trees in the third row of the poster and that of the banana itself on folio 35 of the Parma codex, with its characteristic skin of a dark yellow hue marbled with brown patches (Figure 7.2). The Capuchin interest in recognizing signs of the divine presence on earth also transpired in the botanical representations of the bananas in both works, which, transversally cut, reveal, according to the friars, a crucifix.[10]

The third example of the genre is the *Missione in Prattica* itself, which was available for the novices to study in at least three versions, today in the National Library of Lisbon, the Vatican Apostolic Library, and, for the better-known and probably original version, in the Central Civic Library of Turin.[11] The Lisbon manuscript is the copy that was kept in the library of the former Capuchin convent in the city, where it was probably meant to be consulted by the future missionaries in transit to Central Africa, during their compulsory stop in the Portuguese capital. It reproduces the text from the Vatican version but is not illustrated. The Vatican codex was the version sent to the Sacred Congregation of the Propagation of the Faith, the papal institution that sponsored the Capuchin missions.[12] It includes 134 pages of text, plus four pages of illustrations with a total of seven images in landscape format, each characteristically glossed by a few lines of text at their bottom. Different versions of these seven images, along with thirteen other scenes, are in the Turin manuscript, which itself consists of twenty-nine pages, nine of text and twenty of full-page watercolors, measuring 19.5 by 28 centimeters. The images of the *Missione in Prattica* treat mostly of missionary activities and Central African social and religious life but also include depictions of the plants and animals of the region as they relate to the conduct of the missions.

The three examples of the genre of Capuchin Central African didactic manuscripts treat their subject matter in a similar fashion. They are primarily visual documents that convey information through images commented on by a short amount of text. They are mostly concerned with missionary practice and include and organize information as they relate to that activity. For example, the flora and fauna included in the manuscripts were selected based either on the basis of their utility as foodstuff and medicinal ailments or else because of the danger they could represent to the traveling missionaries. Scenes of local or missionary life were carefully chosen and constructed for the edification of the novices, revealing surprising yet acceptable local practices or else denouncing apparently innocuous customs that were in reality, according to the experienced friars, inspired by the devil.

Images, Knowledge, and Culturally Constructed Representation

In the manuscripts, the friars used images as a means to collect information and to communicate knowledge about the natural, social, and missionary realities of Central Africa to novices back in Europe. Their vignettes were attempts to bridge the gap between the invisible and the visible, the known and the unknown. They aimed at making the never-seen species and customs of Central

CÉCILE FROMONT

Africa recognizable to the European eyes and understandable to the European intellects of the future missionaries. The friars mobilized European visual syntax to reveal the Central African environment in images that reproduced or at least approximated their own visual experience in the field. Although their artistic abilities were limited and their style intuitive and clumsy rather than sophisticated, they depicted animals and plants in a matter-of-fact realistic fashion and created carefully composed genre scenes to present local customs and missionary practices.

The precedents for their images belong to a variety of genres from botanical illustrations to travel literature and illustrated catechisms, but none of these categories accurately describes their mode of operation. Unlike illustrations of travelogues, the friars' images did not illustrate a text but rather formed the core of the manuscript itself; their images also intended to provide their readers with practical rather than entertaining, or in a less anachronistic term, "curious" knowledge. In contrast with the illustrated catechisms used in other missionary contexts, the Capuchin codices treated a wider range of themes than catechization alone and aimed primarily at conveying knowledge about Central Africa and Central African thought to Europeans rather than explaining European Christian ideas to local populations.[13] Similarly, the Capuchin images of flora and fauna did not emerge from the scientific, systematic practices of naturalist observation and classification but from the interest of the friars in the gathering of practical or, in their own words, "very useful" advice. Nonetheless, they were composed in a format that used some of the conventions of the botanical illustrations of the period to communicate information successfully. The bananas in Figure 7.2, for instance, are presented in a frontal representation, as a bunch, revealing their most characteristic aspect. In this case, the gloss provides an identification, "banana fruit," and a numbered reading key lists the salient characteristics of the specimen. The number 2 points to the transversal section of the fruit, which has, for the Capuchins, the miraculous quality of representing a crucifix. The text explains how "opening [the bananas] with a knife, a crucifix appears in the inside, as one can see in 2." In both botanical illustrations and the Capuchins' manuscripts, the goal of representation was to enable the viewers to recognize the specimens and to learn about their traits. Paradoxically, this defining issue of viewership is the point in which, despite their similar format, the Capuchin vignettes and the botanical illustrations differed the most. If the scientific images addressed a loosely defined public of scholars, connoisseurs, students, and also in many instances businessmen and colonial administrators, the Capuchin images rendered the natural environment of Central Africa for the use of a well-defined group of members of their order, coming from a few places around the Mediterranean.[14] In the texts, this unified readership allowed a form of translation by correlation in which exotic species were defined by their resemblance to examples commonly known to authors and readers. For instance, potatoes were labeled "turnips of the Congo," the bananas in Figure 7.2 were called "the figs of this country," and flamingos were tagged "water birds as large as geese."[15]

In contrast with the form of translation used in the texts, the Capuchin images seem to follow a logic in which the point of reference is the object of representation rather than the recipient of information. Plants and animals appear to be depicted convincingly "al vivo" or realistically rather than in the composite, correlative manner of the glosses. In some instances, however, the apparent realism of the representations breaks down, often in the description of the most exotic animals. In these examples, the mode of operation of the images surfaces. The authors combined in their vignettes realistic representation from eyewitness observation with elements of composition that were cultural constructions, deriving either from stylistic conventions, from preconceived knowledge, or from the authors' own rhetorical goals. In other words, the watercolors not only documented objects and scenes but they also recorded the intellectual environment of the Capuchins who worked in the Central African mission.

The animals that take a surprising aspect in the vignettes are indeed the ones whose *fama* was the greatest in early modern Europe and about which the Capuchins shared a wealth of accurate and inaccurate information. As observed by Paul Hulton, early modern travelers brought to the new worlds persistent preconceptions that strongly impacted their perception of the animals and plants they encountered in their new surroundings.[16] In the examples presenting very exotic species, knowledge, observation, and representation clash in a manner that reveals the process at play in the formation of the images, namely, the combination of culturally constructed representation with the appearance of simple, descriptive imagery.

The representations of the "unicorn," maybe a rhinoceros, in the *Parma Watercolors* is a striking example of this process (Figure 7.3).[17] In a simple background similar to that of the other specimen presented in the manuscript, a white, horse-like animal stands in profile, a single pointed horn growing from its forehead. "Unicorn" announces the gloss, "here called Bada. They abound in this land and particularly in the kingdom of Benguela; it is swift to the course and charges with the horn lowered as a lance; the said horn has miraculous virtue as anti-poison." Two streams of knowledge are merging in this representation. On the one hand, the author relies on the lore surrounding the fascinating animal described in the Bible and yet to be identified clearly by the travelers and scientists of the seventeenth century. At the time, the existence of the beast was not put into doubt even if debate raged around the reality of the medical properties attributed to its horn.[18] On the other hand, the author uses the Portuguese word Bada to label the animal. Abada or Bada, was the name of the female rhinoceros famously brought to the court of Philip II of Spain via Portugal in the late sixteenth century.[19] The word was probably used in the Portuguese colony of Angola for rhinoceroses. In the friar's vignette, the two strands of knowledge meet and blur into the description of the "unicorn" or "Bada," presumably a rhinoceros, surprisingly depicted as an animal as large as a horse with a large, centrally placed horn on its head—after all, not an inadequate translation of the main characteristics of the animal, if not of its appearance.[20]

It is clear that the author of the watercolors set off in this example to represent what he had not himself observed closely. Yet this image is a good indication of the intellectual environment of the author and of the mode of operation of representation in his work. In this example of the rhinoceros or unicorn, the author uses the format of naturalist representation to present information that proceeds not from observation but from culturally constructed forms of knowledge. In the image, the author blurs the line between the real and the possible in a manner that echoes the other parts of the manuscript in which the vignettes are used not only as descriptions of the local environment but also instructions for the best missionary practices. The didactic properties of images derive from their ability to create an artificial yet observable reality.

Images in and of Missionary Practice

The Capuchins decided to construct their didactic manuscripts around images, a choice that reflected their use of visual tools in the conduct of missionary work in Central Africa. The use of images in catechization is a widespread phenomenon of early modern cross-cultural proselytism. A large part of the Capuchin didactic images themselves was dedicated to the topic. A recommendation by Bernardino d'Asti from the *Missione in Prattica* underlines the way in which imagery was employed in the Capuchin methods of catechization:

> In these places where there will not be a church, the portable altar of Mass can be left exposed all day to public view, to infuse devotion in the people, as these altars are made with a decent baldachin and with *relievo* of a decorative perspective, all of which can be folded and unfolded really easily.[21]

The portable altars, illustrated in the Turin version of the manuscript, as well as in the *Parma Watercolors*, are displayed under a great tree, adorned with a crucifix, candles, and tapestries and made with images in "decorative perspective," that is to say, using illusionistic representation, here suggested on the bottom part of the altar (Color Plate 6). As a whole, the altars function as a central conveyer of "devotion." Bernardino d'Asti argues here, in his text and associated watercolor, that images can serve as edifying tools thanks to their intrinsic properties. Being exposed to Christian images in a Christian setting, he explains, the Central Africans will experience the development of their faith. Moreover, the efficiency of the exposure to Christian images increases with time, as devotion is "infused," getting stronger with length of exposure, the reason why the altar should be displayed all day. Clearly, for d'Asti, images have agency: they are able to have an impact on their viewers.

The Capuchins thought of imagery in a broad sense and called upon a full spectrum of visual tools. They used devotional objects, theatrical staging of Christian art works, permanent as well as ephemeral architectural constructions and ekphrasis in the rhetoric of their sermons. The missionaries also relied on visual communication to bridge language gaps and bypass the limitations of verbal communication. Father Juan de Santiago for instance explained how he and his colleagues would count on the theatricality of their predication style, rather than the rhetorical effects of speech, to convey the substance of the doctrine:

With exterior actions, with tears and other demonstrations that Our Lord inspired to us each one of us tried to signify as he could the strength of the divine Word and of the doctrine, that he preached without being understood, for in the mouth of the interpreters, it would lose most of its substance and form.[22]

In such occasions, devotional objects were also used with the same aim of inducing devotion outside of linguistic communication, by purely visual means. Juan de Santiago continued:

Often times we experienced that the listeners were moved before the interpreter would explain to them the words in their Mosicongo language, and it happened to me once in Pinda that bringing a pious crucifix with very simple words I moved in a small audience more than twelve nobles.[23]

This episode encapsulates how, for the Capuchins, images and visual staging in general were able to convey powerful messages, and in a manner that words, spoken or written, would not have been able to match.

These two properties of images—their ability to overcome language barriers and to impact the viewer's perception—are precisely the ones that are used in the didactic manuscripts as pedagogical tools directed not at the population to be converted but rather at the future missionaries themselves to convey rather than explain the many subtleties of the mission. In the introduction to the Turin *Missione in prattica*, Asti explained the intended function of his guide and its images:

> To the reader. The reason that induced me to represent and describe the organization of our missions in the kingdoms of Congo and Angola and neighboring countries was that I observed that some new missionaries arriving in these missions, thinking that they were promoting in them major progress by reforming what until then had been practiced, did what should not be done in these kingdoms and, on the contrary, caused more destruction than edification. I thus represented in this book the most essential exercises of the mission, with underneath a brief description regarding what was depicted.[24]

Images are for the author both descriptive and prescriptive tools fit to serve his pedagogical intent. He uses them in particular to correct the mistakes committed by the novices due to their misreading of the situations they faced in the new social, religious, and cultural environment of Central Africa. The source of the errors denounced in his introduction resides in the complex nature of the situations encountered by the new missionaries, the true tenor of which may be lost to them either because of cross-cultural misunderstanding or because of the necessary but peculiar adaptations previously introduced to the apostolic practices in the region. Asti uses images to reconcile the assumptions of the novices with the reality of the land and to explicate the beneficial practices they should implement.

The recourse to interpreters in the sacrament of confession offer a useful example of an idiosyncratic practice of the Central African mission. Although many friars learned to speak the local languages and acquired a level of sophistication in the idioms that allowed them to redact dictionaries and grammars, they also univocally agreed on the difficulty of mastering its subtleties.[25] The friars also had to rely on the intercession of interpreters beyond linguistic considerations. As Giovanni da Romano Belotti remarked, "the Blacks are distrustful of the white Europeans . . . so that with the presence of men from their nation as interpreter, and almost as witness and advocate in their defense, thus reassured, they remain more content in particular in the act of the sacramental confession."[26]

7.4. Bernardino Ignazio da Vezza d'Asti, *The Father Missionary . . . Listens to the Sins of the Penitent*, ca. 1750, watercolor on paper, 19.5 x 28 cm. Biblioteca civica centrale di Torino. Sezione Manoscritti e rari, MS 457, f. 11.

On the vignette describing the method for confession in the Vatican Library version of the *Missione in Prattica*, a Capuchin sits on a stool and listens to the sins of a man kneeling next to him. A *mestre*, or local church leader and interpreter, is sitting behind them, overlooking the scene from a short distance. The text, however, corrects the image. The confession scene, it says, "is here not well represented, the interpreter having to sit next to the Father. See page 43 et s."[27] On page 43, Asti renews his warning that "the missionary should not risk hearing confession in this country, without the help of the interpreter."[28] The Turin version of the manuscript presents the correct arrangement in a slightly different composition (Figure 7.4). The friar and the interpreter are sitting side by side, and the penitent addresses his confession to the *mestre*, while the priest carefully oversees the conversation. According to the accompanying text, the same disposition remains valid even in the absence of a language barrier, because it is "the custom of the land."[29]

This rather straightforward instruction about the need to use interpreters in confessions nevertheless warranted the creation of an independent image in the

CÉCILE FROMONT

didactic manuscript. The simple composition centers around the sacrament. The friar, right hand on his heart, is attentively listening to the exchange between his interpreter and the penitent. On the right side of the composition, several men are waiting for their turn, while on the left side those who have already gone through the process are kneeling or standing, chaplet in hand, to do their penance. The scene takes place in the open air, at a short distance from a small village, under a specific tree, distinct from the palms in the background. The text of the image insists on the necessity of using the interpreter but warns the friars against their occasional treachery. The image, in contrast, presents an idealized version of the event in which every participant fulfills his role with piety and decorum.

The image functions at two levels. On the one hand, it is an idealized rendering of the ceremony, a construction rather than a snapshot, providing instructions for the novices. On the other hand, it fulfills a descriptive role presenting the specificities of the mission with a documentary purpose. It aims at teaching efficient catechization methods to the future missionaries but is also sensitive to the many aspects of what Michel de Certeau calls the local "manières de faire," the local practices that shaped the course taken by Catholicism in Central Africa.[30] The way in which the men are dressed, the choice of the location of the ceremony under a particular sort of tree are key elements of the local practice of Catholicism that the author conveys visually. If the author includes these distinctions, it is because Christianity had taken in the region a particular form. The Kingdom of Kongo was not converted under a colonial rule in which Christianization would be synonymous with Europeanization. Rather, the new religion was allowed to develop in Central Africa within the preexisting local political and ritual structures as long as it did not directly clash with the orthodoxy of the Church.[31] In the images such as the one of the confession, the author was able to present the essential practices of the mission in a manner that revealed the complex context of Central African Christianity. In other, colonial, situations, catechization guides could be exclusively prescriptive of the necessary changes to bring to the local customs. In Central Africa, the political and religious situations warranted a more nuanced approach. The Capuchin didactic manuscripts used images to simultaneously describe the environment and teach best practices. This twofold lesson reflected the complexity of Central African catechization in which local mores were not broadly substituted by European Christianity but rather made to converse with the teachings of the new religion.[32]

If part of the Capuchins' work was aimed at changing a number of local ritual practices and at uncovering idolatry, most of their activity was inscribed within Central African, and in particular Kongo, preexisting social and religious structures, Christian or otherwise. To their own accord, they could not "remedy to all the damage that the [sorcerers made] to the Church of God, without the consent of the people, and the secular arm of the Prince."[33] Invited by the Kongo Crown and dependent on the generosity of the people for their subsistence and on the protection of the nobility for their safety, the Capuchins worked from within the social and political fabric of the land. Even in Angola, the grasp of Portugal was in many parts tentative, and the friars did not act with the help of a powerful colonial administration. From this point of view, they had to analyze carefully the societies in which they worked and judge cautiously what constituted acceptable behavior with regard to Catholicism and what did not.

Several chapters of the Vatican *Missione in Prattica* are precisely concerned with these distinctions. Bernardino d'Asti divided the Central African customs in three categories. Chapter 9, titled "Of the Bad Customs of the Kongo People" described practices not yet completely extirpated by the friars "that include idolatry, vain observances, superstitions, and other diabolical customs."[34] It denounced the use of idols, the cult of the devil, and the oath taking instructed by sorcerers. The next two chapters of the book are crucial to understanding the ideological underpinnings of the catechization efforts of the Capuchins. The friars conceived of their evangelization as a promotion of Catholicism from within the Kongo sociopolitical environment, rather than as an external imposition of the religion. Chapter 10 listed the "Good Customs" of the region, namely, "the honest laws . . . that assist the missionary in the progress of the mission."[35] After reminding the reader that the Kongo had always been a kingdom, governed by a king and his laws, however "extravagant, barbarous, and iniquitous" these might sometimes have been, the friar describes with great admiration some "excellent" rules that governed the country. He lauded the severity of the society against thieves, the rules that protected against "the sixth commandment" or murder, the respect "by law" of older people, and contrasted these attitudes to the uses among the "whites" in Europe and all the more among the Europeans who lived in Central Africa. The following chapter is concerned with the "Kongo Customs that Are Indifferent and that the Missionary Must Tolerate."[36] In these pages, d'Asti warns the future missionaries against their own zeal that could lead them to "some inconvenience" by trying to "introduce reforms in matters that do not pertain to their office," regarding customs that "do not do any harm to their Ministry."[37] Examples of indifferent practices include building houses with temporary material, using a man to test food for poison, or wearing imported European clothing the wrong way.

What permeates this last set of recommendations is a very specific view on evangelization in a cross-cultural context. Asti suggests that, within the limits of the Decalogue and of the doctrine of Rome, cultural differences should be tolerated and that Christianization was independent from Europeanization. The friar was not tender in his written descriptions of the Central Africans, describing many local customs as ridiculous and laughable and judging that there was little hope to change the local ways, but he was able to differentiate between the customs and the ability of the people to embrace the "Holy Faith." Echoing d'Asti's considerations, Cavazzi had expressed decades earlier his own opinion that the impossibility to change some of the "corruptions" did not overly matter since they did "not prejudice the essence of the Religion."[38]

The didactic images describing the practice of the Central African mission operate in this context. The scenes they present are the result of elaborate and often subtle cross-cultural negotiations about the place of Christianity in the region and the modalities of its practice. The vignettes' challenge is to convey such complex information across cultures, translating the cultural reality of the mission field into a form of abstract knowledge intelligible by the European novices. In the same manner as images were used on the mission to infuse devotion in the local population, images were also found to be the means by which best to translate and communicate the many and sometimes elusive details of missionary practice.

Picturing Idolatry

In the vignettes describing the flora and fauna and in the images concerned with missionary work, the authors of the didactic manuscripts proved to be keenly aware of the culturally constructed, artificial nature of images and of the singular ability of visual representation to shape perception and understanding. The authors also tackled in their watercolors the challenges of representing the religious practices of one culture with the visual tools of another. They explored the culturally relative nature of images, seeing, and representation, an issue that was also at the center of their preoccupation in their work as extirpators of idolatry, or worship directed to the wrong recipient. As they represented local "idols," the friars faced the paradox of presenting the primarily conceptual religious tools of the Central Africans through the visual solutions offered by mimetic realism, the dominant early modern European mode of representation.

In Central Africa, religious objects were chosen or created according to abstract, conceptual rationales such as the metaphorical, evocative qualities of their names or shapes. In contrast, Christian devotions were iconic, made to resemble visually the object of worship, God, or more often his intercessors, the saints. The friars were surprised that the Central Africans worshiped "the most extravagant things," that they attributed religious value to objects in a manner that escaped the Europeans' understanding.[39] In the course of their apostolate, the Capuchins uncovered idols of all sizes and shapes, from minute items hanging around the neck of infants or small statues "with horns and a savage look" to six-foot wooden figures looking like "mountebanks' merry-andrews" wearing diverse accouterments.[40] They even occasionally entered into large and elaborate structures that they described as similar to "the nativities of our country" for being populated with a crowd of idols.[41] The written descriptions of Central African religious objects provided at the time by the missionaries indicated the composite nature of local devotional paraphernalia. The friars often described the "idols" they encountered as deformed and misshapen images that included monstrous elements such as horns, or as nonrepresentational objects that combined different components "according to each person's form of madness."[42]

In these testimonies, Central African idols or religious art objects combined visual elements following a logic that was conceptual rather than directed at rendering the actual appearance of what they meant to evoke. They were created in a process that aimed at articulating parts into a whole according to the underlying ideas expressed. The perplexing appearance of Central African religious objects, in contrast to the European forms of the time, was encapsulated by Luca da Caltanisetta in his description of a pendant worn by a child. The youth "had around the neck two little idols, which, at first sight [Caltanisetta] thought to be only simple pieces of wood" until a more experienced priest pointed his mistake to him and recognized them as small protective charms.[43] In this episode, the friar was misled by the trust he placed in his ability to recognize the true nature of images by merely looking at them, while the Central African objects he was faced with did not rely on this form of mimetic representation.[44]

The elusive nature of Central African idols to the eye of the European observers is at the core of the construction of the part of the didactic manuscripts dedicated to the uprooting of local religious practices. Though aware of the limitations of observation, the authors of the watercolors still crafted images to convey their knowledge of Central African religious thought to the European novices. As seasoned missionaries, they understood the nature of local practices and knew the importance of being aware not only of their appearance but also of the underlying worldview. At times, idolatry could be uncovered by observation, but in other circumstances, only previous knowledge could pinpoint an otherwise indiscernible practice. To communicate to the new missionaries both categories of information, the friars strategically used European traditions of visual representation to reveal Central African religious thought. They combined in their images Central African rituals and religious objects with European conventions for the representation of idolatry to create a visual message

CÉCILE FROMONT

that used European form to express accurately Central African thought and its correct interpretation.

Color Plate 7 illustrates this process. In a simple landscape evoking a deserted area, three people have come together around an ancient stone altar on which a live goat is standing. One of the men is kneeling, arms extended in worship toward the animal, while to the side of the scene, another man stands carrying a set of weapons, next to a seated, large-breasted woman holding a decorated container. The animal is distinctively alive; its feet are pounding and its mouth is open, as if bleating. "Numerous and infinite are the idols of these wild places and their names are extravagant," explains the author in the text under the vignette:

> I only represent this one because it seems to me the most ridiculous. It is a live goat, very large, with very long horns, black and wooly, possessed by the demon. It talks and answers and is adored by all the Jaga people as a god with the name of zumbi. On the first three days of the new moon it jumps by itself on an altar made of stone and there it stands to be adored. In all, it is a wondrous thing that it stands immobile as if it were of stone until the function is over, then goes to graze wherever it pleases.[45]

The author then carried on describing the many ways in which the devil "deceives these poor blind people" using the animal. As in the natural history vignettes, the author included a numbered key to the image. "1: Zumbi goat, 2: altar, 3: servant of the idol, 4: gourd full of human milk to give to drink to the idol and to wash its mouth as soon as he has spoken, 6: guardian of the idol, 5: weapons, 7: worshiper."

The scene takes place among the Jaga, a people from inland regions of Central Africa known and feared for their military might.[46] In the seventeenth century, at the time of the composition of the watercolor, the Jaga were a distinctively heathen people, violent enemies of the converted Kongo kingdom, and fiercely resisting the advances of the Portuguese from the colony of Angola neighboring their territory. The image offers the viewer a range of accurate ethnographic details. The characteristic axe with a convex blade carried by the "guardian" and the long-necked flask made of a gourd decorated with woven vegetal fibers are both typical and well documented Central African utensils.[47] The author of the watercolor presents the rest of the objects and actions of the image with the same matter-of-fact documentary tone, including the stone altar and the open-mouthed, speaking goat, but he also introduces in his depiction subtle yet powerful visual keys to render his image efficient as a didactic tool able to explain the true nature of the ceremony. The attitude of the worshiper, for example, kneeling with his arms outreached, can be directly read by the European viewers as a gesture of prayer.

The stone altar on which the animal stands is another powerful clue. Rectangular and proportionate to the body of the goat, it becomes what a pedestal would be to a statue in European art and powerfully suggests the idea of a man-made idol. Thanks to this cue, the author introduces the concept of idolatry and attaches it to the live animal, to explain to the viewer that the goat itself is the object of worship, "as a god."[48] Here idolatry is defined as the misplaced worship that should be devoted to the true Christian God but is wrongly directed toward something else, in this case, the live goat. The construction of the vignette makes the object and nature of worship clear, although the scene it presents falls outside the defined categories of idolatry understood as the worship of idols in the form of images. By bringing in European postures such as the gesture of prayer and visual clues such as the altar-turned-pedestal, the author bridges the gap between Central African practices and European visual vocabulary. With this strategic use of imagery, he operates an elaborate cross-cultural translation of the nature of religious practices.

The group of documents analyzed in this essay formed a particular genre defined by its didactic use of images as tools to collect and translate knowledge across cultures. These richly illustrated manuscripts were pedagogical apparatus designed to educate future missionaries about their work in the Central African missions. The manuscripts seem similar in their format to other contemporaneous illustrated genres but markedly differ from them in their modes of operation. Their authors knowingly mixed in their images documentary, realistic representation with constructed, artificial composition to communicate to European viewers the exotic and complex natural, social, and religious environment of Central Africa. In their catechization of the local population as well as in the education of their younger colleagues through their manuscripts, they used visual syntax strategically to translate elusive religious concepts across cultures.

Although composed and consulted over several decades from, to my knowledge, the mid-seventeenth to at least the mid-eighteenth century, the manuscripts were never published.[49] They soon disappeared from circulation only to resurface in the last decades. This essay presents preliminary thoughts on this rich and little-known corpus that, a century and a half after the end of its active use, is still ready to deploy its visual apparatus, this time for the eyes of the modern scholar. With careful consideration of its rich content and complex form, historians and art historians will find in them precious keys for understanding the religious, visual, and conceptual encounters that took place between Europeans and Central Africans in the early modern period.

CHAPTER 8

—៷ш—

European Wonders at the Court of Siam

SARAH BENSON

*. . . and would like to see how different the dresses, costume
and ornaments in other countries are. You would like to see
me; it is exactly the same as I would like to see you.*
—Ok-Phra Wisut Sunthon

With this fragment of dialogue begins the likewise fragmentary journal of Ok-
Phra Wisut Sunthon, known more familiarly as Kosa Pan, Siamese ambassador
to France in 1686–87.[1] The next event in his narration, "Those ladies then
departed," allows us to reconstruct the scene. Kosa Pan is aboard the *Oiseau*,
the ship that has brought him and two coadjutants from Siam on a diplomatic
mission to the court of Louis XIV. There he has been the object of curiosity for
the first French women to get a look at him after his arrival in their country,
and he has assured them that he is just as curious about them. Kosa Pan's polite
address to the women of France introduces a period in the late seventeenth
century of keen mutual interest between the Europeans and Siamese. Thanks to
Kosa Pan's lengthy stay in France, there was an enormous curiosity in Europe
about Siam and the Siamese. While the ambassadors themselves were paying
visits to the great homes of France, touring the Royal Academy of Painting and
Sculpture, and attending performances at the Comédie Française, their likenesses went everywhere else, as collectible printed portraits (Color Plate 8).
News of the ambassadors' activities in France spilled over into special issue after
special issue of the society monthly the *Mercure Galant*. The market was also

quickly flooded with published accounts by the French missionaries and diplomats who had spent time in Siam in the 1680s. Through these images and travel narratives, we can study how Siam was viewed, interpreted, and packaged for a mass audience in Europe.

But what about the other side of this encounter? All that remains of Kosa Pan's diary, which records a Siamese view of France, is a brief fragment, taken down in a borrowed notebook while he awaited a new supply of paper. The missing diary is a poignant emblem of an even vaster archival gap. A series of disasters and historical calamities, ranging from palace fires to the near-total destruction of the Siamese capital by Burmese forces in 1767, has left in its wake almost no documentary and little material evidence from late seventeenth-century Siam. Even Thai scholars have relied on European sources in reconstructing not only the seventeenth-century encounter with Europeans but the history of the Siamese court in general.[2] This chapter proposes one way that we may fruitfully reconstruct the Siamese interest in Europe through these European sources, and this is by focusing on the practice of collecting. My project is to examine a moment in intellectual history, in both Europe and Siam, that was affected by and reflected in the exchange of objects, and with them, the exchange in points of view.

Phra Narai, king of Siam from 1656 to 1688, was an avid collector of the Western and Asian goods traded by the Dutch East India Company and his other diplomatic contacts in Europe. Many of these were luxury items—Chinese ceramics and silks, Persian and Indian textiles, European hats. But Narai and his father, King Prasatthong (1629–56), apparently alone among seventeenth-century Siamese monarchs, had a special interest in Western optical instruments and scientific apparatuses.[3] These were not merely finely crafted and precious trade goods but were closely attached to European intellectual innovations; they were devices that transformed human vision and perception. What evidence there is suggests that Narai actively imported Western modes of seeing along with the instruments that amplified naked vision. Admittedly the Siamese reception of European optical devices and mechanical gadgets is much more difficult to study than is the case for East Asia. In Edo Japan, printed images demonstrate the fashion for acquiring European scientific devices, even when direct contact with the West was forbidden. Siam had no mass media either to diffuse interest in European curiosities within and beyond the court or to serve us now as a record of such interest. In the case of China, actual objects collected from Europe as prestigious curiosities, such as mechanical clocks, still exist, as do Chinese clocks that incorporated European-style mechanisms.[4] While Narai's acquisitions were destroyed or dispersed long ago, the kind of items that appealed to him are listed in the Dutch East India Company records, French Foreign Missions (Missions Étrangères) correspondence, and published narratives by European travelers. Among the objects Narai requested or received as diplomatic gifts were telescopes, spyglasses, clocks, spectacles, mirrors, orreries, and terrestrial and celestial globes.[5] He even acquired natural specimens, among them stuffed birds, that the Dutch East India Company was shipping back from Indonesia to stock the curiosity cabinets of Europe.

Curiosity cabinets brought together man-made artifacts with botanical and zoological oddities. Compared and catalogued in the artificial context of the cabinet, these objects gave rise to new ways of understanding the human and natural worlds. Collecting in seventeenth-century Europe, then, went beyond the pursuit of material objects and was an intellectual and social project. The objects most prized by collectors in the sixteenth and seventeenth centuries had been valued for their rarity; the rules of nature were studied by its exceptions. Curiosity cabinets were the province of "wonder": as a noun, that category of objects that are unusual, novel, or monstrous, but also, as a verb, a ritualized reaction on the part of the viewer. The category of "wonder" or the "marvelous" was central to the Western encyclopedic project of cataloguing the natural and man-made artifacts that global exploration brought back to Europe. By the end of the seventeenth century, however, a less sensational mode of cultural and natural description was coming into vogue. In the very years of Narai's reign, the first natural history of the Indies was being composed by a Dutch East India company bureaucrat, Georg Eberhard Rumpf, who published under the Latinized name Rumphius. He set himself the systematic task of cataloguing the normal range of natural life around him, in all its bizarre forms.[6] No such European naturalist devoted years to studying, or sketching, in Siam, but the accounts of those who passed through in the 1680s also participate in this new attitude. From the point of view of King Narai and his court, it was European objects that were rarities. In part, Narai was turning the tables on the Europeans, who became the exotics in his realm, but by acquiring curious and rare objects from Europe, he was also buying into Western systems of value, scientific study, and diplomacy. In Narai's vanished collections of European wonders are clues to the European vantage points that the Siamese monarch had an interest in acquiring or mastering and those that might have been urged on him by his European contacts.

Narai's Siam, in and out of Context

The Siamese capital at Ayutthaya, on the Chao Phraya River roughly fifty miles north of Bangkok, was a highly cosmopolitan city. Alexandre, Chevalier de Chaumont, who served as ambassador from France to Siam in 1685, was

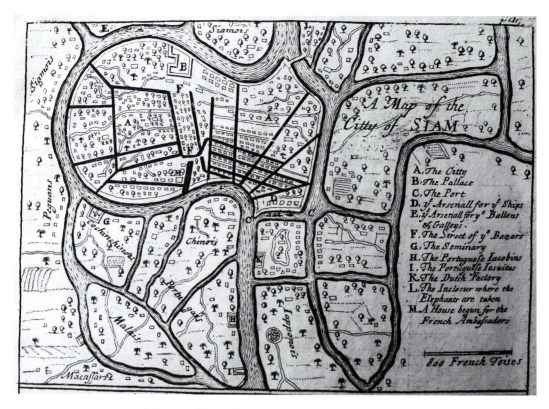

8.1. *A Map of the City of Siam* [Ayutthaya], from Simon de La Loubère, *A New Historical Relation of the Kingdom of Siam* (London, 1693). By permission of the Division of Rare and Manuscript Collections, Cornell University Library.

impressed by the city's international character: "There is no city in the East where is seen more different nations than in the capital city of Siam, and where so many different tongues are spoken."[7] Ayutthaya was both the capital of a Buddhist kingdom and an entrepôt where the Indian, Southeast Asian, European, and East Asian markets intersected. There were communities of Chinese, Japanese Christians, Portuguese, Dutch, Persians, Malays, Peguans (Burmese), and Armenians. A map in Simon de la Loubère's *A New Historical Relation of the Kingdom of Siam* visualizes this mingling of diverse populations among Ayutthaya's canals (Figure 8.1). Chinese served as captains of Narai's trading vessels. One of Narai's chief ministers and confidants was a Greek expatriate who had risen through service in the English East India Company before landing in Siam, a man called Constantine Phaulkon. The European presence in Ayutthaya dated to the second decade of the sixteenth century, when the Portuguese had wrested control of the spice trade out of Malacca. In the early seventeenth century, the Dutch East India Company replaced the Portuguese as the major European trading power in Southeast Asia.[8] Narai cultivated a relation-ship with the French in the 1680s partly to weaken Dutch control of trade in the region. The Europeans were only the latest comers on Pacific trading routes that were centuries or millennia old. The Tai ethnic group, to which the Siamese belong, had risen to power in mainland Southeast Asia only around the thir-teenth century, but they inherited their place in these trans-Asian networks from Khmer and Mon predecessors. Buddhism, Hinduism, and Islam all arrived in Southeast Asia along these trading routes.

Siam was a more successful importer than exporter of the kind of goods through which a culture may broadcast its skill, style, ingenuity, and systems of knowledge. Evaluating opportunities for trade was one aspect of Chaumont's mission of 1685, and he sizes up the goods that come through Siam. Narai, writes Chaumont,

> sends every year to China five or six of these vessels known as junks, of which there are from a thousand to fifteen hundred tons, laden with cloth, coral, and divers other commodities from the coasts of Coroman-del and Surat, such as saltpetre, tin, and silver; he draws thence raw silks, silk lengths, satins, tea, musk, rhubarb, porcelain, varnished works, China wood, gold, and rubies.[9]

Notice that the prime trade of Siam is in exchanging goods between India and China, but, "As to the commodities produced in Siam, there is only tin, lead, sappanwood, ivory, skins of elks and elephants, areca, small pieces of iron, and a good quantity of rice."[10]

Archaeological evidence, much of it from shipwrecks, shows that the Sia-mese did produce ceramics and other wares that were exported for trade to East and Southeast Asia.[11] The Siamese were experts in metal casting, a technique harnessed primarily for producing bronze Buddhas, and, since wood was the basis of most of their architecture, wood carving and carpentry were highly valued arts among the Siamese. European diplomatic visitors report gifts from the king of embellished wooden betel sets, a mark of courtly status. But from 1433, when the Chinese traveler Ma Huan wrote up his impressions of Siam, through 1685, when Chaumont is writing, Siamese exports are typically charac-terized by foreigners as forest products and other raw goods. Chaumont includes as an appendix to his book a long list of diplomatic gifts sent back by King Narai to Louis XIV, so long that the first English translator gave up part way through, protesting himself "weary of relating" them.[12] Among all this generosity there is nothing listed as of Siamese manufacture, although the list includes Chinese and Japanese goods.

The astronomical observations made by Jesuit visitors to Asia allowed for even more precise positionings of Siam on French maps. It remained unclear to Europeans, however, even in the midst of the Siam fever of the 1680s, where Siam was situated culturally. Illustrations in travel narratives and prints made for individual sale picture the Siamese king and courtiers in an imaginative geography. One of these portraits figures Ok-khun Sisawan Wacha, assistant to Kosa Pan, before a landscape of multitiered pagodas, which appear loosely Chinese in inspiration, and an inexplicable pair of camels, when Siam had plenty of its own exotic species to offer, from elephants to tigers and monkeys (Figure 8.2). This visual and topographical confusion suggests how forcibly the international character of Ayutthaya as an eastern bazaar may have struck Europeans. But it also attests a lack of visual models of Siameseness in Europe. Siamese style was unknown in Europe because there was no steady stream of objects making its way into European households to join the Chinese and Japanese ceramics and lacquerware that were by this time common possessions of the nobility and merchant classes.

The wardrobe of Kosa Pan and the other ambassadors is the one exception. Jean-Baptiste Nolin's portrait of Kosa Pan (Color Plate 8) gives as much attention to the clothing as the man, and prints like this one were sometimes hand-colored to give a more vivid sense of Siamese court attire. Siamese headgear, those conical hats that escape the upper limits of Kosa Pan's and Sisawan Wacha's portraits, held a special fascination for the French. The overcoats that the Siamese wore in a Parisian fall and early winter were not, in fact, typical of fashion in Ayutthaya, but the French attempted to imitate Siamese fabrics nonetheless.[13] (These were cottons manufactured in India and decorated with abstract floral patterns made after Siamese designs.) In the absence of large-scale importation of Siamese goods, there was, however, no fashion for "siam-oiserie" as there was for chinoiserie. In fact, the Siamese embassy to France has been cited as sparking further interest in Chinese goods precisely because so many Chinese items were included among Narai's gifts to the French court.[14] The greatest import out of Siam and into Europe was not produced in Siam; it was produced in Europe itself. The major commodity coming out of Siam was information.

The Display of Information in Europe and Siam

Seventeenth-century Western merchants and diplomats produced a rich if sometimes misleading visual record of the people, art, and architecture of Siam. The illustrated accounts that they published furnished readers throughout Europe with a collectible paper museum of Siamese wonders. The Siamese

8.2. *Ok-khun Sisawan Wacha.* Bound with Nicholas de L'Armessin, *Les Augustes representations de tous les roys de France* (Paris, 1688). By permission of the Johns Hopkins University Libraries Special Collections.

memoir of Guy Tachard, one of six Jesuits who accompanied Chaumont's embassy to Siam while en route to China, is an example of how Siam was sold in Europe as information. He published his *Voyage to Siam of the Jesuit Fathers sent by the King to the Indies and China* in 1686, and its full title proclaims the types of data to be extracted from Siam—astronomical, physical, geographical, hydrographical, and historical—and pictures the range of instruments that will yield the necessary data (Figure 8.3). A list of the scientific equipment Tachard's team took from Siam into China follows several pages later:

> we had made for us in that time, two quadrants of ninety degrees, the one of eighteen inches radius, the other of twenty six; three great pendulums with seconds, an instrument for finding out at the same time the right ascension and the declination of the stars; and an equinoctial dial that marked the hours to the very minutes, having underneath a large compass for finding out all hours of the day the declination of the loadstone. All these instruments were to be made use of in astronomical observations.[15]

At a time when the verification of scientific knowledge was increasingly thought to require direct sensory observation—and the little disembodied eyes that hover by the instruments on the title page insist on this—armchair travelers had to rely on hearsay. Rhetorically, both image and list assure readers of the validity of the information presented in the narrative. Tachard's authority is further bolstered by the patronage for his mission. The first chapter begins under a pictorial window into the Royal Academy of Sciences. Founded by Louis XIV in 1666, it was the French answer to the Royal Society of London for the Improving of Natural Knowledge, established by Charles II in Britain earlier in the decade. Natural knowledge, or science, was pursued at the most authoritative levels in these elite clubs, which both lent prestige to and gained prestige from their royal patrons. Shortly before embarkation, Tachard and his fellow Jesuits had been inducted into the Royal Academy. The illustration of the Academy establishes the context in and for which the knowledge contained in this book will be produced and consumed. The activity of the Academy is presented as at once hierarchical and collaborative. Louis's presence and patronage are signaled in the image by an empty throne, marking the authoritarian power of the king to decide even scientific truths. But the space is animated by Academy members who converse, read, and observe. They will in turn produce new works, like Tachard's account of Siam, that reach a wide audience beyond the Academy.

Observing and recording each phase of their travels was just as key an activity for the Siamese ambassadors as for European travelers like Tachard and La Loubère. The Siamese ambassadors whom Narai sent to France in 1686, Kosa Pan, Ok-luang Kanlaya Ratchamaitri, and Ok-kuhn Sisawan Wacha, took notes throughout the day on lacquered mulberry paper. They measured the ships they

SARAH BENSON

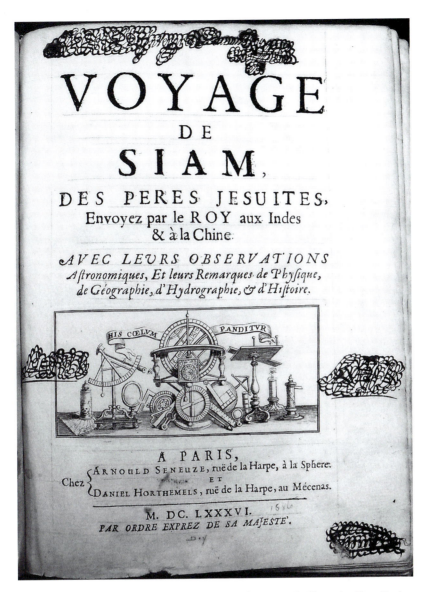

VOYAGE
DE
SIAM,
DES PERES JESUITES,
Envoyez par le ROY aux Indes
& à la Chine.

AVEC LEURS OBSERVATIONS
Astronomiques, Et leurs Remarques de Physique,
de Géographie, d'Hydrographie, & d'Histoire.

HIS COELVM PANDITVR

A PARIS,
Chez { ARNOULD SENEUZE, ruë de la Harpe, à la Sphere.
ET
DANIEL HORTHEMELS, ruë de la Harpe, au Mécenas.

M. DC. LXXXVI.
PAR ORDRE EXPREZ DE SA MAJESTE'.

8.3. Illustration on the title page of Guy Tachard, *Voyage de Siam, des Pères Jésuites* (Paris, 1686). By permission of the Division of Rare and Manuscript Collections, Cornell University Library.

visited and counted trees in the gardens of country estates. Each evening they compared notes, collated their memories, and transcribed a clean version on white paper. On his final audience with Louis XIV, Kosa Pan spoke in flattering terms of the challenge of the task and the plans for the document he and his colleagues had produced:

For us, Great King, overwhelmed . . . at the sight of your profound wisdom and of all the miracles of your reign, our life seems too short, and the whole world too small, to publish what we think about it. Our memory will be taxed to retain so many things. That is why we have gathered with avidity in faithful registers all that we could observe, and we shall finish them with this protestation, that though we say much, still much has escaped us. These memoirs will be preserved for posterity and placed in safety among the most rare and most precious monuments of State. The King our Master will send them as presents to the princes his allies; and in that way the whole Orient will soon know, and all the centuries to come will learn, of the incomparable virtues of Louis the Great.[16]

The catch is that these words are preserved only in French documents. And although we of succeeding centuries do know a great deal about Louis XIV, whether or not we find him virtuous, it is not from the records of the Siamese. With the exception of the fragment of Kosa Pan's diary that opens this chapter, the meticulous accounts of the Siamese ambassadors seem to have been lost in a palace fire in 1744. The French Foreign Missions located and made out another copy, which apparently did not survive the Burmese sack of Ayutthaya in 1767. Without these remembrances, we lose a major opportunity to see Europe over the shoulders of the Siamese and beyond that the possibility of extrapolating a Siamese cultural approach or studied method of observation and recording that we could compare to contemporary European perceptual and mental habits. But the mere existence of the project tells us something about the status and circulation of information in Siam. Kosa Pan describes his document as among the "rare and most precious monuments of State." The microcosm of French culture and court life prepared by the Siamese ambassadors was like the other exquisite and rare objects that Narai collected from Europe. As a curiosity and as testament to the power of Narai, it was to be selectively revealed and shared as a means of garnering prestige. We have so many European accounts of Siam because these were published in numerous editions and translations and fed a popular demand for information about the new worlds with which Europeans had made contact and from which they were bringing back spices, luxury goods, and natural curios. Despite apparently high rates of literacy among Siamese males, most of whom spent part of their boyhood in monasteries, in Siam there was no means of sharing information rapidly such as printing afforded in Europe, China, and Japan.

The circulation of objects and information within the Siamese court was dominated by an etiquette of viewing and display that Europeans found particularly alien. Westerners who visited the Siamese court unfailingly comment on the strict rules that kept the king out of public view. These remarks from the records of the French Foreign Mission are typical: "for the most part Oriental kings almost never show themselves in public" and Narai himself "has but one day a year dedicated to this ceremony."[17] Audience participation was high during the king's public appearances, with as much as 10 percent of the population accompanying the monarch by boat or in procession.[18] Yet, and this always amazed Europeans, the king's subjects were not to look directly at him or his family: "It is forbidden for anyone to look at the king's mother, his wives, or children; and the people turn their faces when the royal family passes. Only strangers or foreign ambassadors are allowed to look at them."[19] An illustration from Tachard highlights the differences in looking and its uses in Siam and in seventeenth-century Europe (Figure 8.4). King Narai is on his elephant, with his attendants prostrated before him. The Europeans made much of the body postures adopted by the Siamese in the presence of their king or someone of higher rank. The fiercely hierarchical Europeans wished to be exempt from these displays of obsequiousness that were not their own. But if Europeans of high rank were sometimes permitted to look upon the king, it was always from below. The Siamese explained that they even limited their homes to a single story so "that no Person may be higher in his own House than the King of *Siam*, when he passes thro the street mounted on his Elephant."[20] Tachard's illustration shows us the customs of the Siamese court while forcing us to transgress. We are allowed to imagine ourselves to be firsthand witnesses, the basis, by European standards, for acquiring true knowledge, while simultaneously violating the Siamese laws of looking. A real firsthand witness would not have witnessed the scene. Where the diplomacy of looking was so different from European custom, so too were the uses of material display and the role of observation in acquiring information.

The Eclipse of Wonder

Simon de la Loubère visited Siam in a second European embassy that accompanied Kosa Pan on his return to Siam in 1687. His account of what he saw there, *A New Historical Relation of the Kingdom of Siam*, first published in 1691, shows a new intellectual attitude that shuns wonder. La Loubère did not come to Siam armed with the scientific equipment that could turn the land and people into quantifiable data, as Tachard had done, but he writes an ethnography that aims to be similarly clear, rigorous, and devoid of hyperbole. A few dozen pages into his description of Siam and the Siamese, La Loubère pauses to make clear his method. It is a passage that comically undermines itself by claiming objectivity while aiming ethnocentric jabs at the Portuguese and Chinese.

P. 288.   *289.*

8.4. Cornelis Martin Vermeulen after a design by Pierre-Paul Sevin, *The King Mounted on His Elephant*, from Guy Tachard, *Voyage de Siam, des Pères Jésuites* (Paris, 1686). By permission of the Division of Rare and Manuscript Collections, Cornell University Library.

I cannot forbear making a remark very necessary, truly to understand the Relations of Foreign Countries. 'Tis that the words, *good, excellent, magnificent, great, bad, ugly, simple,* and *small*; equivocal in themselves, must always be understood with reference to the Phantasie of the Author of the Relation, if otherwise he does not particularly explain what he writes. As for example, if a *Dutch* Factor, or a *Portuguese* Monk do exaggerate the Magnificence, and good Entertainment of the East; if the least House of the King of *China*'s Palace appears unto them worthy of an European King, it must be supposed that this is true, in reference to the Court of *Portugal*. And yet some may doubt thereof, seeing that in truth the Apartments of the Palace of *China*, are no other than Wood varnished on the inside and outside, which is rather agreeable and neat than magnificent. Thus (because it would not be just to contemn every thing, that resembles not what we see in the Court of *France*, and which was never seen before this great and glorious Reign) I have endeavour'd to express nothing in ambiguous Terms, but to describe exactly what I have seen, thereby to prevent the surprising any person by my particular Fancy, and to the end that every one make as true a Judgment of what I write, as if he had performed the Voyage that I had done.[21]

La Loubère expresses a new yardstick of scientific detachment meant to replace wonder in reacting to and assessing the unfamiliar. He concludes, "tho' all Nations act almost on different Principles, the whole amounts almost to the same; and that there is not in any place any thing marvellous or extravagant."[22] In sizing up the intellectual style of the Siamese and the state of their natural history, however, he finds himself in the zone of wonder once again:

But their History of Animals must not easily be credited, they understand not Bodies better than Souls; and in all matters their inclination is to imagine Wonders, and persuade themselves so much the more easily to believe them, as they are more incredible. What they report of a sort of Lizard named *Toc-quay*, proceeds from an Ignorance and Credulity very singular. They imagine that this Animal feeling his Liver grow too big, makes the Cry which has impos'd on him the name of *Toc-quay*, to call another Insect to his succor; and that this other Insect entering into his Body at his mouth, eats the overplus of the Liver, and after this repast retires out of the *Toc-quay*'s body, by the same way that he enter'd therein.[23]

Wonder stymies speech and thought and is the reaction of a simple intelligence, too easily awed by things that can be explained by scientific scrutiny.[24] There is nothing fantastical in the land or people of Siam except in the minds of the Siamese. La Loubère and Tachard manage to work wondrous elements back into their narratives by placing them in Siamese mouths, delivering outlandish pictures of the East to their readers at the same time that they deny any sensationalism on their own part. Those who view the unfamiliar through the lens of wonder, La Loubère suggests, are either old-fashioned Europeans or backward Siamese.

La Loubère's assessment of the state of science, or natural philosophy, reveals less about Siamese habits of mind than about changes in European pedagogy and scientific method. It is La Loubère's own allegiance to a skeptical and academic program of science that he reveals in these passages. Looking for a point of contact with Siamese views in these European sources, one often finds instead a mirror held back up to the face of Europe. For a reader like John Locke, the simultaneous reflection on foreign intellectual histories and self-reflection of European mentalities was enormously valuable. As he was composing the *Essay Concerning Human Understanding,* Locke's thoughts on how the human intelligence assesses information acquired at second hand were informed by the feedback loop of Europeans reporting on Siamese reactions to reports of Europe:

> As it happened to a *Dutch* Ambassadour, who entertaining the King of *Siam* with the particularities of *Holland,* which he was inquisitive after, amongst other things told him, that the Water in his Country, would sometimes, in cold weather, be so hard, that Men walked upon it, and that it would bear an Elephant, if he were there. To which the King replied, *Hitherto I have believed the strange Things you have told me, because I look upon you as a sober fair Man, but now I am sure you lye.*[25]

Between the publication of the first edition of his *Essay* and the fourth edition of 1700, Locke read La Loubère's *A New Historical Relation of the Kingdom of Siam.* La Loubère had written a largely positive account of Buddhist beliefs and morals yet came to the conclusion that the Siamese were atheists. Locke added the example of the godless Siamese to his discussion of "innate principles":

> [There] are Instances of Nations where uncultivated Nature has been left to it self, without the help of Letters, and Discipline, and the Improvements of Arts and Sciences. But there are others to be found, who have enjoy'd these in a very great measure, who yet, for want of a due application of their thoughts this way, want the *Idea,* and Knowledge of God.

'Twill I doubt not be a surprise to others, as it was to me, to find the *Siamites* of this number.[26]

For Locke, failure to have an idea of God meant a failure to have an idea of law, since all law started with God's law. This is, therefore, a failure of reason. On the other hand, people or nations who lack an idea of God neglect to worship. This, on the contrary, is a failure of awe, a failure to have an adequate sense of wonder. Reading the Siamese memoirs of the Abbé de Choisy and La Loubère had given Locke a favorable impression of the Siamese. Siam was a land with a sophisticated artistic and intellectual culture that yet lacked, in Locke's view, the highest degree of either rationality or wonder. In the Christian tradition, rationality and wonder overlapped comfortably, even as an older idea of wonder was replaced by early Enlightenment approaches to science and philosophy.

It is precisely in the context of Christian proselytizing that both wonder and the rationalized vantage point of Western science, framed through the optical devices that Narai collected, were presented to the Siamese king. Any instruction Narai received in the use of Western scientific instruments, even the ones he requested from the Dutch East India Company, would have come through the Jesuit missionaries. The Dutch interest in Siam was never more than economic. Louis XIV, who saw little opportunity for commercial gain in Siam, was instead operating under the dangerously mistaken belief that Narai could be converted to Christianity. The scientific truth that was offered to Narai was also always presented as a religious truth. A thank-you letter written to Narai by the Jesuit Tachard and his colleagues leaves a rare trace of how the Jesuits might have explained their scientific enterprises to Narai:

> The sciences, Sir, that we make profession of, are esteemed all over Europe. Our King does so encourage them, that for their use, he has erected stately observatories, and for their sake given his august name to our companies college where they are taught. We have studied to improve them from our youth upwards, especially astronomy, which best agrees with our inclinations because it raises our minds to the frequent contemplation of Heaven, the habitation of the blessed, and the country we only aspire unto.[27]

The motto on the title page of Tachard's Siamese memoir declares this aim as well: *his coelum panditur*, "by these is heaven revealed." In the sixteenth and seventeenth centuries, wonder had taken on a new role in scientific investigation and experiment. There were several acknowledged shortcomings of early modern naturalism in Europe—it could be cruel, as in the vivisection of animals to expose the workings of the heart or lungs; with the notable exception of navigation, it mostly served no purpose, since there was yet no medical application for new anatomical discoveries or the observation of fleas under the microscope; and it could be distressingly controversial, as in Galileo's telescopic observations of the movements of the planets that led him to side with Copernicus and banish the Earth from the center of the universe. Naturalists turned from matter to the divine to justify their collective enterprise: the ultimate purpose of science was to reveal the intricate wonder of God's creation, from microcosm to the macrocosm, now rendered visible thanks to scientific measuring and optical devices.

Narai was well versed in Siamese astrology and had a close working relationship with his court astrologer, Phra Horathibodi.[28] During the embassy of 1685, Narai had the opportunity to view heavenly bodies from a Western point of view through two imaging devices. In December of that year, a lunar eclipse was visible from Siam, and Tachard and the Jesuits planned to make observations, measuring the progress of the shadow that fell across the moon. Narai was eager to take part. Tachard describes setting up the king with a five-foot telescope, protruding from a window overlooking a gallery where the Jesuits would squat on Persian carpets to plot their observations (Figure 8.5). Narai was pleased to compare what he saw through the microscope to a detailed lunar map and ultimately wanted a better look. So, the Jesuits were allowed to join him with their twelve-foot telescope, perforce standing in his presence to adjust the focus. Narai was impressed enough with Jesuit science that he asked them to build him observatories in Lopburi and Ayutthaya and to send him twelve Jesuit mathematicians to run them. Although he never subscribed to the Christian part of this equation, being a patron, like Louis, to a form of scientific exploration that participated in the divine almost certainly had some appeal for Narai. Building an observatory brought the added benefit of keeping Siam up to date with the Chinese court, for whom the Jesuits had also outfitted an observatory in Beijing.

Collecting Across Cultures in Siam

At the Siamese observatories, the Western scientific point of view would have become a spectacle of interest for Narai's court had not Narai's scientific enterprises come to an abrupt end. In 1688, a revolt toppled the regime of King Narai, who died that year under house arrest. Constantine Phaulkon was tortured and executed. Kosa Pan for a brief time fared well, becoming high chancellor under the new administration of King Phetracha. But this courtier, universally described as handsome in European accounts, lost first his nose and then his life when he fell out of Phetracha's favor. Narai's intimacy with Phaulkon and

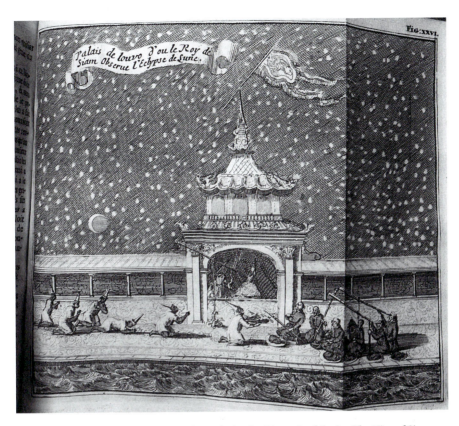

8.5. Cornelis Martin Vermeulen after a design by Pierre-Paul Sevin, *The King of Siam Observes the Eclipse of the Moon from the Palace of Lopburi*, from Guy Tachard, *Voyage de Siam, des Pères Jésuites* (Paris, 1686). By permission of the Division of Rare and Manuscript Collections, Cornell University Library.

his negotiations with the French, who had proved to have military designs on Siam, were factors in the coup, and Phetracha did not continue his predecessor's dalliance with Western scientific ideas. The 1688 revolution may have wiped out any memory of the location where Narai's collections were housed or displayed and whether other members of the court also kept collections of European gadgetry. Even if no Siamese inventory has survived, however, it is telling that there is no record in a European travel account of a visit to Narai's collections. Had any of the ambassadors, merchants, or missionaries been invited to view his cabinet, they would surely have written about it, probably comparing it to collections in Europe.

A rare description of a Siamese display of European objects is offered by Engelbert Kaempfer, a surgeon with the Dutch East India Company. Bound for Japan in 1690, Kaempfer had the opportunity to catch up with Kosa Pan in his home, which was decorated with souvenirs of the embassy to France:

He is a more comely Person, and of better aspect, than I ever met with amongst this black race of mankind who are generally short siz'd and look almost like Monkeys. He is also quick of understanding and lively action, for which reason he was a few years ago sent Ambassador to France, of which Country, its Government, Fortresses and the like, he would often entertain us in his discourses; and the hall of his House, where we had a private audience of him, was hung with pictures of the Royal Family of France, and European Maps, the rest of the furniture being nothing but Dust and Cobwebs.[29]

Kaempfer's description, unreservedly xenophobic, is just about the only evidence that members of the Siamese court had collected European images and objects, in this case portraits and maps, two modes of representation, and knowledge, that were alien to Siam.[30] Kosa Pan, who had crossed the globe to acquire these items, was, however, hardly a typical courtier. Kosa Pan's particular interest in maps is attested by other European sources. Jean Donneau de Visé, in his *Mercure Galant*, reports on Kosa Pan's visit to the Royal Observatory in Paris, where he admired a large map. Although Kosa Pan could not read the French labels, he immediately picked out Siam and showed his companions the route that his ship had taken between Bangkok and Brest.[31] Kosa Pan would seem to have become familiar with European mapping conventions before his arrival in France, but whether he had been exposed to maps in Siam—perhaps the globes in his king's collection—or only later as a curious passenger on board the *Oiseau* is impossible to say.

In the diplomatic gifts that Narai sent the French court, he showed not only his broad interest in scientific and mechanical wonders but also an understanding of the values that Europeans gave to certain classes of objects and the practices through which they collected and displayed them. Chaumont's list of presents sent from the Siamese to the French in 1685 includes Japanese lacquer cabinets, sometimes with sets of nesting drawers, items that were regularly employed by European collectors as small-scale curiosity cabinets; one such item is "an eight-sided Japan chest full of very curious small boxes."[32] Also prominent in the roster of gifts sent on behalf of Narai and his daughter are spring-action automata, mechanical novelties that portrayed Chinese or Japanese figures and seem calculated to feed the curiosity cabinets of Europe: "Two Chinese ladies, each of them on a peacock, carrying in their hands a small silver cup, enamelled, the peacocks by turning a spring walk on a table, according to the way they are placed, the cups staying upright in their hands"; "Two Chinese horsemen carrying in their hands two small cups, who walk by a motion by springs, all of silver in the Chinese fashion"; "A silver crab bearing a cup on its back and which walks about because of a spring"; "Two ladies of Japan, gilded and enamelled silver, each of which carries a small cup in her hands, and which move by springs"; "A Chinese lady of silver and amber which moves by springs."[33] European clockworks were manifestly not the first mechanical novelties known in Siam. The cup-bearer automaton is a technology that dates at least to the sixth century in China.[34] Narai pursued his collecting across his full range of cultural contacts, and it does not seem to have been his aim to create for himself a facsimile of a European cabinet of curiosities, governed by European standards for the production of knowledge.

Narai's collection was likely not, in the contemporary European sense, a collection at all. Instead, the foreign objects that he acquired may have been stored for use only on ceremonial occasions, as part of the complex choreography in which his own presence was revealed to and screened from his subjects. Dutch East India Company merchants report that Narai sometimes asked to borrow foreign goods for display in his processions and visits to make merit at Ayutthaya's temples.[35] Narai frequently annoyed the Dutch East India Company by failing to pay his bills for the expensive items that he ordered. The king, however, may have expected to receive these as gifts for allowing the Dutch to do business in his state, in effect turning the Dutch into a tributary nation. Siamese kings also expected human tribute, and in the establishment of a new city or court, Siamese chronicles always speak of the number of artisans who would be part of the king's retinue. Tachard and Chaumont were accompanied to Siam by French craftsmen who were expected to stay at the court: a clock-maker, glassmaker, and fireworks engineer. And in asking for twelve more Jesuits to run his observatory, Narai was not only bowing to European expertise but harnessing it for his own glorification, since kings commonly sent their artisans to a more powerful leader. Both Narai and his father are generally called usurpers, but this was not an unusual mode of succession in Siam. Although the eldest son often inherited his father's title, Siamese kingship did not adhere to a simple pattern of primogeniture. The status of chief or king was earned by the ability to attract supporters and to deploy objects that embodied kingly power, traditionally regalia adopted from Indic monarchs.[36] In the 1680s, it is too early to speak of trading in Indic signs of power for a cult of modernity, but because of the constant flow of new ideas and objects across Southeast Asia's trade routes, there was a high value placed on being up to date and "contemporary."[37]

Perhaps one of the last functioning curiosity cabinets in true Baroque fashion, combining the collecting of bizarre natural artifacts with cutting-edge scientific research, is the Museum of World Insects and Natural Wonders in Chiang Mai, Thailand. The proprietors, Manop and Rampa Rattanarithikul, have identified two dozen species of mosquito and display these and the four hundred other mosquito species native to Thailand carefully catalogued alongside fanciful objects from the natural world, such as petrified wood or stones in fantastical shapes. The museum's somewhat idiosyncratic and anachronistic pairing of taxonomic classification with the category of wonder is a revival rather than a survival from the seventeenth century. Still, this curiosity cabinet thriving as a tourist attraction in modern Thailand, and combining Eastern, Western, scientific, and folkloric modes of reading nature, furnishes a parable for the reception of Western scientific wonders in Southeast Asia three hundred years ago. The Siamese court was one in which there was a constant exposure to, and often great tolerance for, novel ideas and belief systems. The ability to acquire and control valuable foreign objects was a mark of royal power for a Siamese king. It was Narai's innovation to bring Western scientific devices into his creation of a royal image. Although we cannot know what was revealed to Narai when he looked at his world through European lenses, both he and the Europeans who wrote about his kingdom were testing their own intellectual traditions against mutually novel ideas of wonder.

Plate 1 (above). Gottfried Bernhard Goetz, *America*, Augsburg, ca. 1750, engraving, 46.7 x 71.3 cm. Courtesy of the John Carter Brown Library at Brown University.

Plate 2 (below). Johann Wolfgang Baumgartner, *America*, ca. 1750, oil on canvas, 25 x 38 cm. Augsburg, Städtische Kunstsammlungen-Deutsche Barockgalerie.

Plate 3. Juan Sánchez Cotán, *Quince, Cabbage, Melon and Cucumber*, ca.1602, oil on canvas, 27 1/8 x 33 1/4 in. San Diego Museum of Art. Gift of Anne R. and Amy Putnam.

Plate 4. Juan de Valdés Leal, *Vanitas*, 1660, oil on canvas, 51 3/8 x 39 1/16 in. Wadsworth Atheneum Museum of Art, Hartford, Connecticut. The Ella Gallup Sumner and Mary Catlin Sumner Collection Fund.

Plate 5. *Caritanira Amir*, early seventeenth century, red lacquer top board and f.1, ink Javanese carakan script on lontar (palmyra) palm, given by William Herbert, 3rd Earl of Pembroke, 1629. Bodleian Library MS Java b.2(R).

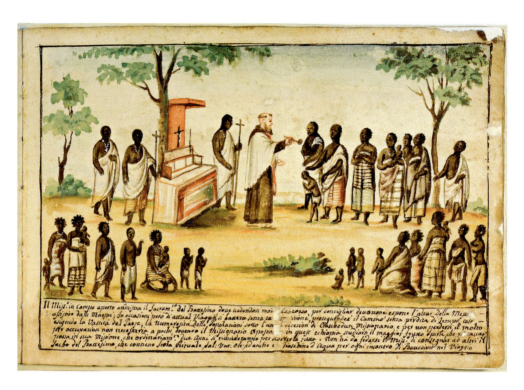

Il Miss.º in Campo aperto amministra il Sacram.ᵗᵒ del Battesimo doue uedendosi moi assiguro dalli Maestri. In occasioni pero d'actual Viaggio si batteza senza ta uiguendo la Uastita del Paese, la Numerosità delle popolazioni sono l'un per occupazion non necessarie a pochi, douendo il Missionario Apostos. pioso in sua Missione, che ordinariam.ᵗᵉ due Anni si uidueranno per scorrerla tutte sache del Battesimo, che contiene Scola Rituale dal Vas: olei, ed anche e

capporso, per conciliar deuozione espone l'altar della Messa pr. Visione, proseguendasi il Camino senza perdita di Tempo, cose ur. tezion di Chischedun Missionario, e per non perdersi il molto in quest echiopia iudiari il maggior fronto sparte che si uauag. Non ha da fidarsi il Miss.º di consegnar ad altri il sacramento d'Acqua per ogni incontro il Battesimi nel Viaggio

uisli e insinin sino ordinarios li Bestj di questi deserti e strangardi sono i loro nomi, pongo solo questo perciò a me pare il più vidicolo, e questo un capris.... son Grande, con Chiad. Millo lungo, nero e sempre inginiato dal demonio questa parla e risponde, e da essi i Giassi addna... son nome di Bani, i più assini giorni nella luna solea epli Moderni in un albero fatto di pietra e lisia facendosi parla e......

OOC, PRAVISOUTSONTHOON RAATCHATHOUD.

Ambassadeur du Roy de Siam, envoyé au Roy, il etoit frere du defunt Barcalon ou premier Ministre du Roy de Siam, homme d'Esprit, qui a toujours été auprès de son frere dans toutes les affaires. Il reçut Mr le Chevalier de Chaumont Ambassadeur du Roy a l'entrée de la riviere de Siam, et l'accompagna par tout. Ils firent leur entrée Solennelle dans Paris par la porte St Antoine le lundy XII Aoust 1686 dans un Carosse de sa Majesté, ils furent reçu par Mr le Marechal Duc de la Feüillade.

Dessiné sur le naturel. A Paris, Chez Nolin, rue St Jacques, a l'Enseigne de la Place des Victoires. Avec Privilit du Roy.

Plate 6 (facing page, top). Bernardino Ignazio da Vezza d'Asti, *The Missionary in Open Land*, ca. 1750, watercolor on paper, 19.5 x 28 cm. Biblioteca civica centrale diTorino. Sezione Manoscritti e rari, MS 457, f. 4.

Plate 7 (facing page, bottom). Unknown artist, *Many and infinite are the idols of these deserts*, ca. 1663–87, watercolor on paper, 24 x 34 cm. Private collection, f. 83. Photograph by the author.

Plate 8 (above). Jean-Baptiste Nolin, *Ok-Phra Wisut Sunthon* [Kosa Pan], 1686. Hand-colored etching. By permission of the James H.W. Thompson Foundation, Bangkok.

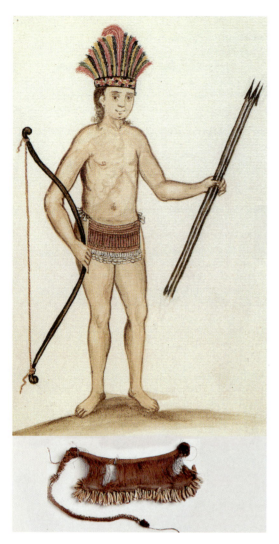

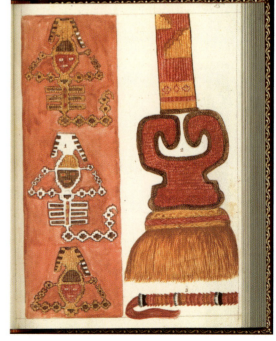

Plate 9 (above). "Indian Warrior," in Baltasar Jaime Martínez Compañón, *Trujillo del Perú*, vol. ix, f. 21 (top), and the garment depicted in the illustration (bottom). Real Biblioteca, Patrimonio Nacional, Spain, and Museo de América, Madrid.

Plate 10 (right). Three prehispanic textiles from the north coast of Peru, in Baltasar Jaime Martínez Compañón, *Trujillo del Perú*, vol. 9, f. 24. Patrimonio Nacional, Spain.

Costumes du Peuple.

CHILI

Plate 11. " Costumes du peuple. Chili," drawing by Philipoteaux and engraving by Saulnier after sketches made by Louis Choris (ca. 1859?). In Louis Choris, *Voyage pittoresque autour du monde avec des portraits de sauvages d'Amérique, d'Asie, d'Afrique et des îles du Grand océan, des paysages, des vues maritimes et plusieurs objets d'histoire naturelle* (Paris, 1822).

Plate 12. Creator unknown, *Récolte du maguey à San Martino*, from the album *Mexique*, 1865, assembled by Louis Falconnet. Research Library, The Getty Research Institute, Los Angeles (93.R.20).

PART III

—ɯ—

COLLECTING PEOPLE

CHAPTER 9

—⚹—

Collecting and Accounting: Representing Slaves as Commodities in Jamaica, 1674–1784

TREVOR BURNARD

When Thomas Thistlewood died in late November 1786, he was eulogized in an obituary in the *Cornwall Gazette* on December 16, 1786 as follows:

> In Westmoreland, on Thursday the 30th of November, in the 65th year of his age, Thomas Thistlewood, Esq., a gentleman whose social qualities, during a residence of upwards of thirty years in that parish, had greatly endeared him to a whole circle of his neighbours and acquaintances and whose attainments, in many branches of natural knowledge, in which he was peculiarly communicative, rendered him a most desirable companion to men of science.[1]

Thistlewood was a gentleman collector, with a wide-ranging interest in "many branches of natural knowledge," a follower of Linneaus and his classificatory systems and an obsessive recorder of all types of information. These included the books he read, the letters he wrote and received, the plants he introduced into Jamaica and tended in his showpiece garden, the women he had sex with, and the weather that he experienced.

But, despite his eulogist, he was hardly a "gentleman," in either origins or behavior, though he was certainly a collector. What he is notorious for was his willingness to record in his private diaries multiple interactions with slaves. Because he was a list maker and a collector and thus attuned to the enumerating and classifying undercurrents of the Enlightenment, he preserved his diaries of his life in Jamaica, diaries that, along with thirty-seven years of very precise weather measurements and some other accompanying material, have been fortuitously saved for posterity. These diaries have been mined by historians of slavery to examine white mastery in the tropics. They show Thistlewood to have been a harsh master, a sadist, and a more than occasional rapist.[2]

His obituary, however, which depicts him as a socially gregarious man of parts and a parish-level intellectual, does not mention Thistlewood's extensive involvement with slavery. It is a silence characteristic of eighteenth-century engagement with this institution. Eighteenth-century people in plantation societies were hardly indifferent to slavery. Nevertheless, when they thought about slaves and slavery, they did so in the abstract, treating slavery as an intellectual or political problem, rather than as a negotiated relationship between two sets of mutually antagonistic people.[3] The idea of collecting material about slavery was incomprehensible, although, as James Delbourgo notes, more collecting of slave-related material was done than we might think.[4] In general, however, slaves were invisible in the intellectual life of eighteenth-century Europe, especially as people whose ideas, material creations, and material constraints were worth collecting and displaying.[5] The number of individual slave lives in the Americas we can reconstruct even partially is so small as to raise real questions of representation. Slaves were always present, always crucial to white self-definition in societies where slaves were present, but that presence was seldom thought worthy of including in intellectual discourse. Even less was the material life of slaves worth saving or preserving.[6]

To take one example of the dissonance between what Thistlewood thought about slaves and his interest in intellectual achievement, we can compare his reaction to the executions of slave rebels and the death of his closest intellectual friend, Dr. Anthony Robinson, in 1768. Thistlewood thought Robinson "a good natural philosopher and the greatest botanist that ever was in Jamaica, his genius perfectly adapted to examining plants" and mourned his death intensely "walking out alone and weeping bitterly." He recalled fondly the spring of 1761 when he and Robinson had amused themselves by "drawing Birds, Plants etc.," some of which drawings Thistlewood carefully copied into his commonplace book. At that very time, however, whites in western Jamaica were wreaking terrible revenge on slaves captured during Tacky's revolt of 1760, the largest and most dangerous eighteenth-century slave revolt in British America. A few weeks before Thistlewood met Robinson, Apongo, or Wager, a remarkable man whom Thistlewood considered "the King of the Rebels" was condemned to "hang in Chains 3 days then be took down and burnt." A few weeks after Thistlewood met Robinson, he noted in his diaries, rather casually, that he had allowed one of his slaves to give "witness against Allen's Quamina: he is to be hang'd at the estate, his head Cutt off, and Body burnt." Less than a fortnight after Robinson's death and while he was still grieving over the loss "of my friend Dr A.R.," Thistlewood went to the local town to post some letters home and talk with a friend about the best way to grow roses. On the way home, he noted with little comment that "they were hanging two rebel Negroes." The event was so unremarkable as to attract virtually no attention.[7]

Slaves were incidental to how Thistlewood imagined himself—a member of the petit Enlightenment in the tropics. In his commonplace books, he virtually never wrote about slavery. He merely noted, but did not comment upon, James Ramsay's pioneering 1784 tract on abolitionism, which he read soon after publication.[8] On the other hand, he copied out large passages on electricity from the American guru of the phenomenon, Benjamin Franklin. Given that he had contemplated, in his first year in Jamaica in 1750, removing to Philadelphia, it is not entirely implausible that he might, especially with his skills in scientific experimentation, have come to the great man's attention.[9] Certainly, the meteorological historian Michael Chenoweth, who rates Thistlewood extremely highly as an accomplished early modern chronicler of tropical weather conditions and thus an important figure in the history of science, imagines Thistlewood conversing with Thomas Jefferson, a fellow climate enthusiast.[10]

Similarly, slaves are seldom represented in the great collections established by people with West Indian connections. Three major British collectors derived their wealth from the West Indies. Christopher Codrington established one of the finest libraries in England with the proceeds of profits from slavery, the Codrington Library at All Souls, Oxford. The library at Eton College was also established from a legacy of an old boy and West Indian planter. William Beckford, III, the wealthiest man in late eighteenth-century England, was an obsessive collector of Orientalism, and his estate eventually formed a key part of the Wallace Collection. The most important collection made by a man with West Indian connections was, of course, that made by Sir Hans Sloane, who parlayed a brief but lucrative visit to Jamaica in the late seventeenth century into a career at the very heart of London's scientific community, with his collections forming the basis of the British Museum and the British Library. But none of these collectors showed much interest in slavery, in Africa, or in Africans, despite the centrality of slavery to providing the means whereby collections could be established. In this respect, all three collectors are similar to Thomas Jefferson, whose library formed the starting point of the Library of Congress. As these institutions have developed over the centuries, the links between their origins in slave-derived profits and their subsequent development have become even more blurred.[11]

Endemic racism is one reason so little material was collected on slavery. Just as significant, however, as an impediment is the nature of slavery itself. Slaves had very little possessions, and those that they did possess did not survive. The paraphernalia associated with the slave trade and with slavery that whites developed was also hardly worth keeping, and given that much of the most distinctive bits was related to punishment, collecting slave-related material was in itself morally dubious, suggesting a prurient interest in either torture or sexuality. Slavery was a permanent institution but a transient culture, with few artifacts produced out of slavery having any aesthetic value.[12]

Such paucity of surviving materials is problematic for people wishing to memorialize the legacy of slavery for the present, as museum curators know well. The difficulties inherent in marking the institution of slavery are canvassed in Elizabeth Kowaleski Wallace's book on Britain and the modern memory of the slave trade. Wallace examines depictions of slavery created at the Merseyside Maritime Museum, the William Wilberforce Museum in Hull, and the Bristol Slave Trade Trail. She notes that, despite the best efforts of curators at the Merseyside Museum to respect African agency when devising their innovative and intelligent display on slavery and despite their efforts to resist the essentializing and dehumanizing notion of the African slave, in the end "they were hampered by a Western ethnographic temporalising practice that persistently sees African history as out of time." The problem becomes acute when curators try to show how slaves resist slavery because the objects they inevitably choose to accompany human voices talking of slave resistance are inevitably instruments of torture—shackles, chains, branding irons, and a "punishment collar," a cast-iron brace designed to keep the head tortuously upright. As Marcus Wood notes, these artifacts of torture can create "interpretive traps." When the object of torture is displayed as an abstract item, one divorced from a narrative context in which the human being who suffered is made apparent, the slave emerges as "an object afflicted, not as object capable of describing his or her affliction."[13]

But for all sorts of reasons, we cannot allow slavery to be forgotten; thus, we want to create displays of slavery that show the institution in its full variety. All sorts of museums are thinking about how to do this with the materials they have at hand. One such museum is the National Maritime Museum in Greenwich, which has acquired from the collector and dealer Michael Graham-Stewart of London an impressive archive of material relating to slavery that forms the basis of a new exhibit in its recently formed Atlantic Worlds gallery. As one might expect, the collection is diverse and unrepresentative. It is heavily weighted to the eighteenth and even more so the early nineteenth century and to pictorial representations of slaves. Nothing in the collection seems to have been produced by a slave, nor is there anything that suggests that slaves were able to construct a rich culture during captivity.[14]

To me, the most interesting items are items that historians of slavery encounter everyday in the archives but which they seldom consider from the perspective of art history or material culture. These are documents listing slaves for legal purposes. One such document is a one-page listing of slave names, probably dating from the mid-eighteenth century in the British islands of the Lesser Antilles. It is described in the National Maritime Museum's catalogue of the Graham deposit as a "List of Slaves to be Delivered."[15] It shows how slaves were both humans and also commodities. By enumerating and then listing slaves, noting men first, then women, then boys, then girls, the writer was signaling to some unknown person and also to the slave carrying the list that slaves were commodities that could be individually priced. Even if, as is likely, the slave carrying the list was illiterate, one can presume that he or she would have been able to understand the purpose of the document carried.[16]

Lists of slaves are hardly unusual and have survived in great numbers, mostly in legal records connected to property. The business of slavery generated large quantities of paperwork, a surprising amount of which has survived. In Jamaica, for example, we find references to slaves noted in wills, where testators specified which slaves were to be left to which devisees and occasionally indicated which fortunate slaves would be freed on their master's death; in deeds; in poll tax lists; in manumission records; and in transcripts of sales of slaves. Historians have mined these records extensively over many years in order to establish the essential lineaments of slave life. Usually they have used the material contained in these records as data for larger investigations without examining in great detail the record itself as an artifact that in its very construction tells us something significant about slavery.[17]

The form and content of such documents changed over time. African chattel slavery was an institution that was essentially created fresh in the Americas, even if it obviously had European and indeed African precedents.[18] It took many years for Europeans to establish rules, procedures, and assumptions about how slaves were to be recorded in documents. Indeed, collecting information about slaves for purposes of accounting for what they did, what they were worth, and for how they were to be conceptualized was not something that came naturally to planters—records from the seventeenth century about slavery and the plantation economy are notably less revealing than records from the eighteenth century and the early nineteenth century. Because the form and content of documents relating to slave property evolved over time, close analysis of their structure and meaning allows historians to trace changing patterns of slave representation by slave owners.

The best documents to trace changing representations of slaves as peculiar and particular pieces of property are estate records and inventories of personal possessions of recently deceased people taken soon after death. Estate records, especially from the mid-eighteenth century onward, when John Ward argues significant technical improvements in reporting functions occurred, mirroring improvements in accounting practice in Europe, contain the fullest details of slaves and their lives.[19] By the end of the eighteenth century, estate records could be very extensive, although some of the most basic elements of accounting, such as double entry bookkeeping, were not adopted until the very end of slavery. The accounting model usually chosen to run sugar estates was the ancient "master and steward" or "charge and discharge" system adopted from the administering of large aristocratic and gentry estates in England. The method was designed to ensure the preparation of periodic statements, showing what the steward had received and disbursed.[20]

In this system, as Barry Higman notes, accounts kept by overseers, attorneys, and merchants were an essential record and a key source of information for projections and planning. In the case of Jamaica, plantation accounts, created in the island, played a significant role in the managing of the plantation economy. According to the leading Scottish accounting textbooks of circa 1750, published by William Gordon and John Mair, three main types of books were kept: the boiling house book (a daily record of sugar potted), the still house book (rum produced), and the plantation book (listing produce sent off the island, goods acquired, and the numbers of slaves and free people on the property and their annual increase and decrease). Journals sometimes contained information overlapping that in a diary and generally included inventories, lists, and a record of cash transaction.[21]

The object, St. Domingue coffee planter P. J. Laborie argued in 1798, was to enable the planter to "balance accounts with himself and to be able to refer to notes upon occasion." Laborie believed

> the journal must contain a state of the Negroes and cattle, a state of the birth and deaths, the number, dates, and various kinds of plantations, the daily works and employments of the Negroes, ordinary as well as extraordinary; the state of the crops day by day; the deliveries of coffee, as well as the price of sale and amount, as stated in the factor's letters; lastly the state of the provisions, tools, utensils, and cloaths delivered to the Negroes.[22]

Without making their reasoning explicit, by the second decades of the nineteenth century, attorneys compiling such records sometimes included lists of enslaved people valued in money terms according to principles that depended on age, sex, color, health, and disposition. These valuations were essentially predictions of the productive potential of the enslaved and of the prices they might be sold for in the market. The principles were similar to those applied to livestock. The Gale-Morant papers of 1778 are an early and good example of this form of accounting practice. These list slaves by name, value, age, and ethnicity. An even better one is the account book for the Old Montpelier estate for the years 1824 to 1828. It contains copies of official returns; extensive lists of the enslaved people, with comments on their health and character, as well as their occupations and the "increase and decrease" among them; and a listing of slaves by where they lived and with whom they lived.[23]

It is only recently that scholars have begun to look at estate records as particular texts that inform about intentions behind accounting practices. The role of accounting and accountants was long viewed in neutral or amoral terms. Scholars wrote accounting history from a technical view, concerned to identify the origins of particular methods of bookkeeping without being especially concerned about the uses to which these methods were put once developed. Recently, however, this focus has been challenged by the rise of "critical accounting," a movement within accounting history that interrogates accounting and accounting practice within a historical and moral context. To what extent, it has been asked, should accountants use their specialized skills to uphold morally abhorrent practices? Studies of plantation slavery fall naturally within this net. The keepers of accounts are seen by accounting historians such as Richard Fleischmann, Thomas Tyson, and David Oldroyd as active agents in the efficient and profitable exploitation of enslaved people, not merely the keepers of record. This critical approach, as Barry Higman argues, is parallel to the approach taken to slavery by social and economic historians in the 1960s and to recent examinations of slavery in the development of human resources and modern management.[24]

What critical accounting historians have reminded us is that there is no obvious accounting reason slaves were presented in estate records in the way they were. In particular, it is difficult to understand why so many lists of slaves attach a monetary value to individual slaves. As Fleischman, Oldroyd, and Tyson note, there was no compelling reason such as a government tax on slaves by value that made the valuing of slaves a necessary activity. They speculate that regular valuations of slaves may have been necessary for purposes of insurance, although the evidence that slaves were insured is relatively scarce. I have not come across any firm in Port Royal or Kingston offering insurance to slaveowners against their slaves, although it is not impossible to imagine that such schemes did exist. After all, buying a slave was an expensive proposition and if a slave died before being "seasoned" for plantation work, then a slaveowner would suffer a considerable loss. The records of one estate—Blubber Valley Plantation in Antigua in 1784—suggest that insuring slaves did occur. Fleischman, Oldroyd, and Tyson suggest on this estate the going rental rate of slaves was 10 percent with any insurance premium or risk lying with the renter. It is more likely, however, that slaveowners wanted their slaves valued regularly in order that they could ascertain fair wages for slaves sent out for hire. The hiring of slaves, as Heather Cateau has argued, was very common and resulted in considerable income.[25] Thomas Thistlewood, for example, derived the majority of his income in the 1770s and 1780s from hiring out most of his slaves to sugar planters during harvest season.

They also argue that valuing slaves was part of the agency information that owners required in order to improve their management of estates. As W. T. Baxter notes, "accounting started as a means of keeping track of debtors, creditors and cash; and this is still its main task, without which business would collapse." By the 1780s, progressive planters were becoming more aware that they could not make the best returns from their estates if they did not have accurate updating of the amount of capital that they had and how that capital changed from year to year. Slaves generally comprised in Jamaica over 50 percent of the nonlanded value of planters' estates and thus knowing whether the capital invested in slaves was rising or falling was useful to know. Planters were beginning to follow the advice put forward by agricultural improvers such as Arthur Young, whose prescriptions to British farmers show that it was best agricultural practice by the end of the eighteenth century to calculate income, taking into account the increase or decrease in the value of implements and livestock. The aim, Young suggested, was for improved record keeping to be used as a means of measuring and then improving performance.[26]

The problem with using estate records to examine patterns of slave description is that estate records as described above all date from the late eighteenth century onward. By this date, the principles behind how slaves were described and ordered had become established. We get a much better idea of the principles behind how slaves were described from an analysis of inventories. These date from the third quarter of the seventeenth century and are available in large numbers throughout the eighteenth and nineteenth centuries. An analysis of these documents from Jamaica between 1674 and 1784 shows, first, that slaves were valued carefully from before the advent of the large-scale plantation; second, that valuations of slaves marched in line with valuations of livestock, with which slaves were usually grouped; and, third, that changes over time in the presentation of slaves as particular forms of property were considerable and significant.[27]

These inventories can be read without reference to other documents, but their meaning and significance are heightened if they can be placed in a longer temporal context. The first inventories that survive in Jamaica come from the mid-1670s and are sketchy in details compared to later inventories, especially in how they describe slaves. I have examined inventories from several periods in Jamaican history in order to trace changes in the depiction of slaves over time and have done an intensive survey of inventories from one year, 1775, in order to canvass the varieties of ways in which slaves were presented after a century or more of slavery in English Jamaica. What these records show is both continuity and change. The descriptions of slaves became more elaborate over time, but even from the start of settlement it seems clear that white Jamaicans thought that slaves were special types of property, different from all other types of property and, thus, needing to be presented differently in listing of possessions but also akin to other types of property, livestock in particular. Looking at changing descriptions of slaves over time should give us a better insight into how slaves were viewed as commodities.

What does this examination of how slaves were represented in inventories over time reveal? The most obvious conclusion is that over time slaves became more differentiated and more information was made available by appraisers about the individual characteristics of slaves. In the first volume of inventories preserved at the Jamaica Archives, slaves (invariably termed Negroes or Indians or "Negro and other slaves" rather than slaves) were seldom named and were often grouped together by gender. Thus, the appraisers of John James, in 1674, noted that he owned "Two Negro women" worth £40 and "one Negro man." There was no difference in this inventory between how a slave was described and how livestock was described—James owned "A horse," worth £7 and a Mare and a young colt, worth £12. Only occasionally in seventeenth-century inventories, as in the inventory of Alexander Pitt in 1674, were slaves named. Pitt owned "Two negro women named Hanah and Polly" and "a negro man named Kingston." "A Mulatto boy," however, was listed but not named. Slaves were not often grouped by gender, as the inventory of Benjamin Whatcomb shows. When they were grouped by gender, however, the ways slaves were listed are interesting. Robert Freeman was one of the first and largest planters in Jamaica. His 85 slaves are divided into men, women, boys, and girls. Alone among early inventories, other additional information was added. Several slaves are given modifiers to their names, reflecting either ethnicity (Coromantee Tom, Ebo Dick) or physical characteristics (Black Robin, Long Robin). The only reason this was done was to differentiate between slaves with the same names. It does not seem to have affected the value of the slaves listed; indeed, Freemen's appraisers did not assign individual values to any slave. They seem to have listed slaves by name for identification purposes only.

The link between how livestock and slaves were described is strong, as can be seen in the inventory of John Blair from 1705, where slaves are described on the same page as mules and "neat cattell" in what was a deliberate form of presentation—"stock and other livestock" was a form sometimes used. Nevertheless, by the early eighteenth century, the listing of slaves by name was becoming more common, as can be seen in the inventory of John Guy in 1703. In this inventory, each slave was listed by name and price with men first, followed by women. Children were not differentiated from adults and when still attached to their mother were not given names, as in "Bassgow and child." Not all planters did this. Robert Phillips grouped together slaves by gender in much the same way as he grouped livestock. Gender, however, remained a crucial divider between humans and livestock. Cattle and horses were seldom specified by sex; slaves increasingly were.

Family links were attenuated. Few slaveowners bothered to record family details and, when they did so, were vague about details, like the appraisers of Nicholas Richardson, who in 1703 noted that Richardson owned seventeen negro women, of whom six had suckling children. The only family link that counted was the link between mother and child, and that was almost always confined to a mother and a suckling child. More often than not, the woman was named but not the child, perhaps the absence of a name for infant children reflecting the low likelihood of slave infants reaching adulthood. Indicative of such assumptions is the fact that the prices of women named with suckling children were no more than the prices of women without children. In John Guy's inventory, for example, Bassgow was valued at £30, the exact value assigned to Grace, Abba, and Venus, £10 less than Catalina and £20 less than the most valuable female slave, Nanny. Nanny had a child but so too did Bassgow, suggesting that the value of a suckling child was close to minimal.

By 1723, more and more slaves were listed by name in inventories. They were often grouped by value rather than by anything else, that is, all slaves worth £50 were grouped together, regardless of gender. By 1746, not listing slaves by name was the exception rather than the rule. Nevertheless, not much more information than name and value was given. The appraisers of Mathew Hughes distinguished between slaves who were sailors, slaves who were house slaves or had a trade, and those who worked on the mountain or on the pen, presumably as field laborers. Males and females, however, were jumbled together, and it is not clear if all children are noted as such. It is noticeable that Hughes's appraisers gave as much care to describing his horses as they did to describing most of his slaves. The horses were each listed by name (Diment, Marquand, Crop, and

Sorrill) although, unlike slaves, they were not individually differentiated by price. William Vassall's 1746 inventory is a good example of standard accounting practice in describing slaves just before accounting practices started to become more codified and more detailed. His appraisers divided his slaves into Negro men, women, boys, and girls, with each category being valued individually higher than in the next category. A few slaves are distinguished by modifiers, but this is unusual and inconsistent. The children he owned were valued as part of a collective unit rather than as individuals and are not assigned to parents. A few slaves are noted as being old and past labor. He also added a few more pieces of information about slaves provided so as to differentiate between slaves with similar names. Thus, his appraisers listed Old Sampson and Little Sampson and Coromantee Hector and Papaw Hector. Three working slaves were noted as "old," while one woman slave—Sampson's Bess—was denoted by reference to the man who was her partner. Children were noted by name, unlike earlier inventories, but they were not individually differentiated by price. Eight named boys were valued jointly as worth £45.

By the mid-eighteenth century, some assumptions regarding how slaves were viewed by white owners had become clear. First, it was by mid-century good practice to name slaves and to value them individually. Vassall's slaves were grouped together by gender but not by price—the most valuable slaves were the 37th and 43rd slaves mentioned. A few distinguishing characteristics of slaves were noted, but these were generally used to distinguish between slaves with a similar name. Second, the major distinction between slaves was gender rather than value or ethnicity or health or disposition and character. Virtually no inventories listed slaves with reference to the family groups they were part of. Only one inventory before 1750—Abraham Richardson's 1726 inventory— and one after 1750—Thomas Thistlewood's in 1787—broke down slaves into family groups. It means that we need to revise an assumption by Fleischman about how slaves were appraised—the listing of slaves by gender only suggests that slaves did not march past the appraiser and were then valued as they promenaded. If slaves were brought forward for inspection and valuation, they were divided beforehand into specific groups, defined by gender and whether they were adults or children.[28]

The question we need to ask is why slaves needed to be valued individually. It had not been necessary in slave appraisements in the seventeenth century, and it was a time-consuming and cumbersome process to list slaves in the laborious way that the appraisers of William Vassall listed them. One argument might be that it reflected a growing appreciation of slave individuality by owners. Thinking of slaves as individuals should not be interpreted as a softening of slave conditions—they probably declined in the first half of the eighteenth century as the African slave trade expanded and as a larger percentage of slaves lived on large sugar-producing estates.[29] The price of a slave included a large number of variables, most of which are not noted in the inventories but which must have been examined before an appraiser made up his mind about slave value. The gap between the most valuable slave and the least is £90—a considerable sum given that the average price for a healthy male slave was £55–60. This suggests that purchasers of slaves were very discerning about how much they would pay for individual slaves and that they were not prepared to pay above market price just for the convenience of getting a job lot of slaves. The only reason slaves would be valued so carefully and so individually would be that Jamaica had an active internal slave market, in which slaves were frequently purchased and sold. If slaves were to go directly to inheritors, then they would need to be individually valued. What the ordering of slaves in inventories suggests to me is that it reflects a normal pattern of sale of property in a vendue sale. Vendue sales, or auctions of secondhand goods held frequently but irregularly and at people's homes rather than in an assigned space given over to trade, were a British-American invention—markets based on auction did not exist in Britain, where people generally bought retail from shops or at regularized markets. It is clear from occasional inventories where items owned by testators are listed alongside who purchased these items as goods that one of the functions of creating a comprehensive inventory was to allow a vendue sale to take place so that inheritors could inherit cash or credit rather than goods. Appraisers valued slaves in the ways that they did and listed slaves as they did because this reflected normal patterns of purchasing at vendue sales. They used all sorts of criteria in coming to a decision as to the value of slaves, but they did not bother communicating this to others, probably because individual inspection of slaves could reveal why a slave was valued as it was. Moreover, it was only a secondary purpose of inventories to provide agency information in the period before widespread absenteeism and while planters were indifferent to keeping accurate accounts.[30]

Another reason slaves may have been valued individually is because slaves, as people, were fundamentally different from livestock. In the main, one sheep or cow is as good as another (it is a little more difficult to say this for a horse, which is one reason horses were occasionally valued individually, although very few names of horses are listed until the late eighteenth century), and there is little reason either to differentiate between prices or to treat them as anything other than a collective. One probably needed to brand cows and sheep, as one did with slaves, in order to locate them if they wandered off or were stolen, but for purposes of establishing wealth and passing on such wealth to inheritors,

TREVOR BURNARD

one did not need to know much more information about cows and sheep than how many cows or sheep there were and what their total value was. Slaves, however, were human and could run away of their own accord. It was thus good to have a record of their name and value if they did abscond from a property. Moreover, the work slaves depended much more on intelligence, capacity, and willingness than was the case for livestock; thus it was necessary to know which slave was which if slaves were to be sold or divided among several inheritors.

By the third quarter of the eighteenth century, changes in how slaves were described and listed in inventories were beginning to occur. A few inventories, such as those of Gilbert Mathison, William Leacock, and John Nelson Kentish, began to give agency information about the slaves so that, for the first time, we can begin to break down slave value by various criteria or variables. Mathison's inventory lists occupation and groups slaves in a hierarchical way by virtue of both gender and occupation. Thus, the most important and valuable slave, Cuffee, a driver worth £200, was listed first. Elderly watchmen were listed after women working in the field. A few slaves were listed by ethnicity or race—Creol Mary, Conga Sarah, and Mulatto Susannah—but the inconsistency of such descriptions suggests that these monikers were used to distinguish slaves with similar names from each other. Leacock's inventory lists ages, as does that of John McLeod, the best inventory in regard to the information conveyed in the whole period of study. Kentish lists not only the names and values of individual slaves with some information on occupation but does the same for horses—the first such equation between livestock and slaves made in a Jamaican inventory. By the 1780s, three or four inventories a year were listing livestock—both horses and cattle—by name.

Nevertheless, the increase in agency information in the 1770s is limited. Most inventories listed slaves either by name only, as with Francis Darcy, or in alphabetical order, by gender, as with Edward Clarke. An examination of inventories made in 1775 indicates that few appraisers gave out consistent information about anything other than name or price. John McLeod's inventory gives information about name, age, occupation, health, and value. John Nixon gives information on all these except age. Four other inventories give consistent information about occupation. Otherwise, information on slave characteristics is sparse and inconsistent. Over one-third of inventories in 1775 give no more information than name and value. Of the 49 inventories, besides the six where agency information is consistent, where some details are occasionally given about individual slave circumstances, 24 note occupations, 20 note details of family (mothers and children only except for one slave man, Essex, belonging to Gilbert Mathison, who is noted as having three sisters), and 10 mention race or ethnicity. Only 7 inventories noted slaves who were runaway—whether that underestimates actual runaways is uncertain—and just one inventory made it clear that two slaves were "new" Negroes.

It is unwise to make too many conclusions about the meaning of the presentation of slaves in inventories because we have little to no information about what principles guided appraisers in their practices besides tradition and experience. But I think we can make some conclusions about patriarchy, hierarchy, family, and commodification. That the most significant division was by gender, with adult men presented first and girls presented last, indicates that whites accepted a degree of male dominance among their slave populations.[31] Not only were men valued more highly than were women, but their placing at the head of slave lists indicates that planters thought that slave men were entitled to some superiority over slave women. Not surprisingly, when plantations began to become more occupationally specialized, with planters training slaves to be tradespeople rather than hiring white tradesmen and expanding drivers and house slaves, the great majority of skilled positions were assigned to men. Patriarchal themselves, slaveowners accepted that slave men had some patriarchal privileges over women. A second conclusion is that slave society became more hierarchal over time. In the seventeenth century, slaveowners did not distinguish between slaves when valuing them. Experience taught them that the intelligence, capacity, strength, and skills of slaves varied enormously from slave to slave and that slaves could be individually priced with a good deal of precision. Eventually, slaveowners, most of whose capital was tied up in slaves, tried to maximize these advantages by training their best slaves into trades, thus accentuating the gap between the most highly valued slaves and the least valued. Descriptions of slaves gradually became more hierarchical with the most valuable slaves placed first and the least valuable slaves placed last. In short, slaveowners' human resources skills seem to have improved over time. A third conclusion concerns family and is essentially negative. Slaveowners saw slaves as property first, profit-producing people second, and family members hardly at all. Lists of slaves are singularly unrevealing about family relationships in Jamaica and that lack of revelation tells us a great deal about slaveowner indifference to slave family formation. Finally, slave lists tell us how completely slaves were commodified right from the start of settlement and how that commodification became refined and expanded over time. One of the most lamentable ironies in this examination of changing practices of representation over time is that what Philip Morgan has told us in his investigations of Thomas Thistlewood's diaries is correct: the gap between Africans and animals in the white Jamaican's mind was distressingly small.[32] Here we see continuity rather than change. The first inventories treated slaves and livestock as interchangeable

TREVOR BURNARD

pieces of property by not giving either individual names. The latter inventories treated livestock and slaves as interchangeable pieces of property by listing animals by names—more and more of which were similar to slave names—in the same way that they did for slaves. Africans were peculiar types of humans and peculiar types of animals—less the Adam and Eve who gave names to animals than the animals who were so named.[33]

In sum, slaves were collected and were valued but were seldom esteemed. The true brutality of Jamaican slavery does not lie in the abundance of evidence—some of which survives in the form of artifacts—of constant violence against slaves and frequent instances of torture through tools designed to give sadistic pleasure to the people wielding such tools. It lies in both the care and also the casualness by which slaves were listed, evaluated, and described in the thousands of lists of slaves that were created in order to prove that slaves were owned, that slaves were property. Owners of slaves and their representatives were most concerned about enslaved people as commodities, which is why slave lists detail prices with attention and with increasing accuracy and discrimination over time. But owners were little concerned about slaves as people. They were uninterested in their family circumstances, their places of origin, or their character or health. A slave list tells us more about the actual conditions of slavery and the attitudes that owners had toward slave than the few bits of material culture evidence that have survived and have been passed down to the present day. These "collections" of slaves that are abundant within the records relating to slavery do not just provide us with information about prices or numbers of slaves: they are significant material artifacts in their own right.

CHAPTER 10

—ɯɯ—

"Collecting Americans": The Anglo-American Experience from Cabot to NAGPRA

PETER C. MANCALL

"[The English] will not give a doit to relieve a lame begger, they will lay out ten to see a dead Indian."
—William Shakespeare, *The Tempest*, II:2

In the early modern era, some European visitors to the Western Hemisphere thought they would take indigenous Americans home with them. Christopher Columbus was the first to do so, but soon after, Sebastian Cabot did the same thing, as did many Europeans who traveled to the Americas before the mid-eighteenth century. Historians have tended to understand the movement of Americans across the Atlantic Ocean as a portent of incipient slavery, the development of long-distance diplomacy, or the expression of a European craving to understand the "other."[1] But this particular population movement can also be understood as a problem in the history of collecting: Europeans were keen to collect American bodies, alive and dead, and that passion continued for five hundred years.

Scholars have already paid enormous attention to early modern European understandings of Native American bodies. But questions relating to American bodies long predated modern scholarly inquiries. Why, many early modern Europeans wondered, did natives die in such large numbers from diseases that had little impact on newcomers? One classic early modern expression of this problem came from William Bradford, governor and historian of the English colony at Plymouth in the early decades of the seventeenth century. Observing a devastating epidemic of smallpox among Americans in 1634, Bradford noted that "by the marvelous goodness and providence of God, not one of the English was so much sick or in the least measure tainted with this disease, though they daily did these offices for them many weeks together."[2] Other Europeans also recognized that Americans died from a multitude of diseases once invaders arrived. This observation led to speculation about the nature of American bodies and disputes over the causes of mortality. At times, as in Roanoke in the mid-1580s, natives and newcomers offered competing theories about the causes for American fragility.[3]

Over time these discussions became more elaborate. Americans died because they would not embrace Christianity; they lived in squalor and their residences bred infection; they were culturally inferior and had no effective way to cope with the changes to their lives and the effects of these changes on their bodies.[4] By the late twentieth century scholars settled on the theory of so-called virgin soil epidemics: Americans died because they lacked immunities to newly arriving infectious disease agents.[5] This antiracist theory, to use the notion of the physiologist Jared Diamond, purportedly explained American deaths without any reference to culture or religious practice and had the added benefit of embracing basic epidemiological principles. Unfortunately, as the psychiatrist/historian David Jones has revealed, the theory is also wrong. Many Americans could have survived the arrival of these pathogens had they not also suffered from invasion and the resulting breakdown of their economies, including the ability of members of a community to provide care for others. Americans died not only because they lacked immunities but their bodies also succumbed because Europeans' understanding of them precluded sustained efforts to tend to the afflicted.[6]

The European (and later Anglo-American) desire to understand Americans' bodies and especially the widespread mortality continued for centuries. Recent explanations for the steep decline in the number of Americans from 1492 to circa 1900 pivot on changes in diet, for example, as well as the introduction of infectious diseases.[7] The growth of the Euro-American population also put stresses on indigenous communities, especially when individuals or groups had to move to new locales, a circumstance that often meant adjusting their economies and rituals to new circumstances (such as the presence or absence of certain animals). Europeans also introduced commodities, notably firearms and alcohol, which invariably contributed to American population decline because of the increase in violence that followed colonization.[8] Taken together, the combination of what the historian Alfred Crosby referred to as the "Columbian Exchange" (the movement of biological matter across the early modern world) and Europeans' inability (or reluctance) to provide even minimal palliative care led to a crisis in the Americas. That crisis focused on the body of Americans. It unfolded long after Europeans had begun their systematic investigation into the nature of those bodies, during a time when Europeans eagerly collected myriad American artifacts.

Europeans understood, of course, that the human body was corruptible. It was impossible in the early modern era to collect living specimens for permanent display. The best to be hoped for, judging from the collecting practices that emerged, was for a period of observation of the living, followed by scrutiny of remains, either as skulls and bones or perhaps mummified bodies.[9] In this way, Europeans combined their culture of collecting, evident in the similar practice of gathering materials for a cabinet of curiosity, with their fascination with the body. But decaying bodies placed specific demands on Europeans who sought objects for study. They responded to the challenge by depicting Natives visually, describing their bodies textually, and poring over their skeletal remains. The keeping of mortal remains was a practice that survived for centuries and has only recently been challenged in the United States through cases brought forward by indigenous communities employing the authority they now possess under the Native American Graves Protection and Repatriation Act (known as NAGPRA). As a result of this legislation, the culture of collecting Americans, within the boundaries of the United States at least, has recently shifted from its early modern moorings. The views of Native Americans now shape discussion of the keeping of early American bodies.

The first American bodies to travel across the Atlantic Ocean to Europe belonged to individuals taken captive by Columbus on his first voyage. Columbus was fascinated with the Natives he found, including the fact that they were humans and not monsters. "Until now I have not found any monstrous men in these islands, as many had thought," he wrote. "On the contrary, all these people are very good-looking: they are not black as in Guinea, but have flowing hair, and they do not make their homes in places where the rays of the sun are too strong." He had heard rumors that cannibalistic monsters inhabited an island he did not visit, but he never saw them. His contacts were people, some of whom he captured. "When I arrived in the Indies, I took some of these people by force in the first island I found, so that they might learn our language and give me news of what existed in those parts." These individuals played their roles well, and for reasons Columbus did not explain, he brought them back to Europe. By interrogating them, he found that they believed the Europeans came from heaven. "I am bringing them with me now," he wrote in his first formal report on his voyage, "and they still think I come from heaven, despite all the conversation they have had with me." From the start, Columbus recognized

PETER C. MANCALL

that Natives differed from Europeans culturally but also that they did not lack the human capacity for intellectual achievement—at least, as he understood the situation, they knew of heaven. His act was not, then, an effort to display these captives but instead to bring them to a place where they might be educated and then eventually employed.[10]

The first Americans to reach England came with Sebastian Cabot, probably in 1502. Like Columbus, Cabot did not aim to capture but instead to examine these individuals and to determine their capabilities. The earliest and most explicit reference to these experimental subjects can be found in an ancient London chronicle kept by Robert Fabian. The account, as it was retold in 1589 by the younger Richard Hakluyt, the tireless promoter of colonization, noted that, when they arrived, they were "clothed in beasts Skins, and did eate rawe flesh, and spake such speech, that no man could understand them, and in their demeanor like to brute beasts, whom the King kept a time after." But after the King "kept" them for a while, these Americans had changed their ways. Two years later, Fabian reported, "I sawe two appareled after the maner of Englishmen in Westminster palace, which that time I could not discerne from Englishmen, till I was learned what they were," though he admitted he did not hear them speak. Nonetheless, the experience of collecting these Americans had had a specific effect: held, with or without their consent (the historical record is silent on what they felt about their time in London), these individuals proved themselves capable of changing their ways. With serious refinement, the bodies of Americans could become indistinguishable from those of the English.[11]

After the voyages of the Cabots, the English essentially lost interest in the Americas for almost a century. English fishing ships still trolled for cod off the North Atlantic shelf, and invariably some of these sailors and fishermen made contact with Americans, but there is scant evidence of them having done so. In the meantime, other Americans were traveling back to Europe on board continental ships. Before 1530, American captives had arrived in Portugal, France, and Spain, and by the early seventeenth century, some had even reached Denmark.[12] The most famous were the Tupinambas taken by the French to Rouen to greet King Henri II in 1550, an event that generated a solitary image and a brief description in a pamphlet published in 1551. The French collected and displayed these Americans; their hosts even created an elaborate venue for their presentation to the French, including a drama in which the French soldiers dressed like so-called "Tagaberres" and staged a "war" with the Tupis. The Natives constituted a living theater, moving memorabilia of a distant culture.[13]

These Brazilians in France were among many Americans to arrive in Europe during the century following Columbus's first voyage. By the early seventeenth century, perhaps 1,600 Americans had been to Europe, and artists were already at work providing visual depictions of them, as Hans Weigel did with his portrait of an indigenous Brazilian family (see Figure 10.1).[14] Most of these travelers went to the Continent, but some landed in England despite apparent English disinterest.

Among Britons eager to collect Americans were Martin Frobisher and his crew. During Frobisher's 1577 journey in search of the Northwest Passage—he had first gone into the North Atlantic the year before—he (or those who chronicled his voyage) became fascinated with the fur-clad Inuit they met in the North Atlantic. Among those who wrote about the venture was Dionyse Settle, whose account was one of three "true" reports detailing Frobisher's journey. Settle's account provided the kinds of detail that could only come from someone who was actually on the spot. He marveled at rocks that gleamed with gold, though he reminded his readers of the proverb that "All is not golde that glistereth." He wrote about how some of the sailors put spiders into the horn of a narwhal, where they died. Settle also described a small battle between the English and the Inuit, three of whom leaped into the sea and died after they were hit with arrows—a strategy they followed in an effort to avoid capture. Settle, who wrote that the English would have saved them, concluded that they were "altogether voyde of humanitie, and ignorant what mercy meaneth, in extremeties looke for no other than death." While most of the survivors fled, two women could not escape; one had a small child and the other was too old. Some of the English believed the elderly Inuk was a witch or a devil, so they pulled off her buskins to find out if she had cloven feet. Finding that she was human, and arguing that she was deformed and ugly, they released her. Many Europeans might have believed that Americans were capable of cultural conversion, but at least some still held to the idea that they were not fully human. Like Columbus, they wondered if the residents of this frozen world were among the monstrous races that their literature had taught them could be found at the ends of the earth.[15]

The Inuit seemed to be cautious in their dealings with the English, though Settle recognized that the Natives were familiar with visitors, with whom they had traded. When the English left pen, ink, and paper for several English sailors who had been left behind in 1576, the Inuit waited for them to leave the area, then picked up the goods. Settle also told about an apparent Inuit plan to capture a few English to trade them for the man, woman, and child taken in captivity on the ships.[16] Settle's account described the material culture and appearance of the Inuit, and emphasized that "there is no flesh or fishe, which they finde dead (smell it never so filthily) but they will eate it, as they finde it, without any other dressing"—a feature of their daily lives that he found "loathsome."[17]

PETER C. MANCALL

BRASILIENSIVM VEL HOMINVM
in Peru habitus.

CLXXXI.

Die Wilden Leuth auß Brasilien / oder von den newen Insulen.

Also gehen die Wilden Leuth/
Männer vnd Weiber beider seidt.

So wohnen in Brasilien/
Oder den newen Insulen.

10.1. A Tupinamba family, from Hans Wiegel, *Habitus Praecipuorum Populorum, Tam Virorum Quam foeminarum Singulari arte depicti* (Nuremberg, 1577). Huntington Library.

When the captured Inuit arrived in England, they quickly became objects of public fascination. Artists sketched the man Collichang (or Kalicho), the woman Egnock (or Arnaq), and her infant (Nutaaq). Lucas de Heere from Ghent, who also painted English men and women,[18] depicted the man holding an oar for his kayak and a bow and arrow (a kayaker in action can be seen in the background). An unknown artist, possibly the same John White who would become famous in the 1580s for his water colors of the Carolina Algonquians of Roanoke, painted portraits of each of them, in addition to a scene of a battle fought in the North Atlantic between Frobisher's men and the Inuit.

Collichang, Egnock, and her infant did not last long in England. The queen herself wanted to visit them, but they died before she had a chance. Collichang died first, the victim, so it seems, of an infection caused by a broken rib. While there remains some dispute about the cause of that injury, which he perhaps suffered when he was taken captive, there is no doubt that he sustained it. How can we be so sure? Because a physician named Edward Dodding performed an autopsy on him. Once Dodding finished his work, the English decided to bury Collichang. But before they placed his body into the ground, they first brought Egnock to see his corpse. They did so because they wanted to prove to her that the English were not cannibals and had no desire to consume the flesh of Americans. They apparently had no obvious desire to keep or display the physical remains of their captives. Egnock attended the funeral with the physician Dodding. Four days after Collichang's funeral, Egnock was also buried at St. Stephen's Church in Bristol. The English took the infant to London, but it died several weeks later, foiling the queen's desire to meet these captives.[19]

Nonetheless, English artists made sure that these three Americans would not be forgotten. In addition to the watercolor portraits, which might have been done in England, there are also two engravings depicting the Inuit "family" living in England (see Figure 10.2). (Though the English did not realize it at the time, the man and woman had apparently not met before they were taken prisoner.) Or, to be more precise, artists engraved images of what they imagined to be the common activities of the Inuit. Collichang can be seen riding in a kayak; Egnock and her child remained on the land. These images appeared in books published in France and Germany in the early 1580s, guaranteeing the spread of information American's capabilities to the Continent.[20]

While the English continued to receive Americans as visitors, the collecting of them shifted, as the Frobisher experience suggested, from the actual body to visual depictions of bodies. One English artist scheduled to go to America in 1582, whose main task was to provide maps of the region, received explicit instructions about how he was to draw the Natives he met, paying particular attention to "the figures and shapes of men and women in their apparel[.]"[21]

10.2. Europeans were fascinated by Inuit brought by explorers, including a man, woman, and child captured and taken to England by Martin Frobisher. Engravings of them engaged in re-creations of their customary practices—such as spear fishing from a light weight kayak (so light it could be held in one arm)—attracted at least two printers' attention. From *La navigation du capitaine Martin Forbisher* (La Rochelle, 1578). Huntington Library.

The most famous set of images appeared in the illustrated account of Thomas Harriot's *A Briefe and True Report of the New Found Land of Virginia*. Originally published without illustrations in 1588, and again as text only in Hakluyt's *Principall Navigations, Voiages, and Discoveries of the English Nation* in 1589, the book appeared in 1590 with a series of engravings by Theodor de Bry based on watercolors done by John White in Roanoke in the mid-1580s. Virtually all the de Bry images set the figure of the Carolina Algonquian subject in domestic contexts of everyday labors. These are not formal portraits (though the figures appeared in poses that sent specific messages to European viewers) but instead ethnographic evidence, each image providing details about bodies in action. One exceptional image, last in the collection (Figure 10.3), featured a single

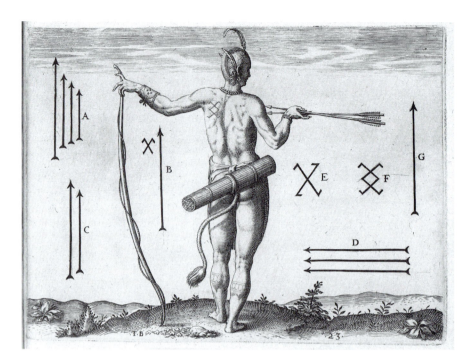

10.3. English visitors to modern North Carolina in the 1580s took notice of the ritual tattoos on the bodies of local Carolina Algonquians, and their interest prompted the Flemish engraver Theodor de Bry to add this picture at the conclusion of his suite of images of these indigenous Americans. From Thomas Harriot, *A Briefe and True Report of the New Found Land of Virginia* (Frankfurt-am-Main, 1590). Huntington Library.

man with a tattoo on his back identified as a "cheefe man of Pomeiooc, and Aquascogoc," two Algonquian towns. Unlike the others, he stands on bare ground with no action in the background. The text notes that the "inhabita[n]ts of all the cuntrie for the most parte have marks rased on their backs, wherby yt may be knowen what Princes subjects they bee, or of what place they have their originall." The image explains the signs employed in the region and the names of the towns "that they might more easelye be discerned." The caption, which could have been written by Hakluyt (who shepherded the book into production in Frankfurt in four languages in 1590), continued, "Which industrie hath god indued them withal although they be verye simple, and rude. And to confesse a truthe I cannot remember, that ever I saw a better or quieter people then they."[22]

In the decades following the doomed settlement in Roanoke, the English established their own colonies in eastern North America and, as a result, had more extensive contact with Americans. To be sure, the colonial experience was often devastating to the bodies of the English, especially in the Chesapeake region where local diseases and tainted water killed newcomers with rigorous efficiency during the early years of the seventeenth century.[23] But the newcomers prevailed and the English understanding of Native bodies shifted from the few individuals who crossed the Atlantic to the numerous individuals encountered on a daily basis in the nascent colonies. Though some Americans continued to travel to England, most famously the Powhatan Pocahontas who went with her husband John Rolfe in 1616, reports from eastern North America conveyed much more information than actual encounters with Americans in Europe. Pocahontas, of course, did become known; stories about her circulated widely, and she became the object of one of the best-known portraits of any American during the colonial period. That image, of Pocahontas rechristened Rebecca (Figure 10.4), revealed the same malleability of the American body that Fabian's report had acknowledged: these people might seem foreign, and it remained a mystery why so many of them continued to die when English settlers arrived, but they could also be converted. Or at least they could be made to look like an English man or woman, even if they tended to live abbreviated lives in their new environments. Pocahontas herself died before she could return to Virginia with Rolfe and their son.

The English who looked on American bodies in these formative years all shared the belief that the indigenous peoples of North America were human beings who, under the proper tutelage, could be civilized. They were not identified as a racialized "other" incapable of conversion, nor were they monsters who lived beyond human experience. As the English cleric William Crashaw put it, the English in Virginia would extract various material goods but would offer to the Natives

1. *Civilitie* for their bodies,
2. *Christianitie* for their soules.

"The first to make the[m] *men*," Crashaw added; "the second *happy men*; the first to cover their *bodies* from the shame of the world: the second, to cover their *soules* from the wrath of God." Crashaw argued that all the observable evidence indicated that the Americans were "of the same constitution, & the sons of Adam, and that we had the same Maker, the same matter, the same mould."[24] The lessons the English learned from the Americans that they collected revealed that differences between Europeans and Americans were due to environment and were thus impermanent.[25]

During much of the seventeenth and eighteenth centuries, English and Anglo-Americans paid less attention to the bodies of Americans than previously. In the colonies, the most obvious sense of collecting Americans was

10.4. "Matoaka als Rebecca"—or Pocahontas after her marriage to John Rolfe and her adoption of English clothing. From John Smith, *The Generall Historie of Virginia, New-England, and the Summer Isles* (London, 1624). Huntington Library.

associated with the brutality of scalp bounties—the payments allocated by provincial governments to colonists who killed Indians and brought their scalps in as proof. Such violent collecting of American bodies (or body parts) was not limited to men; in 1697, Hannah Dustan became a colony-wide heroine when she scalped ten Natives during her escape from her captivity.[26] The declining

PETER C. MANCALL

interest in Americans as specimens invariably reflected the fact that Natives were now peoples who had to be dealt with on a regular basis.

Still, some Americans traveled to England, where they often became spectacles even during diplomatic missions. The most famous of them were the four so-called "Indian Kings," young emissaries of the Five Nations of the Iroquois who traveled to England in 1710. The Iroquois had come on matters of state business, and they met with Queen Anne in their efforts to secure funding for their ongoing conflict with New France.[27] During their journey, English artists rendered portraits of them, and, like the engravings in Harriot's book, these images too circulated in printed form (see Figure 10.5). One anonymous engraving "The True Effiges of the Four Indian Kings Taken from the Original Paintings Done by [John Verelst]" identified each of them by their place of origin: Tee Yee Neen Ho Ga Row, the so-called "Emperour of the Six Nations" was followed by Sa Ga Yean Qua Rah Tow, "King of the Maquas," ETow ohKaom, "King of the River Nation" (the term for the Mohawks), and O Nee Yeath Towno Riow, the "King of Ganajoahhore."[28]

Paintings of these individuals, by Verelst and others, depicted them as if they had just emerged from the forest. Significantly, while European artists emphasized the indigenous look of each—and none did so more effectively than the anonymous engraver of the effigies—the full-length portraits display these Iroquois wearing a mixture of European and American clothing and carrying some European trade goods. For those in England who could not actually see the Indian kings during their procession, the paintings and engravings revealed them as objects of English fascination. In this sense, they were hardly unique; Europeans had long been interested in visual depictions of the residents of other parts of the world, and, as others have argued, some of the representations of Americans (such as the de Bry engravings of White's watercolors) drew explicitly on a visual language developed to depict the human body in classical antiquity and on contemporary understanding of what a portrait was supposed to convey.[29] The visual representations of Americans in English collections thus served a specific cultural purpose: the American body needed to be known so that the human residing within it could be civilized.

The expansion of English settlements in the mainland slowly shifted Anglo-American understandings of American bodies. During the early colonial period, the English wrote extensively about the nature of American cultures, often with the explicit goal of shaping strategies to "reduce" Natives to civilization. If colonizers could understand indigenous beliefs about property, gender roles, political arrangements, economy, and spirituality, then the newcomers and their descendants could hatch strategies designed to eliminate any vestiges of savage

Tee Yee Neen Ho Ga Row Emperour of the Six Nations

10.5. John Verelst, "Tee Yee Neen Ho Ga Row, Emperor of the Six Nations," one of the four so-called "Indian Kings" who toured England in the early eighteenth century (London, 1710). Huntington Library.

life. Theorists of colonization drew on an extraordinary body of literature that had begun in ancient times, gathered new evidence during the medieval period, and exploded during the age of European discovery. By the end of the seventeenth century, European scholars had essentially laid the groundwork for the modern discipline of anthropology, with its attention to interpreting cultures and their developments.[30]

But what had happened to English fascination with the bodies of Americans? The era of collecting living specimens like those described by Fabian and Settle had long passed. The English, who needed Native allies against the French during the Seven Years' War (among other conflicts), had long abandoned the idea of collecting and displaying living Americans for mere entertainment or even for science. Any cultural imperative toward collecting Americans gave way to the more practical considerations of cementing alliances with Native groups. Since the fate of English armies in wars on the American mainland depended to a large extent on their ability to maintain friendly ties to local Natives, who in the best of circumstances would fight side by side with the English (and who might at least be persuaded to stay neutral), the English could not risk capturing individual Americans for the purposes of display. Though it is true that Anglo-American colonists did periodically engage in the capture of Natives for the slave trade, they did so only in limited circumstances in which they calculated that those hauled into bondage did not have allies who could seek revenge.[31]

But when Anglo-Americans and their English correspondents began to realize that the population of Natives was still declining during the eighteenth century, many observers became interested once again in collecting Americans. As early as the first decade of the eighteenth century, the Carolina explorer John Lawson had recognized the destructive impact of the Europeans' arrival on Native peoples. "The Small-Pox and Rum have made such a Destruction amongst them, that, on good grounds, I do believe, there is not the sixth Savage living within two hundred Miles of all our Settlements, as there were fifty Years ago," he wrote. "These poor Creatures have so many Enemies to destroy them, that it's a wonder one of them is left alive near us." Lawson, for his part, believed that Americans had much to teach Anglo-Americans; he even encouraged intermarriage, an effort that would preserve American bodies and further the conversion of America.[32] But he also thought that the opportunity for cultural contact was rapidly disappearing as Natives died off.

Lawson's ideas reflected a sympathetic understanding of American demography and culture. His interest was less in collecting Americans themselves than in bringing civilization into the wilderness and in preserving aboriginal languages and cultures of the Americas. Two generations later, another Anglo-American venturing into the woods took a very different approach. That explorer was Thomas Jefferson, who among his many attributes was also an amateur archaeologist.

During the early to mid-1780s Jefferson lived mostly in Paris, serving the diplomatic interests of the new nation. While there he wrote a book, published in London in 1787 as *Notes on the State of Virginia* (it had earlier been published in an unauthorized edition in Paris). It is a remarkable study, and the only full-length book that Jefferson ever published during his lifetime, though it represented a small fraction of his writings. In the book, Jefferson provided an overview of the indigenous peoples of Virginia, including a sympathetic (if brief) rendering of their history. After noting that he knew "of no such thing existing as an Indian monument," he acknowledged that there were "Barrows, of which many are to be found all over this country." Jefferson summarized local expertise in Native architecture before he conducted his investigations. "[Barrows] were of different sizes, some of them constructed of earth, and some of loose stones," he wrote. "That they were repositories of the dead, has been obvious to all: but on what particular occasion constructed, was matter of doubt." Jefferson reviewed the various theories that he had heard about these barrows, mentioning that some believed they contained warriors only, while others suggested that they were for the founder of a particular settlement and still others argued that it was a local custom for the people to collect "at certain periods, the bones of all their dead, wheresoever deposited at the time of death."[33]

After rehearsing these theories, Jefferson went to work. There was, it turned out, one of these barrow tombs in his "neighborhood," specifically in the floodplain of the nearby Rivianna River on the site of a former Native community. Jefferson decided he would excavate it: "For this purpose I determined to open and examine it thoroughly." He described the general size of the chamber and then reported what he found. "I first dug superficially in several parts of it, and came to collections of human bones, at different depths, from six inches to three feet below the surface," he recalled. "These were lying in the utmost confusion, some vertical, some oblique, some horizontal, and directed to every point of the compass, entangled, and held together in clusters by the earth. Bones of the most distant parts were found together, as, for instance, the small bones of the foot in the hollow of a scull, many sculls would sometimes be in contact, lying on the face, on the side, on the back, top or bottom, so as, on the whole, to give the idea of bones emptied promiscuously from a bag or basket, and covered over with earth, without any attention to their order." Jefferson disdained the chaos of the find, but he persisted in his efforts to examine what he found. "The bones of which the greatest numbers remained, were sculls,

PETER C. MANCALL

jaw-bones, teeth, the bones of the arms, thighs, legs, feet, and hands." He added that he found some ribs too, along with some vertebrae.[34]

Jefferson could have stopped after this survey of what he saw, but instead he decided he would examine these mortal remains more carefully. His comments emphasized his deductions about the strength of the actual bones. "The sculls were so tender, that they generally fell to pieces on being touched," he wrote. "The other bones were stronger." Jefferson became fascinated by the mortal remains of children, including an infant. "This last furnishing decisive proof of the burial of children here, I was particular in my attention to it. It was part of the right-half of the under-jaw. The processes, by which it was articulated to the temporal bones, were entire; and the bone itself firm to where it had been broken off, which, as nearly as I could judge, was about the place of the eye-tooth." He provided details about the size and then described its appearance. "This bone was white, all the others of a sand colour. The bones of infants being soft, they probably decay sooner, which might be the cause so few were found here."[35]

After this detailed examination of a selection of the remains, Jefferson changed his strategy. He reported that he made "a perpendicular cut through the body of the barrow" so that he could "examine its internal structure." The cut was wide enough to walk though, and Jefferson paid careful attention to what he saw. "At the bottom, that is, on the level of the circumjacent plain, I found bones; above these a few stones, brought from a cliff a quarter of a mile off, and from the river one-eighth of a mile off; then a large interval of earth, then a stratum of bones, and so on." In one end he saw four strata of bones, and three strata at the other. He observed that the bones closest to the surface of the ground showed the least decay and that there were no holes in any of them, a sign that the dead did not in all likelihood die from a bullet or an arrow. There were, he estimated, the remains of one thousand humans in the barrow—a number so large that it was impossible (in his opinion) to contain only warriors who fell in battle. He also believed that the findings contradicted a local tradition that such barrows were

the common sepulcher of a town, in which the bodies were placed upright, and touching each other. Appearances certainly indicate that it has derived both origin and growth from the accustomary collection of bones, and deposition of them together; that the first collection had been deposited on the common surface of the earth, a few stones put over it, and then a covering of earth, that the second had been laid on this, had covered more or less of it in proportion to the number of ones, and was then also covered with earth; and so on.

He had come to this conclusion based on his observations of the number of remains in the grave, the fact that there were multiple layers of bones, the presence of infants there, and the fact that the bones were in no obvious position.[36]

Jefferson's investigation of this collection of bones did not end with his physical examination of it. He also reported that the site must have been well known since a generation earlier a group of Natives left their path and made a detour to the site, where they remained and apparently made "expressions which were construed to be those of sorrow" before continuing on their way. He added that there were other barrows in the vicinity, including one near the Shenandoah River. And then he added one more detail, which suggests his sense of the value of these collections of Native bones: "Both of these have, within these dozen years, been cleared of their trees and put under cultivation, are much reduced in their height, and spread in width, by the plough, and will probably disappear in time." Jefferson did not make much of that observation; instead he wrote about investigations about the origins of Native Americans—he agreed with those who believed the Americas had been peopled by migrants crossing the Bering Straight—and recommended intensive study of indigenous languages to understand the point at which a common language split into regional variations.[37] Yet his casual observation that settlers of European origin were dismantling barrows—clearing them of trees, sinking ploughs into them, and presumably destroying their contents in the process—suggests that in the late eighteenth century, at least, Americans had little obvious desire to collect the remains of Americans. These bones were the stuff of the past: worthy of description, as Jefferson himself demonstrated, but not of display. He never mentioned if he even kept any of the remains he excavated.

During the first years of the nineteenth century, the casual attitude toward Native bodies evident in the Anglo-American population changed again. The shift did not occur randomly. Instead, during the years when the United States government was using its force to eliminate Native Americans from the eastern portion of the continent—a process that would reach its culmination in the so-called "Removal" period of the 1830s—Euro-Americans spent a great deal of time and energy studying human remains, including of indigenous Americans.[38] Eventually some began to argue that the indigenous peoples of their new country were on the road to extinction. No one held to that view more strongly than the artist George Catlin, who in the 1830s traveled into the American West to paint Indians before they were all gone. He wrote that the tribes of the red men of North America, as a nation of human beings, are on their wane, that (to use their own very beautiful figure) "they re fast travelling to the shades of their fathers, towards the setting sun"; and that the traveller who would see these people in their native simplicity and beauty, must needs be hastily on his way to the prairies and Rocky Mountains, or he will see them only as they are now seen on the frontiers, as a basket of *dead game*—harassed, chased, bleeding and dead; with their plumage and colours despoiled; to be gazed amongst in vain for some system or moral, or for some scale by which to estimate their true native character, other than that which has too often recorded them but a dark and unintelligible mass of cruelty and barbarity.[39]

Catlin believed that the way to remember this disappearing people was to paint them before they disappeared. His gallery of North American Indians was meant to show the opposite of the images generated in Roanoke by John White and later engraved by de Bry. Those behind the sixteenth-century images— Harriot, White, Hakluyt—wanted to prove that it would be possible to convert Americans into English men and women. The images thus showed the potential for conversion and that the Carolina Algonquians were farther along in the process than the original inhabitants of Britain when the Romans arrived. Catlin's collection of images, by contrast, was a testimony to the corruptible body. Natives had to be painted and their customs recorded because they would soon be gone.

One of Catlin's contemporaries was Samuel George Morton, a naturalist who also developed an extraordinary interest in collecting Americans (in addition to promoting the field of natural history).[40] But Morton had a very different way to remember Americans: he chose to collect their skulls. When he died in 1851, his collection exceeded one thousand skulls, many of them extracted from Indian graves by Morton's associates. As the historian Ann Fabian has written, "Morton measured his skulls, but he also cleaned, polished, varnished, and labeled them and then put them on display, inviting the public to visit his collection, free of charge, on Tuesdays and Saturdays."[41]

Morton did not collect his skulls for their aesthetic value. Instead, like other naturalists in the nineteenth century, he believed that systematically collecting the physical remains of Americans would provide clues to the differences between human races. This was a concept that was mostly foreign to the Elizabethans, who believed that perceptible differences between peoples were due to environmental conditions (such as climate), not inborn differences. Morton believed that differences could be detected in the shape and size of human crania, so he measured his vast collection. He also relied on those who supplied him with skulls to tell him where they obtained their specimens, and some of his correspondents mentioned to him that some of the bones came from recently deceased Natives; one source in Indiana even spoke about the anticipated acquisition of skulls from two headmen "as soon as the Indians are removed from our neighborhood."[42] The morality of Morton's willingness to accept such remains needs to be put in context. Though he dismissed American intellectual capacities, he nonetheless recognized the importance of Indian graves. "No offence excites greater exasperation in the breast of the Indian than the violation of the graves of his people," he wrote in 1844, "and he has even been known to disinter the bones of his ancestors, and bear them with him to a great distance, when circumstances have compelled him to make a permanent change of residence."[43] For what he believed was the greater good of building his collection of Americans, then, Morton violated American cultures.

Morton approached his collection with the purportedly objective eye of a scientist. He was concerned, as he wrote in one essay, to examine the "osteological structure" of Native Americans, "as seen in the squared or rounded head, the flattened or vertical occiput, the high check bones, the ponderous maxillæ, the large quadrangular orbits, and the low, receding forehead." Having examined 400 of these skulls, he was "astonished to find how the preceding characters, in greater or less degree, pervade them all."[44] Those similarly shaped crania contained brains apparently incapable of reaching the heights of European civilization, or so Morton argued. Their deficiencies could be found in architecture, among other areas. "They have made no improvement in the construction of their dwellings, except when directed by Europeans who have become domiciliated among them," he wrote in his 1844 *Inquiry into the Distinctive Characteristics of the Aboriginal Race of America*; "for the Indian cabin or the Indian tent, from Terra del Fuego to the river St. Lawrence, is perhaps the humblest contrivance ever devised by man to screen himself from the elements." Though some Americans apparently possessed greater intellectual abilities—Morton called them "demi-civilized nations"—the limitations were more apparent than any abilities.[45]

Morton's most famous work, and the one that revealed him as a collector of Americans, was his *Crania Americana*—a highly technical scientific treatise comparing the skulls of different aboriginal peoples. Published in 1839, it included precise measurements for thirteen aspects of each skull: longitudinal diameter, parietal diameter, frontal diameter, vertical diameter, intermastoid arch, intermastoid line, occipito-frontal arch, and horizontal capacity (all measured in inches); internal capacity, capacity of the anterior chamber, capacity of the posterior chamber, and capacity of the coronal region (all measured in cubic

PETER C. MANCALL

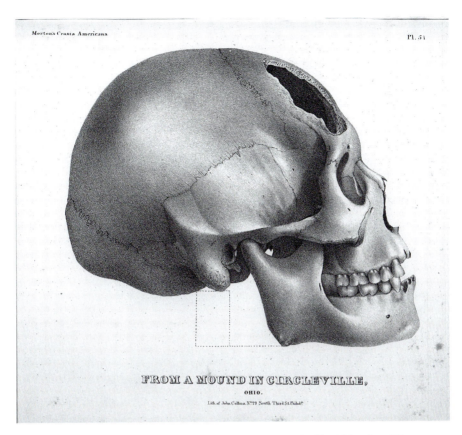

FROM A MOUND IN CIRCLEVILLE,
OHIO.
Lith. of John Collins, N.°79 South Third St. Philad.ª

10.6. Skull taken from a Native American grave in Circleville, Ohio, from Thomas
Morton, *Crania Americana; or, A Comparative View of the Skulls of Various Aboriginal
Nations of North and South America* (Philadelphia, 1839). Huntington Library.

inches); and facial angle (measured in degrees). The book's greatest treasure
was its appendix, which consisted of seventy-two full-page plates, each carefully
rendered from a skull that must have been in his personal collection (Figure
10.6).[46] In the pages of this volume, Morton focused on the races of humankind
and emphasized that "The American Family" was essentially a single "race": "it
may be assumed as a fact that no other race of men maintains such a striking
analogy through all its subdivisions, and amidst all its variety of physical circumstances." Morton came to this conclusion through analysis of his collection.[47]

After Morton's death, the skulls went to the Academy of Natural Sciences in
Morton's hometown of Philadelphia. When Europeans decided that they would
commemorate the four-hundredth anniversary of Columbus's voyage to the
West in 1892, curators there packed forty of the Natives' skulls and sent them to
be exhibited in Madrid. The display was a success and received a silver medal.

But the reception in Philadelphia was not the same: when the skulls returned, the museum's curators decided that they should no longer be put on display, so they sent them to storage. Eventually, the museum at the nearby University of Pennsylvania acquired Morton's collection. As Fabian has reported, "The old skulls are now shrouded in bubble-wrap and sealed in plastic containers, awaiting repatriation" under the terms of NAGPRA.[48]

Curators at the Academy of Natural Sciences in Philadelphia might have become squeamish about the thought of displaying Morton's skulls when they came back from Madrid, but many museum directors apparently felt otherwise. Curators and the celebrated anthropologist Alfred Kroeber collaborated (or conspired, depending on one's view) to display Ishi, the "last" of the Yahis, in the Anthropology Museum in San Francisco from the time he was "discovered" in Butte County in 1911 until his death in 1916. He immediately became a star attraction; perhaps 24,000 people came to see him build fires and string bows in the first six months he was exhibited to the public.[49] While his case was extraordinary because Ishi was still alive while he was on display, the fact of an American's corporeal presence in a museum was fairly common in the twentieth century. When the Cheyenne elder William Tallbull went to the Smithsonian's Museum of Natural History in 1986 to reclaim a pipe, he found out that the museum contained bones from 18,000 individuals.[50] Most of the bones there, like the human remains found in other museums, were kept in cabinets, presumably according to an organizational scheme that made sense for scientific study of the remains.

Scholars have, of course, long since abandoned the racialist sensibilities of Morton and his ilk. Presumably no one today would display an individual as the last of a dying species. Instead, physical anthropologists and archaeologists, often employing sophisticated imaging equipment, have studied these remains to understand the long-term health and illness of Native Americans.[51] One modern data set combines details from over 12,000 skeletons, the vast majority of them Native Americans.[52] There are likely still thousands of Americans whose remains, once interred in the earth, now lie on metal shelves in museum storerooms.

In the age of NAGPRA, many Native peoples are in the process of repatriating the physical remains of their ancestors from the filing cabinets of illustrious museums. Though some notable cases have generated famous disputes, such as the ongoing battle for the so-called Kennewick Man (currently housed in the Burke Museum at the University of Washington in Seattle), most efforts by indigenous peoples to reclaim their ancestors have aroused far less acrimony. Some scientists might regret the loss of the materials through which they believe they can better understand human evolution and especially the development of

PETER C. MANCALL

certain ailments. But the politics of the moment give preference to Natives. It is too soon to know the final results, but it is possible that the European fascination with the collecting of Americans might be coming to a close after 500 years. Perhaps the English and their Anglo-American followers have finally gotten over their desire to see dead Indians.

PART IV

—ᴡ—

EUROPEAN COLLECTIONS OF AMERICANA
IN THE EIGHTEENTH
AND NINETEENTH CENTURIES

CHAPTER 11

—〰—

Spanish Collections of Americana in the Late Eighteenth Century

PAZ CABELLO CARRO

This essay surveys some of the many late eighteenth-century collections of Spanish Americana, attempting whenever possible to match extant objects that are held today in contemporary museums to the inventories and textual descriptions that survive from when they were originally gathered. Although archaeological curiosities were shipped from the Indies to Europe before the eighteenth century and it is known that the Spanish Crown maintained American collections, those early collections seem to have perished in the 1734 fire at the Reales Alcázares in Madrid, which destroyed most of the royal palace. Thus, a new era of royal collecting of Americana began in the second half of the eighteenth century, particularly in the last three decades of the century. In 1752, acting on a proposal from the naval officer Antonio de Ulloa—considered an expert on American topics given his travels in Ecuador between 1736 and 1744 as part of the joint Franco-Spanish geodesic expedition—King Ferdinand VI created the Royal Cabinet of Natural History.[1] Shortly thereafter, however, Ulloa left Madrid for South America and the cabinet languished. In 1771, Charles III created another Cabinet of Natural History, based on his acquisition of the collection of Guayaquil-born Spanish naturalist Pedro Franco Dávila. Ulloa's collection was integrated into the new cabinet. During the second half of the century, both Ulloa and Dávila prepared orders for collectors to contribute to the royal cabinet and offered guidance on how to gather and ship materials. Ulloa, who had observed and written about Peruvian tombs, drafted a set of rules on how to conduct archaeological excavations. Dávila, the cabinet's director until his death in 1786, drew up instructions for gathering, preparing, and shipping natural history items.

At the end of the Napoleonic occupation of Spain, in 1813 and 1814, the French sacked the Cabinet of Natural History, destroying both documentation and artifacts in the collection. In 1815, the cabinet's name was changed to the Museum of Natural Sciences; the historical collections were undisturbed until an inventory was completed in 1860. In 1867, the museum's collection was split, with the historical and American collections transferred to the newly created National Archaeological Museum. In 1941, after an earlier attempt was foiled by the outbreak of the Spanish Civil War, the Museum of America was created in Madrid, and the Royal Cabinet's American and Oceanic collections, originally gathered in the eighteenth century, reside there today.[2]

Early Archaeological Excavations in Peru

A list of objects sent by the king to the cabinet under Dávila includes details of a collection of archaeological objects from the northern coast of Peru. Consisting of three hundred earthenware pots in the shapes of animals, fruits, and people, as well as silver and wooden pieces, this collection matches the inventory of a shipment made by the viceroy of Peru in 1765; it also corresponds to a drawing of an excavation dug in 1764, which appears in the ninth volume of natural history drawings collected years later by Baltasar Jaime Martínez Compañón, bishop of Trujillo in Peru from 1779 to 1791. The schematic drawing shows a stratigraphic cut-away view of a tomb on a stepped hillock. A slip of paper in the collection explains that this is the Huaca de Tantalluc in Cajamarca. In the eighteenth century, the province of Cajamarca extended almost to the coast, which explains the materials in this collection, which are typical of the northern Peruvian coast.

The three hundred pots listed in the document, characteristic of the Chimu culture, were soon confused with another three hundred pots from the same zone and culture that the bishop of Trujillo shipped some years later—the museum's old inventories mistakenly refer to six hundred pots assembled by Bishop Martínez Compañón, even though an extant detailed inventory, made by the bishop himself, clarifies that this latter shipment consisted of a total of three hundred pots.

I have identified other pieces from the Tantalluc tomb in addition to the three hundred pots. These pieces include gold and silver figurines, silver vessels, earthenware vessels of diverse shapes with silver-leaf appliqués, and a set of seven polychrome wooden vessels in gradually decreasing sizes, easily recognizable as *keros*, or ritual wood vessels. Interestingly, while the three hundred pots are apparently of pre-Columbian origin, some of these other pieces seem to belong to a later period: small elements in the silver decorations of the ceramic vessels indicate Spanish influence, and *keros* are usually considered to date from the postconquest period. Furthermore, the drawing of the excavation depicts some bodies within the tomb who are wearing apparel that reflects the Spanish presence and the adaptation of some indigenous customs to European ways.[3] The contents of the tomb, therefore, suggest that rich burial rites were performed in the indigenous fashion years after the appearance of the Spanish.[4]

The excavation of the Huaca de Tantalluc in 1764 was one of the earliest in the Americas. We do not know for certain who directed it, but a likely candidate is Miguel Feijoo, the author of a book published in 1763 on the natural history of Trujillo del Peru that also discusses archaeological findings in the area.[5] Feijoo had been *corregidor*, or mayor, of Trujillo; after he served in that post, he resided in Lima at the same time as Martínez Compañón. Martínez Compañón was subsequently named bishop of Trujillo, and it was in Trujillo that he seems to have followed in Feijoo's archaeological footsteps. Seizing the opportunity offered by a pastoral visit to his diocese in 1782–90, Martínez Compañón ordered a nine-volume natural history of Trujillo (Color Plate 9). He dedicated the ninth volume to archeology (as discussed by Lisa Trever and Joanne Pillsbury in this volume), and it is there that the aforementioned diagram of the 1764 excavations appears.[6]

Excavations in the Mayan city of Palenque

The best-known archaeological excavations conducted in the Americas in the late eighteenth century were undertaken in the Mayan city of Palenque in 1784, 1785, and 1787. Captain Antonio del Río, who undertook the third—and the most famous—of these excavations prepared a report and a number of drawings that were only published in 1822 in London, as a result of the Napoleonic invasion of Spain. It was not known at the time that the excavations had been performed according to detailed instructions and a deliberate archaeological policy. In the early nineteenth century, the Spanish Crown organized a highly ambitious fourth archaeological expedition to explore the ruins of Mexico; the expedition, which concluded its work in Palenque, was directed by Guillaum Dupaix. After Mexico declared its independence from Spain, the objects collected during this expedition went into the first Mexican museum. The drawings prepared as part of the project were published in 1831 in London by Lord Kingsborough, and Dupaix's story was published in 1844 in Paris. Yet, amid this seemingly rich documentation of the expedition, one important detail was lost:

the fact that Dupaix's archaeological trip and the excavations preceding it had their origins in an enlightened and very deliberate Spanish policy.

Some time ago, I examined the Palenque collection in the Museum of America, identifying previously undetermined artifacts and establishing that the three initial Spanish expeditions (previous to that led by Dupaix) displayed continuity and followed a methodical, preconceived plan. The planning was the work of José Estachería, governor and chief justice of the Guatemala Court, and of Juan Bautista Muñoz, a historian of the Spanish viceroyalties, member of Spain's Royal Academy of History, and the creator of the Archive of the Indies (Archivo de Indias), a central repository for all documents on the Indies. The exploration of Palenque began in the following manner:

> The priest of Palenque spread the news that there were ruins nearby, and the authorities inquired into the matter. They were intrigued, because it was known that monumental ruins were not typical of the small Mayan kingdoms of the conquest period. The files contained only one report from 1576 mentioning the existence of the ruins of a major city, which made the authorities believe that the Mayans' past was much more important than the picture Spanish chronicles had drawn. The governor of Guatemala, José Estachería, sent the mayor of Palenque, José Antonio Calderón, in 1785 to draw up a detailed description of the site accompanied by drawings. Calderón gave an account of a considerable number of ruins and made some simple drawings, in which the palace and the reliefs on the different temples can be recognized. Estachería was in contact with Juan Bautista Muñoz, who, as a historian of the Indies, was master of a considerable store of information and was giving Estachería instructions.[7]

Following Muñoz's recommendations, Estachería sent architect Antonio Bernasconi to the ruins in 1785. The elderly Bernasconi prepared a report on four large sheets of paper, each containing several drawings and maps with explanatory slips of paper. Following Muñoz's instructions and using the previous trip by the mayor of Palenque as his guide, Bernasconi drew the area, the palace, the temples, and a number of associated objects. (A careful comparison of his drawings with pieces in the Museum of America collection revealed a small collection whose original site it has been possible partly to reconstruct.)

Muñoz submitted his report, and Governor Estachería drew up careful, detailed instructions on where and how to excavate. Bernasconi had by now died, so Estachería sent his only available officer, Captain Antonio del Río, accompanied by draftsman Ricardo Almendáriz, to Palenque in 1787 to lead the excavation. Del Río adhered to his instructions to the letter. He followed his predecessors' routes and dug where he was asked to dig. Not accurate, but nonetheless perfectly recognizable, the drawings show the Palace of Palenque, its reliefs, and the bas reliefs of the uncovered temples. In his 1787 report, del Río explained where he had dug and what he had found, and these details enable us to reconstruct the excavation and to identify the location where the recovered objects once lay and the reliefs and temples Almendáriz drew.[8] The most significant items unearthed were vessels, two spear points, and two eccentric knives that were found in the Temple of the Inscriptions, the Temple of the Cross, and the Temple of the Foliated Cross. The samples of the reliefs from the palace and the Temple of the Inscriptions are particularly interesting, as is a stone stele with glyphs, the companion to another stele that Bernasconi drew (now in the Museum of America), both of which were in the palace.

One outstanding piece, known as the Madrid Stele, consists of one of the two legs of the throne of the king of Palenque. It has been thought that the stele depicts an underworld deity who, with his upraised hand, holds up the world and the royal throne. However, the figure is actually King Pakal of Palenque himself, with his characteristic protruding nose and flat cheekbones, which can be seen in other portraits of this monarch and on the stele over his tomb in the Temple of the Inscriptions, as well as in the great circular relief over Pakal's throne commemorating his enthronement.[9]

Collections from the Scientific Expeditions to South America

Between 1777 and 1788, naturalists Hipólito Ruiz and José Pavón carried out a botanical expedition to Peru and Chile. For the first five years, Ruiz and Pavón were accompanied by French collector and naturalist Joseph Dombey, who had agreed to hand over to the Spanish Crown one half of everything he collected and all truly unique pieces. The logs of Ruiz, published in the twentieth century, supplement the information and point toward possible provenances of the objects.[10] Another list of Dombey's objects was drawn up in Madrid by Spanish naturalist Juan de Cuéllar, who was later sent on a long scientific expedition to the Philippines, where he gathered a collection that has yet to be identified.[11] These lists have enabled us to reconstruct part of the collection gathered in Chile and Peru by the members of this expedition.

Although the expedition was a botanical one, the participants did collect archaeological objects. Some items seem to have been picked up from the ground or perhaps during superficial cleaning excavations, such as the stone axes and the characteristically Incan star-shaped puzzles, which are listed as made by the *indios gentiles* (heathen Indians) of Peru, a name used for both the pre-Columbian indigenous peoples and the non-Christianized or uncivilized Indians of the time. According to the description in Ruiz's log, these materials must have been gathered in late 1787 and early 1788 in the province of Jauja, near Tarma. The log discusses the ruins of Tarmatambo Castle and the visible remains of an ancient settlement nearby, described as pierced by the royal Incan road that runs in a straight line from Cuzco to Quito. The expedition sent back some bronze knives and some small leaves, which could have come from the aforementioned locations. The vessels that the expedition collected, however, seem by their Chancay style to have been gathered at the coast, perhaps from the excavations at Pachacamac, near Lima, where the expedition probably also found an *uncu*, or feather shirt. Like a good botanist, Ruiz described how the ears of corn found in graves sprouted after being planted. The collection contains some of these same small ears of corn, as well as some stone ears of corn used in the pre-Hispanic world as fertility symbols.

Among the expedition's ethnographic collections, the outstanding items are a number of feathered hats and pieces of fabric adorned with feathers for decorating horse trappings. The latter were given to the expedition by a local governor for the Natural History Cabinet in Madrid. The viceroy of Peru also sent the cabinet a few objects that had already been gathered by other expeditions, such as blankets of bark from the Pacific islands and a number of feathered helmets from Hawaii.[12]

The prize pieces in the collection put together by Dombey are a number of hats made by the now-extinct Pehuenche Indians from the outskirts of Buenos Aires; a variety of bolas and objects from the pampas; and a collection of vessels by the Santiago de Chile nuns—the only items of colonial craftwork among the collection, perhaps because their profuse gold decoration must have seemed out of the ordinary to "Dombey." The magnificent Incan *uncu* dates from the early colonial era, and its fine state of preservation and motifs associated with royalty indicate that it was never buried and was instead probably acquired from a member of the high Cuzco nobility.

Around the same time that Ruiz, Pavón, and Dombey ventured to Peru and Chile, a number of other expeditions were also mounted. In 1785 and 1789, for instance, Antonio de Córdoba commanded expeditions to the Strait of Magellan. Among the explorers were officers such as Dionisio Alcalá Galiano and Ciriaco Cevallos, who later participated in the first part of the Malaspina expedition (1789–94) and in the voyage of the schooners *Sutil* and *Mexicana* to the American Northwest. Published logs of some of these expeditions may have been written by Alcalá Galiano and Cevallos. The logs of the expedition to Tierra del Fuego contain descriptions of the indigenous people (now extinct), their limited goods, and the exchanges made with them, which helped create a small collection that I have partly identified.[13]

In 1794, the brothers Christian and Conrad Heuland conducted a mineralogical and zoological expedition that presumably gathered archaeological or ethnographic objects, although practically nothing is known of such items. José Celestino Mutis, living in Santa Fe de Bogotá, then the capital of the Viceroyalty of New Granada, conducted a lengthy botanical expedition (1783–1816). Ancient labels indicate that he must have gathered and sent some of the seed decorations kept today in the Museum of America. Mutis's expedition must have been responsible for sending the Royal Cabinet an exceptional series of six paintings depicting *mestizaje* (miscegenation) human types from Quito and its surroundings, signed by painter Vicente Albán in 1783.

A collection of clothing and skins from the Indians of the North American plains, which was kept in the early nineteenth century in the Public Library in Toledo, Spain, testifies to an expedition to the lands of northern Mexico, now southern United States, which were in the process of being explored and colonized in the eighteenth century. The Toledo Public Library used to house the collections of Cardinal Borbón and Francisco Antonio de Lorenzana, first bishop of Mexico and then archbishop of Toledo. Lorenzana did important work in Mexico collecting pre-Columbian antiquities; thus, it seems likely that the Indian artifacts were part of Lorenzana's collection and had been gathered in the eighteenth century, which makes them extremely rare.

Expeditions to an Unknown World:
The Pacific Northwest Coast

Eighteenth-century Spanish journeys to the northern Pacific coast resulted in the discovery and first explorations of the American Northwest and Alaskan coast. Other navigators from other countries immediately followed in the wake of the Spanish explorers, each seeking to secure control of part or all of the newly discovered region. At the same time, the Russians, advancing through Siberia to the Kamchatka peninsula, pushed on eastward and thus penetrated the American lands of Alaska.

The abundance of skins in the region led Russian traders to finance expeditions to America, and Antonio de Ulloa immediately reported to the Spanish government this breach into their territory. To track the Russians, in 1761 Spain began to keep permanent ambassadors at the Russian court, who discovered that Russian expeditions were heading eastward to coasts imagined to be the still-unknown coasts of western America. The Pacific Northwest was the only part of the world, except for the polar regions, that was still unexplored; it seemed like the end of the world, the place farthest from any European port, so inaccessible that in order to reach it from Europe it was necessary to sail around Tierra del Fuego.

In the eighteenth century, Spain, which had consolidated its presence in the core areas of America, began to extend feelers through the sparsely inhabited peripheral zones, such as the lands of Río de la Plata and the lands south of there, and to spread northward to colonize the belt of land spanning Florida, Texas, New Mexico, and California, which formed part of the viceroyalty of New Spain, with its capital in Mexico City. At the same time, England was aggressively seeking naval hegemony and predominant influence over the maritime trade in the Atlantic and the Pacific, an ambition that brought it into continuous confrontation with Spain. Responding to the English threat, in 1726 first José Patiño and then Zenón de Somodevilla, marquis de la Ensenada, launched a bid to develop the navy and to spur Spanish progress in naval science and industry.

Within this context, news of a Russian presence in what seemed to be the lands lying north of Alta California (then in the process of being colonized) prompted Spain to organize a series of expeditions to the north of the California settlements. Although precise instructions were written for each separate venture, all sets of instructions told the explorers to determine the scope of Russian expansion, ratify the rights of the king of Spain to the American lands by taking possession of any new places found, explore and map the new coasts, and report on them. Every expedition had to keep two logs, sending one to the viceroy on reaching port. The explorers had strict orders to treat the native peoples with sensitivity and patience and to avoid any confrontation. Although not widely known to historians, many of the explorers were also ordered to collect objects for the Royal Natural History Cabinet.[14]

While a team of midshipmen trained at the naval school in Cádiz, Viceroy Antonio María de Bucareli ordered pilot Juan Pérez, who used to provision the new California colonies of San Diego, Monterrey, and San Francisco, on the first exploratory voyage. The viceroy gave him copies of maps printed in Saint Petersburg in 1758 and 1773 and a set of precise instructions. Pérez departed in January 1774, from San Blas, Mexico, on the frigate *Santiago*, with Esteban Martínez as his second-in-command. Friar Junípero Serra disembarked in San Diego, while in Monterrey Friar Tomás de la Peña and Friar Juan Crespi joined the ship. To avoid the southwest currents and some unknown stretches of coast, Pérez set a course out to sea, straight north, until he arrived at what is now known as the Dixon Entrance, north of the Queen Charlotte Islands, which he called the Santa Margarita Islands.

11.1. Bird sculpture made of carved bone, collected by Juan Pérez in 1774. Museo de América, Madrid.

Friar Juan Crespi and Friar Juan de la Peña wrote the journey's logs, which are in the Archive of the Indies, Seville, and in the Toledo Public Library. The friars described a variety of exchanges and encounters, such as when several canoes full of indigenous peoples appeared, wearing headdresses and singing, with whom "a fair" was quickly arranged. The scarcity of water forced the *Santiago* to sail southward until it reached an anchorage, a small island that the crew called "San Lorenzo de Nutka" on the western coast of today's island of Vancouver.[15] Crespi described how, when the Spanish were preparing to take on fresh water at the beach on what came to be known as Nootka, about fifteen canoes drew up. Some women in the canoes began to trade skins and "painted reed hats . . . the pyramidal top is finished off with pear-shaped balls, and some woven of a thread very like hemp, with fringe of the same thread." The objects that interested these Indians were red ribbons and an assortment of shells from the beaches of Monterrey. Bad weather and scurvy forced the expedition to return to Mexico, though it hugged the coast and mapped as it went.

A document entitled "Inventory of the items swapped with the Indians discovered at the height of 55 degrees and 19 minutes by the individuals on the frigate *Santiago* assigned to explore the northern coast of California that was sent to H.M. by the Viceroy of New Spain" (Mexico City, December 1774) describes some objects matching those described in the logs. Two hats have been identified, as has "a species of bone bird with a cracked upper beak recovered from an Indian woman who wore it round her neck with a portion of tiny teeth apparently from a small alligator" (Figure 11.1). These are the oldest objects from the Northwest coast gathered by the first expedition to visit that area. They were later mixed up with objects gathered by the Malaspina expedition.

In the following year, 1775, a second expedition left, its crew including part of a contingent of midshipmen who had arrived in Mexico with modern scientific equipment to facilitate the reconnaissance work. There were two ships in the expedition: the *Santiago*, now under the command of Bruno de Hezeta, with Juan Pérez and Esteban Martínez serving as pilots, and the schooner *Sonora*, captained by Juan Francisco de la Bodega y Quadra, with Antonio Mourelle as first mate. The ships sailed close to the island of Vancouver, of which they took possession in July. Only a few days later, due to bad weather and illnesses among the crew, the *Santiago* embarked on its return journey, during which Juan Pérez died of fever, while the *Sonora*, despite its precarious situation, continued northward.

The *Sonora* sailed past the latitude reached the year before, until the crew spied Mount St. Elias. Although forced by scurvy to turn back, they explored the coast on their return journey: the Alexander Archipelago, the island of Floridablanca (now one of the islands in the Queen Charlotte Archipelago), and the island of Vancouver. In their logs, Bodega y Quadra and Mourelle describe their contacts with the indigenous peoples, recording several exchanges, some as far north as off Mount St. Elias.[16] The *Sonora* arrived back in San Blas, in late November. Mourelle's log, published in London, was used by Captain James Cook on his third and last voyage in 1778, when he explored the Alaskan coasts and disembarked at Nootka. There is no evidence of objects collected on this expedition in 1775.

The results of the voyages in 1774 and 1775 were studied, and then, in May 1776, a third expedition was readied. New ships had to be bought and built. With orders to reach 70N and equipped with a sophisticated method of navigation, in February 1779, the corvettes *Princesa*, under the command of Ignacio de Arteaga, head of the expedition, with Fernando de Quirós as first mate, and *Favorita*, captained by Juan de la Bodega y Quadra, again with Mourelle as his first mate, departed. In early May, they reached Bucareli Bay in the Prince of Wales archipelago, where the expedition spent two months mapping and describing the country. Two months later, they pressed on northward, reaching as far north as the previous expedition. After arriving at Carmen Island (now Kayak Island), they sailed along the coast until they disembarked in a harbor that they called "Santiago" on La Magdalena Island (now Hinchinbrook Island); they hugged the coast of Quirós Island (now Montague Island), exploring what is now known as Prince William Sound, all Inuit lands. In August, they reached Regla Island, which is perhaps today's Chugash Island on the Kenai Peninsula. Scurvy forced them to return, and when in late November they reached their home port, Spain and England were at war.

The expedition members interacted each day with the indigenous people who approached them during the two months they spent at Bucareli Bay. In his log, Mourelle tells of several exchanges with the native peoples of the Bucareli area and describes the traded objects in minute detail. These included "morions in the figure of the head of some very fierce animal" and "whistles that they played like the flute." "And of everything," Mourelle recounts, "the Commanders took that which they judged particular, leaving the rest to trade by our peoples." What did they acquire? We know that, on arriving in Mexico, Juan de la Bodega y Quadra wrote a set of letters to the viceroy, describing in one that he had delivered to Commissioner Francisco Hijosa the trifles collected during the expedition. We know, too, that he sent a chest containing Indian objects to the court. A document dated July 18, 1780, states that Joseph Ivargoyen, bookkeeper at the Factoría de Tabacos company in Guadalajara, sent from that city to the viceroy, for the Royal Cabinet, another collection that included "2 stone figures that are believed to have been an idol of the Indians. Some instruments used by the Indians lately discovered to the Northwest of California. They are comprised of a cape, a breastplate, a back plate, two arrows, a stone ax and a bag with some small sticks with which said Indians play."[17]

The Museum of America has among its collection several suits of armor, two of them complete; a fine ax with a highly decorated green stone blade; and several sets of gaming sticks. Which of them did Bodega y Quadra send? Let us see his log:

> The Indians, whose martial genius without doubt made them think long on defensive weapons, present themselves at functions of war with a breastplate and back plate made of narrow boards and knitted by many threads that weave them together, leaving them flexible to conform to the body, leaving the arms free to movement; around their neck they wear a wide, thick, gorget-shaped fold of wood that covers them up to the immediacy of the eyes, and on their head a morion that they regularly make in the figure of a fierce animal. From the waist down they wear a wooden apron and on their back a fine hide that covers them to their ankles.[18]

"The offensive weapons they generally use," Bodega continues, are "hatchets of flint and of another green stone, so hard that, in chopping any piece of wood, it knows no notch whatever in its edge." These descriptions match the ensemble of an ax (accession no. 13916) and full set of armor made up of a breastplate and back plate (13914), helmet (13913), and collar (13908) on display at the Museum of America (Figure 11.2).

11.2. Tlingit helmet. Museo de América, Madrid.

A fourth journey was made nine years later, in 1788, to Inuit and Russian lands. After the United States declaration of independence in 1776, Spain, harassed by England in the Atlantic and eager to recover the British-held enclaves of Minorca and Gibraltar, threw its support behind the former English colonies and declared war against Britain in 1779. The exigencies of wartime temporarily disrupted plans for a fourth expedition, with officers who had been assigned to the voyage to the Northwest being sent to other posts. Fresh reports of Russian settlements in the Aleutians, Prince William Bay, and Nootka, however, reanimated Spanish plans. In March 1788, the frigate *Princesa* and the packet boat *San Carlos*, commanded by Gonzalo López de Haro and by Esteban Martínez, respectively, departed. They sailed straight to Prince William Bay, where they traded with the Inuit people, and then pushed up Cook Inlet.[19] At last they located the first Russian settlement and gathered information about the locations of Russians anchorages and trading posts. They sailed past Kodiak Island and Unimak and Unalaska islands in the Aleutians, trading with the indigenous Inuit people and with the Russians as they went. They returned in September with the news that the Russians intended to set themselves up the following year at Nootka harbor on Vancouver Island. Some Pacific Inuit items

PAZ CABELLO CARRO

were likely gathered on this voyage, but no documentary evidence of any items remains.

The 1788 Nootka Conflict and the Expedition of 1790

The Russians were known to want to settle in Nootka, much farther south from the places in Alaska they usually frequented, in order to check the English trade in otter skins that the Russians had dominated until 1786. Apprehensive of a Russian move, Spain quickly armed a fifth expedition and dispatched it northward in 1787. The commander, Esteban Martínez, had instructions to establish a permanent settlement on Nootka, employ all means to earn the goodwill of the locals, and behave urbanely with Russians and Englishmen. In May 1787, the expedition reached Nootka. Friendly relations with the local chief, Chief Maquinna, were resumed. A fort and large huts began to be built, trenches were dug, and six defensive batteries were installed on the point at the mouth of the harbor.[20]

On July 2, the packet boat *Argonaut* put into port. The *Argonaut*, property of a British trading company, the South Sea Company, and commanded by "Jaime Colnet" (James Colnett), also bore instructions, given to him in Macao by Colnett's employers, to establish an outpost in Nootka. As Colnett refused to recognize Spanish authority and the primacy of the Spanish settlement, Martínez took Colnett and his ship prisoner and sent them to San Blas. The same fate shortly befell Thomas Hudson, captain of the sloop *Princess Royal*, belonging to the same company. So began the well-known Nootka Incident and another war with England. The episode marked an end to the first cycle of Spanish expeditions to the Northwest and the beginning of a brilliant second age, which was to prove to be the high point of Spanish presence in the area.

According to documents at the Spanish National Museum of Natural Sciences, in Madrid, on March 4, 1790, the king's baili, Antonio Valdés, sent the Cabinet of Natural History four chests containing a shipment that the commander of Nootka harbor had dispatched on July 9, 1789. The chests contained the skins of some animals from the northern California coast and some curios and adornments from there and from the Sandwich Islands—more particularly, "some curios that the Indians of Meza or Sandwich Island weave": two feather blankets in "crimson and yellow of the sort Tayana Rey uses on Owihee Island," two short feathered capes for women, three feathered caps "of morion-like make," and a dress of the sort used by locals of San Lorenzo de Nutka harbor. In a document at the National Archaeological Museum (a copy of an original lost in 1936), we find "reports of what was sent by Estevan Josef Martínez." A note explains that "these objects were transferred by order of the King on March

21, 1790, to the Royal Cabinet of Natural History in union with skins of various animals of the Northern Coast of California, in four chests."

Why was Esteban Martínez able to send to Spain not only skins from California and garments from Nootka but also feathered capes and caps and other objects from the Sandwich Isles? The answer is not hard to find: the South Sea Company ships stopped at the Sandwich Isles en route from Macao to Nootka. The same anonymous Franciscan author of the *Relación de los hechos acaecidos en Nutka en 1788* records that "among Captain Colnet's [sic] crew there came an Indian of said [Sandwich] Ysles, a lad of some twenty years, who following the other sailors went to our ships."[21] He almost certainly took with him the feathered capes of the Hawaiian kings and some of the feathered hats kept at the Museum of America, whose provenance and history has confounded historians for many years.

In the same year, 1789, the new viceroy, Revillagigedo, and Bodega y Quadra arrived in Mexico in the same ship, together with a new group of officers trained at Cádiz and assigned to San Blas. Their objective was to secure the department of San Blas, whose harbor was Mexico's port of departure for the north Pacific; to supply the settlements of the two Californias; to support the new colony in Nootka; to renew the explorations interrupted by the war; and to resolve the Nootka conflict.

The viceroy sent a well-manned expedition, the sixth, under the command of Francisco de Eliza, with the frigate *Concepción*, the packet boat *San Carlos*, and the sloop *Princesa*, which departed in February 1790. After provisioning the Californian *presidios* (strongholds), they arrived at Nootka, where Eliza settled in, sending Salvador Fidalgo in the *San Carlos* to explore farther north. Fidalgo reached La Magdalena Island, explored Prince William Sound, and visited the Russian settlement at Cook Inlet, filling in gaps in cartographic and geographical knowledge as he went, until bad weather forced him to return. In the meantime, Sub-lieutenant Manuel Quimper reconnoitered Juan de Fuca Strait and the entire complicated coastline of the area around Nootka and Vancouver. There is no documentary proof that this sixth expedition produced any artifacts for the Cabinet.

The 1792 Border Expedition to Nootka

The Nootka Incident perched Spain and England on the precipice of an unwanted war. Seeking to step back from the edge, the count of Floridablanca orchestrated several negotiations, including the aforementioned expedition to Nootka led by Bodega y Quadra. Bodega y Quadra was to meet with an English delegate in Nootka in an effort to draw the borders *(límites)* and determine the specific points of the dispute between Spain and England. Before he left, Bodega y Quadra had the opportunity to meet with the English sailors taken prisoner in the Nootka conflict, Colnett, Hudson, and Temple; he conversed with the outgoing and incoming viceroys; and he carefully prepared his expedition and directed the building of ships such as the schooners *Sutil* and *Mexicana* (whose voyage is described later in this chapter).

Bodega y Quadra's expedition sailed out of San Blas in February 1792 and returned in February of the following year. Of considerable size, the expedition was made up of the frigates *Santa Gertrudis*, *Aránzazu*, and *Princesa* and the schooner *Activa*. It spent five months in Nootka, but its activities went beyond diplomatic negotiations. Bodega y Quadra finished fortifying the harbor, raised buildings, and even planted a vegetable garden. He sent the frigate *Princesa*, under Salvador Fidalgo's command, to explore the coasts of Juan de Fuca Strait and many points on the coast; in the event, Fidalgo's expedition went so far as the Sandwich Islands. The *Aránzazu* was dispatched, under Jacinto Caamaño's command, to explore the waters north of Nootka. Caamaño exchanged gifts and developed a steady, cordial relationship with the community of Chief Jammisit, apparently of the Haida people.

Meanwhile, in Mexico, a lengthy botanical expedition to the New World was under way, directed by naturalist Martín Sessé. Viceroy Revillagigedo, who had probably conversed with Bodega y Quadra about the latter's plan for a scientific expedition during their journey together from Spain to Mexico, sent the naturalist José Mariano Mociño—a participant in Sessé's expedition—to Nootka. Mociño spent five months in Nootka, working under the direction of Bodega y Quadra and with the assistance of a draftsman, Echevarría, and a surgeon, José Maldonado, who had some knowledge of botany and natural history. The result of Mociño's studies and classifications was a series of botanical and zoological plates that are today kept at the Ministry of Foreign Affairs together with other documents from this expedition and ethnographic drawings from Mociño's studies. Mociño wrote a treatise on Nootka, the first study of the area, providing detailed descriptions of its natives' customs. He learned the native language and included a vocabulary at the end of his study, which was published in 1913 under the title *Noticias de Nutka* (News from Nootka).

Among the collections at the Museum of America is a series of items that seem to have come from Nootka and that have been traditionally ascribed to the collection made by the Malaspina expedition, which, during its brief stay in Nootka, made some magnificent drawings, although no records indicate that the Malaspina expedition collected and shipped any items from Nootka. Furthermore, I learned that an inventory drawn up by Florencio Janer in the mid-nineteenth century contained some items from the Pacific Northwest that Janer described as having been gathered by the expedition of Ruiz and Pavón, who had explored much further south, the viceroyalty of Peru. These objects, which were listed as Peruvian, were hats and large masks that were clearly of Nootkan manufacture and were listed later as having been sent by the Malaspina expedition. Knowing the unreliability of the data in the nineteenth-century inventory, I investigated. I discovered that before Mociño fled Spain in 1815 and went into exile in France with the botanical plates from his voyage, he deposited in Ruiz and Pavón's office some chests containing part of his collection. Mociño died on his return voyage to Madrid in 1818, and his description of how the hats were made was lost until the publication, more than a century later, of his *Noticias de Nutka*. After Pavón died in 1840, the goods in his office were sent to the Royal Cabinet, where they remained packed up until around 1855, when Janer opened and inventoried them. Believing all the chests to belong to Ruiz and Pavón's Peruvian expedition, he understandably misattributed the objects from Nootka.

We have, therefore, a new collection parallel to the one Captain Cook gathered a few years before, a collection that tallies with Mociño's descriptions and with the Mociño expedition drawings at the Ministry of Foreign Affairs. The objects in the collection must have belonged to or been related with the family of Chief Maquinna, who was drawn by the Malaspina expedition during the few days that it was in Nootka at the same time as the limit-drawing expedition (Figure 11.3). Almost as an anecdote, it may be mentioned that, in one drawing from this expedition (featuring a large mask that formed part of the collection), Maquinna is shown at a dance given in honor of Bodega y Quadra, who is shown seated with his officers next to a civilian in a top hat (Mociño). As the event is recounted in the logs of both Bodega y Quadra and Captain Vancouver (who was England's envoy to negotiate the peace), we know that Vancouver was there as well (younger and seated at Bodega's side). And we know also from the two navigators' logs that, returning from this celebration, they baptized the island as Quadra and Vancouver Island, a name that remained on Spanish maps until quite recently, while on English maps it ended up as Vancouver Island.

The Malaspina Expedition and the Expedition
of the Schooners *Sutil* and *Mexicana*

Alejandro Malaspina and his second-in-command, José Bustamante, on board the corvettes *Descubierta* and *Atrevida*, embarked on one of the most significant expeditions of the eighteenth century in 1789. On their five-year scientific, political, and discovery-oriented mission, they followed the entire coast of South America, sailed up to Alaska and then out into the Pacific to the Philippines

11.3. Portrait of the "Chief of Nutka" (Maquinna), Malaspina expedition. Museo de América, Madrid.

and Australia, stopping at Lima before making their way back to Spain. This very well-known, thoroughly studied expedition made drawings, most of which are kept today at the Museum of America, to which they were donated in the mid-twentieth century by Carlos Sanz.

In 1792, the Malaspina expedition visited Nootka while Bodega y Quadra's limit-drawing expedition was also there. The Malaspina expedition also coincided with the expedition of the schooners *Sutil* and *Mexicana*, commanded by Dionisio Alcalá Galiano and Cayetano Valdés, officers trained in the midshipmen's school, who had local experience and had participated in the first part of the Malaspina expedition.[22] The log of this expedition was published (in 1802) as an anonymous tale, preceded by a lengthy introduction describing all the Spanish voyages to northern California since the first in the fifteenth century, with details taken from their navigation logs.

The *Sutil* and *Mexicana* left Acapulco in March 1792 and sailed for Nootka harbor, where they arrived in May. Bodega y Quadra and the corvette *Aránzazu*, commanded by Caamaño, were already in Nootka when the schooners arrived. Alcalá Galiano and Valdés and their crews made astronomical and physical observations while maintaining cordial relations with Chief Maquinna's community. In their logs, they describe the character and leadership capacity of Maquinna, the rather tense relations the indigenous community had with the Europeans from other ships, and the community's complicated relations with neighboring indigenous peoples. The expedition then explored Juan de Fuca Strait, where it ran across Fidalgo, who was part of the Bodega y Quadra expedition, and, later, Englishmen from the expedition run by Captain Vancouver, who was on his way to meet with Bodega y Quadra.

The *Sutil* and *Mexicana* fostered close relations with Tetaku, a chief who inspired great fear in the area. Their logs describe the customs of and differences between various local communities (Mociño, the naturalist, provided them with many of the details they relate about the Nootka settlement). The expedition traded with the indigenous people, acquiring objects such as a mantle, bows, arrows, clubs, and paddles. In northern Nootka, it found Nootka-speaking indigenous people whose chief wore "a hat very similar to that which we had seen the year before on the chief of Mulgrave Port . . . who esteemed it greatly because he had taken it from his enemies in a battle. We bought it," they tell in the *Relación* of 1802. On another occasion, they regretted not having been able to buy more utensils and weapons from other native people, which strongly suggests that this expedition gathered its own collection, although we have no documentary record that any of the objects acquired were shipped to the Royal Cabinet.

Despite the lack of such records, it seems certain that the objects from the Pacific Northwest that made their way into the Royal Cabinet were acquired during the voyages of the *Sutil* and *Mexicana* and the other expeditions that this chapter has described. Although the catalog of the 1892 Madrid exhibition commemorating the four-hundredth anniversary of the discovery of America attributed the Northwest coast collections in the Royal Cabinet to the Malaspina expedition, this was a mistake—and an error that was repeated throughout the twentieth century. Comparisons revealed that the descriptions of objects in the logs of the Malaspina expedition do not tally with the shipping lists, the drawings, and the pieces held today in the Museum of America. However, the objects in the museum do tally with the shipping documents for objects from the other expeditions we have mentioned in this chapter.

Spain eventually abandoned the Nootka enclave, which became forgotten and depopulated. Spain also abandoned its ambitions to control the coast of the Pacific Northwest and Alaska. In the early nineteenth century, Spanish political influence dwindled as Spain was buffeted by the French invasion and other turbulent political events, and finally vanished with the independence of its former viceroyalties. Nevertheless, for twenty years in the late eighteenth century, Spanish sailors and scientists explored and mapped some jagged, intricate coastlines and made contact with indigenous societies at the pinnacle of a thousand-year tradition. The maps, logs, drawings, and objects collected by these intrepid explorers offer us a window onto their world.

—ᴙᴙ—

Martínez Compañón
and His Illustrated "Museum"

Lisa Trever and Joanne Pillsbury

As bishop of the intendancy of Trujillo, Peru, during the 1780s, the Basque priest Baltasar Jaime Martínez Compañón y Bujanda (1737–97) created what was surely the most systematic and best-documented collection of natural history and pre-Columbian art and artifacts assembled in late eighteenth-century Peru.[1] In 1788 and 1790, the bishop sent box upon box of flora, fauna, metals and minerals, northern Peruvian antiquities, ethnographic objects, and colonial artworks from Cartagena, across the Atlantic, to the Bourbon crown in Spain.[2] Although the current location of the natural history collections is unknown, fortunately many of the artifacts the bishop collected survive today in Madrid's Museo de América, where they have recently been studied by Paz Cabello Carro.[3] The bishop's endeavors are best understood as part of a broader tradition of Enlightenment-era efforts to document and order the world in encyclopedic form, although traces of an earlier paradigm of collecting remain in his work's occasional attention to the monstrous and the marvelous. Not just an imperialist project to document and collect examples of all aspects of northern Peru, the bishop's work also often relies on the production and visualization of local, creole, and indigenous South American knowledge.

Born in the village of Cabredo in the province of Navarre, Spain in 1737, Martínez Compañón was ordained a priest in 1761 and shortly thereafter completed a doctorate in canon law. In 1767, Charles III appointed him cantor of the cathedral in Lima, Peru. He spent a decade there, serving as rector of the Santo Toribio Seminary and as secretary to the Sixth Lima Provincial Council.

He was named bishop of Trujillo in 1778 and thereafter dedicated nearly a dozen years to the documentation and reform of that province. In 1791, Martínez Compañón left Peru to become archbishop of Santa Fé de Bogotá, where he remained until his death in 1797.[4]

We consider Martínez Compañón's work as a collector to be two-fold. On the one hand, in Peru he collected thousands of natural and cultural objects on behalf of Charles III for his newly opened Royal Cabinet of Natural History in Madrid, which had been founded in 1771. On the other hand, during the course of the three-year inspection tour (*visita pastoral*) that inaugurated his tenure in Trujillo, the bishop oversaw the creation of a series of over 1,400 watercolor illustrations by local artists who systematically depicted nearly every aspect of the natural and social worlds of Trujillo. Through these illustrations, Martínez Compañón also collected the *likenesses* of Andean natural history specimens and artifacts (for example, Color Plate 10 and Figure 12.1). This graphic collection, or paper museum, which today survives in Madrid's Biblioteca del Palacio Real under the modern title *Trujillo del Perú*, complements the bishop's collections of objects, but it also exists as a corpus of visual knowledge independent of the things themselves.[5]

Although Martínez Compañón never wrote a text to accompany these images, the bishop's nine volumes of illustrations remain an astonishingly rich source for the study of northern Peru in the late eighteenth century.[6] The first volume documents the region's demography, illustrates civil and ecclesiastical institutions and personnel, and includes maps and plans of cities, towns, and churches. The second volume is largely ethnographic and illustrates the ethnic and social categories current in eighteenth-century Peru, as well as a variety of local costume, industry, craft, dance, and music. Volumes three and four contain botanical illustrations, which are arranged according to their non-Linnaean, common or indigenous names (Figure 12.2). The fifth volume is devoted to medicinal plants, many examples of which were remitted to Spain in 1788. Volume six illustrates "quadrupeds, reptiles, and insects."[7] Volume seven contains illustrations of birds, and volume eight illustrates marine life. The final volume of illustrations is devoted to Andean antiquities and contains maps and plans of Inca, Chimú, and Moche archaeological sites within the bishopric, as well as representations of burials, ancient textiles, metal and wood artifacts, and a vast array of ceramic vessels.[8]

Martínez Compañón's own words indicate that he envisioned this extensive documentary project as a kind of graphic museum in itself.[9] In 1785, at the completion of his *visita*, the bishop wrote to the viceroy of Peru, Teodoro de Croix, stating that he had assembled a collection of those "productions of nature" and "curiosities of the art of the heathens [*gentiles*]" that he could

12.1. Chimú (top) and Moche (bottom) ceramic vessels from the north coast of Peru, in Baltasar Jaime Martínez Compañón, *Trujillo del Perú*, vol. 9, f. 95. Patrimonio Nacional, Spain.

acquire and that he planned to arrange the materials as a museum [*museo*], which he believed would be a first, since, as he writes, no other bishop in the Americas had formed such a museum.[10] The Jardín Botánico was founded in Lima in 1778, by order of a *real cédula* from Charles III, but the first public museum did not open in Peru until after independence in 1822.[11] But in this letter to the viceroy, Martínez Compañón continues by saying that he has assembled a history of the diocese, which he plans to title the "Historical, Physical, Political, and Moral *Museum* of the Bishopric of Trujillo, Peru" (our

12.2. *Ampihuasca*, in Baltasar Jaime Martínez Compañón, *Trujillo del Perú*, vol. 3, estampa 153, Patrimonio Nacional, Spain.

emphasis). This letter suggests that the bishop intended *both* the collections of objects *and* the illustrations of those objects to constitute his "museum"; the objects and the images were conceived as two parts of a single enterprise of collecting.[12]

The term "museum" in contemporary usage usually refers to a place, particularly a building, but in the past the term has had other associations. The Greek word *mouseion*, place of the Muses, originally referred to a school, library, or a place connected with the arts more broadly. Through time, the word came to denote a gathering of information, including drawings. Particularly with the advent of printing in the sixteenth century and the expansion of scientific observation in the seventeenth century, drawing became an essential part of the practice of observation and the recording of information. Pictures became not just an aid to observation but an end in themselves.[13] The idea of a museum as a collection of manuscripts or illustrations took extraordinary shape in the work of Cassiano dal Pozzo (1588–1657) in the seventeenth century. The concept of a "paper museum" (*museo cartaceo*) has its origins in the Academy of Linceans, a scientific organization founded by Federico Cesi (1585–1630) in 1603.[14] Cassiano compiled the greatest collection of scientific illustrations of the time, a paper museum of some twenty-three bound volumes containing hundreds of drawings of antiquities, as well as a remarkable group of natural history drawings. In the eighteenth century, Lorenzo Boturini Benaduci's (1702–51) well-known collection of indigenous Mexican manuscripts was called the "Museo Indiano."[15] Furthermore, the term "museum" in the seventeenth and eighteenth centuries could refer even to the results of travel and the gathering of manuscripts or other information in volumes.[16]

This essay seeks to place Martínez Compañón's "museum"—that is, both the collections of tangible objects and the collection of their representations on paper—within broader traditions of collecting and illustration in the viceroyalty of Peru. We find that the bishop's project draws heavily on European precedents for the systematic acquisition of knowledge but that the contents of his paper museum are at times unexpected in a late eighteenth-century encyclopedic work and may be attributed to the specific historical circumstances of their facture.

Traditions of Collecting in Peru

A primary objective of our research on Martínez Compañón's northern Peruvian collections of objects and images has been to reconstruct the intellectual circumstances that gave rise to and shaped his endeavors. The story of Spain's collecting of and from its viceroyalties is well established, but the history of collecting in Peru and for Peruvians remains largely unwritten. To situate Martínez Compañón's work as a collector, let us turn to a history of Peruvian collecting.

Collecting, in its broadest sense, was not new in the Andes when the first Europeans arrived in the sixteenth century. The earliest historical accounts of the Inca Empire include descriptions of activities that may be considered collecting, including the acquisition and maintenance of everything from fine textiles to mummies.[17] The capital of Cusco was filled with valuables from the empire, and no gold, silver, or precious textiles could be taken out of the city once they were brought in. Provincial populations were obliged to send one of their principal cult objects to the capital where they were integrated into the state religion—and held hostage, should the provinces fail to abide by imperial demands.[18] Royal mummies were kept and venerated by their descent groups.[19] Normally kept in the palaces they occupied during their lifetimes, along with objects associated with their reigns, the mummies were on occasion brought out to visit other mummies, advise the living through the assistance of oracles and servants, and participate in rituals in the main plaza of Cuzco.

Objects of gold and silver, and even mummies, continued to be collected after the arrival of Spaniards in the late 1520s. But most Europeans prized the value of the metals more than any aesthetic qualities of the Andean works. Francisco Pizarro engineered the collection of the famous room of gold and two of silver as the ransom for the Inca emperor Atahualpa. Most of the metal objects collected at the time of the conquest—and into the early viceregal period—were melted down, rendering their collection merely an economic by-product of imperialism. Inca mummies, curiously, had something of a display afterlife in the century following the arrival of Europeans.[20] In 1559, Viceroy Andrés Hurtado de Mendoza, Marqués of Cañete, charged the chief magistrate (*corregidor*) of Cusco, Polo Ondegardo, with the task of rounding up and confiscating all the royal mummies of the Inca kings and their effigies (*huauques*).[21] In Inca times, these royal effigies or "brothers," made of gold, silver, wood, stone, and other materials, would stand in for a ruler during his lifetime and were then retired at his death and maintained with his mummy. Some of the mummies collected by Polo Ondegardo were sent to Lima where they were on display in the Hospital de San Andrés until at least 1638. Presumably the effigy "brothers" and other associated objects were melted down or destroyed earlier.

In the sixteenth and seventeenth centuries, ritual objects associated with "heathen superstitions" were regularly sought out and destroyed as part of anti-idolatry campaigns waged by the Church. It is one of the ironies of ancient American art history that some of the best descriptions of pre-Hispanic objects come to us via manuals designed to assist the clergy in the search and destruction of these "idols."[22] There were some exceptions to these destructive practices, and indeed we know of rare examples where objects of indigenous manufacture were sent back to Europe as curiosities.[23] Viceroy Toledo, for example, collected Inca regalia as well as fine Andean cloth.[24]

Wills and last testaments can provide data on the sorts of objects owned by Andeans in the early modern period, but in general these listings indicate objects of daily or ritual use, not necessarily items purposely gathered as a "collection" in the modern sense.[25] There are some exceptions, however. The Ortiz de Zevallos family of Lima, for example, amassed an important collection of Peruvian antiquities in the eighteenth century. And, in the case of Pedro Bravo de Lagunas y Castillo, a Lima judge (*oidor*) who lived in the first half of the eighteenth century, one finds the purposeful creation of a collection that contained both European paintings and Peruvian antiquities.[26]

The first national museum in Peru opened in 1822, but already in 1793, an article in Lima's protonationalist newspaper the *Mercurio peruano*, published by the city's Sociedad de Amantes del País, mentioned in passing the society's desire to establish a natural history museum in Lima.[27] The ornithological, zoological, and mineralogical collections that José Rossi y Rubí, a prominent member of the society and regular contributor to the *Mercurio* who wrote under the pen name Hesperiophylo, had collected from various regions of Peru would have served as the foundation for such a museum.[28] Nevertheless, historical descriptions of early modern natural history collections created in Peru, and for Peru, remain relatively few.

Most of our information on collecting centers instead on accounts of Europeans gathering natural specimens and cultural curiosities in the Andes to be sent back across the Atlantic. Charles V and Philip II of Spain were great collectors, and we know that, as early as 1572, Philip II received a collection of paintings and curiosities assembled by Viceroy Toledo in Peru. As mentioned above, the viceroy also collected for himself, especially items of a European nature but made in Peru, such as ecclesiastical silver and fine linens. Items sent to Philip II were Andean in type as well as manufacture and included tunics typically worn by Andean men (*uncu*) and textile head ornaments that denoted high status (*borlas*). The king was also sent more exotic items, such as medicinal bezoar stones, "little idols" (*idolillos*), and other natural and manufactured curiosities.[29]

Natural history collections sent to Spain have received more attention, in part because the crown considered such collections to be of great scientific and economic importance and in part because the men who created them were meticulous in their documentation. The Spanish Jesuits José de Acosta (1540–1600) and Bernabé Cobo (1580–1657) were the most prominent writers on natural history in early modern Peru, though as far as we know, they did not create collections of botanical or zoological specimens.[30] Later naturalists, explorers, and collectors, such as Louis Feuillée (1660–1732), Amédée François Frézier (1682–1773), Charles-Marie de La Condamine (1701–74), José Celestino Mutis (1732–1808), Alessandro Malaspina (1754–1810), Hipólito Ruiz (1754–1816), and José Antonio Pavón (1754–1840?),[31] have been discussed at length and with insight by both Paz Cabello Carro, Daniela Bleichmar, and others.[32] These figures constitute the intellectual tradition from which Martínez Compañón drew and to which he contributed. One may reasonably assume that the bishop had some contact with Ruiz and Pavón during their 1777–88 survey of the plant life of Peru and Bolivia, and we know with certainty that, at least by 1792, the bishop had a collegial relationship with the naturalist Mutis, who directed the royal botanical expedition of the viceroyalty of Nueva Granada (Colombia) from 1783 until his death in 1808.[33] In overall form, the bishop's collections and visual encyclopedia of Trujillo were profoundly shaped by an established history of collecting in Peru and by the waves of new scientific methods arriving in South America from Europe in the mid- to late eighteenth century.

Martínez Compañón's *Trujillo del Perú*

Martínez Compañón's own collecting and documentary project began as a traditional ecclesiastical survey of the bishopric, initiated in 1781 with the dispatch of two questionnaires, which queried the state of the regional churches, as well as the area's natural resources, local industries, and cultural traditions.[34] The bishop might have begun his project with the spirit and methodology of a traditional *visita*, but, by the mid-1780s, his work had become something far more extensive, and much more visual, than any other American *visita*. The creation of 1400 illustrations would have been unheard of in the context of a traditional *visita*—particularly in Peru, where, unlike in Mexico, very few included images of any kind, even maps.[35]

One of the most important aspects of the bishop's pastoral work was regional reform. During his tenure, he initiated an array of civic works, including the building of new roads, churches, and dozens of new schools for Native children. Many of these Enlightenment-era reforms remained only at the blueprint stage, but the impetus behind the detailed plans was a desire to create what Emily Berquist has called a "practical utopia."[36] The employment of Native or local illustrators in his documentary project may also be understood as part of the bishop's greater reform project and his desire to join political economy with natural history.

Furthermore, one may also consider Martínez Compañón's work more broadly within the context of the eighteenth-century Bourbon reforms, which sought to reassess and strengthen Spanish American administration and the economic exploitation of natural resources. Of particular interest to the Bourbon crown was the cinchona (or *cascarilla*) plant, which one finds among the bishop's many botanical illustrations and in the 1788 inventory of objects sent to Madrid.[37] Quinine extracted from cinchona bark was used to treat malaria and other tropical fevers since at least the seventeenth century.[38] Samples of minerals and metals from northern Peru that the bishop also remitted to Spain reflect the late eighteenth-century Bourbon interest in identifying new and potentially lucrative mines in the Americas.[39] An illustration of the Hualgayoc mines near Cajamarca is found in the bishop's first volume of drawings and again in the second volume.[40] The repetition of this drawing underscores the importance of these mines to the bishop and the crown at the time.

In addition to scientific and economic materials, Martínez Compañón collected many objects from the ancient Andean past. Elsewhere we argue that an essential impetus behind this part of the bishop's work was his awareness of Charles III's interest in antiquities.[41] The monarch's sponsorship of the excavations at Heculaneum and Pompeii earlier in the eighteenth century was well known by the late 1760s, and Martínez Compañón was clearly interested in discovering his own American antiquity on the north coast of Peru. Several royal orders commanding the collection of natural history specimens were issued from Madrid in the eighteenth century, but a request drawn up in 1777 by Antonio de Ulloa for the second Royal Cabinet was particularly specific in its requests for the reconnaissance of ruins and the collection of ancient objects.[42]

Martínez Compañón's documentation of the pre-Hispanic ruins and antiquuities of northern Peru may have been directly influenced by the work of La Condamine and the Spanish naval officers, Jorge Juan and Antonio de Ulloa, whose *Relación histórica* one finds in the bishop's library.[43] Although Juan and Ulloa's account and the bishop's work address many of the same types of subjects, the former was less concerned with Native art and artifacts and featured far fewer images than the latter. One might also compare Martínez Compañón's illustrations of Andean artifacts to an engraving from Frézier's *Relation du voyage*, which includes a rendering of three prehispanic ceramic vessels (Figure 12.3).[44] Unlike Martínez Compañón's illustrations, this image was derived from the popular genre of Inca portraits rather than based on observation and collections.

The extraordinary visuality of Martínez Compañón's documentary work may be a reflection of the bishop's engagement with broader Enlightenment-era concerns. The remarkable scope of his project reflects the expansive scientific and cultural interests of his day, as well as those of his predecessors such as Cassiano dal Pozzo. The range and thoroughness of his nine volumes speaks not only to an impetus to reform a world but also to encapsulate it.[45] The bishop may have modeled the encyclopedic—often alphabetic—layout of his multiple volumes of illustrations on the French *Encyclopédie* of Denis Diderot and Jean Le Rond d'Alembert, whose multiple volumes of text and plates circulated widely after their publication between 1754 and 1772.[46] Shared concerns and conventions are most evident in the depictions of natural history—especially

A Incas, ou Roy du Perou. B Coia ou Reine. ces deux figures ont été dessinées
d'après vn tableau fait par les jndiens du Cusco
C jndien du Perou D jndienne portant la mantilla E leurs maisons.
F moitié du plan de la Bicharra ou fourneau abruler de l'herbe Icho G profil de Bicharra
H differentes formes de vases trouves dans les tombeaux des anciens jndiens

12.3. The Incas of Peru, including ceramics from pre-Hispanic tombs (H), in
Amédée-François Frézier, *Relation du voyage aux côtes du Chily et du Perou, fait
pendant les annes 1712, 1713 & 1714* (Paris, 1732), pl. 31, opposite p. 247. Houghton
Library, Typ 715.32.405.

botany—and in the images of industry and technology in the two sets of
works.[47]

Yet, despite its identification as a product of Enlightenment-era traditions
of scholarship, Martínez Compañón's work also contains some evidence of an
antiquated interest in the prodigious, the monstrous, and the miraculous that

creates an intellectual tension in the illustrated volumes. For the most part, the natural history illustrations are highly conventional, and specimens are presented according to strict visual formulae (for example, Figure 12.2). But the fantastic occasionally commingles with the rational as traces of the preternatural linger within the bishop's collection of naturalist illustrations.

For example, in the sixth volume, among the drawings of reptiles and snakes, one finds a fantastic depiction of a bicephalic serpent, called *omeco-machacuai* (Quechua meaning "howler-monkey snake"), which twists around a thorny *catahua* tree [*Hura crepitans* or sandbox wood] and at once consumes both a monkey at top and a small deer below (Figure 12.4).[48] The mythical bicephalic serpent called Machacuay or Amaru was revered as a dangerous entity and represented by a dark cloud constellation in pre-Hispanic Peru.[49] Without an explanatory caption or accompanying text, one is left to wonder how to interpret an image like this. Might the legendary beast in the illustration be a vision brought on by the catahua tree or its leaf—so clearly illustrated at right? Is the Indian ingesting some form of this plant that he has harvested (note the basket in his hand and the knife on the ground beside him)? Ethnographic evidence suggests that the plant is sometimes mixed into hallucinogenic *ayahuasca* and consumed in order to gain special access to shamanic knowledge.[50] The ethnobotanical and ethnopharmaceutical uses of catahua leaves, seeds, and resin are many.[51] The resin is a powerful fish poison, strong enough to kill an anaconda (or even an omeco-machacuai?). In his 1788 inventory of botanical specimens remitted to Spain, Martínez Compañón notes that the sap of the catahua plant is used by the Peruvian Indians to facilitate the extraction of carious teeth.[52] If the bark is punctured, caustic sap can spurt out, burn the skin, and cause temporary blindness if it contacts the eyes. The danger of this aggressive tree covered in exaggerated spikes can be understood in the image as analogous to that of the ferocious monkey-and-deer-eating snake. Whatever the precise relationship between the fantastic serpent, poisonous tree, and attentive Indian, what is certain is that such an image of a monstrous, mythological creature is considerably removed from the more academic presentations of flora and fauna elsewhere in the volume and in other naturalist works of the late eighteenth century.

Monsters and prodigies appear occasionally elsewhere in the bishop's otherwise normalized series of plants and animals. At the end of the seventh volume, the volume on birds, one encounters the image of a small, pathetic body of a young bird with two wings and four legs, which is simply glossed "monstrous chicken."[53] Natural marvels and monstrous creatures are relatively common in late medieval and Renaissance collections, catalogues of curiosities, and illustrated broadsides. For example, a cat with two bodies from Ulisse Aldrovandi's collection is illustrated in Lorenzo Legati's 1677 catalogue of the Museo

LISA TREVER AND JOANNE PILLSBURY

12.4. *Omeco-machacuai*, in Baltasar Jaime Martínez Compañón, *Trujillo del Perú*, vol. 6, estampa 83, Patrimonio Nacional, Spain.

Cospiano.[54] But by the late eighteenth century such popular curiosities had mostly vanished from the pages of natural history catalogues and treatises.

Nestled within the illustrations of fruit-bearing trees in the bishop's fourth volume, as if they were botanical specimens like those that come before and those that follow, one finds drawings of a "naturally formed figure of a crucifix" and "naturally formed crosses"[55] (Figures 12.5 and 12.6). Throughout the sixteenth and seventeenth centuries, plants that mimicked human forms were often pictured in books of natural history and curated in cabinets of curiosities. Human forms seen in the roots of the mandrake were especially remarked on, and these plants were sometimes illustrated as fully anthropomorphic in Renaissance herbaria.[56] Legati's catalogue of the Museo Cospiano also illustrates a root that roughly resembles a human figure and a stone marked with the cross.[57] But, by the late eighteenth century, these objects, along with other marvels, are rarely found in scholarly volumes.[58] There is, however, an important difference between these Italian and Peruvian examples of naturally-formed religious icons. Unlike the illustrations in the Museo Cospiano, Martínez Compañón's natural crucifix and crosses are shown planted or nestled within landscapes. Yet the planting of the crucifix is precarious at best, and one soon notices that it bears neither leaves nor fruit. Not a tree at all, the crucifix—if such a thing ever existed and was collected—appears instead as a Y-shaped branch, broken off, dried out, and perhaps curated.[59] Yet in the illustration, the gesture of planting is nevertheless important, and the crucifix is represented as if it were emerging from the Peruvian soil.

The bishop's naturally formed icons point to an archaic tradition of collecting curiosities, but their inclusion in this botanical volume may also refer to his pastoral desire to present evidence of the active hand of God in the Americas. Such images might have been out of place in other eighteenth-century naturalist works, but their presence is important within Martínez Compañón's project, which marries both scientific and ecclesiastical objectives. The bishop was probably familiar with the engraved illustration of another natural American crucifix, discovered in a cinnamon tree in the Limache Valley of Chile, which Alonso de Ovalle (1601–51) included in his *Histórica relación del reyno de Chile*, published in Rome in 1649 (Figure 12.7).[60] Ovalle explains the appearance of that natural crucifix thus: "As our faith is beginning to set roots in the New World, the creator of Nature has caused this grand and new argument to emerge in the trees themselves."[61] It is reasonable to think that the Peruvian bishop also may have included his own images of natural religious icons emerging from the Peruvian land to prove the piety of his bishopric, in which Christian icons grow just like palms and cedars. Such an argument can be seen to underlie the bishop's entire scholarly production. By placing his naturally formed crucifix and crosses here at the end of the series of wood-bearing trees (and not in his ecclesiastical or ethnographic volumes), Martínez Compañón naturalizes the occurrence of the miraculous, as if to reaffirm Augustine's theology, which saw all forms of nature as part of God's miracle, and extend it to this South American bishopric.[62]

E. 92

Figura de un Crucifijo naturalmᵗᵉ formada.

12.5. "Naturally formed crucifix," in Baltasar Jaime Martínez Compañón, *Trujillo del Perú*, vol. 4, f. 92. Patrimonio Nacional, Spain.

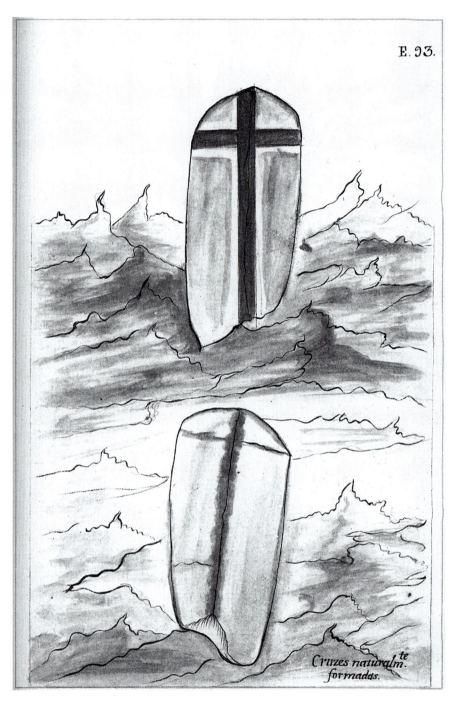

12.6. "Naturally formed crosses," in Baltasar Jaime Martínez Compañón, *Trujillo del Perú*, vol. 4, f. 93. Patrimonio Nacional, Spain.

Vera Effigies cuiusdam Arboris, quæ in hunc modum et figurā crucis et Crucifixi creuiße inuenta est in Regno Chilēnsi in America, vbi in valle Limache colitur magña populi deuotione ab anno Dñi 1634.

12.7. The Crucifix of Limache, Chile, in Alonso de Ovalle, *Histórica relación del reyno de Chile* (Rome, 1646), opposite p. 58. Houghton Library, *SC6.Ov145.646h.

Both creole and indigenous concerns and forms of knowledge are elsewhere apparent in Martínez Compañón's collection of illustrations. As already observed, the nomenclature of plants and animals does not follow the Linnaean system but often draws on indigenous language and knowledge.[63] For example, an illustration of a liana is labeled with its Quechua name *ampihuasca* (Figure

12.2),[64] but only in the description of a botanical sample in the 1788 inventory does one find a Spanish translation of the name of the South American plant: "bejuco del veneno" (venomous liana), which Indians use to poison their hunting arrows.[65] As Susan Scott Parrish writes, in colonial American natural history, the Native American embodies a dangerous, double role: at once possessor of knowledge and also object of scientific scrutiny.[66] Such a doubling of knowledge of/by Native Americans is evidenced in Martínez Compañón's opus by two pairs of images found in the volume on fish and in the ethnographic volume.[67] A nearly identical pair of images of Indians fishing appears in both volumes, although the pair in the ethnographic volume appears to have been copied by a different artist, *after* the pair in the volume on marine life. In the marine volume, the images are indexed as "Fishing net" and "a different kind of fishing net,"[68] but in the ethnographic volume these same images are both labeled "*Indians* fishing with a net" (our emphasis).[69] The object of illustration thus shifts from the technology of fishing (as known and practiced by Peruvian Indians) to the indigenous fishermen themselves. The doubling of knowledge by/of the Indians is brought into focus by the repetition of images across this classificatory divide. If the pair of fishing images was indeed first drawn for the volume on fish (and only later included to represent Indians fishing), then the agency of the Indians as keepers of knowledge and collaborators in the bishop's documentary project can be understood to precede their examination as ethnographic objects. Images like these reveal that indigenous collaborators were more than informants, or even illustrators, and were fundamental in the formation of Martínez Compañón's graphic presentation of his Peruvian diocese.

Although the impetus for the creation of Martínez Compañón's physical and visual collections was Charles III's call for collections from the New World viceroyalties, there is something qualitatively different about the bishop's *Trujillo del Perú* in its profound emphasis on visual production. The nine volumes of watercolors are not only unlike the works of his predecessors in Peru, but they are also unlike those of his contemporaries in Mexico—individuals who were responding to a similar set of impulses from Spain and the Americas.[70] The vast scope and intensely visual character of Martínez Compañón's opus likely developed out of his keen personal interests in, and knowledge of, Enlightenment-era scholarship. Nevertheless, despite its many debts to European books and illustrations, Martínez Compañón's illustrated museum also exhibits the important contributions and concerns of creole and indigenous Peruvian collaborators. Sent to Spain in 1803, these volumes disappeared into the royal library until their rediscovery in the late nineteenth century. Now published in its entirety, Martínez Compañón's graphic collection remains a largely untapped source of visual information on late-eighteenth-century Peru. This late colonial work must be approached, however, with a critical eye and appreciation of the particular motivations and intellectual traditions—both imperial and popular, Bourbon and Peruvian, scientific and theological—that informed its production.

CHAPTER 13

—꩜—

Europe Rediscovers Latin America: Collecting Artifacts and Views in the First Decades of the Nineteenth Century

Pascal Riviale

The disciplines of anthropology and archaeology underwent a spectacular development in the nineteenth century: the entire world could now be studied and classified. A major focus of this ambitious scientific project was the Americas. The artifacts and images that explorers and collectors brought back from the Americas documented peoples and cultures that were profoundly different from anything known in Europe.

Due to colonial Spain's and Portugal's efforts to control the circulation of ideas, merchandise, and information between Latin America and Europe, little information about the indigenous history of Latin America reached Europe before the early nineteenth century.[1] Countries such as France had sent observers such as Louis Feuillée and Amédée François Frézier to South America and had participated in a few scientific expeditions, such as those led by Charles-Marie de Lacondamine and Joseph Dombey in the eighteenth century, but these travelers gathered only fragmentary data. As a consequence, European has to rely chiefly on old Spanish chronicles and scarce travel accounts to form an impression of the southerly part of the New World.

In the first decades of the nineteenth century, as the countries of Latin America achieved independence, the situation changed drastically: European nations, as well as the United States, saw the possibility of direct access to those countries and began to establish independent relationships with the new republics. In that sense, this period witnessed a kind of rediscovery of Latin America.

Most of Europe believed that Spain had neglected the scientific study of its colonies, a belief that was reinforced by the so-called black legend, which depicted Spanish rule in the New World as brutal, fanatical, superstitious, and anti-intellectual. Thus, in the first decades of the nineteenth century, archeologists and ethnographers from countries such as Great Britain, France, and the United States saw themselves as having to embark on a task previously neglected: the scientific exploration of America. This chapter addresses the following questions: What were the principal motivations for this research? How did research take place? What were the major results of the collecting activities of this period?

New Republics Opened to New Appetites: The Political and Scientific Context

Just after the emancipation of the Latin American republics, European powers (mainly Great Britain, France, and Prussia) sought to substitute for the old colonial masters. They sent diplomatic missions to make contact with the new governments; financial investors established themselves in the cities; and adventurers began to explore the lands with an eye toward commercial gain. In Mexico and Peru, most of the mining industry fell into the hands of European capitalists. In Brazil, Prince Regent João VI and, later, Emperor Pedro I opened the country to new ideas and foreign investors. Within a few years, the European presence was considerable.

In the wake of the naval expeditions of James Cook, Louis-Antoine de Bougainville, Jean-François de Lapérouse, and other eighteenth-century navigators, a new wave of expeditions was organized to explore the natural resources and the historical and anthropological mysteries of this part of the world. The diversity and strangeness of the peoples encountered threw doubt on existing anthropological theories. Various authors defended the idea of the plurality of human races, and even human species, and proposed different classifications of humans.[2] Eager to confirm or confound these theories, researchers collected a variety of scientific material—mainly skulls, but also artifacts—that Europeans could use to interpret the cultural origins of American peoples.

This desire to gather anthropological specimens emerged within a much larger program for a systematic inventory of the natural world, a program initiated in the eighteenth century in the belief that collecting specimens from the three kingdoms of nature (animal, vegetable, and mineral) would lead to a global classification system that in turn would enable humans to understand the origin, organization, and future of the world.

Philadelphian Samuel George Morton systematically measured series of skulls brought to him by travelers and navigators. His studies seemed to confirm the hypothesis of a specific human species in the Americas, and his work had a major influence on subsequent anthropological theories and research.[3] For instance, the peculiar shape of some skulls discovered by travelers in Peru and Bolivia was misinterpreted as evidence of a physically distinct people (in fact, the strange shapes were the result of artificial deformations practiced by pre-Columbian populations in the Andes). British diplomat Joseph Barclay Pentland was one of the first to note this curiosity; he considered South Americans to be a distinct race of humans, and Morton used Pentland's observations to support his theories.[4]

The debates on the classification of humans continued until the second half of the nineteenth century. James Cowle Prichard defended the unity of human species but noted the extraordinary shape of some Andean skulls (Figure 13.1). Dr. Peter Wilhelm Lund wrote to the Geographical Society of Paris in 1844 to declare that the human remains he had discovered in Lagoa Santa (Brazil) had the specific characteristics of the American race and were associated with skeletons of extinct gigantic animals, thus proving the extraordinary antiquity of these people.[5]

The descriptions and images brought to Europe by travelers testified to the diversity, complexity, and originality of ecosystems in the New World. An Amazon rain forest scene drawn in Brazil by the Count of Clarac in 1817 showed Indians walking through gigantic luxuriant vegetation such as one might imagine to have been the landscape at the beginning of humanity. The scene became a model for the representation of tropical nature in the next decades, inspiring artists such as those produced by Henri Taunay, Jean-Baptiste Debret, Araujo Porto-Alegre, and Johann Moritz Rugendas (Figure 13.2).[6]

Given the physical dissimilarities between the Old and the New Worlds, it was not absurd to believe very specific human races had emerged in America. Even so, some paleontologists studying prehistoric remains discovered in Europe in the 1820s and 1830s were able to establish a possible connection between these remains and those found in the Americas:

> We learned from M. Coupery that seven canoes displaying great similarity to the pirogues of the savages from America were discovered at the bottom of a peat bog, in England. This fact, of which we have another example in Lancashire, added to the carib heads discovered in prehistoric alluvial deposits in various countries, seems to prove that the first inhabitants of the world belonged to this race, which is now confined to the torrid zone.[7]

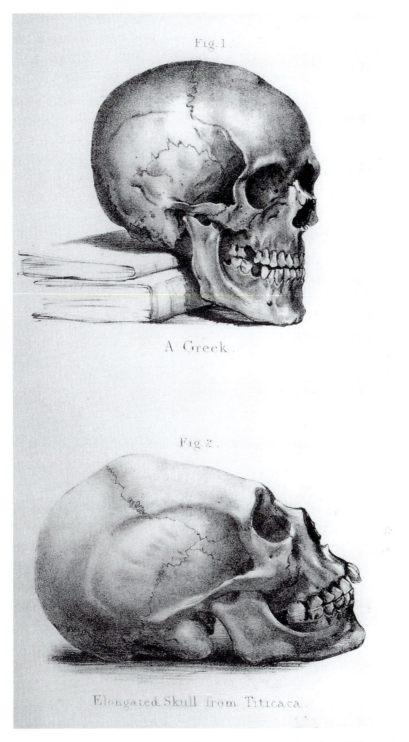

Fig. 1.

A Greek.

Fig. 2.

Elongated Skull from Titicaca.

13.1. Comparison between a Greek skull and an elongated skull from Titicaca, in James Cowles Prichard, *Researches in the Physical History of Mankind* (London: Sherwood, Gilbert, and Piper, 1836), vol. 1, figs. 1 and 2.

13.2. "Forêt vierge près de Manqueritipa," lithography by A. Joly, in Johan Moritz Rugendas, *Voyage pittoresque dans le Brésil* (Paris: Engelmann, 1835).

As physical anthropology developed, so too did ethnology and ethnography during these years. William Edwards founded the Société Ethnologique in Paris in 1839 to promote his conception of ethnology as the "science of races," a science built on other disciplines such as anatomy, geography, linguistics, ethnography, and history. The mission of the society was to gather, coordinate, and publish "observations that help know the different races of men that are scattered on the Earth."[8] Similar societies were founded throughout Europe and quickly developed a network to exchange information on anthropological matters.

A few decades after the first contacts were made by Europeans with people living in the Pacific islands, navigators observed dramatic changes in these societies, which were at risk of imminent extinction. In France in the 1820s, intellectuals and scientists proposed the foundation of a museum that would serve as a "conservatory of human cultures": it would contain artifacts from around the

PASCAL RIVIALE

world and would allow future scientists to study those peoples who were fast disappearing:

> Today the appearance of the globe offers a general tendency to present a nearly European physiognomy . . . how useful would it be to conserve for the future monuments of an ever-changing industrial state! In a century how shall we be able to know about the arts of a people who still exists today, but will have disappeared tomorrow.[9]

This intellectual and scientific trend led to the creation of the Naval Museum in the Louvre Palace in 1830. Although this museum was created to celebrate the glory of the French marine forces, a large section was dedicated to the "primitive" and faraway cultures encountered by naval expeditions—especially French ones.[10] In 1850, the institution was transformed into a genuine ethnographical museum. Similar repositories were being constructed in other parts of Europe: in 1845, the Museum of American Antiquities was created in Copenhagen by Charles Rafn (based on a preexisting collection of Eskimo artifacts, it was quickly expanded through the acquisition of antiquities from North America, Mexico, the Caribbean, Peru, and Brazil); in 1847, the Museum of Ancient Weapons, Armors, and Art Objects, founded in Brussels in 1835, was transformed into the Royal Museum of Armors, Antiquities, and Ethnology; in Great Britain, various scientific societies set up their own museums. As early as 1824, William Bullock opened a Mexican museum in London that promoted public interest in pre-Columbian antiquities.[11]

The study of ancient civilizations from Mexico and Central and South America was directly affected by the emergence of Egyptology. After the Napoleon Bonaparte's military expedition in Egypt and Jean-François Champollion's studies of the hieroglyphic system, interest in archaeological activities in Egypt and, more generally, in the whole Middle East increased, as did the number of travelers with a taste for antiquities.[12] In this new environment, the study of the pre-Columbian history of America took on a different meaning. Although Spanish chronicles of American civilizations described marvelous cities, incredible treasures, and powerful empires, the origin of these cultures had not been satisfactorily explained by chroniclers and historians. In the early nineteenth century, various authors began to compare people from the New World with antique civilizations from Egypt and the Near or Middle Orient, finding amazing points of similarity. Such discoveries stimulated the appetite for collecting and bringing back to Europe more American documents and artifacts to feed studies; further explorations, some researchers anticipated, would uncover the

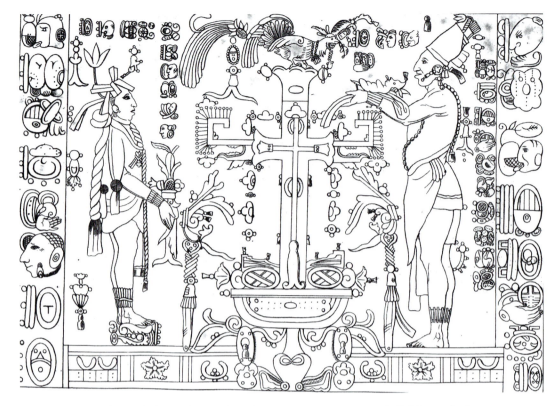

13.3. "Bas relief de Palenque; le milieu est occupé par une croix," lithography by Mantoux, in David Baillie Warden, *Recherches sur les antiquités des Etats-Unis de l'Amérique Septentrionale* (Paris: Everat, 1827), pl. XVII.

mystery of the existence of advanced civilizations in the New World. The discovery of Mayan ruins and their artworks stirred great speculation. European archeologists could not resist the temptation to compare Mayan glyphs with Egyptian hieroglyphic writing, and the discovery of a relief from Palenque with a cross excited the imagination of more than one historian (Figure 13.3).

First Investigations in Latin America

The opening of the borders of Latin American nations and the competition between industrial powers to conquer those new commercial markets provoked an increasing flow of travelers, migrants, and adventurers to America. At the same time, European nations were sending naval vessels to the Atlantic and Pacific coasts to protect their diplomatic and commercial interests; more than a few of the officers aboard the warships joined in the fashion for collecting pre-Columbian artifacts and either sent accounts of their discoveries to Europe or donated what they had found to European learned societies.

The French Naval Pacific Station, for instance, was established between 1821 and 1823, creating a permanent French naval presence along the Pacific coast of America. Officers and crew members took advantage of their ports of call to collect every curiosity they could find. For example, in 1838, France was engaged in a serious diplomatic conflict with Mexico and flexed its military muscle by sending its fleet to Fort San Juan de Ulloa, near Veracruz. Sometime later, Captain Cosmao Dumanoir brought back to France a fine collection of ceramics excavated on the Isle of Sacrificios (opposite Veracruz).

Mariners from all nations were bitten by the collecting bug. Captain Evan Nepean of the Royal Navy, for instance, followed in Dumanoir's footsteps and collected antiquities from the Isle of Sacrificios (his collection was donated to the British Museum in 1844).[13] Some of the very early Peruvian collections brought to Europe in the first part of the nineteenth century were gathered by mariners, as well as by diplomats, engineers, and merchants.[14]

Scientific institutions quickly recognized the potential in these amateur enthusiasts and began to compile compendiums of instructions for archeologically minded travelers and mariners. In 1818, the French minister of marine asked professors from the national Museum of Natural History to write directions for naval officers to guide them in their scientific research. The third edition of this guide, published in 1839, included an anthropological section.[15] Many scientific societies published their own instructions for members and correspondents. Although to us today these texts demonstrate how vague was early nineteenth-century knowledge of pre-Columbian civilizations, at the time they contributed greatly to nonprofessional enthusiasm for exploring American history and civilizations.

For example, naturalist Alcide d'Orbigny was sent to South America on an ambitious exploring journey in 1826. The French Museum of Natural History in Paris and the Musée de la céramique in Sèvres gave d'Orbigny specific guidelines instructions for gathering artifacts. As Alexandre Brongniart, director of the Musée de la céramique, recalled, "I urged him to collect for the ceramics collections of Sèvres every piece of pottery that could teach us about the state of ceramic arts among Indigenous before the conquest and in modern times."[16] After his return to France, d'Orbigny wrote a book about South American peoples that spanned various scientific fields (archaeology, anatomy, linguistics, ethnohistory, natural history). The volume would have a major impact on his contemporaries' vision of pre-Columbian history. In particular, he identified and put into archeological content the ancient Aymara ethnic group, thereby disproving part of Morton's anthropological theories about the American races.[17]

Morton's theories were also dented by archaeological activity in Mexico and Central America. Just after the colonies declared independence, a report about the pre-Columbian site of Palenque written by Antonio del Rio was published in London, revealing an unknown civilization to the European public.[18] Meanwhile the Mexican museum in London, founded by William Bullock in 1825, together with Bullock's published account of travel in Mexico, increased scientific curiosity in the region.[19] The Geographical Society of Paris organized a contest to reward the best archaeological investigation of Mexico. Several travelers and adventurers vied for the prize, including Latour-Allard, Maximilian Franck, Carl Nebel, Johann Moritz Rugendas, Jean Frederick Waldeck, Henri Baradère, and José Galindo. In addition to their attempts to explore the Mayan country, these adventurers visited various collections in Mexico City and sent their sponsoring European scientific societies accounts, descriptions, and drawings of the incredible variety of the antiquities to be found in the country.[20] A few years later, Nebel and Waldeck published travel albums that became popular for the quality of their lithographs.[21] Meanwhile, Father Baradère brought to France drawings of pre-Columbian objects and monuments (which had been made years before under the direction by Guillermo Dupaix for the king of Spain). This led to two major publications: *Mexican Antiquities*, published in London between 1831 and 1848, and *Antiquités mexicaines*, published in Paris between 1834 and 1843. These books had an immediate impact, as could be seen in a comment offered in *Annales de Philosophie Chrétienne*:

> The *Annales* have been the first to announce the importance of American discoveries, for the solution of various historical and philosophical objections made, last century, against the authority of Religion and of the Bible. . . . The new publication that we announce today compels attention by the significance of the new documents that it presents so as to support our historical beliefs, and by the beauty and the number of the plates that it contains. An ancient world, formerly hidden from everybody's eyes, is now, so to speak, revealed to our eyes, put down on paper, in an imperishable manner, in this great historical museum.[22]

The editors of *Antiquités mexicaines* tried to promote an international scientific expedition to Mexico. The first voyage, the editors proclaimed, would be conducted by an "association of princes of Europe." A later proposal envisaged French and British scientists forming a Commission of Transatlantic Exploration that would also include representatives from Spain, Prussia, and Denmark: "We consider that the scientific participation of Europe is essential."[23] In the event, the *Antiquités mexicaines*' grand plans came to nothing.

Various other projects did come to fruition, however, including several supported by individual European governments. These expeditions had political as well as scientific goals and sought to demonstrate a nation's leading role in the furtherance of science. When the American John Lloyd Stephens and his British fellow-traveler Frederick Catherwood arrived in British Honduras in October 1839, British Superintendent Alexander MacDonald sent a dispatch to Colonel Secretary Lord John Russel, informing him that he, MacDonald, had organized a small expedition to beat the American to the Mayan ruins at Palenque. "The ruins form now a great object of interest among the enlightened in the United States, and I am led to understand that similar sentiments pervade the curious in Europe."[24] Patrick Walker and John Caddy reached Palenque before Stephens and sent an official report to the British administration.

The published accounts of the discoveries enhanced the already widespread interest in the area. Stephens's account, enhanced by splendid drawings by Catherwood, became wildly popular.[25] In 1841, the Austrian Emmanuel Friedrichstahl and then the American Benjamin Moore Norman visited the Mayan ruins in the same region.[26] Interest was so great that, in 1842, George Ure Skinner, a Scottish merchant living in British Honduras, proposed that the British Museum purchase Mayan ruins. (Stephens had made a similar suggestion a few years before, with the idea of founding a museum dedicated to pre-Columbian antiquities.)

Whatever their motivations, these expeditions resulted in large numbers of indigenous artifacts being shipped from Latin America to Europe. Several travelers who had participated to the contest organized by the Geographical Society of Paris brought back important collections of antiquities from Mexico to France. Latour-Allard's and Franck's collections of artifacts were acquired by the French government, while drawings associated with these antiquities were sold in London.[27] The collections were first housed in the Naval Museum and eventually formed the embryo of the Musée Américain founded in the Louvre Palace in 1850.[28]

The establishment of the Musée Américain marked the official recognition of the Americanist field of research. It also demonstrated a desire to show the public a visual representation of the "other." Engraved and lithographic plates that depicted these unknown areas and cultures formed an integral part of the collections.

Images of a New World

In 1839, when Superintendent Mac Donald wrote to Lord John Russel to announce that he had organized an expedition to Mayan ruins, he specified that "the pencil of Lieut Caddy will illustrate the journey and I am fully assured that the views taken by him will convey to your Lordship's mind a perfect idea of the appearance of Polenki [Palenque]."[29]

Since the first expeditions to America, drawings had been used to support and extend the written accounts of what the explorers had observed. In the eighteenth century, with major oceanic expeditions under way and in the broader context of science rationalization, the visual documentation of discoveries was systematized. Drawing became part of a naturalist's work. The instructions for naturalists prepared by scientific institutions in the eighteenth and nineteenth centuries did not fail to mention the value of illustrations as a means of identifying natural species observed and collected and of providing a better and more vivid understanding of the environment and peoples encountered. The habit of visually recording findings was soon extended from official expeditions to individual enterprises. Not only did travelers collect artifacts and natural specimens, but they also brought back pictures that allowed scientists and the public to visualize virtually unknown countries, their exotic peoples, and their strange customs (Figure 13.4). Some of these images were drawn on the spot or after a journey by the travelers themselves; others were purchased from local artists.[30] First intended as a personal souvenir of a journey, some of these drawings were eventually published in volumes that excited the imagination of the public. Just as ethnographic museums were developed to present extinct or unknown civilizations to the public, illustrated books (thanks to technological innovations such as lithography or wood engraving) showed Europeans what life was like in far-away lands.

Although these illustrations depicted the material culture of indigenous societies, the publishers often had to adapt to the aesthetic taste of their readers as well as to provide some context. Thus, this period saw the development of so-called picturesque albums, which included not only archaeological or ethnographical views but also landscapes and cityscapes, depictions of people dressed in local costumes or engaged in particular types of work, and romantic representations of "genre scenes."[31] Some images, like those of Chilean costumes drawn by Louis Choris during Otto von Kotzebues's expedition to the Pacific in 1815–17, were widely reproduced in popular editions and engravings for years afterward (Color Plate 11).[32]

This process of wider dissemination is illustrated by the case of travel albums executed after drawings made in Brazil in the first decades of the nineteenth century. Numerous artists and expeditions ventured to Brazil, including the French artistic mission, with painters like Jean-Baptiste Debret and Nicolas-Antoine Taunay, and the scientific missions of Prince Wied Neuwied, Johann

13.4. "Momie d'un chef coroudo [coroado]," engraving by Cazenave after a drawing by Jean-Baptiste Debret, in Ferdinand Denis, *L'Univers: Histoire et description de tous les peuples. Brésil* (Paris: Firmin-Didot, 1837).

Baptiste von Spix, and Carl Friedrich Philipp Martius and of Baron von Langsdorff. Luxurious publications of the drawings done by Debret, Neuwied, and Johann Moritz Rugendas had a great influence on the representation of indigenous Brazil: some of those images—like the "dance of the Puris"—would become "classic" ethnographical views of Brazil (Figure 13.5).[33] Other Latin

13.5. "Danse des Purys," lithography by V. Adam and V. Lecamus, in Johann Moritz Rugendas, *Voyage pittoresque dans le Brésil* (Paris: Engelmann, 1835).

American countries were equally known by the images produced and published by travelers: Mexico (Nebel, Waldeck, Claudio Linati), Peru and Bolivia (d'Orbigny), La Plata (Emeric Essex Vidal, d'Orbigny), Chile (Claude Gay, Choris).[34] Similar images were also reproduced in the illustrated press and popular publications.[35] The images were published not only to entertain but also to instruct—to teach children and families of the growing bourgeoisie what far-distant parts of the world looked like.

The taste for exotic views was widespread, and images of the Americas appeared in various media. Exhibitions with painted panoramas became popular: when William Bullock opened his exhibition "Ancient and Modern Mexico" in London in 1825, he used a panoramic backdrop of a Mexican landscape; a year later, in 1826, he exhibited a panoramic view of Mexico City in Robert Burford's Leicester Square rotunda. In 1836, Robert Burford displayed a panorama of Lima in London, based on a drawing made by Lieutenant William Smyth.[36] Panoramic wallpapers were produced using "exotic scenes." The

French manufacturers Dufour and Jean Zuber created a Brazilian panoramic wallpaper based on drawings by Rugendas.[37] Porcelain plates with American motifs, such as the "Service forestier" by the manufacture de céramiques in Sèvres, were also produced during this time.

Conclusion

The first investigations into the Americas unveiled unknown cultures. Ethnographical museums were founded using collections of artifacts brought back from these trips, while illustrated descriptions of the land and peoples of Central and South America allowed European scientists and collectors to visualize these foreign regions.[38] Museums, books, paintings, and prints presented the wider public with images of distant indigenous cultures. Artists not only produced entertaining images for a fascinated public but also provided rich documentary material for scientists working in such fields as archeology, ethnography, and natural history.[39]

These collections also contributed to an invented image of those countries. The beginnings of this "visual economy" (to use a phrase coined by Deborah Poole) contributed to the development of stereotyped representations of Latin America, some of which endured until the end of the nineteenth century.[40] A dearth of sources and the absence of a reliable scientific context, however, limited the extent to which collected artifacts and images really improved European knowledge of this part of America. Travelers were asked to gather and send collections and documents, but no one questioned the origin of these materials or the way in which collections were formed. This is why we now face so many problems with the cultural identification of these first museum collections. For instance, among the antiquities brought by d'Orbigny are mochica ceramics from the north coast of Peru—where he never ventured. These artifacts probably belonged to a very old collection gathered by a bishop of La Plata that d'Orbigny purchased when he was in Bolivia. In the first decades of the nineteenth century, Europeans were unable to imagine the actual cultural diversity of pre-Columbian Peru, so all the objects that travelers collected were considered to be part of a relatively homogeneous Peruvian culture and a relatively uncomplicated Peruvian history.

Another problem generated by the increasing interest of travelers in pre-Columbian antiquities was the plundering of archaeological sites and the production of forgeries. This forgery industry began very early. As director of the Musée de la Manufacture de céramique in Sèvres, Alexandre Brongniart ordered travelers and officials to collect ceramics for his museum. In 1844, in his *Traité des arts céramiques*, he noted that "People in Payta, on the north coast of Peru, imitate the ancient black potteries."[41] Indeed, the Peruvian collections of the museum in Sèvres still contain ceramics representing caimans that were brought by mariners in the first half of the nineteenth century and that are obviously fake. In this first phase of the rediscovery of Latin America, however, everything was so new that very few people shared Brongniart's suspicions. Even the smallest relic brought to Europe was considered to be an authentic part of a scientific treasure.

CHAPTER 14

—ᚹᚹ—

Image and Experience in the Land of Nopal and Maguey: Collecting and Portraying Mexico in Two Nineteenth-Century French Albums

Megan E. O'Neil

Pensée.
Pays du nopal et du maguey; terre de
Montezuma et de Malinche! Son souvenir
me domine! Les années prèvent finir,
ma main dessécher, mon coeur vieller,
mais moi vivant je ne l'oublierai jamais.
Pour rien au monde je ne voudrais l'effacer
de ma mémoire.
　　　　—Louis Falconnet, *Mexique, 1865* (3r)

These words mark the beginning of *Mexique, 1865*, an album of Louis Falconnet, a French officer in Emperor Maximilian's military cabinet during the French "Intervention" or occupation of Mexico in the mid-1860s, when Maximilian of Habsburg was placed by Napoleon III as the "emperor" of Mexico.[1] Although in Mexico on official business, Falconnet makes the rhetoric of the album personalized, both in this poem and in the original watercolors, hand-written descriptions, collected *cartes de visite*, and even a scrap of cloth pasted on the album's paper pages.[2] In this "Pensée," Falconnet claims that never would he efface Mexico from his memory, and the album becomes the vehicle for preserving such memory. As a material record or cache of distilled memories, the album is made into a place to store memories and to create a vision of Mexico, its people, its history, its food, and also a record of the individual's experience of it.

The idea of individual experience is made explicit by the album's organization as a journey through space and time, for the album's contents are literally framed by textual and graphic synopses of Falconnet's physical journey: a list of places visited on the first page of the album and a geologic cross-section of the route from Veracruz to Mexico inserted at the end. Yet established types—whether of people, scenes, objects, or images—mediate his experience of Mexico, and the personal experience is thus subordinated to normative classification, categorization, and representation. At times these people, places, and objects are individualized and prioritized, as in the case of known historical or political figures or of famous antiquities such as the Aztec Calendar Stone. On the other hand, the specific individual or object is usually subordinated to the type, as in the collecting and display of *tipos mexicanos* or *tipos populares*, in which the individual Mexican—primarily those of the lower working class in the urban environment—is effaced by and transformed into a category (Figure 14.1). Moreover, although set up as a personal narrative, many of the personal experiences are represented by mass-produced images or have been mediated by them, for many of the hand-painted scenes and drawings are copies, tracings, or emulations of particular images or of genres that had been used to depict Mexico's people and places and suggested or shaped what the outsider was to see, know, experience, and collect while in Mexico.

Nevertheless, this complex, rich album is laced with striking personal touches, intended to embody or represent a personal journey. What we find, then, is that the selection, use, and engagement with established imagery and mass-produced media allow Falconnet not only to engage with collective experience but also to create personal memory. A contemporaneous album, made by an unknown Frenchman, shows analogous organization and material and even contains some of the same *cartes de visite* as Falconnet's album (Figure 14.2).[3] This album is of a genre made expressly for collecting *cartes de visite*, with manufactured windows designed to hold the small photographs, which were produced and sold in considerable quantities in the second half of the nineteenth century.[4] Although much smaller and less lavish and containing only *cartes de visite*, this album includes images of what was expected to be experienced or known about Mexico.[5] And despite their vast differences, the two albums both portray the personal through the collective, distilling Mexico into a series of images that are collected and set within a personal narrative. Yet there is a rupture in the relatively formulaic representation of Mexico toward the end of the Falconnet album, when the pages turn to the execution of Maximilian.

MEGAN E. O'NEIL

14.1. Creator unknown, *Mexico—le marchand de bonbons, l'aguador et l'hacendado*, from the album *Mexique, 1865*, assembled by Louis Falconnet. Research Library, The Getty Research Institute, Los Angeles (93.R.20).

This event alters the album's subject matter, organization, and mode, changing from nostalgia for Mexico to representations of the brutal nature of the execution, with explicit and implicit criticism of Mexico as a result.

In this essay, I explore these two albums of nineteenth-century Frenchmen's experience in and representation of Mexico, in which they—one named, the other anonymous—collect and display images and memories of experiences that engage and integrate with the collective. Here, practices of collecting and display are used to satisfy desires to preserve personal memory, to create representations of Mexico, and to display or narrate particular episodes of history. The use of and engagement with established types and mass-produced materials give them the tools to create these narratives; yet the personal becomes emptied, for it is one-sided and isolated from Mexico and its people, places, and objects. In particular, collected images mediate both actual experiences and their representation, for even the hand-crafted images—such as drawings or watercolors—copy or emulate other images and their material substrates. In fact, at times the collected memories constitute more of an engagement with other images of

14.2. Creator unknown, *Aguador ou Porteur d'Eau de Mexico*, from the *Album of Mexican and French Cartes de Visite*. Research Library, The Getty Research Institute, Los Angeles (2000.R.25).

Mexico and with new media and genres (such as photography and the *carte de visite*) than with individualized persons, places, or things within Mexico; they may be personal memories, but they are removed, cushioned, and buttressed by the collective, analogous—perhaps—to the experience of the foreign diplomat moving through privileged spaces of the Mexican landscape.

Louis Falconnet's album, *Mexique, 1865*, bound in rich red leather with gold, ornamented lettering, is explicit in its nature as a travel narrative. It is a person-alized narrative, beginning with a photograph of Falconnet with a caption iden-tifying why he was in Mexico: "Mexico. 1865. Employé du Cabinet de S.M. L'Empereur Maximilien 1er."[6] The "Pensée" at the beginning (see the epigraph, at the start of this chapter) essentially lays out his goals for this album. Those words, written in calligraphic script at the bottom right of the page, comprise a romantic engagement with Mexico's present environment and past history—the motifs of nopal, maguey, Montezuma, and Malinche, two natural products and two historical indigenous people, or four elements unique to Mexico—and the visitor's desire to retain memories of this place, even as his body ages.

The next pages (4r and 4v) bear a detailed list of places in his journey, which the album follows closely, that is, until the vagaries of history—the execution of Maximilian—intervene, for although the itinerary ends in Brest, Brittany, on April 8, 1867, two months before the execution, the album addresses the execution as well. The format and placement of this itinerary are crucial, though, to establishing the album's organization, and this movement through space is emphasized by notes about geographical elevation and markers of time, including dates of embarkation and disembarkation (embarked on the *Tarn*, the name of the ship, on May 4, 1865; disembarked at Veracruz June 16, 1865) and the number of hours journey in between cities within Mexico (99 hours from Veracruz to Mexico; 53 hours from Mexico to Querétaro), which call attention to the physical and temporal movement across the landscape of Mexico. Moreover, pasted in the back cover of the album is a diagram of the elevation profile of the land route from Veracruz to Mexico City, which depicts the journey from a different perspective, here the physical movements up, down, and across Mexico's varied terrain.[7] Between these items portraying travel in decidedly different but complementary ways are numerous original watercolors, *carte de visite* photographs, handwritten narratives, and lithographs, which are deployed as material forms or symbols for memory and experience of that journey.

In the initial pages of the album, we see movement through space and time on Falconnet's journey from Europe to Mexico, with watercolor paintings of Gibraltar, showing a British fort (5r), and Santa Cruz de Teneriffe in the Canaries, showing a mountain and sea scene with the city tucked in (6r), and a map of the Greater and Lesser Antilles (7r). This map and another of Cuba, later in the album, appear to be meticulously hand-copied and colored, and a caption on the Cuba map—"copié à la Havane"—suggests that Falconnet or someone working with him was copying maps seen or collected during the journey. Like other images that they either copied or emulated, these maps allowed Falconnet to personalize and display his experiences in the album, and here the mediation is made explicit, the collecting of personal memories enacted through copying of previously existing images.

Also in this section of the journey to Mexico are four images of women in Martinique; these are the first examples in this album of "types" of people in the Americas, a genre with which the album's contents engage extensively. In particular, there are four paintings of Martinique women, two to a page on facing pages (7v and 8r). The left-hand set shows two women with their labor identified: "Blanchisseuse" and "Marchande de fruits," and the latter wears a basket of fruit on her head. Both images show dark-skinned women on white backgrounds, with bright colors adorning them: yellows in the dress of both, and red, green, pink, and yellow in the fruit of the fruit seller. The paintings in the right-hand set, in contrast, show women against dark backgrounds, as if standing against a studio backdrop, and the right-most one has a lighter glow behind her on the backdrop (Figure 14.3). Although made by hand, brush, and paint, these look very much like contemporaneous photographs, particularly the genre of types of people that were distributed in the *carte de visite* format.[8] Later in the album, Falconnet incorporates a number of *carte de visite* photographs, which portray types of people in Mexico. Here, though, he does not use a collected photograph; instead, by using paint to emulate the latest technology, he engages with the media of painting and photography and with the *carte de visite* genre and thereby further integrates his personal experiences with a larger collective, whose distributed images have enabled or inspired the creation of new images.

The next section of the album is the largest one, narrating Falconnet's experience within Mexico. Just before his disembarkation in Veracruz, Mexico (the same place where many Europeans had entered Mexico for centuries) is a hand-written narrative about the Aztecs, with a focus on their migration stories and the founding of Tenochtitlan. It is an appropriate beginning for his own travel narrative to integrate the Aztec travel narratives en route to Tenochtitlan, for Tenochtitlan—which had been transformed into the City of Mexico—was one of Falconnet's destinations as well. Starting with the Aztec past also is similar to other contemporary books and albums that do the same, as this history—even if treated cursorily—was seen to be an important part of understandings or representations of Mexico's present in a variety of contexts. In other words, the album's narrative structure—including looking to the Aztecs for the nation's origins—is modeled after the collective, from both published and unpublished accounts.

This migration story is followed by pages of watercolors and drawings of landscapes, city scenes, and people on the journey from Veracruz to Mexico City; in subject matter, material, and execution, these engage with both the personal and the collective. The first is a pencil sketch of a large boat arriving at Veracruz. The initials L.F. (Louis Falconnet) appear in the bottom right corner of the pasted-in image, identifying authorship of the scene. In this drawing are French soldiers holding backpacks and bayonets, moving from the large ship to smaller boats to take them to shore. A sign on the large ship names it as "Tarn," the name mentioned in the itinerary as well, and this detail personalizes

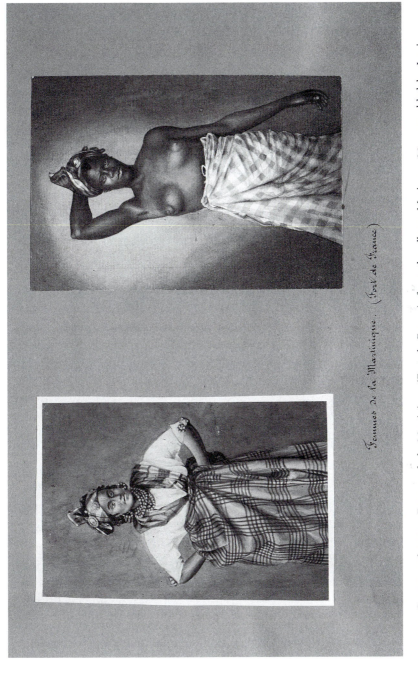

Femmes de la Martinique. (Fort de France)

14.3. Creator unknown, *Femmes de la Martinique (Fort de France)*, from the album *Mexique*, 1865, assembled by Louis Falconnet, 8r. Research Library, The Getty Research Institute, Los Angeles (93.R.20).

the image and the journey, again connecting the itinerary with the images of that journey. Following is another pencil sketch, here of the Plaza Mayor of Veracruz, with a perspective from above. A caption in pencil, added later next to the inked caption but in a similar hand, specifies "d'Hotel de Ville," identifying the image as the view one would see from a room or balcony of that building. People in various types of dress and engaging in various activities—one man on a horse, holding a flag, a water seller carrying jars, well-dressed women walking in pairs, one set with a man approaching them—populate the plaza and the sidewalks; birds fly above, and ships are visible in the distance on the water beyond the architecture. Although the particular perspective and the "d'Hotel de Ville" caption situate the artist's experience in the act of making the drawing (which thereby personalizes the scene for the viewer, who can imagine Falconnet taking a break from his official duties to capture this scene of daily life), his drawing is a modified version of Edouard Pingret's *Boceto de la Aduana de Vera Cruz*, having both a similar format and comparable depictions of architecture, figures in the plaza, and birds flying above.[9] This may have been a scene that Falconnet or an artist near him viewed and wanted to capture, but Pingret's earlier work mediated the representation.

Moreover, many of the landscape and city scenes in Falconnet's album are emulations of particular works or genres of paintings by earlier and contemporary artists working in Mexico. For example, a number of the album's paintings from this section from Veracruz to Mexico portray landscape or city scenes in which the landscape or architecture is expansive and comprises most of the composition, with very small people populating sections of these images, usually in the foreground or middle ground of the composition. Such compositional formats are similar to paintings such as the Italian painter Pedro Gualdi's *Exterior de la Catedral Metropolitana* of 1840 or the French painter Pingret's *Vista del Castillo de Chapultepec y el barrio de San Miguel* of 1852. These earlier paintings provided inspiration and form for the representation of Falconnet's journey through Mexico, another example of the personal engaging with the collective.

Following these grand landscapes are five pages (12v–15v) concerning the manufacture of pulque, an alcoholic drink native to Mexico made from the agave or maguey plant, which was made and consumed by Mexico's indigenous peoples both before and after the Spanish Conquest. Falconnet appears to have had a keen interest in pulque, whether for his personal consumption or simply because it was unique to Mexico, shown not only in these pages but also in the comments on the itinerary that mark two places in particular as renowned for their pulque: "Rancho de San Bartolo. Renommé por su pulque fino" and "San Martino. Pulque très recherché." These two locations, in fact, are the ones that appear on these pages amid other descriptions and depictions. For example, on the left of the first double-page spread (12v and 13r) is a handwritten description of *Agave Americana*, and on the right is a watercolor image of lines of agave plants at the Hacienda San Bartolo. The next double layout, whose organization is parallel to the previous one, concerns the harvesting of maguey and the fabrication of pulque: the left is a handwritten description of the process, and the right is a pencil sketch colored with watercolors, captioned "Récolte du maguey à San Martino," which shows a man using a long gourd to suck the juice from the maguey plant (Color Plate 12). This last image is one that is clearly copied from either Pingret's oil painting of *El Tlachiquero* or—more likely—from one of the widely distributed *cartes de visite* of this particular type, staged photographs that essentially copied this painting, with some variation.[10] Again, this is another example of Falconnet or a companion artist using previously established images, types, and compositions from a larger collective to capture and display memories of personal experiences.

These examples give a taste of what is a larger pattern in this album—numerous original drawings and paintings that depict places and people that Falconnet and his entourage might have seen on their journey. Their images, though, were shaped by previous images that typified Mexico and actually guided visitors' experiences—what to expect, what to see, what not to miss, or how to understand what one saw. Furthermore, as demonstrated by the images in Falconnet's album, these previously distributed images allowed visitors to give form to what they saw when in Mexico, such that the inspirations for and categorizations of experience, understanding, and representation were intertwined.

This idea becomes even clearer in the section of the album that takes place after Falconnet's arrival in Mexico City; here are a series of drawings, paintings, and photographs of *tipos populares*, images of types of working-class people, predominantly in urban environments in Mexico, including tortilla makers and sellers of water, flowers, fruit, meat, coal, and ceramics, whom visitors would have encountered as they moved through Mexico's cities.[11] In contrast to the landscape and architecture scenes, where humans were sublimated in favor of larger expanses of nature and buildings, these focus on humans, with only one or two to an image. Nevertheless, these are not individuals but types, and any human individuality is sublimated to a category. In particular, these people are unnamed and are categorized instead according to their labor, both by the captions that name them—fruit seller, bird seller, or *atole* seller—and by the items appearing in the image relating to their work (Figures 14.1, 14.2).

The album contains a wide variety of these types, which visually engage with the genre of the *tipos populares*—to the point of emulating particular ones, even as there is creativity and personalization of some of the scenes. In addition, as if to emphasize the engagement with the genre, or simply to add to the collection, the paintings and drawings are intermingled with actual *carte de visite* photographs, including one of an "Aguador" (water seller) on the same page as "Le marchand de bonbons" and "l'hacendado" (Figure 14.1). The "Aguador" was a particularly common type, having appeared in painted form (Pingret's *Aguador*, in oil) and in wax figurines, in addition to the *carte de visite* photographs.[12] Although there were multiple versions of the "Aguador" type, the "Aguador" in Falconnet's album is the same *carte de visite* as that in another album in the Getty's collections, to be discussed later (Figure 14.2). Other pages within this section feature even more *carte de visite* photographs, including "Tortilleras" and "Arriero, Conducteur de mules," that Falconnet—or someone traveling with him—collected while in Mexico. That these *carte de visite* photographs of *tipos populares* are intermingled with painted and drawn ones suggests that both collecting images of what one might see and representing what one saw could be parallel—if not intertwined—modes of narrating personal experience. Furthermore, by collecting *cartes de visite*, Falconnet also engaged in the larger practice of the collecting of these images, thus connecting with other outsiders journeying through Mexico who were intrigued by this new mode of the distribution of images.[13]

Moreover, the engagement not only with the genre but also with the medium of *carte de visite* photographs again becomes apparent with a drawing that explicitly emulates the photographic medium and the particular style of many contemporaneous *cartes de visite*. In particular, on one page of the album is a drawing—entitled "Famille Indienne"—of a man bearing a large basket of corn and a woman holding a baby on her back and carrying a water jar. The style of the drawing roughly emulates the contemporary photographic medium, particularly in the use of light and shadow and the absence of background and landscape, the figures placed against the white backdrop of the page (Figure 14.4).[14] Furthermore, the drawing depicts laboring Mexican peasants with the icons of their identity being implements of labor—nearly ubiquitous in the *carte de visite* genre. Moreover, this drawing is on the right-hand side of a double-page spread and is juxtaposed with actual *carte de visite* photographs—the "Tortilleras" and "Arriero" images mentioned above. This juxtaposition further emphasizes the engagement and play with the medium and the representation, perhaps even demonstrating the mastery of the artist's hand in emulating and recreating the newest medium.

In addition to these types of people, this section of the album also contains sets of images concerning other aspects of Mexico: antiquities from the pre-Hispanic past, fruits and vegetables, and city scenes and landscapes. Although

14.4. Creator unknown, *Famille Indienne*, from the album *Mexique, 1865*, assembled by Louis Falconnet. Research Library, The Getty Research Institute, Los Angeles (93.R.20).

the larger album organization is according to the movement of the journey through space and time, these categorical sets appear within the time spent in Mexico, inspired—most likely—by things seen and experiences had during this time.

The implicit transition between contemporary places and people and the pages on antiquities comes in the form of the Chapultepec Palace that, as noted in a caption, was Maximilian's residence. Very much a part of Falconnet's contemporary day, it forms an appropriate transition from the French-Mexican present to the Aztec past, for Chapultepec had also been the location of the Mexica Tlatoani's—or emperor's—palace when the Spaniards arrived in the sixteenth century. The section on antiquities is relatively small, seven pages compared to the thirty of the previous section, yet these again contain both the "greatest hits"—places and monuments that appeared in numerous other albums and publications as what was to be seen or experienced in Mexico—and some lesser known items.

Although Falconnet or his entourage may or may not have seen these objects—whether on the streets of Mexico or in the National Museum—the images in the album are both original paintings and drawings and ones that were mass-produced and distributed.[15] For example, the first image is the Aztec Calendar or Sun Stone, identified in captions both as "El Calendario. Le Calendrier" and "Piedra del Sacrificio," making reference to the Mexica practice of human sacrifice. The Calendar Stone was certainly the most famous and published of all pre-Hispanic New World monuments—both in the nineteenth century and today. Discovered in the Mexico City Zocalo in 1790, it was displayed for years on the side of the cathedral in the city's center (until it was moved to the National Museum in 1885) and was one of the not-to-miss attractions for locals and tourists alike. By the time of this album, circa 1865–67, a cast of the Calendar Stone—along with one of the Coatlicue sculpture—had been displayed in England (at William Bullock's Egyptian Hall in London in 1824) and had been published numerous times in Mexico, Europe, and the United States.[16] The Calendar Stone in Falconnet's album, in fact, appears to be a lithograph removed from one of these books; on the opposite page is a handwritten description of the monument.

The last monument in this antiquities section is another sculpture of widespread distribution, the Coatlicue sculpture, which appears in an original drawing. This monument is a gruesome sculpture with human hands, hearts, and a skull hanging from the necklace of this large, decapitated creature whose skirt is of serpents and whose hands and feet end in large claws. The lines of this drawing of Coatlicue are less sure than those of the other drawings and paintings of places and people in the album. This likely is the result of the Aztec aesthetic confounding this artist, for the imagery and manner of representation contrast greatly with the romantic landscapes and genre scenes elsewhere in the album.

The album includes another set of pre-Hispanic objects—mostly figurines—whose outlines are penned on a large piece of paper that has been folded into fourths and taped into the album (Figure 14.5). On this paper are drawings of twelve objects from the ancient Maya civilization (though not identified as such), arranged as if on display. Yet this drawing is a copy of another artist's work, the lines traced from a contemporary lithograph (from 1865), its production thus analogous to many other drawings and paintings in the Falconnet album.[17] On the facing page are two *cartes de visite*, each with three smaller-scale antiquities. The left card has three Aztec sculptures (though they are unidentified in the album) that were drawn and then photographed to produce the *carte de visite*. The card on the right has three small photographed figurines, probably made of ceramic, at least one a nineteenth-century version of a pre-Hispanic figurine. This right-hand card with the three figurines is similar to a card in another French album, to be discussed later, and may well have been a popular *carte de visite*. In both albums, these are unidentified and simply stand in for pre-Hispanic objects, more generalized and less particular objects than the renowned Calendar Stone and Coatlicue sculptures.

In contrast to the unidentified figurines in the *cartes de visite*, the objects on the fold-out drawing are numbered, and a legend below attempts to identify each of them (for example, "1, Chef Aztèque . . . 5, Femme en terre cuite . . . 9, Enfant du soleil . . . 11, Soldat jetant le cri de guerre"). The numbering and labeling of the objects are similar to the 1865 image from which it may have been copied, though the numbers are rearranged and the identifications changed. Number 1, for example, is labeled as "Chef Aztèque," although the text accompanying the 1865 image identifies the source of these objects as Jonuta and connects the ruins and figurines of that region to others in southern Mexico and Yucatán (such as Palenque, Uxmal, and Mayapan).[18] These places are now known to be from the ancient Maya civilization, though the confusion and blending of pre-Hispanic cultures in the nineteenth century was not uncommon. Although there were distinctions coming to the fore between the Aztec and Maya regions, for example, there was still much progress to be made concerning chronological associations of the various cultures and their relationships to modern cultures and languages, and it was not uncommon for pre-Hispanic objects to be identified as Aztec, regardless of their actual cultural or geographical provenance. An additional example of this practice appears in another image of pre-Hispanic objects in the Falconnet album: a painting of three vessels the artist may have seen in the National Museum that was placed

14.5. Creator unknown, antiquities [title devised] from the album *Mexique*, 1865, assembled by Louis Falconnet. Research Library, The Getty Research Institute, Los Angeles (93.R.20).

in the album next to the Coatlicue image. Although identified as "Aztèques," these three vessels actually come from northern Mexico, from in or around the site of Casas Grandes, outside the Aztec Empire. It would not be until the late nineteenth century that we see more deliberate attempts to distinguish antiquities from one another, both because of advances in science, anthropology, ethnology, and archaeology and recognition of regional distinctions and the diverse makeup of Mexico.[19]

The last set of images in the Mexico City section concerns Mexican fruits and vegetables, with original watercolors of cherimoya (originally an Andean fruit), avocado, and chiles, among others. Each is shown with attention to detail, and most of the fruits are shown both whole and peeled, to show both exterior and interior of the plants, thereby following older traditions of botanical illustrations (of the type Daniela Bleichmar discusses in her chapter in this volume). This emulation of scientific illustration is yet another example of Falconnet (and his companion artist or artists) engaging with other forms of representation, which give the visual vocabulary to represent sights and experiences from the Mexican journey.

After these series of people, objects, and plants in Mexico City, the album resumes its movement through space, with a set of paintings of places, people, and activities taking place in and around Querétaro. Here we see much texture and variety of both material and representation and get more of an idea of *place*, personalized through Falconnet's time in Querétaro, which as a place is allowed to take on its own character, similar to but different from Mexico City, even as some of the people in the Querétaro section are again reproduced though types, as in the "Aguador," "Indien jouant la cuerda," and the "Garçon de boucheries" [55r]. These three images have been pasted on the same page of the album and are made up of a combination of media: the "Indien jouant la cuerda," which is centered on the page, is an original drawing, and the other two are *carte de visite* photographs, the "Aguador" being one of the most popular of this series of types. Notably, this version of the "Aguador" *carte de visite* is an alternate version, different from the one in the Mexico section, for here the man bears his water jugs on a cart rather than on his body.

The next section of the album moves more rapidly through space and time, for it covers Falconnet's departure from Mexico and return to France by way of Cuba and Madeira. Before the album's departure from Mexican territory, though, are a few pages concerning the Battle of Camerone, which had taken place near Puebla in 1863, a legendary battle for the French in Mexico.[20] Falconnet was not in Mexico when this battle took place, but it had become part of his personal experience, for it was an event of major significance from the collective experience of the French Foreign Legion.

Falconnet's departure from Mexican territory is narrated through a map of Cuba and woodcuts of Havana, Cuba, and Funchal, Madeira; these correspond to the "retour en France" on February 17, 1867, of his stated itinerary and are parallel to the images of Gibraltar and Santa Cruz de Teneriffe, from the beginning of his journey. With this set of images, then, the album returns more explicitly to the physical and personal mode of the journey through space and time. And as in the rest of the album, the stops in this journey are represented through engagement with previously established or mass-produced images, such as a map of the Island of Cuba, which bears the caption "Copié à la Havane," and woodcuts of the Havana cathedral and an aerial view of Havana. The inscription "Copié à la Havane" makes explicit the interaction between the personal and the collective that I have argued fills this album. In these many examples, both implicit and explicit, collective experience and representation are used to mediate and represent the personal experience, aiding in the act of representation for the stated purpose of retaining personal memories.

Falconnet's journey is now completed, but the album is not finished, taking on a direction not expected in the meticulous recording of places on the itinerary at the beginning of the album, which ended at Brest, Brittany, on April 8, 1867. In the last third of the album are materials related to the execution of Maximilian, which took place on June 19, 1867. Although Falconnet was in Mexico as part of Maximilian's cabinet, Maximilian had played an extremely small part in the earlier sections of the album. This section, therefore, embodies a severe shift of focus, concentrating on historical particulars as opposed to views and types seen or experienced within Mexico. Moreover, even though Falconnet had left Mexico by the time of Maximilian's execution, it had become part of his Mexican experience.

Nevertheless, as opposed to the lovingly detailed and singular watercolors and drawings of the previous sections of the album, Falconnet relies on mass-produced *carte de visite* photographs and collected memorabilia in order to tell Maximilian's and his companions' story.[21] These include *cartes de visite* of Maximilian and Carlota and of other individuals, places, or things associated with the execution: the conservative Mexican generals executed with Maximilian, the site of the execution, Edouard Manet's painting of the execution, the firing squad, and Maximilian's bullet-ridden vest, in addition to Benito Juárez and Ignacio Comonfort, Mexicans who opposed the French presence in Mexico.[22] Although Falconnet does not record his own opinion of this event, he did insert a French newspaper clipping that is most critical of Mexico, "ce malheureux pays," stating that "L'exécution de l'infortune Maximilien vient de marquer le Mexique d'un sceau funèbre et d'une réprobation universelle." Finally, on one of the last pages is the *carte de visite* of Carlotta mourning Maximilian.

This assemblage of Maximilian memorabilia and photographs is followed by blank pages, as if there was nothing more to be narrated about Mexico or this major rupture in France's relations with Mexico.

Inside the album's back cover, though, are two more items. These are large foldouts, one a reproduction of a postconquest Aztec calendar diagram (the original owned by Frenchman Eugène Boban), the other an elevation profile of the land route from Veracruz to Mexico City. Both are fitting ends to this travel narrative, whose overall structure was of an individual moving through the time and space of a journey. In particular, although Falconnet likely did not know this, the Aztec Calendar diagram represents movement through time as a movement through the physical space of the universe. The elevation diagram, on the other hand, is a schematic representation of the journey Falconnet made and depicted in the first half of his album, and the dramatic changes in elevation make his experiences all the more impressive. Again, though, this elevation diagram results from someone else's experience of the landscape, which has been transformed into a scientific abstraction of it; like many other images in the album, this image from the collective fittingly complements Falconnet's personal narrative.

Whereas the album's ending summarizes the journey itself, recall that the album began with a poem about memory. These opening and closing materials meaningfully complement the materials on the inside, which are organized according to the time and location in which Falconnet and his entourage experienced them. These materials include both collected photographs and original paintings and drawings that were inspired or mediated by other images, some of them widely distributed. In this album, then, we see the intersection of personal and collective memory and experience, both in how the collective experience may drive the personal—steering someone to visit and see certain places, people, or things—and how collective experiences and representations allow individuals to make sense of their own experiences and find a way to preserve them, such that mass-produced memories in the end become quite personal. Kept in his home or parlor, perhaps, this assemblage of items could have helped Falconnet codify and preserve his own memories, so that Mexico, the land of nopal and maguey, as he called it, would not be effaced from his memory.

Another album—also in the Research Library of the Getty Research Institute—drives this point home much more poignantly, for it is made up only of mass-produced *carte de visite* photographs. Although functioning as a memory book for an individual's experience in—or about—Mexico, it is comprised only of collected images and is very much outside space, place, and even time, as its sections cover what were considered highlights of Mexican history, people, and places, thereby both different from and similar to Falconnet's album.

The *Album of Mexican and French Cartes de Visite* is a small album bound in leather with a gold clasp and contains *cartes de visite* from Mexico in the 1860s and France in the 1880s. The compiler is unidentified and may have traveled to Mexico as part of the French Intervention or was simply interested in Mexico. The album is organized into five sections, though this organization is implicit, with no section titles or textual explanations, other than short captions identifying the photographs. The album in a way serves as a travel narrative, recording elements from Mexico (and, later, from France), but it is organized not spatially or chronologically, as if through a journey, but by implicit categories. The categories within the Mexican section of the album are the following: Mexican antiquities/the pre-Hispanic past; Mexican historical and political figures from the nineteenth century; and *tipos Mexicanos*, similar categories to those interspersed within Falconnet's travel narrative. The French section is comprised first of French historical and political figures from the eighteenth century and then of what appear to be personal relations, including the compiler's grandfather in a photograph dated 1880.

The first section (1r–3r) is comprised of *carte de visite* photographs of objects from or about the ancient Mexican past, here only referred to as "Aztec." Beginning the album in the pre-Hispanic past provides a foundation and historical depth for the place of Mexico, rooted in an ancient, romantic, exotic Aztec past. As I mentioned earlier, such a beginning is not uncommon for such albums or books about Mexican history in general and is analogous to Falconnet's beginning his narrative with an account of the Aztec migrations. Two pictures portray wax figurines—collectibles themselves—of what are called a "Dieu Astèque" and a "Princesse Astèque," and the "Aztec God" has been classicized, for he wears what appear to be Greek hunting gear and a shield with a lion face (Figure 14.6).[23] These open (1r) and close (3r) this section, and between them are photographs of antiquities, some generalized and some particularized. First are two cards of "Idoles Astèques," each with three terra cotta figurines set next to each other, similar to one of the *cartes de visite* in Falconnet's album. Some—if not all—are modern productions and may have been sold either as copies of ancient figurines or as authentic antiquities. Regardless, these are generalized objects and are presented simply as types of objects grouped together with other objects of the very same type. Undoubtedly, they also were collected as such generalized types, without much concern to particularities of culture, chronology, or meaning. On the other hand, page 2v contains the "Calendrier Astèque," the Aztec Calendar Stone or Sun Stone, one of the most famous of New World pre-Hispanic monuments, which also had been in Falconnet's album and likely appeared in other personal albums as well (Figure 14.6).

　　　　　MEGAN E. O'NEIL

Mexique   Mexique

Calendrier Astèque   Princesse Astèque

14.6. Creator unknown, *Calendrier Astèque* and *Princesse Astèque*, from the *Album of Mexican and French Cartes de Visite*. Research Library, The Getty Research Institute, Los Angeles (2000.R.25).

Section two of the Album (3v–7r) contains *carte de visite* photographs of Mexican historical figures, both political and military. Analogous to the book as a whole, which starts with the Aztec past as its foundation, this section begins with Miguel Hidalgo y Costilla, the priest whose actions began the War for Independence from Spain, essentially the founder of the modern Mexican nation.[24] The Album's third section (7v–17r) is the largest and contains Mexican *tipos populares,* predominantly workers or vendors, young Indians (and named as such), and a middle-class woman. Some photographs are of people, and others are of wax figurines of people, these being objects that also were collected. Here, then, we see that it is the type that matters, not the individual, for photographs of objects representing types can stand in for photographs of people representing analogous types, and they are placed side by side without any conceptual distinction between them. As opposed to the album's section containing photographs of political or military figures, in which the individual is identified, singled out, and glorified, each person in this section is subordinated to the type or the profession to which he or she belonged. Such photographs captured the types of Mexican people the French would have encountered on the street. A part of their everyday life and travels, part of the sights and sounds of the cities and countrysides, they were different and foreign, characteristically Mexican, whose only identity, at least seen from the outside, consisted of the goods produced or sold.

The fourth section of the album is comprised of French historical figures, including Jean-Marie Roland de la Platière and Jacques Necker, eighteenth-century figures from the French Revolution, some unidentified individuals, and Eugenie and Napoleon III, empress and emperor of France, 1852–70. Finally, there is a turn toward the personal, for one of the cards in this last section, with a photo of an older man on the front, has, written in pencil on the back, "Grand-père 1880."[25] Other pictures in this last section are of young boys and a clergyman, though they are unidentified (at least as can be seen on the outside pages. Another personal touch is the addition of the engraved calling card of Madame Michel Roux, upon which is added in ink, "Voeux de bonne année," another marker of a visit, an experience. The final card bears a picture of a boy on one side and a poem, titled "Jacques Inaudi," by Jean Serrazin.

In summary, this album, although depersonalized because we have no record of its compiler, is certainly a personal affair, in which the individual places himself at the juncture of both personal and collective experiences, each adding to this collection or compilation of memories. Some of these memories—which perhaps functioned as mnemonic devices for storytelling—are particular and others are generalized and generate a picture not only of personal experience but also of the collective experiences of visitors to Mexico or those simply interested in Mexico, created through the collection, selection, and display of images within albums.

The modes of integrating the personal with the collective in order to create and represent individual experience are not exclusive to these two albums or to nineteenth-century France or Mexico and, instead, are very much a part of wider human experience and expression, for they are a fundamental part of the creation and re-creation of memories, where the personal and collective intermingle, each shedding light on or modifying the other, and also are akin to histories of representation, which often draw on visual precedents to make experience visible. Moreover, the standards displayed in these albums of what the visitor should see or experience while in Mexico continued in an analogous way into the twentieth century and until today, when people visit many of the same places Falconnet and his contemporaries visited and display the same objects in their photo albums, the Aztec Calendar Stone, for example, appearing in all Mexican guidebooks and in hundreds of digital photographs posted on Flickr.com alone, one of our era's personal—and collective—photo albums.

NOTES

—⁓—

INTRODUCTION

1. Hernán Cortés, *Letters from Mexico*, trans. Anthony Pagden (New Haven, Conn.: Yale University Press, 1986),110–11; Silvio Bedini, *The Pope's Elephant* (New York: Viking, 1997).

2. James Axtell, "Europeans, Indians, and the Age of Discovery in American History Textbooks," in *Beyond 1492: Encounters in Colonial North America* (New York: Oxford University Press, 1992), 197.

3. Oliver R. Impey and Arthur McGregor, eds., *The Origins of Museums: The Cabinet of Curiosities in Sixteenth- and Seventeenth-Century Europe* (Oxford: Clarendon Press, 1985).

4. Among the vast literature on early modern collecting, see Horst Bredekamp, *The Lure of Antiquity and the Cult of the Machine* (Princeton, N.J.: Markus Wiener, 1995); Lorraine Daston and Katharine Park, *Wonders and the Order of Nature, 1150–1750* (New York: Zone Books, 1998); John Elsner and Roger Cardinal, eds., *The Cultures of Collecting* (London: Reaktion Books, 1994); Paula Findlen, *Possessing Nature: Museums, Collecting, and Scientific Culture in Early Modern Italy* (Berkeley: University of California Press, 1994); Thomas DaCosta Kaufmann, *The Mastery of Nature: Aspects of Art, Science, and Humanism in the Renaissance* (Princeton, N.J.: Princeton University Press, 1993), esp. chap. 7; Joy Kenseth, ed., *The Age of the Marvelous* (Hanover, N.H.: Hood Museum of Art, Dartmouth College, 1991); and Krzysztof Pomian, *Collectors and Curiosities: Paris and Venice, 1500–1800* (Cambridge: Polity, 1990).

5. Topsell, *Historie of Four-Footed Beastes* (London, 1607), quotation at sig A3r.

CHAPTER 1. SEEING THE WORLD IN A ROOM:
LOOKING AT EXOTICA IN EARLY MODERN COLLECTIONS

An earlier version of this essay appeared as Daniela Bleichmar, "Looking at Exotica in Baroque Collections: The Object, the Viewer, and the Collection as a Space," in Mar Rey Bueno and Miguel López-Pérez, eds., *The Gentleman, the Virtuoso, the Inquirer: Vincencio Juan de Lastanosa and the Art of Collecting in Early Modern Spain* (Cambridge: Scholars Publishing, 2008): 63–77. I thank Drs. Rey Bueno and López-Pérez for introducing me to these materials and including me in the conference they coorganized on Lastanosa in Huesca in summer 2007.

1. On Lastanosa, see Carmen Morte García and Carlos Garcés Manau, eds., *Vincencio Juan de Lastanosa (1607–1681): La pasión de saber* (Huesca: Instituto de Estudios Altoaragoneses, 2007); Nicolás García Tapia, Jesús Carrillo Castillo, and José Luis Peset, eds., *Tecnología e imperio: Turriano, Lastanosa, Herrera, Ayanz: ingenios y leyendas del siglo de oro* (Madrid: Nivola, 2002); *Signos. Arte y cultura en Huesca: De Forment a Lastanosa, siglos XVI–*

XVII (Huesca: Gobierno de Aragon, Diputación de Huesca, 1994); and Ricardo del Arco y Garay, *La Erudición aragonesa en el siglo XVII en torno a Lastanosa* (Madrid: Góngora, 1934).

2. Beds were often the most expensive possession listed in household inventories; luxurious beds such as are described in Lastanosa's residence could be worth more than works or art or other collectibles. See Rafaella Sarti, *Europe at Home: Family and Material Culture, 1500–1800* (New Haven, Conn.: Yale University Press, 2002), and Patricia Fortini Brown, *Private Lives in Renaissance Venice: Art, Architecture, and the Family* (New Haven, Conn.: Yale University Press, 2004).

3. Juan Francisco Andrés de Uztarroz, *Descripción de las Antigüedades i Jardines de don Vincencio Iuan de Lastanosa, hijo i ciudadano de Huesca, ciudad en el Reino de Aragon* (Zaragoza: Diego Dormer, 1647); Andrés de Uztarroz, *Descripción del palacio y los jardines de Vincencio Juan de Lastanosa* [1650?], Hispanic Society of America (New York), MS. B-2424, ff. 24r–51v; *Narración de lo que le pasó a Don Vincencio Juan de Lastanosa a 15 de octubre del año 1662 con un religioso docto y grave*, Hispanic Society of America (New York), MS. B-2424, ff. 52r–79v; *Catálogo de la biblioteca de Vincencio Juan de Lastanosa* (Sparvenfeld Catalogue [1640–62?]), MS. U-379, Royal Library, Stockholm. I am extremely grateful to the organizers of the conference "Lastanosa: Arte y Ciencia en el Barroco," held in Huesca from May 28 to June 2, 2007, for making their transcriptions of these four documents available to me. I have followed their lead in discounting a fifth account of the collection, *Las tres cosas más singulares que tiene la Casa de Lastanosa en este año de 1639*, Biblioteca Nacional de España, MS. 18727-45, whose authenticity they have questioned. All mention and citations of these documents in my paper refer to these transcriptions. All translations in this essay are mine.

4. The word *exotica* does not appear in the descriptions of the Lastanosa collection and does not seem to have been in common use in Spanish since no form appears in Sebastián de Covarrubias's *Tesoro de la lengua castellana o española* (Madrid, 1674). However, the 1677 catalogue of the Bolognese *Museo Cospiano*, which combined the collections of Ulisse Aldrovandi and Ferdinando Cospi, refers to "Libri, Volumi, Carte, e Scritture Esotiche." Lorenzo Legati, *Museo Cospiano: Annesso a quello del famoso Vlisse Aldrovandi e donato alla sua patria dall'Illustrissimo Signor Ferdinando Cospi* (Bologna, 1677), 184. The *Oxford English Dictionary* records the first appearance of "exotick" in English in 1599, with a meaning related to magic and witchcraft; by 1646, the term had gained the current connotation of having to do with a foreign origin. The word "exotica" is recorded for the first time in English usage only in 1876.

5. Andrés de Uztarroz, *Descripción del palacio y los jardines*, ff. 28r, 26r, 37v.

6. See, for instance, Joy Kenseth, "A World of Wonders in One Closet Shut," in Joy Kenseth, ed., *The Age of the Marvelous* (Hanover, N.H.: Dartmouth College Art Museum, 1991), 80–101, 81.

7. The idea of the collection as a narrative is explored in Mieke Bal, "Telling Objects: A Narrative Perspective on Collecting," in John Elsner and Roger Cardinal, eds., *The Cultures of Collecting* (London: Reaktion Books, 1994), 87–116.

8. Andrés de Uztarroz, *Descripción del palacio y los jardines*, ff. 47r–47v.

9. *Narración de lo que le pasó a Don Vincencio Juan de Lastanosa*, f. 75v.

10. Among the vast literature on Kircher, see Paula Findlen, ed., *Athanasius Kircher: The Last Man Who Knew Everything* (New York: Routledge, 2004), and Daniel Stolzenberg, ed., *The Great Art of Knowing: The Baroque Encyclopedia of Athanasius Kircher* (Stanford, Calif.: Stanford University Press, 2001).

11. *Catálogo de la biblioteca de Vincencio Juan de Lastanosa*, Royal Library, Stockholm, MS. U-379, f. 102v. On Lastanosa's library, see Karl-Ludwig Selig, *The Library of Vincencio Juan de Lastanosa: Patron of Gracián* (Geneva: Droz, 1960).

12. I thank Arianna Opsvig for bringing these two examples to my attention.

13. Benjamin Schmidt discusses the exotic mode in the context of Dutch visual culture at the time in "Inventing Exoticism: The Project of Dutch Geography and the Marketing of the World, Circa 1700," in Pamela Smith and Paula Findlen, eds., *Merchants and Marvels: Commerce, Science, and Art in Early Modern Europe* (New York: Routledge, 2002), 347–69, and "Mapping an Exotic World. The Global Project of Dutch Geography, Circa 1700," in Felicity Nussbaum, ed., *The Global Eighteenth Century* (Baltimore: Johns Hopkins University Press, 2003), 21–37. For an illuminating discussion of the role of geography in the history of art, see Thomas DaCosta Kaufmann, *Toward a Geography of Art* (Chicago: University of Chicago Press, 2004).

14. Lorenzo Legati, *Museo Cospiano*, book 3, chap. 2, 191; and *Inuentario semplice di tutte le materie esattamente descritte che si trouano nel museo Cospiano: non solo le notate nel libro gia stampato e composto dal sig. Lorenzo Legati, ma ancora le aggiunteui in copia dopo la fabrica* (Bologna, 1680), 16.

15. See, for instance, Horst Bredekamp, *The Lure of Antiquity and the Cult of the Machine* (Princeton, N.J.: Markus Wiener, 1995).

16. Martin Kemp, "'Wrought by No Artist's Hand': The Natural, the Artificial, the Exotic, and the Scientific in Some Artifacts from the Renaissance," in Claire Farago, ed., *Reframing the Renaissance: Visual Culture in Europe and Latin America 1450–1650* (New Haven, Conn.: Yale University Press, 1995), 175–96.

17. Kemp argues in "'Wrought by No Artist's Hand'," 180–81, that "a complex fluidity, ambiguity, and diversity of meaning characterizes the viewing of such items even in a number of apparently similar contexts in Renaissance societies, and that such viewing undermines any propensity to characterize them neatly in terms of the kind of historical 'meta-realities'—such as power, colonialism possession, oppression, patriarchy, Eurocentrism, and otherness—which now tend to be taken as having a privileged explanatory power."

18. Kemp, "'Wrought by No Artist's Hand'," 185.

19. Paula Findlen, *Possessing Nature* (Berkeley: University of California Press, 1994); Thomas DaCosta Kaufmann, *The Mastery of Nature: Aspects of Art, Science, and Humanism in the Renaissance* (Princeton, N.J.: Princeton University Press, 1993), esp. chap. 7; and *Court, Cloister, and City: The Art and Culture of Central Europe, 1450–1800* (Chicago: University of Chicago Press, 1995); Kryzstoff Pomian, *Collectors and Curiosities: Paris and Venice, 1500–1800* (Cambridge: Polity Press, 1990); Kenseth, ed., *The Age of the Marvelous*; Lorraine Daston and Katharine Park, *Wonders and the Order of Nature, 1150–1750* (New York: Zone Books, 1998).

20. The classic discussion of the importance of situating the eye historically is Michael Baxandall's powerful concept of the "period eye," in *Painting and Experience in Fifteenth-Century Italy: A Primer in the Social History of Pictorial Style* (Oxford: Oxford University Press, 1988 [1972]). On space-specific viewings in early modern Europe, see, for example, Randolph Starn, "Seeing Culture in a Room for an Renaissance Prince," in Lynn Hunt, ed., *The New Cultural History* (Berkeley: University of California Press, 1989), 205–32.

21. See, for instance, Ivan Karp and Steven D. Lavine, eds., *Exhibiting Cultures: The Poetics and Politics of Museum Display* (Washington, D.C.: Smithsonian Institution Press, 1991), esp. Michael Baxandall, "Exhibiting Intention: Some Preconditions of the Visual Display of Culturally Purposeful Objects," 33–41.

22. Francesco Imperato, *Discorsi intorno a diverse cose naturali* (Naples, 1628), sig. 3, quoted in Findlen, *Possessing Nature*, 31.

23. Kenseth, "A World of Wonders," 81.

24. Reproduced in Peter C. Mancall, ed., *Travel Narratives from the Age of Discovery: An Anthology* (New York: Oxford University Press, 2006), 401–3.

25. Mancall, ed., *Travel Narratives*, 401–3.

26. Objects in large princely collections were often arranged according to their material—this method was recommended by Samuel Quiccheberg and practiced in the Munich cabinet of Duke Albrecht V (1528–79), and Ferdinand II's at Ambras Castle. Size and shape were also important governing principles. See Kenseth, "A World of Wonders," 84–85.

27. Samuel Quiccheberg, *Inscriptiones, vel, Tituli theatri amplissimi, complectentis rerum universitatis singulas materias et imagines eximias* (Munich, 1565). On the memory theater, see Frances Yates, *The Art of Memory* (Chicago: University of Chicago Press, 1966).

28. Benedetto Ceruti, *Musaeum Francisci Calceolarii* (Verona, 1622), and Paolo Maria Terzago, *Musaeum Septalianum* (Tortona, 1664).

29. "Hay en esta misma pieza tres estantes de arcabuces y mosquetes con todos sus aderezos, algunos raros por la forma de los caños y cajas, y variedad de pistolas de exquisitas hechuras . . . armas de mucha antigüedad, instrumentos belicos, ballestas de caça, carcajes con madrazos, ballestas de guerra con carcajes con flechas y dardos con lancillas, y casquillos de acero. Arcos de caça y pelea, los primeros con turquesas para hacer los bodoques, los de guerra con aljavas y flechas. Anillos de marfil. Una bocina de bronce. Otra de marfil de casi una bara de largo, de un Rey del Japon, los dos tercios estriados y el ultimo escamado; remata en una cabeza de cayman, tiene asida con la boca la cabeza de un rey. Una estorica, arma de la Reyna de las Amazonas, de la qual hace memoria el Padre Acuña en la relacion referida. Dos catanas, una del Rey de los Tartaros, guarnecida de carai y bronce dorado, con primorosissimas lavores de relieve; diosela a don Vincencio Juan de Lastanosa el Excelentisimo Señor don Fernando de Gurrea Aragon y Borja, Duque de Villa Hermosa. La otra catana es de los chinas, la cuchilla como rayo, toda gravada de aguas, remata esta y tiene y sirve de empuñadura un diablillo. / Un puñal del Rey don Pedro el III de Aragon, con que se corto los dedos quando corto los Privilegios de la Union. Ay otra copiosa variedad de armas antiquissimas, como son petos, coraças, rodela de acero de Milan, de madera de Salamanca, otras muchas pieças assi de las que se platican en la guerra como en las justas y torneos," Andrés de Uztarroz, *Descripción del palacio y los jardines*, ff. 47r–47v, my emphasis.

CHAPTER 2. COLLECTING GLOBAL ICONS: THE CASE OF THE EXOTIC PARASOL

1. Johannes van Keulen published one of the most popular maritime atlases on the market, the *Nieuwe Lichtende Zee-Fakkel*, which first appeared in Amsterdam in 1681 and continued to be published, in various editions and translations, throughout the eighteenth century. Many of these editions can be traced in C. Koeman and P. C. J. van der Krogt, *Atlantes Neerlandici* ('T Goy-Houten: HES & De Graaf, 1997).

2. Further cases are plentiful, yet see, for example, the palm tree that forms the backdrop to an Inuit camp site—meant to be in maritime Canada—in Arnoldus Montanus's highly influential geography of the Americas, *De nieuwe en onbekende wereld* (Amsterdam, 1671), 101. This and other habits of early modern tropical iconography are discussed in Florike Egmond and Peter Mason, "'These Are People Who Eat Raw Fish': Contours of the Ethnographic Imagination in the Sixteenth Century," *Viator: Medieval and Renaissance Studies* 31 (2000): 311–60.

3. Beth Lord, "Foucault's Museum: Difference, Representation, and Genealogy," *Museum and Society* 4 (March 2006): 1–14; and Tony Bennett, *The Birth of the Museum: History, Theory, Politics* (London: Routledge, 1995).

4. The bibliography is growing: see Horst Bredekamp, *The Lure of Antiquity and the Cult of the Machine: The* Kunstkammer *and the Evolution of Nature, Art, and Technology*, trans. Allison Brown (Princeton, N.J.: Princeton University Press, 1995); Paula Findlen, *Possessing Nature: Museums, Collecting, and Scientific Culture in Early Modern Italy* (Berkeley: University

of California Press, 1994); Krzysztof Pomian, *Collectors and Curiosities: Paris and Venice 1500–1800*, trans. Elizabeth Wiles-Portier (Cambridge: Cambridge University Press, 1990); Ken Arnold, *Cabinets for the Curious: Looking Back at Early English Museums* (Aldershot: Ashgate, 2006); Oliver Impey and Arthur Macgregor, eds., *The Origins of Museums: The Cabinets of Curiosities in Sixteenth- and Seventeenth-Century Europe* (Oxford: Oxford University Press, 1985); Ellinoor Bergvelt and Renée Kistemaker, *De wereld binnen handbereik: Nederlandse kunst- en rariteitenverzamelingen, 1585–1735* (Zwolle: Waanders, 1992); Lorraine Daston and Katherine Park, *Wonders and the Order of Nature, 1150–1750* (New York: Zone, 1998); Peter Mason and Florike Egmond, *The Mammoth and the Mouse: Microhistory and Morphology* (Baltimore: Johns Hopkins University Press, 1997).

5. The theme of a European global moment ca. 1700—at least in terms of a descriptive engagement with the world—is broadly explored in Felicity Nussbaum, ed., *The Global Eighteenth Century* (Baltimore: Johns Hopkins University Press, 2003); see, more particularly (in the Nussbaum volume), Benjamin Schmidt, "Mapping an Exotic World: The Global Project of Dutch Geography, Circa 1700," 19–37.

6. Several examples could be cited, the most pervasive involving ceramics: see C. J. A. Jörg, *Interaction in Ceramics* (Hong Kong: Urban Council, 1984). It seems worth pointing out that, while texts may rank as the most commonly cited sources on the exotic world, this may have more to do with our own intellectual predilections—scholars like to read and collect books—and factors such as material preservation, change in taste, and academic training than with the indubitable and widespread presence of material objects pertaining to the non-European world.

7. Cf. Philip Baldaeus, *Naauwkeurige beschryvinge van Malabar en Choromandel* (Amsterdam, 1672), frontispiece, and the map of South Asia in R. and J. Ottens, *Atlas maior* (ca. 1730), n.p.

8. *Iconologia overo Descrittione di diverse imagini cavate dall'antichità & di propria inventione, trovate & dichiarate da Cesare Ripa Perugino, Cavaliere de Santi Mauritio & Lazaro. Di nuovo revista, & dal medesimo ampliata di 400 & più Imagini et di Figure ad intaglio adornata* (Rome, 1603); and note that the original edition of 1593 appeared without any illustrations. On Ripa, see Hugh Honour, *The New Golden Land: European Images of America from the Discoveries to the Present Time* (New York: Pantheon, 1975); and E. H. Gombrich, *Symbolic Images* (London: Phaidon, 1972), 126–45. On the trajectory of such iconography more broadly, see Peter Mason, *The Lives of Images* (London: Reaktion, 2001).

9. On the development of the allegorical "America," especially in the context of Flemish art, see Benjamin Schmidt, *Innocence Abroad: The Dutch Imagination and the New World, 1570–1670* (Cambridge: Cambridge University Press, 2001), 123–42.

10. Gottfried Bernhard Goetz, *America* (Augsburg, ca. 1750); and for the "iconic" image of Africa, cradling a cornucopia in her right arm (as in the Goetz engraving), see the frontispiece, by Johannes Visscher after Nicolaes Berchem, to the volume on "Africa" in Joan Blaeu, *Atlas Maior* (Amsterdam, 1664). The allegory of Africa done for the Goetz series, it might be added, included several figures bearing feathered (i.e., "American") headdresses, while "Africa" herself sits under the very paraphernalia that had by this time (ca. 1750) become closely attached to "America": the parasol. The images are reproduced (yet erroneously captioned) in Susan Danforth, ed., *Encountering the New World 1493 to 1800* (Providence, R.I.: John Carter Brown Library, 1991), 7, 67.

11. Along with the allegorical figure, an alligator, and a parrot, the Alcora *America* (ca. 1770) also includes a conspicuously large ladle clasped in "America's" right hand like a weapon (not removable for use), which bears no obvious connection to the Ripa icon. Compare also the porcelain figure of similar dimensions manufactured by the Meissen factory

around this time (ca. 1750), which quite closely resembles the Goetz engraving—yet offers a porcelain-white-skinned America. Both figures are reproduced in Hugh Honour, *The European Vision of America* (Cleveland: Cleveland Museum of Art, 1975), cat. 142, 148 (and note that the dating and authenticity of the Alcora *America*, now in the Cooper-Hewitt Museum of Design in New York, has sometimes been questioned).

12. Many of these images—including the famous allegorical ceiling frescoes done by Giovanni Battista Tiepolo for the Residenz, Würtzburg—are discussed more extensively in Honour, *European Vision*, 131–56. See also Rachel Doggett, ed., *New World of Wonders: European Images of the Americas, 1492–1700* (Washington, D.C.: Folger Library, 1992).

13. This genre is understudied, yet see, for example, on the Dutch case, Jaap van der Veen, "Dit Klain Vertrek Bevat een Weereld Vol Gewoel: Negentig Amsterdammers en hun Kabinetten," in Bergvelt and Kistemaker, *Wereld binnen handbereik*, 232–58, especially "Bijlage 1" (313–34), which lists collections with their catalogues (when they exist).

14. Pieter van der Aa, *La Galerie agreable du monde*, 66 pts. (Leiden: Pieter van der Aa, ca. 1729). Note that many of the engravings in this lavish picture book—it contains around 4,000 illustrations, annotated with only meager text—have trompe l'oeil frames, and the putative reader (or better, browser) might be imagined touring the virtual "gallery." Compare also Romeyn de Hooghe, *Les Indes Orientales et Occidentales et autres lieux* (Leiden: Pieter van der Aa, 1710), where many of the engravings originate.

15. Simon de Vries, *D'eedelste tijdkortingh der weet-geerige verstanden: of De groote historische rariteit-kamer* (Amsterdam: Daniel van den Dalen, 1694), and de Vries, *Groot historisch magazyn: Rijcklijck opgevuld met keur van aenmercklijcke stoffen, natuerwonderen, en sonderlinge geschiedenissen* (Amsterdam: Aert Dircksz Ooszaen, 1688). On the astonishing production of de Vries, see Arianne Baggerman, *Een drukkend gewicht: leven en werk van de zeventiende-eeuwse veelschrijver Simon de Vries* (Amsterdam: Rodopi, 1993).

16. Petrus Nylandt, *Het schouw-toneel der aertsche schepselen, afbeeldende allerhande menschen, beesten, vogelen, visschen* (Amsterdam: Marcus Willemsz. Doornick, 1672); Levinus Vincent, *Wondertooneel der nature* (Amsterdam: François Halma, 1706); and Abraham Ortelius, *Theatrum orbis terrarum* (Antwerp: Gilles Coppens de Diest, 1570).

17. Joseph Roach, *Cities of the Dead: Circum-Atlantic Performance* (New York: Columbia University Press, 1996), especially chap. 3 (73–118).

18. Arjun Appadurai, "Disjuncture and Difference in the Global Cultural Economy," *Public Culture* 2, 2 (1990): 1–24; and see also Joseph Roach, "The Global Parasol: Accessorizing the Four Corners of the World," in Nussbaum, *Global Eighteenth Century*, 91–106 (cited 94).

19. Roach, "Global Parasol," 96, citing Helen Wallis and Sarah Tyacke, eds., *My Head Is a Map: Essays & Memoirs in Honour of R. V. Tooley* (London: Francis Edwards, 1973).

20. William Vincent's *Indian Queen* was first published ca. 1683 and several more times through 1729. Further details can be found at the National Portrait Gallery Web site (NPG D19498).

21. Aphra Behn, *Oroonoko: or, The Royal Slave. A True History* (London: Printed for William Canning, 1688).

22. In brief, we know from archival records that Behn herself provided the feather garments for Dryden's *Indian Queen*, which comprised genuine artifacts retrieved from Surinam, where she briefly lived; and that these props were recycled for her own *Widow Ranter*, which Dryden had a hand in staging. If many of the props were what I earlier called "ersatz," then the feather-wear in this print counts as the real McCoy. See T. W. Craik et al., *The Revels History of Drama in English, 1660–1750* (New York: Methuen, 1976), 5: 145.

23. On consumption and colonialism in the context of Behn's work, see Laura Brown, "The Romance of Empire: *Oroonoko* and the Trade in Slaves," in Felicity Nussbaum and

Laura Brown, eds., *The New Eighteenth Century: Theory, Politics, English Literature* (New York: Methuen, 1987), 41–61.

24. What few examples can be found appear in publications of relatively limited circulation. See, for example, the title-page woodcut of Francisco de Xerez, *Verdadera relacion de la conquista del Peru* (Seville: Bartholome Perez, [1534]), a copy of which belongs to the John Carter Brown Library, Rhode Island (call no. B534 X61).

25. "The Meeting of Cortés and Montezuma," from the *Conquest of Mexico* series, second half of seventeenth century, Jay I. Kislak Collection in the Library of Congress. The scene shows Cortés leaving for Syle De Istalpalapa.

26. Lionel De Fonseka, "The Karave Flag," *Ceylon Antiquary and Literary Register* 7 (July 1921), n.p.

27. Some of these images are more fully referenced in Fonseka, "Karave Flag."

28. "Be sure and hold her parasol over her; and clear a way for her if she's hemmed in by the crowd; fetch a stool to help her on to the couch; and unlace or lace up the sandals on her dainty feet" (*Ars Amatoria*, II, 209–12).

29. See Elkanah Settle, *The Empress of Morocco, A Tragedy* (London: William Cademan, 1673). The parasol is illustrated in one of the original "sculptures" (engravings) included in the printed version of the text, inserted between pages 13 and 14.

30. On Visscher, see Paul van den Brink and Jan Werner, eds. *Gesneden en gedrukt in de Kalverstraat: de kaarten- en atlassendrukkerij in Amsterdam tot in de 19e eeuw* (Utrecht: HES, 1989). The America map replaced Willem Blaeu's best-selling *Americae*, which dated from the 1610s. Note that Joan Blaeu, who headed the firm after Willem's death, adapted a variation of Berchem design for the "America" allegory that Blaeu used for the volume in his *Atlas major* (ca. 1660s) dedicated to the Western Hemisphere.

31. The Dutch context of what will become an essentially European image is missed by most critics. Jorge Cañizares-Esguerra touches on this allegory in *Puritan Conquistadors: Iberianizing the Atlantic, 1550–1700* (Stanford, Calif.: Stanford University Press, 2006), where he correctly identifies its Christian component, yet he misses the punning allusion to gold and thus its commercial message (and the role of Berchem in its design).

32. The drawings are reproduced in Cassandra Bosters, Jan Frederik Heijbroek, and Marijn Schapelhouman, *Kunst in kaart: decoratieve aspecten van de cartografie* (Utrecht: H & S, HES Uitgevers, 1989), 80–81.

33. Many of these can be traced in Koeman and van der Krogt, *Atlantes Neerlandici*.

34. Johann Hübner, *Zemnovodnago kruga kratkoe opisanie. Iz staryia i novyia gegrafii po voprosam i otvietam chrez IAgana Gibnera sobranoe* (A short description of the terraqueous globe. Collected by Johann Hübner from ancient and modern geography by way of questions and answers) (Moscow, 1719). Ogilby published the map, with a revised dedication, in the context of his larger project of geography, for which he leaned heavily on Dutch publications—in this case, Montanus's *Nieuwe en onbekende wereld* (Amsterdam, 1671). Justus Danckerts' map—*Recentissima Novi Orbis sive Americae Septentrionalis et Meridionalis Tabula* (ca. 1697)—simply expunges the upper, dedicatory cartouche. A map signed by F. de Wit, *Novissima et Accuratissima Septentrionalis ac Meridionalis Totius Americae Descriptio*, dated varyingly ca. 1680–1700, has a version of Berchem's lower cartouche in reverse (cf. the copy at the John Carter Brown Library: Cabinet B670/1.4). For Danckerts, de Wit, and Schenk—all prominent cartographers—see the entries in Koeman and van der Krogt, *Atlantes Neerlandici*.

35. Hendrik Donker, *Pas-caert van Guinea vertoonende de Tand-kust, Qua Qua-Kust en de Goud kust* (Amsterdam, ca. 1688).

36. Craig Clunas, *Pictures and Visuality in Early Modern China* (London: Reaktion, 1997), 46. Clunas develops this idea from Carlo Ginzburg's discussion of erotic imagery, where

Ginzburg makes a distinction among related sets of images that circulate in distinct spheres, such as private and public, and that have varying resonances, accordingly: "Titian, Ovid, and Sixteenth-Century Codes for Erotic Illustration," in *Clues, Myths, and the Historical Method*, trans. John Tedeschi and Anne C. Tedeschi (Baltimore: Johns Hopkins University Press, 1989), 77–95.

37. For Shah Jahan, see Olfert Dapper, *Asia: of Naukeurige beschryving van het rijk des Grooten Mogols, en een groote gedeelte van Indiën . . . beneffens een volkome beschryving van geheel Persie, Georgie, Mengrelie en andere gebuur-gewesten* (Amsterdam: Jacob van Meurs, 1672); for the samurai, see Arnoldus Montanus, *Gedenkwaerdige gesantschappen der Oost-Indische Maetschappy in 't Vereenigde Nederland, aen de Kaisaren van Japan* (Amsterdam: Jacob van Meurs, 1669), and also van der Aa, *Galerie agreeable* (tome 56); for the Chinese women, see Olfert Dapper, *Gedenckwaerdig bedryf der Nederlansche Oost-Indische Maetschappye, op de kuste en in het keizerrijk van Taising of Sina* (Amsterdam: Jacob van Meurs, 1670); and for the Floridians (likely Seminoles), see Montanus, *Nieuwe en onbekende wereld* (Amsterdam, 1671).

38. *Pinacotheca Bettertonaeana: or, a Catalogue of the Books, Prints, Drawings, and Paintings of Mr Thomas Betterton, that Celebrated Comedian, lately deceased* (London, 1710).

39. The phenomenal production of Jacob van Meurs is discussed in Benjamin Schmidt, "Accumulating the World: Collecting and Commodifying 'Globalism' in Early Modern Europe," in Lissa Roberts, ed., *Collecting Points: Centres of Accumulation and the Production of Knowledge in the Early Modern Period* (London: Palgrave, 2011). See also John Wills, Jr., "Author, Publisher, Patron, World: A Case Study of Old Books and Global Consciousness," *Journal of Early Modern History* 13 (2009): 375–433; and Isabella H. van Eeghen, "Arnoldus Montanus's Book on Japan," *Quaerendo* 2 (1972): 250–72.

40. See Johannes Nieuhof, *L'Ambassade de la Compagnie Orientale des Provinces Unies vers L'Emperour de la Chine, ou Grand Cam de Tartarie* (Amsterdam: Jacob van Meurs, 1665). Van Meurs also published a Dutch edition that year: *Het gezantschap der Neerlandtsche Ost-Indische Compagnie, aan den grooten Tartarischen Cham, den tegenwoordigen keizer van China*. For further details on this highly influential work, see John Landwehr, *VOC: A Bibliography of Publications Relating to the Dutch East India Company, 1602–1800* (Utrecht: HES, 1991).

41. One of the best examples may be in the "portraits" of the non-European peoples governed by the Dutch in Brazil and painted by Albert Eckhout, which are replicated by a host of followers in painting, print, tapestry, ceramics, and more. These exotic "American" types landed in depictions of both the East and West Indies—most strikingly in a series of Delft-made tableaux showing imagery that would otherwise come under the rubric of "chinoiserie." On Eckhout, see Quentin Buvelot, ed., *Albert Eckhout: A Dutch Artist in Brazil* (The Hague: Royal Cabinet of Paintings Mauritshuis, and Zwolle: Waanders Publishers, 2004). For a sample of the delftware, see "Tile Panel with Chinese Ornament and Africans" in the Rijksmuseum, Amsterdam (Object number BK-NM-12400-443).

42. Anonymous, French clock with Robinson Crusoe and Man Friday, bronze, partly gilt (ca. 1810), Museo degli Argenti, Palazzo Pitti, Florence. The clock is reproduced in Honour, *New Golden Land*, 154 (ill. 151).

43. The Asian geography is Dapper, *Gedenckwaerdig bedryf*, for which see Ogilby's English version, published as the *Atlas Chinensis* (London, 1671), 436; and compare John Stalker, *A treatise of Japaning and varnishing, being a complete discovery of those arts* (Oxford: John Stalker, 1688), 18. For the wallpaper, see Otto Pelka, *Ostasiatische Reisebilder im Kunstgewerbe des 18. Jahrhunderts* (Leipzig: Hiersemann, 1924), plates 70–76. A Leipzig painted cabinet, also discussed by Pelka (plates 77–86) contains a separate scene of torture taken from the title page of Nieuhof's *L'Ambassade*; and a pastiche of self-mutilation scenes, which is taken from an altogether different volume on the practice of Islam in Syria.

1. See also Anna Maria Rao, "Antiquaries and Politicians in Eighteenth-Century Naples," *Journal of History of Collections* 19 (2007): 165–75.

2. John Douglas, quoted in Bernard Smith, *European Vision of the South Pacific, 1768–1850: A Study in the History of Art and Ideas* (Oxford: Clarendon, 1960), 130. I owe this quotation to Giuseppe Pucci, *Il Passato Prossimo* (Rome: Nuova Italia Scientifica 1993), 170.

3. Francis Bacon, *Sylva sylvarum* (London, 1627).

4. Denis Diderot, preface to Nicolas Antoine Boulanger, *L'antiquité dévoilée par ses usages* (Amsterdam, 1756), my translation.

5. Walter Charleton, *Chorea Gigantum, or the Most Famous Antiquity of Great Britain* (London: 1725), 4.

6. Michael Hunter, *John Aubrey and the Realm of Learning* (London: Duckworth, 1976), 181.

7. On these points, see also Peter C. Mancall, "Collecting Americans," this volume.

8. For this study, I have relied on the complete collection of the voyages of de Bry published in 1990 in Berlin. Gereon Sievernich, ed., *The America—de Bry, 1590–1634: America oder die Neue Welt. Die entdeckung eines Kontinents in 346 Kupferstichen, Bearbeitet und herausgeben von Gereon Sievernich* (Berlin: Casablanca, 1990).

9. There is a considerable body of work dealing with John White. I refer to the catalogue of his works by Kim Sloan, ed., *A New World: England's First View of America* (Chapel Hill/London: University of North Carolina Press/British Museum Press, 2007).

10. Quoted in Arthur Williamson, "Scots, Indians, and Empire: The Scottish Politics of Civilization, 1519–1609," *Past & Present* 150 (1996): 50n6.

11. Sigismund Meisterlin, *Eine schöne chronik* (Augsburg, 1457).

12. E. S. Piccolomini, *Operae quae extant* (Basel, 1551), 685.

13. T. D. Kendrick, *British Antiquity* (London: Methuen, 1950), 121; Stuart Piggott, *Ancient Britons and the Antiquarian Imagination: Ideas from the Renaissance to the Regency* (London; Thames and Hudson, 1989).

14. Quoted in Williamson, "Scots, Indians, and Empire," 56; see also Roger Williams, *The Hireling Ministry None of Christ's* (London: 1652), reprinted in Perry Miller, *Roger Williams: His Contribution to the American Tradition* (New York: Atheneum, 1974), 200. One might read this text with William Crashawn, *A Sermon Preached in London* (London, 1610), 3: "What the English offered the inhabitants of Virginia was: 1, *Civilitie* for their bodies, 2, *Christianitie* for their Soules."

15. Williamson, "Scots, Indians, and Empire,"58; see also Anthony Pagden, *The Fall of Natural Man: The American Indian and the Origins of Comparative Ethnology* (Cambridge: Cambridge University Press, 1986), 38–39.

16. John Mair, *Historia majoris Britanniae tam Angliae quam Scotiae* (Paris: 1521), as quoted in Williamson, "Scots, Indians, and Empire," 60.

17. John de Fordun, *Chronica gentis Scotorum*, ed. W. K. Skene (Edinburgh: 1871–72), 42; and Willamson, "Scots, Indians, and Empire," 61.

18. See also further the interesting article by Daniel Schavelzon, "La primera illustración di un sitio arqueológico in Argentina, Patagonia (1615)," in Mariano Ramos and Eugenia Néspolo, eds., *III Jornadas de arqueología e historia de las regiones pampeana y patagónica* (Luján: Universidad Nacional de Luján, 2003), 247–49.

19. See De Bry, *America* from Schouten's *Travel*, 346.

20. Alain Schnapp, *The Discovery of the Past* (London: British Museum Press, 1996), 16.

21. See note 6, above.

22. José Alcina Franch uses the term *archaeologist* as equivalent to *antiquarian* in José Alcina Franch, *Arqueólogos o anticuarios: Historia antigua de la arqueología en la América española* (Madrid: Ediciones del Serbal, 1995).

23. Alcina Franch, *Arqueólogos o anticuarios*, 20.

24. D. R Reinsch, ed., *Kritoboulos d'Imbros: Critobuli Imbriotae Historia* (Berlin: de Gruyter, 1983), 170.

25. David A. Lupher, *Romans in a New World: Classical Models in Sixteenth-Century Spanish America* (Ann Arbor: University of Michigan Press, 2003), 238.

26. Quoted in Angel Losada, *Fray Bartolomé de las Casas a la luz de la moderna crítica histórica* (Madrid: Tecnos, 1970), 276.

27. Alcina Franch, *Arqueólogos o anticuarios*, 24.

28. Alcina Franch, *Arqueólogos o anticuarios*, 3.

29. Diego Duran, *Historia de las Indias de Nueva España* (1581); *Historia de las Indias de Nueva España y Islas de Tierra Firma* (Madrid: Biblioteca Nacional, manuscript); reprint, 4 vols. (México: Editora Nacional, 1951).

30. Jorge Cañizares-Esguerra, *How to Write the History of the New World* (Stanford, Calif.: Stanford University Press, 2001).

31. Duran, *Historia de las Indias de Nueva España*, 2: 556.

32. Quoted in Canizares-Esguerra, *How to Write the History of the New World*, 66.

33. Cañizares-Esguerra, 67, and Diego de Landa, *Relación de las cosas de Yucatán* (Madrid: Historia, 1985), 54–55, 145–46.

34. Alcina Franch, *Arqueólogos o anticuarios*, 48; see also Duran, *Historia de las Indias de Nueva espana y Islas de Tierra Firma*. In the exercise of his holy office, Diego de Landa did not hesitate to use extreme violence to repress Indians suspected of remaining faithful to their traditions; Cañizares-Esguerra, 67.

35. Alcina Franch, *Arqueólogos o anticuarios*, 46–47.

36. Alcina Franch, *Arqueólogos o anticuarios*, 46.

37. Marie de Testa and Antoine Gautier, "De l'établissement des Pères capucins à Constantinople à la fondation de l'école des jeunes de langues (1626–1669)," in *Drogmans et diplomates européens auprès de la Porte ottomane* (Istanbul: ISIS, 2003), 43–46.

38. Lupher, *Romans in a New World*, 231.

39. Lupher, *Romans in a New World*, 230; see also Francico del Paso y Troncoso, ed., *Epistolario de Nueva España 1505–1818*, vol. 4 (México: Porrua, 1939), 150–179.

40. Quoted in Serge Gruzinski, *The Conquest of Mexico* (Cambridge: Polity Press, 1993), 16.

41. Francico del Paso y Troncoso, *Epistolario de Nueva España*, 166; see also Gruzinski, *Conquest of Mexico*, 20.

42. Cañizares-Esguerra, *How to Write the History of the New World*, 64.

43. Enrique Florescano, *Memory, Myth, and Time in Mexico* (Austin: University of Texas Press, 1994), 126–31.

44. Gruzinski, *Conquest of Mexico*, 60.

45. Cañizares-Esguerra, *How to Write the History of the New World*, 75.

46. Cañizares-Esguerra, *How to Write the History of the New World*, 72; see also, José de Acosta, *Historia natural y moral de las Indias* (Sevilla, 1590), bk. 6, chap. 8, 402.

47. See Schnapp, *Discovery of the Past*, 122–77.

48. See Alcina Franch, *Arqueólogos o anticuarios*, 20.

49. Francis Bacon, *Novum Organum* (Leipzig: Melzer, 1840).

50. Alcina Franch, *Arqueólogos o anticuarios*, 50–52.

51. Daniel Schálvelzon, "La primera excavación arqueológica en América: Teotihuacan en 1675," *Annales de Anthropologia* 20, 1 (1983): 121–34.

52. Alcina Franch, *Arqueólogos o anticuarios*, 50. Sigüenza develops these points in "Teatro de Virtudes politicas." See also María Auxiliadora Fernández, "The Representation of National Identity in Mexican Architecture: Two Case Studies 1680–1889" (Ph.D. dissertation, Columbia University, 1993), 103–204; and Anthony Pagden, "Identity Formation in Spanish America," in Nicolas Canny and Anthony Pagden, eds., *Colonial Identity in the Atlantic World, 1500–1800* (Princeton, N.J.: Princeton University Press, 1989), 51–95.

53. Schnapp, *Discovery of the Past*, 157.

54. Schnapp, *Discovery of the Past*, 205.

CHAPTER 4. AZTEC REGALIA AND THE REFORMATION OF DISPLAY

1. "Auch hab jch gesehen die dieng, die man dem könig auß dem neuen gulden land hat gebracht: ein gancz guldene sonnen, einer ganczen klaffter braith, deßgleichen ein gancz silbern mond, auch also groß, deßgleichen zwo kammern voll derselbigen rüstung, desgleichen von allerley jhrer waffen, harnisch, geschucz, wunderbahrlich wahr, selczsamer klaidung, pettgewandt und allerley wunderbahrlicher ding zu maniglichem brauch, das do viel schöner an zu sehen ist dan wunderding. Diese ding sind alle köstlich gewesen, das man sie beschäczt vmb hundert tausent gulden werth. Und ich hab aber all mein lebtag nichts gesehen, das mein hercz also erfreuet hat als diese ding. Dann ich hab darin gesehen wunderliche künstliche ding und hab mich verwundert der subtilen jngenia der menschen jn frembden landen. Und der ding weiß ich nit außzusprechen, die ich do gehabt hab." Albrecht Dürer, *Schriftlicher Nachlass*, ed. Hans Rupprich (Berlin: Deutscher Verein für Kunstwissenschaft, 1956), 1: 155. For early modern aesthetics and the marvelous, see Stephen Greenblatt, *Marvelous Possessions: The Wonder of the New World* (Chicago: University of Chicago Press, 1991), esp. 79–80; and Lorraine Daston and Katharine Park, *Wonders and the Order of Nature* (New York: Zone Books, 1998).

2. "Ha ordenado de venir en esta cibdad los monederos de todos sus reinos y hecho traer el oro y plata de las Indias para que aquí se labre por escudos." Martín de Salinas, *El emperador Carlos V y su corte según las cartas de Don Martín de Salinas, embajador del infante Don Fernando (1522–1539)* (Madrid: Fortanet, 1903), 648. Martín de Salinas was Archduke Ferdinand's secretary and ambassador at the court of his brother Emperor Charles V.

3. Following J. H. Elliott's *The Old World and the New, 1492–1650* (Cambridge: Cambridge University Press, 1970), scholars have argued for the New World's lack of impact on ideas and cultural production in sixteenth-century Europe. See the influential essays by Anthony Pagden, *European Encounters with the New World* (New Haven, Conn.: Yale University Press, 1993), chap. 1; and Michael T. Ryan, "Assimilating New Worlds in the Sixteenth and Seventeenth Centuries," *Comparative Studies in Society and History* 23 (1981): 519–38.

4. Julius von Schlosser, *Die Kunst- und Wunderkammern der Spätrenaissance* (Leipzig: Klinkhardt & Biermann, 1908), 20–49; also Krzysztof Pomian, *Collectors and Curiosities: Paris and Venice, 1500–1800*, trans. Elizabeth Wiles-Portier (Cambridge: Polity Press, 1990), 37–39. For the transition, see essays by Thomas DaCosta Kaufmann, "From Treasury to Museum: The Collections of the Austrian Habsburgs," and Anthony Alan Shelton, "Cabinets of Transgression: Renaissance Collections and the Incorporation of the New World," in John Elsner and Roger Cardinal, eds., *The Cultures of Collecting* (Cambridge, Mass.: Harvard University Press, 1994), esp. 137–41, 178–81.

5. Arjun Appadurai terms such competitions for symbolically valuable material objects "tournaments of value" in "Introduction: Commodities and the Politics of Value," in Appadurai, ed., *The Social Life of Things: Commodities in Cultural Perspective* (Cambridge: Cambridge University Press, 1986), 21.

6. "Den grosten schatz hat er allein / Von silber gold vnnd edel stein / Von perlein gut auch köstlich gwant / Als nie keim fursten ward bekannt / Davon tzu gotes dienst vnnd eer / Vil geben hat vnd gibt noch mer." Franz Winzinger, *Albrecht Altdorfer Graphik* (Munich: R. Piper, 1963), 70–74 and Eduard Chmelarz, "Die Ehrenpforte des Kaisers Maximilian I," *Jahrbuch der Kunsthistorischen Sammlungen des Allerhöchsten Kaiserhauses (JKSK)* 4 (1886): 289–319.

7. Hermann Wiesflecker, *Kaiser Maximilian I.: Das Reich, Österreich und Europa an der Wende zur Neuzeit* (Munich: Oldenbourg, 1986), 5:304.

8. Franz Winzinger, *Die Miniaturen zum Triumphzug Kaiser Maximilians I* (Graz: Akademische Druck, 1972–73), 1:28–29, 2:50–51.

9. For this tradition, see Karl Leyser, "The Tenth Century in Byzantine-Western Relationships," 116–17, and "Frederick Barbarossa, Henry II and the Hand of St. James," in *Medieval Germany and Its Neighbors 900–1250* (London: Hambledon, 1982), 222; Patrick Geary, "Sacred Commodities: The Circulation of Medieval Relics," in Appadurai, ed., *The Social Life of Things*, 169–94.

10. Michael Baxandall, *The Limewood Sculptors of Renaissance Germany* (New Haven, Conn.: Yale University Press, 1980); Robert W. Scribner, "Popular Piety and Modes of Visual Perception in Late Medieval and Reformation Germany" (1989), reprinted in Scribner, *Religion and Culture in Germany, 1400–1800*, ed. Lyndal Roper (Leiden: Brill, 2001), 104–28; and more recently, Scribner, "Ways of Seeing in the Age of Dürer," in Dagmar Eichberger and Charles Zika, eds., *Dürer and His Culture* (Cambridge: Cambridge University Press, 1998), 93–103.

11. For the French and Hungarian crowns, see Ernst Kantorowicz, *The King's Two Bodies: A Study in Medieval Political Theology* (Princeton, N.J.: Princeton University Press, 1957), 339. Sergio Bertelli's more recent *The King's Body: Sacred Rituals of Power in Medieval and Early Modern Europe*, trans. R. B. Litchfield (University Park: Pennsylvania State University Press, 2001), emphasized the embodiment of sacral kingship. Carlos Eire surveyed the literature on the more ambiguous case of Castile in *From Madrid to Purgatory: The Art and Craft of Dying in Sixteenth-Century Spain* (Cambridge: Cambridge University Press, 2002), 354–59.

12. For early sixteenth-century depictions of Charlemagne wearing the regalia, see Maximilian's geneaological project in Simon Laschitzer, "Die Heiligen aus der Sipp-, Mag- und Schwägerschaft' des Kaisers Maximilian I," *Jahrbuch der Kunsthistorischen Sammlungen des Allerhöchsten Kaiserhauses* 4 (1886): 50; for Albrecht Dürer's portrait (ca. 1511–13) of Charlemagne, see David H. Price, *Albrecht Dürer's Renaissance* (Ann Arbor: University of Michigan Press, 2003), 102–10; and Christopher S. Wood, *Forgery, Replica, Fiction: Temporalities of German Renaissance Art* (Chicago: University of Chicago Press, 2008), 149–52.

13. *Die kronung des allerdurchleuchtigsten vnd großmechtigisten Fursten vnd herren Herren Karls Romischen vnd Hispanischen Konigs* (Leipzig: Stöckel, 1520), and Hartmannus Maurus, *Coronatio Invictissimi Caroli Hispaniarum Regis Catholici in Romanorum Regem* (Nuremberg: Peypus, 1523).

14. "da hab ich gesehen alle herrlich köstlichkeit, deßgleichen keiner, der beÿ vns lebt, köstlicher ding gesehen hat [there I have seen such lordly splendor. No one who lives in our time has seen more splendid things]," Dürer, *Schriftlicher Nachlass*, 1: 159. Dürer also applied a more moderate version of this descriptor to sacred space, calling the abbey of St. Michael's in Antwerp "alß jch nie gesehen habe [that which I have never seen]," 1: 152.

15. *Ein warhafftiger tractat wie man das hochwirdig heiligthum verkündt und geweist in der heiligen stadt Trier im thum . . .* [1513] and *Diss hernachgetrucktes wirdig Heyltum: ist funden worden / Im hohen altar im Thumbe zu Trier* [1512].

16. "die vil heiligthums und zierde in ir beschlossen," Julia Schnelbögl, "Die Reichskleinodien in Nürnberg, 1424–1523," *Mitteilungen des Vereins für Geschichte der Stadt Nürnberg (MVGN)* 51 (1962): 156.

17. Schnelbögl also details the relationship between emperor and city as negotiated through the imperial relics, 78–159; see also Johannes Müllner, *Die Annalen der Reichstadt Nürnberg von 1623*, ed. G. Hirschmann (Nuremberg: Stadtrats zu Nürnberg, 1984), 244–46; and *Heiligthum und Gnade* (1493; fasc., Nuremberg: Medien & Kultur, 1979) ff. Aiii′–Av′.

18. Annette Weiner, "Cultural Difference and the Density of Objects," *American Ethnologist* 21 (1994): 391–403; and Arjun Appadurai, "Introduction: Commodities and the Politics of Value," 13–24. Weiner and Appadurai's focus on material objects and value inspired a plethora of studies on materiality and value.

19. J. M. Minty, "Judengasse to Christian Quarter: The Phenomenon of the Converted Synagogue in the Late Medieval and Early Modern Holy Roman Empire," in Robert W. Scribner and Trevor Johnson, eds., *Popular Religion in Germany and Central Europe, 1400–1800* (New York: St. Martin's, 1996), 58–86. Examples include the Hagia Sophia in Istanbul and the cathedral in Córdoba.

20. Hernán Cortés, *Carta de relacion enbiada a su majestad del emperador nuestro señor por el capitan general de la nueva spaña llamado Fernando Cortes* (Seville: Cromberger, 1522).

21. See Robert W. Scribner, "Why Was There No Reformation in Cologne?" in Scribner, *Popular Culture and Popular Movements in Reformation Germany* (London: Hambledon, 1987), 220, for Maximilian's refusal to grant the archbishop of Köln his regalia. For Charles's maneuverings with ecclesiastical and secular princes, see Adam Wrede, ed., *Deutsche Reichstagsakten, jüngere Reihe (RTA)*, vol. 3 (Gotha: Perthes, 1901), 234; and *Warhafftig anzaygung wie Kaiser Carl der fünft ettlichen Fürsten auff dem Reychstag zu(o) Augspurg im M.CCCCC.-XXX jar gehalten/ Regalia und Lehen under dem fan gelihen . . .* [1530], ff. Aiii–Aiii′.

22. Gülru Necipoglu, "Süleyman the Magnificent and the Representation of Power in the Context of Ottoman-Habsburg-Papal Rivalry," *Art Bulletin* 71 (1989): 412–13.

23. Peter Martyr Anglerius, *De nuper sub d. Carolo repertis insulis, . . .* (Basel: 1521), 36–39. A full list of the gifts to Charles and his mother Juana was published in Karl A. Nowotny, *Mexicanische Kostbarkeiten aus Kunstkammern der Renaissance* (Vienna: Museum für Völkerkunde, 1960), 20–25.

24. *Provinciae sive regiones in India occidentali* (1520), ff. civ′–dii. The Venetian Francesco Corner also reported these events in *Italian Reports on America, 1493–1522*, Repertorium Columbianum 10 (Turnhout: Brepols, 2001), 76–77, 130–31.

25. Hernán Cortés, *Letters from Mexico*, trans. Anthony Pagden (New Haven, Conn.: Yale University Press, 1986), 100–101; "Las quales de mas de su valor eran tales y tan maravillosas que consideradas por su novedad y estrañeza no ternian precio ni es de creer que alguno todos los principes del mundo de quien se tiene noticia las pudiesse tener tales y de tal calidad." Cortés, *Carta de relacion* (1522), f. bvi.

26. Hernán Cortés, *Les coutrées des îles et des paysages, trouvés et conquis par le capitaine de très illustre, très pussant, et invincible Charles élu empereur romain* (Anvers: Hoocstraten, 1522), f. civ.

27. Cortés, *Carta de relacion* (1522), ff. bii–biiii, bviii–c.

28. Archivo General de Indias (AGI), Patronato 180, ramos 84, 85, 88.

29. Carina L. Johnson, "Negotiating the Exotic: Aztec and Ottoman Culture in Habsburg Europe, 1500–1590" (Ph.D. dissertation, University of California at Berkeley, 2000), discusses Cortés's spiritual map of Castile, 102–4.

30. Cortés, *Carta de relacion* (1522), f. aiiii and José Miguel Morán and Fernando Checa, *El Coleccionismo en España. De la cámara de maravillas a la galería de pinturas* (Madrid: Cátedra, 1985), 17.

31. The verbal capitulation was discussed in the main body of the 1522 *Carta de relacion*, while news of the conquest of Tenochtitlan was inserted as a postscript to that letter and

detailed in Cortés, *Carta tercera de relacion* (Seville: Cromberger, 1523), printed in March 1523.

32. Dagmar Eichberger, *Leben mit Kunst, Wirken durch Kunst: Sammelwesen und Hofkunst unter Margarete von Österreich, Regentin der Niederlande* (Turnhout: Brepols, 2002), esp. 167–85, 417–35. Deanna MacDonald, "Collecting a New World: The Ethnographic Collections of Margaret of Austria," *Sixteenth Century Journal* 33 (2002): 649–63 discusses the position of Margaret's collection in the development of the *Kunstkammer.*

33. M. Michelant, "Inventaire des vaisselles, joyaux, . . . etc., de Marguerite d'Autriche . . . 9 juillet 1523," *Compte Rendu des Séances de la Commission Royale d'Histoire* 3rd ser. 12 (1871): 5–78, 83–136; Heinrich Zimerman, "Urkunden und Regesten aus dem K. u. K. Haus-, Hof- und Staats-archiv in Wien," JKSK 4 (1885): 93–123; M. Michelant, "Inventaire des joyaux, ornements d'église, . . . etc. de Charles-Quint, . . . de mai 1536," *Compte Rendu des Séances de la Commission Royale d'Histoire* 3rd ser. 13 (1872): 199–368; and Joycelyne G. Russell, *Diplomats at Work: Three Renaissance Studies* (Wolfeboro Falls, N.H.: Alan Sutton, 1992). Alfred Kohler, *Antihabsburgische Politik in der Epoche Karls V* (Göttingen: Vandenhoeck & Ruprecht, 1982), 98–159.

34. For feather plumes in military garb, see J. R. Hale, *Artists and Warfare in the Renaissance* (New Haven: Yale University Press, 1990), 42–73. For their use in processions, see Necipoglu, "Süleyman the Magnificent"; Pia Cuneo, *Art and Politics in Early Modern Germany* (Leiden: Brill, 1998), 162–76; and Johannes Müllner, *Die Annalen der Reichsstadt Nürnberg von 1623, Teil III,* ed. M. Diefenbacher (Nuremberg: Stadtrats zu Nürnberg, 2003), 469, 483, 487.

35. Österreichische Nationalbibliothek (ÖNB), Codex 7871, was kept by several of Ferdinand's Castilian courtiers.

36. ÖNB Codex 7871, ff. 1–59, 77–111; and Carl Eduard Förstemann, *Neues Urkundenbuch zur Geschichte der evangelischen Kirchen-Reformation,* reprint (Hildesheim: Georg Olms, 1976) 121, 127.

37. "Ornamento" was used to designate ceremonial and clerical robes in Isabel of Castile's collections; *Testamentaría de Isabel la Católica,* ed. Antonio de la Torre (Valladolid: 1968), 264–336. In sixteenth-century central European pamphlets on spectacle, the term was often used to refer to the emperor's ceremonial robes and other regal adornments. *Geschichts Beschreybung/ Unsers aller gnedigisten Herrn/ des Rö. Kayser Carls des fünfften Belehnung . . .* [1530]; and later, *Habitus Praecipuorum Populorum, Tam Virorum Quam Foeminarum Singulari arte depicti. Trachtenbuch: Darin fast allerley und der fürnembsten Nationen/ die heutigs tag bekandt sein / Kleidungen / beyde wie es bey Manns und Weibspersonen gebreuchlich / mit allem vleiß abgerissen sein / sehre lustig und kurtzweilig zusehen* (Nuremberg: Hans Weigel, 1577).

38. ÖNB Codex 7871, ff. 196–99′.

39. "la yndia nueva mente fallada de que hera señor montezuma que agora se llama la nueva españa"; ÖNB Codex 7871, f. 197′.

40. "se pone el sacerdote quando quere sacrificar a los dioses o ydoles," ÖNB Codex 7871, f. 198.

41. Necipoglu, "Süleyman the Magnificent," 411–15.

42. *RTA,* vol. 4, ed. A. Wrede (Gotha: Perthes, 1905), "hat Verdinando als stathalter die reichsstend in die redt herfordern lassen," 262, also 54, 102, 176–77. ÖNB Codex 7871, 197′–98. For Ferdinand's motives, see Paula Fichtner, *Ferdinand I of Austria* (Boulder, Colo.: Eastern European Monographs, 1982).

43. *RTA,* 4: 290–95. The Edict of Worms (1521) banned Martin Luther's teaching in the Holy Roman Empire. For vivid details of the diet, see Förstemann, *Neues Urkundenbuch zur Geschichte der evangelischen Kirchen-Reformation,* 152–57. For anti-Habsburg political sentiments, see Kohler, *Antihabsburgische Politik,* 70–97.

44. Andreas Bodenstein von Karlstadt, *Von abtuhung der Bylder* (Schyrlentz, 1522), f. aii′, and Diepold Peringer, *Eyn sermon gepredigt vom Pawren zu Werdt// bey Nürnberg / am Sonntag vor Faßnacht / von dem freyen willen des mennschen/ auch von anrüffung der hailigen* (Augsburg, 1524), includes an attack on Herod's appearance in regal vestments, f. iiii. For iconoclasm in the early Reformation, see Lee Palmer Wandel, *Voracious Idols and Violent Hands: Iconoclasm in Reformation Zurich, Strasbourg, and Basel* (Cambridge: Cambridge University Press, 1995).

45. Staatsarchiv Nuremberg (StAN), Ratsbuch 12, f. 229′; and Ratsverlässe 701, ff. 13–13′. *RTA*, 4: 44, 242, 738–44; and Günter Vogler, *Nürnberg 1524/25. Studien zur Geschichte der reformatorischen und sozialen Bewegung in der Reichsstadt* (Berlin: Deutscher Verlag der Wissenschaften, 1982), 60–61.

46. Uwe Müller, "Herzog Wilhelm V. und das Reichsheiltum," *MVGN* 72 (1985): 118–29; StAN, Krönungsakten 1, ff. 101–13.

47. See Alfonso de Valdés, *Diálogo de las cosas ocurridas en Roma* (Madrid: Espasa-Calpe, 1969), 121–25; and David Goodman, *Power and Penury: Government, Technology and Science in Philip II's Spain* (Cambridge: Cambridge University Press, 1988), 16, 44.

48. Hernán Cortés, *Praeclara Ferdinandi. Cortesii de Nova Maris Oceani Hyspania Narratio Sacratissimo. ac Invictissimo Carolo Romanorum Imperatori. . . .* (Nuremberg: Peypus, 1524), ff. aii, xlix.

49. Hans-Otto Keunecke, "Friedrich Peypus (1485–1535)," *MVGN* 72 (1985): 1–65.

50. Cortés, *Praeclara*, ff. aiii–aiv.

51. The *Praeclara*'s subtitle is "In qua Continentur Plurima scitu, & admiratione digna Circa egregias earum provintiarum Vrbes, Incolarum mores, puerorum Sacrificia, & Religiosas personas, Potissimumque de Celebri Civitate Temixtitan Variisque illius mirabilibus," f. ai, also aiii–aiv.

52. "Idolum lapideum," "Templum ubi sacrificant," "Capita sacrificatorum," Cortés, *Praeclara*, foldout map.

53. Martin Luther, *Vom Kriege widder den Türken* [1529], *Luther's Werke*, vol. 30:2 (Weimar: Hermann Böhlau, 1909).

54. StAN, Krönungsakten 1, ff. 101–21, and SI Losungsamt 134, no. 19; Albrecht Kircher, *Deutsche Kaiser in Nürnberg* (Nuremberg: V. die Egge, 1955).

55. Müllner, *Die Annalen der Reichstadt Nürnberg von 1623*, Teil III, 487; and Müller, "Herzog Wilhelm V. und das Reichsheiltum," 118–19.

56. Wandel, 116; StAN, SI Losungsamt 131, no. 22; Carl Christensen, "Iconoclasm and the Preservation of Ecclesiastical Art in Reformation Nuernberg," *Archiv für Reformationsgeschichte* 61 (1970): 220; Gerald Strauss, *Nuremberg in the Sixteenth Century* (Bloomington: Indiana University Press, 1976), 184–86.

57. Josef Kohler, ed., *Die Carolina und ihre Vorgängerinnen* (Halle: Verlag des Waisenhauses, 1900), 91–92.

58. Haus-, Hof-, und Staatsarchiv, Austria (HHStA), Hofsachen, Karton 103 ff. 123–38.

59. Pedro de Madrazo, "Über Krönungsinsignien und Staatsgewänder Maximilian I. und Karl V. und ihr Schicksal in Spanien" *JKSK* 9 (1889): 446–64 and for context, Regine Jorzick, *Herrschaftssymbolik und Staat* (Vienna: Geschichte und Politik, 1998), 78–98.

60. *La conquista del Peru, llamada la nueva Castilla* (Seville: 1534); Francisco de Xérez, *Verdadera relacion de la conquista del Peru* (Seville: B. Perez, 1534); and *Newe Zeytung aus Hispanien und Italien* [1534] in Habsburg territories. AGI Patronato Real [2460] Leg. 93 n. 4 r. 4; HHStA, Belgien PA 25 [1533], ff. 150–50′.

61. See Xérez, esp. f. Bii′ for Atahualpa's sovereignty, and Alonso de Santa Cruz, *Crónica del Emperador Carlos V*, vol. 3 (Madrid: Patronato de Huérfanos de Intendencia é Intervención Militares, 1922), chap. 34, 164–73.

62. "son de ver. . . . porque cosa que fasta oy no se ha visto en *Indias* otro semejante ni creo que lo hay en poder de ningun Principe," *Libro primero de Cabildos de Lima*, vol. 3, *Documentos* (Lima: 1888), 127.

63. "algunas piezas de las más estrañas e de poco peso," *Libro Primero de Cabildos de Lima*, 128.

64. *Libro Primero de Cabildos de Lima*, 129–30. For slightly varying lists of Pizarro's presentation, see Xérez, f. [cvii']; Rafael Loredo, *Bocetos para la Nueva Historia del Perú: Los Repartos* (Lima: D. Miranda, 1958), 42–43; "Nouvelles certaines des Isles du Peru. Lyon, 1534," trans. Raul Porras Barrenechea, *Las Relaciones primitivas de la conquista del Perú*, Universidad de San Marcos, Instituto Raúl Porras Barrenechea 3 (Lima: 1967), 76–77.

65. Salinas, *El emperador Carlos V*, 562.

66. Contarini's description is in *Relazioni degli ambasciatori venetia al senato*, ed. Eugenio Alberi 1:2 (Florence: Clio, 1840), 52–53; Las Casas, *Apologetica Historia Summaria*, vol. 7, *Obras completas* (Madrid: Alianza, 1992), 592–93; and for sixteenth-century European aesthetic reaction to Mexican featherwork, see Alessandra Russo's "Plumes of Sacrifice: Transformations in Sixteenth-Century Mexican Feather Art," *Res* 42 (2002): 227–49, esp. 236–37.

CHAPTER 5. DEAD NATURES OR STILL LIFES?
SCIENCE, ART, AND COLLECTING IN THE SPANISH BAROQUE

The authors gratefully acknowledge the support of the project "Science, Court and Empire: Natural Knowledge and the Spanish Monarchy in the Modern Period (1600–1800)" (HUM2004–02590), the FPU Predoctoral Grant Program from the Spanish Ministry of Education and Science, and the Fundación Esquerdo and the Residencia de Estudiantes, Madrid.

1. See Jens Høyrup, "Reflections on the Baroque in the History of Science," *Physis: Rivista Internazionale di Storia della Scienza* 34 (1997): 675–94, a review of Gunnar Eriksson, *The Atlantic Vision: Olaus Rudbeck and Baroque Science* (Canton, Mass.: Science History, 1994). Giuseppe Olmi and Paula Findlen, among others, have produced noteworthy contributions on the Italian case: Olmi, *L'Inventario del mondo: Catalogazione della natura e luoghi del sapere nella prima età moderna* (Bologna: Il Mulino, 1992); Findlen, *Possessing Nature: Museums, Collecting, and Scientific Culture in Early Modern Italy* (Berkeley: University of California Press, 1994); and Findlen, ed., *Athanasius Kircher: The Last Man Who Knew Everything* (London: Routledge, 2004). There is an ongoing project on baroque science at the Unit for History and Philosophy of Science of the University of Sydney.

2. Pamela Smith, "Art, Science, and Visual Culture in Early Modern Europe," *Isis* 97 (2006): 83–100. For the particular issue of science and still-life painting, see, for example, Olmi, *L'Inventario del mondo*, part 1.

3. See Norman Bryson, *Looking at the Overlooked: Four Essays on Still Life Painting* (London: Reaktion Books, 1990), chap. 1.

4. Pliny, *Natural History*, XXXV, 36.

5. Regarding the Spanish case, see William B. Jordan and Peter Cherry, *Spanish Still Life from Velázquez to Goya* (London: National Gallery, 1996); and Cherry, *Arte y naturaleza: El bodegón español en el siglo de Oro* (Madrid: Fund. apoyo Historia Arte Hispánico, 2000). The characterization of this genre, as we will see later, is similar in many cultures, but its designation varies: *Pittura di cose piccole, still-stehende Sache, nature reposeé, bodegones*.

6. Harold J. Cook, *Matters of Exchange: Commerce, Medicine, and Science in the Dutch Golden Age* (New Haven, Conn.: Yale University Press, 2007); Svetlana Alpers, *The Art of Describing: Dutch Art in the Seventeenth Century* (Chicago: University of Chicago Press, 1984).

7. José María López Piñero, *Ciencia y técnica en la sociedad española de los siglos XVI y XVII* (Barcelona: Labor, 1979).

8. Jonathan Brown, *Kings and Connoisseurs: Collecting Art in Seventeenth-Century Europe* (New Haven, Conn.: Yale University Press, 1995), trans. into Spanish as *El triunfo de la pintura: Sobre el coleccionismo cortesano en el siglo XVII* (Madrid: Nerea, 1995).

9. See Findlen, *Possessing Nature*; Lorraine Daston and Katharine Park, *Wonders and the Order of Nature: 1150–1750* (New York: Zone Books, 1998).

10. Brown, *Kings and Connoisseurs*, chap. 3. For a more precise account of Philip IV and his collecting practices, see José Miguel Morán and Fernando Checa, *El coleccionismo en España: de la cámara de maravillas a la galería de pinturas* (Madrid: Cátedra, 1985), 282–306; and the monograph V. V. A. A., *Tras el centenario de Felipe IV* (Madrid: Fundación Universitaria Española, 2006).

11. Jonathan Brown and John H. Elliott, *A Palace for a King: The Buen Retiro and the Court of Philip IV* (New Haven, Conn.: Yale University Press, 1980).

12. Benito Navarrete, "Fuentes iconográficas para el Salón de Reinos del Buen Retiro," in V. V. A. A., *Tras el centenario de Felipe IV*.

13. Fernando Rodríguez de la Flor, *La península metafísica: Arte, literarura y pensamiento en la España de la Contrarrefroma* (Madrid: Biblioteca Nueva, 1999).

14. S. Speth-Holterhoff, *Les Peintres flamands de cabinets d'amateurs au XVIIe siècle* (Brussels: Elsevier, 1957); Zirka Filipczak, *Picturing Art in Antwerp: 1550–1700* (Princeton, N.J.: Princeton University Press, 1987).

15. Brown, *Kings and Connoisseurs*, 147–84.

16. Ernst H. Gombrich, *Art and Illusion: A Study in the Psychology of Pictorial Representation* (London: Phaidon, 1983).

17. See, for example, Marcus B. Burke, *Collections of Paintings in Madrid, 1601–1755*, 2 vols. (Los Angeles: Provenance Index of the Getty Information Institute, 1997).

18. Fernando Checa, ed., *El Real Alcázar de Madrid: Dos siglos de arquitectura y coleccionismo en la corte de los Reyes de España* (Madrid: Nerea, 1994).

19. Art historian Javier Portús chose the phrase as the title for an exhibition on still life paintings at the Prado Museum. See Javier Portús, ed., *Lo fingido verdadero* (Madrid: Museo del Prado, 2006).

20. Wilma George, "Alive or Dead: Zoological Collections in the Seventeenth Century," in Oliver Impey and Arthur MacGregor, eds., *The Origins of Museums: The Cabinet of Curiosities in Sixteenth and Seventeenth Century Europe* (Oxford: Clarendon Press, 1985), 245–56.

21. Silent objects present a mute contrast to the "talking objects" discussed in Lorraine Daston, ed., *Things That Talk: Object Lessons from Art and Science* (New York: Zone Books, 2004), esp. "Introduction." See also Daston, ed., *Biographies of Scientific Objects* (Chicago: University of Chicago Press, 2000).

22. Jean Baudrillard, *El sistema de los objetos* (México: Siglo XXI, 2004), 98.

23. Baudrillard, *El sistema de los objetos*, 108–11.

24. Bryson, *Looking at the Overlooked*, chap. 2.

25. Vicente Carducho, *Diálogos de la pintura* (Madrid, 1633); Francisco Pacheco, *Arte de la pintura* (Seville, 1649).

26. Charles Sterling, *Still Life Painting from Antiquity to the Present Time* (Paris: Pierre Tisné, 1959), 71.

27. Jordan and Cherry, *Spanish Still Life*, 30.

28. For the Spanish baroque tradition, see Enrique Valdivieso, *Vanidades y desengaños en la pintura española del Siglo de Oro* (Madrid: Fundación de apoyo a la Historia del Arte Hispánico, 2002).

29. Harold J. Cook, "Time's Bodies: Crafting the Preparation and Preservation of Naturalia," in Pamela Smith and Paula Findlen, eds., *Merchants and Marvels: Commerce, Science, and Art in Early Modern Europe* (New York: Routledge, 2002), 230.

30. Fernando Rodríguez de la Flor, *Barroco: Representación e ideología en el mundo hispánico (1580–1680)* (Madrid: Cátedra, 2002), *Pasiones frías: Secreto y disimulación en el barroco hispano* (Madrid: Marcial Pons, 2005), and *Era melancólica: Figuras del imaginario barroco* (Barcelona: José J. de Olañeta, 2007).

31. Another example of a comparison between anatomy and vanitas painting is M. J. López Terrada and F. Jerez Moliner, "El *Atlas anatómico* de Crisóstomo Martínez como ejemplo de *vanitas*," *Boletín del Museo e Instituto Camón Aznar* 56 (1994): 5–34. On the Spanish microscopist, see Nuria Valverde, "Small Parts: Crisóstomo Martínez (1638–1694), Bone Histology, and the Visual Making of Body Wholeness," 100 (2009): 505–36.

32. Rodríguez de la Flor, *La península metafísica*, chap. 6.

33. Cook, "Time's Bodies," 229–31.

34. The treatise was published in Madrid in 1640. On Juan Eusebio Nieremberg, see Juan Pimentel, "Baroque Natures: Nieremberg, American Wonders and the Preter-Imperial Natural History," in Daniela Bleichmar, Paula De Vos, Kristin Huffine, and Kevin Sheehan, eds., *Science in the Spanish and Portuguese Empires, 1500–1800* (Stanford, Calif.: Stanford University Press, 2008), 93–112.

35. Søren Kierkegaard, *Either/Or* (1843); Joseph Leo Koerner, "The Mortification of the Image: Death as a Hermeneutic in Hans Baldung Grien," *Representations* 10 (1985): 52–101.

36. Julie V. Hansen, "Resurrecting Death: Anatomical Art in the Cabinet of Dr. Frederik Ruysch," *Art Bulletin* 78, 4 (1996): 663–79.

37. The literature on flower painting and its relation to "scientific" illustrations is large. In the Spanish context, see, for example, María José López Terrada, *Tradición y cambio en la pintura valenciana de flores (1600–1850)* (Valencia: Ajuntament, 2001).

38. Claudia Swan, "Ad vivum, naer het Leven, from the Life: Defining a Mode of Representation," *Word and Image* 11 (1995): 353–72.

39. Brian W. Ogilvie, *The Science of Describing: Natural History in Renaissance Europe* (Chicago: University of Chicago Press, 2006).

40. Alfonso Pérez Sánchez, *Pintura española de bodegones y floreros* (Tokyo: National Museum of Western Art, 1992), 13.

41. Lissa Roberts, "A World of Wonders, a World of One," in Smith and Findlen, *Merchants and Marvels*, 404.

42. Anne Goldgar, *Tulipmania: Money, Honor, and Knowledge in the Dutch Golden Age* (Chicago: University of Chicago Press, 2007).

43. Agnes Arber, *Herbals: Their Origin and Evolution: A Chapter in the History of Botany, 1470–1670* (Cambridge: Cambridge University Press, 1986).

44. López Terrada, *Tradición y cambio*, 100–101, which follows Sam Segal's approach in *Flowers and Nature: Netherlandish Flower Painting of Four Centuries* (The Hague: SDU, 1990).

45. Paula Findlen, "Inventing Nature: Commerce, Art, and Science in the Early Modern Cabinet of Curiosities," in Smith and Findlen, *Merchants and Marvels*, 307.

46. For the Spanish case, see, for example, María José López Terrada, "Hernández and Spanish Painting in the Seventeenth Century," in Simon Varey, Rafael Chabrán, and Dora B Weine, eds., *Searching for the Secrets of Nature: The Life and Works of Dr. Francisco Hernández* (Stanford, Calif.: Stanford University Press, 2000), 151–69. An interesting example of this would be the case of Luis Meléndez (1716–80): his still-life paintings, which frequently feature elements from the New World, were commissioned as part of the decoration of the prince's Cabinet of Natural History, at the end of the eighteenth century. Again, we find natural specimens and paintings sharing the same space: "art and nature together under the same roof," according to the inscription that Charles III ordered for the frontispiece of the Royal Cabinet of Natural History (today the Academy of Fine Arts) in Madrid. For the Dutch case, see, for example, Julie Hochstrasser, *Still Life and Trade in the Dutch Golden Age* (New Haven, Conn.: Yale University Press, 2007).

47. Simon Schama, *The Embarrassment of Riches: An Interpretation of Dutch Culture in the Golden Age* (London: Collins, 1988); Sam Segal, *A Prosperous Past: The Sumptuous Still Life in The Netherlands, 1600–1700* (The Hague: SDU, 1989).

48. Pérez Sánchez, *Pintura española de bodegones y floreros*, 93.

49. For botany, see Londa Schiebinger and Claudia Swan, eds., *Colonial Botany: Science, Commerce, and Politics in the Early Modern World* (Philadelphia: University of Pennsylvania Press, 2005).

50. Findlen, "Inventing Nature," 299.

51. Findlen, "Inventing Nature," 299.

52. Smith and Findlen, "Commerce and the Representation of Nature in Art and Science," in Smith and Findlen, *Merchants and Marvels*, 15.

53. As discussed in Sachiko Kusukawa and Ian Maclean, eds., *Transmitting Knowledge: Words, Images, and Instruments in Early Modern Europe* (Oxford: Oxford University Press, 2006); Wolfgang Lefèvre, Jurgen Renn, and Urs Schoepflin, eds., *The Power of Images in Early Modern Science* (Basel: Birkhäuser, 2003); and Pamela Smith, *The Body of the Artisan: Art and Experience in the Scientific Revolution* (Chicago: University of Chicago Press, 2004).

54. Brian S. Baigrie, ed., *Picturing Knowledge: Historical and Philosophical Problems Concerning the Use of Art in Science* (Toronto: University of Toronto Press, 1996).

55. Smith and Findlen, "Commerce and the Representation of Nature in Art and Science," 3.

56. Olmi, *L'Inventario del mondo*, part 1; Bryson, *Looking at the Overlooked*, 85.

CHAPTER 6. CRYING A MUCK: COLLECTING, DOMESTICITY, AND ANOMIE IN SEVENTEENTH-CENTURY BANTEN AND ENGLAND

Epigraphs.—Anon., *A Most Execrable and Barbarous Murder done by an East-Indian Devil, or a Native of Java-Major in the Road of Bantam, Aboard an English Ship called the Coster, on the 22 of October last, 1641* (London: Thomas Banks, 1642), 3; *Bujangga Manik*, old Sundanese palm-leaf manuscript, western Java, ca. early sixteenth century, ll. 1–7, Bodleian Library, Oriental, MS. Jav.b.3(R), f. 1, trans. J. Noorduyn, *Three Old Sundanese Poems* (Leiden: KITLV, 2006), 241. The manuscript copy may date from the late sixteenth or early seventeenth century; the Bodleian acquired it in 1627.

1. Boise Penrose, "Some Jacobean Links Between America and the Orient," *Virginia Magazine of History and Biography* 48, 4 (October 1940): 289; Walter Lippmann, *New Republic* (February 17, 1917): 60. Lippmann's actual terms were "western world," "Atlantic Powers," and "Atlantic community." In 1941, Forrest Davis wrote of the "Atlantic System"; Davis, *The Atlantic System: The Story of Anglo-American Control of the Seas* (New York: Oxford University Press, 1941); Lippmann, *U.S. War Aims* (Boston: Little, Brown, 1944). See Bernard Bailyn, *Atlantic History: Concept and Contours* (Cambridge, Mass.: Harvard University Press, 2005), 6–7.

2. Miles Ogborn, *Global Lives: Britain and the World, 1550–1800* (Cambridge: Cambridge University Press, 2008), esp. 131–40; Linda Colley, *The Ordeal of Elizabeth Marsh: A Woman in World History* (London: Harper, 2007).

3. Dennis Flynn and Arturo Giraldez, "Cycles of Silver: Global Economic Unity Through the Mid-Eighteenth Century," *Journal of World History* 13, 2 (Fall 2002): 391–427; Kenneth Pomeranz, *The Great Divergence: China, Europe and the Making of the Modern World Economy* (Princeton, N.J.: Princeton University Press, 2000), 190 and passim; Andre Gunder Frank, *ReOrient: Global Economy in the Asian Age* (Berkeley: University of California Press, 1998). William Schell frames this as a kind of symbiosis in "Silver Symbiosis: ReOrienting Mexican Economic History," *Hispanic American Historical Review* 81, 1 (2001): 89–133. See also the important critique by Robert Brenner and Chris Isett, "England's Divergence from China's Yangzi Delta: Property Relations, Microeconomics, and Patterns of Development,"

Journal of Asian Studies 61, 2 (May 2002): 609–62, which argues that domestic issues about property (agrarian capitalism in England) drove this divergence. The outlines of this debate come from Adam Smith, "Of Systems of Political Economy," *The Wealth of Nations* (London: Strahan and Cadell, 1776), bk. 4, chap. 1.

4. Cf. David O'Hara, *English Newsbooks and the Irish Rebellion, 1641–1649* (Portland, Ore.: Four Courts, 2006); and Joad Raymond, *The Invention of the Newspaper: English Newsbooks, 1641–1649* (Oxford: Oxford University Press, 1996).

5. For a methodology of the sociology of the book, see Adrian Johns, *The Nature of the Book: Print and Knowledge in the Making* (Chicago: University of Chicago Press, 1998), and Miles Ogborne, *Indian Ink: Script and Print in the Making of the English East India Company* (Chicago: University of Chicago Press, 2007). On print in relation to time and space, see Benedict Anderson, *Imagined Communities: Reflections on the Origin and Spread of Nationalism* (London: Verso, 1991).

6. Sir Francis Drake introduced the word as "cricke, a dagger" along with thirty-two other Javanese words, noting that they "bought reasonable store." Richard Hakluyt, *The Principall Navigations, Voyages, Traffiques and Discoveries of the English Nation* (London: 1600), III, 741–42. See also Edmund Scott, *An Exact Discourse of the Subtilties, Fashions, Pollicies, Religion, and Ceremonies of the East Indians, as well Chyneses as Javans, there abyding and dweling* (London: W.W. for Walter Burre, 1606), unpaginated, in William Foster, ed., *The Voyage of Sir Henry Middleton* (London: Hakluyt Society, 1943), 171.

7. Scott, *Exact Discourse*, April 1604, 106–7, 110; Arthur MacGregor, *Tradescant's Rarities: Essays on the Foundation of the Ashmoleon Museum* (Oxford: Clarendon Press, 1983), 150–66. My thanks to Annabel Gallop and Arthur MacGregor for pointing me toward these.

8. Pamphlets from the 1580s routinely gave the motivation for such murders as the "foraine juristiction" presiding over Catholic belief: see *A True Report of the Late Horrible Murther Committed by William Sherwood* (London: 1581), B3. "Bloody," "barbarous," and "execrable" were all common title adjectives in the genre.

9. Largely due to Stamford Raffles. Personal conversation with Annabel Teh Gallop. For Cope's collection, see *Thomas Platter's Travels in England, 1599*, trans. Clare Williams (London: J. Cape, 1937), 171, 173.

10. Paula Findlen, *Possessing Nature: Museums, Collecting and Scientific Culture in Early Modern Italy* (Berkeley: University of California Press, 1994), 94. The attribution of this shift to Descartes and Galileo can be found in Krzysztof Pomian, *Collectors and Curiosities: Paris and Venice, 1500–1800* (London: Polity Press, 1990), 46–78.

11. For diverse senses of "curiosity" in Europe, see Neil Kenny, *The Uses of Curiosity in Early Modern France and Germany* (Oxford: Oxford University Press, 2004). On the complexity of collecting as it relates to exchange at a global level in this period, see my "On the Movement of Porcelains: Rethinking the Birth of the Consumer Society as Interactions of Exchange Networks, China and Britain, 1600–1750," in John Brewer and Frank Trentmann, eds., *Consuming Cultures, Global Perspectives: Historical Trajectories, Transnational Exchanges* (Oxford: Berg, 2006), 95–122.

12. C. A. Bayly, *The Birth of the Modern World, 1780–1914* (Oxford: Blackwell, 2004), 49; John Richards, *The Unending Frontier: An Environmental History of the Early Modern World* (Berkeley: University of California Press, 2003), 1, 90–97. On domesticity, see also the argument about the devolution of royal authority and the "modern tendency toward conceptual division" in Michael McKeon, *The Secret History of Domesticity: Public, Private and the Division of Knowledge* (Baltimore: Johns Hopkins University Press, 2005), xxiv, 48; and Julia Adams's attention to the tension between patriarchal patrimonialism and lateral fraternal (or sibling-like) alliances and rivalries, especially with regard to the English and Dutch East India Companies in *The Familial State: Ruling Families and Merchant Capitalism in Early Modern Europe* (Ithaca, N.Y.: Cornell University Press, 2005), 127–36.

13. For the feudal thesis, see Johan Talens, *Een feodale samenleving in koloniaal vaarwarter: Staatsforming, koloniale expansie en economische onderontwikkeling in Banten, West-Java (1600–1750)* (Hilversum: Uitgeverij Verloren, 1999); and Ota Atsushi, *Changes of Regime and Social Dynamics in West Java: Society, State and the Outer World of Banten, 1750–1830* (Leiden: Brill, 2006). For the cosmopolitan argument, see Anthony Reid, "The Cosmopolitan City as an Asian Maritime Tradition," paper presented at the symposium "Towards the Construction of Urban Cultural Theories," Osaka City University, March 2006, http://ucrc.lit.osaka-cu.ac.jp/200603sympo/index_e.html, accessed 5/10/06; and Reid, *Southeast Asia in the Age of Commerce, 1450–1680* (New Haven, Conn.: Yale University Press, 1993), 2: 66.

14. Scott, *Exact Discourse*, 83; Guildhall MSS, Court of Aldermen Repertory, 29 (1609), 13v–14, cited in Paul Griffiths, *Lost Londons: Change, Crime and Control in the Capital City, 1550–1660* (Cambridge: Cambridge University Press, 2008), 309. Thanks to Paul Griffiths for additional information about this citation. For a time after 1642, the pamphlet's spelling "a muck" prevailed, so Andrew Marvell wrote, "Like a raging Indian. . . . he runs a mucke (as they call it there) stabbing every man he meets." *The Rehearsal Transpros'd* (London: Nathaniel Ponder, 1672), 59.

15. For the most recent scholarship on Scott's famous description of torture, see Eric Hayot, *The Hypothetical Mandarin: Sympathy, Modernity, and Chinese Pain* (Oxford: Oxford University Press, 2009), chap. 1.

16. Scott, *Exact Discourse*, 121–22, 168.

17. On the ways that both Marcel Mauss's and Claude Lévi-Strauss's conceptions of exchange downplay the problem and question of keeping, see Annette Weiner, *Inalienable Possessions: The Paradox of Keeping-While-Giving* (Berkeley: University of California Press, 1992); and Maurice Godelier, *L'Énigme du don* (Paris: Libairie Arthème Fayard, 1996).

18. Claude Lévi-Strauss, *The Way of the Masks*, trans. Sylvia Modelski (London: Cape, 1983), 184; *Anthropology and Myth* (Oxford: Blackwell 1987), 153–55; "Maison," in Pierre Bonte and Michel Izard, eds., *Dictionnaire de l'ethnologie* (Paris: PUF, 1991), 435. See also Janet Carsten and Stephen Hugh-Jones, eds., *About the House: Lévi-Strauss and Beyond* (Cambridge: Cambridge University Press, 1995); and Charles Macdonald, ed., *De la hutte au palais: sociétés "à maisons" en Asie du sud-est insulare* (Paris: CNRS, 1987).

19. For an introduction to the complex vocabulary surrounding the Javanese house, see P. A. Koesoemo Joedo, "Het Javaansche Voorerf" and Sastra Amidjaja, "Het bouwen van Javaansche huizen," *Djawa* 4 (1924): 105–17.

20. Benedict Anderson, "The Idea of Power in Javanese Culture," in Claire Holt, ed., *Culture and Politics in Indonesia* (Ithaca, N.Y.: Cornell University Press, 1972), 12–13.

21. Bodleian Library, Western MSS, *Benefactors' Register*, 1: 261.

22. Cf. Tom Beaumont James, "James, Richard," *Oxford Dictionary of National Biography* (London: Oxford University Press, 2004); online ed., January 2008.

23. Bodleian Library MS Jav.b.3. It has recently been translated by J. Noorduyn in *Three Old Sundanese Poems*, ed. J. Noorduyn and A. Teeuw (Leiden: KITLV, 2006), 241–76. I have followed Noorduyn's translation, checking the transcription in relation to the Oxford manuscript.

24. This particular set of tropes highlights why David Sabean proposes the phrase "ideologies of the house," because focusing on the house tends to idealize certain models of masculinity. *Property, Production and Family in Neckarhausen, 1700–1870* (Cambridge: Cambridge University Press, 1990), 88–116, 249, 429. On the vital house, see Roxana Waterson, *The Living House: An Anthropology of Architecture in Southeast Asia* (Kuala Lumpur: Oxford University Press, 1990), 115–37.

25. On varieties of wood and their significance, see Ann Kumar, *Java and Modern Europe: Ambiguous Encounters* (Richmond, Va.: Curzon Press, 1997), 127–28.

26. Portuguese accounts pick up on this. Cf. Fernão Mendez Pinto, *Peregrinacam de Fernam Mendez Pinto* (Lisbon: Pedro Crasbeeck, 1614), trans. Rebecca Catz, *The Travels of Mendes Pinto* (Chicago: University of Chicago Press, 1989), 28, 49, 111–12, 247, 331, 414.

27. Teeuw, *Three Old Sundanese Poems,* 143. Teeuw notes, following Noorduyn, how "localized" all these concepts are, rather than referring to a broader Indian/Sanskrit canon (145); J. Noorduyn, "Some Remarks on Javanese Chronogram Words: A Case of Localization," *Bijdragen tot de Taal-, Land- en Volkenkunde* 149 (1993): 309.

28. Following Jacques Derrida, *Given Time*, vol. 1, *Counterfeit Money*, trans. Peggy Kamuf (Chicago: University of Chicago Press, 1992), 147.

29. Bodleian Library MS Laud Or. Rolls a. 1. Similar pepper receipts survive in the Sloane Collection (donated 1753 in the British Museum, Sloane 1035 in Javanese) between Si Cina Kamasan and Ratu Kilenm with a partially legible English name [—anes]; and most interestingly Sloane 1403A and 1403E (on thick bamboo) in Javanese and Chinese.

30. British Library, India Office Records, Factory Records, Java G/21/3–2, vol. 1, March 11, 1625, ff. 163–65. The present and letter that went with it are described in W. N. Sainsbury, *Calendar of State Papers, Colonial Series, East Indies, China and Persia, 1625–1629* (London: Longman, 1884), 576, 645–66. Charles's response to the first letter is transliterated from the Malay in Leiden University Cod. Or. 8514. A second letter in Malay from Pangéran Ratu to Charles I responding to its loss is PRO SP 102/4/50. See Annabel Teh Gallop, "Seventeenth-Century Indonesian Letters in the Public Record Office," *Indonesia and the Malay World* 31, 91 (November 2003): 418–21.

31. Pangéran Anom of Banten to Charles I, 1635, PRO SP 102/4/37; British Library, India Office Records, Factory Records Java, G/21/3–2, vol. 3, 352r, 353f. See also in the same volume, "Consultation held in Bantam," June 19, 1635, ff. 360r–362.

32. Canto 39.27. See Husein Djajadiningrat, *Critische beschouwing van de Sadjarah Banten* (Haarlem: Enschede, 1913), 51.

33. National Library, Jakarta MS KBG 105 Arab.; microfilm copy Leiden University, F. Or. A. 14a.

34. Kirti Chaudhuri, *The English East India Company: The Study of an Early Joint-Stock Company, 1600–1640* (London: Frank Cass, 1965), 166, citing Court books for August 1640.

35. *Calendar of State Papers, Venice*, vol. 25, *1640–2*, ed. Allen Hinds (London: Public Record Office, 1924), 74; Robert Ashton, *The Crown and the Money Market* (Oxford: Clarendon Press, 1960), 178–79, 184. On Charles I and the EIC, see Robert Brenner, *Merchants and Revolution* (Cambridge: Cambridge University Press, 1993), 306–12, 374–81.

36. Cartwright to the EIC, Bantam, March 13, 1642–43, British Library, India Office Records, E/3/18, no. 1819, ff. 1–2; and December 9, 1643, E/3/18, no. 1847, f. 3.

37. *Dagh-register gehouden int casteel Batavia vant passerende daer ter plaetse als over geheel Nederlandts-India, anno 1640–1641* (Batavia: Landsdrukkerij, 1887), 448, 470.

38. When Sir Francis Drake visited Java in 1579, he emphasized the *slametan* as a "common assembly." Hakluyt, *Principal Nauigations*, III, 739. On the *slametan*, see Clifford Geertz, *Religion in Java* (London: Free Press, 1960), 11–15.

39. *Execrable and Barbarous Murder*, 5.

40. Émile Durkheim, *Suicide: A Study in Sociology*, trans. John Spaulding and George Simpson (New York: Free Press, 1951), 219–28, 246, 254.

41. Kojin Karatani, *Architecture as Metaphor: Language, Number, Money*, trans. Sabu Kosho, ed. Michael Speaks (Cambridge, Mass.: MIT Press, 1995), 116–20, 134–35, 162–66.

42. Thomas Browne, *Religio Medici, Hydriotaphia, and the Garden of Cyrus,* ed. Robin Robbins (Oxford: Clarendon Press, 1972), 47. The coinage of "suicide" is on p. 46 in the same section. The text appeared in two pirated editions in 1642 and then in an authorized one in 1643.

Research for this paper was made possible by support from an Andrew W. Mellon Fellowship from the Center for Advanced Study in the Visual Arts, from the Conseil Régional de la Martinique, and from the Michigan Society of Fellows. I would like to thank Servus Gieben for granting me access to the collections of the Museo Francescano and express my deepest gratitude to the private collectors who have generously welcomed me into their homes to study the images discussed in this essay.

1. The three volumes of the Araldi Manuscript are in a private collection in Modena, Italy. Their illustrations have been published in Ezio Bassani and Giovanni Antonio Cavazzi, *Un cappuccino nell'Africa nera del seicento: I disegni dei Manoscritti Araldi del Padre Giovanni Antonio Cavazzi da Montecuccolo*, Quaderni Poro 4 (Milano: Associazione Poro, 1987), 89.

2. Two volumes of the Cadornega Manuscript are in the Academia das Ciências of Lisbon under the call number MS Vermelho 77; the third volume is in the British Library in London, Ms. Add. 15183. A later copy of the three volumes is also in the Bibliothèque Nationale in Paris, MS Portugais 2 to 4.

3. The Turin *Missione in prattica* manuscript has been published as an appendix in Michele Angelo Guattini, Dionigi Carli, and Francesco Surdich, *Viaggio nel Regno del Congo*, Fascino dell'ignoto 15 (Cinisello Balsamo (Milano): San Paolo, 1997). Most of its images also appeared in Paolo Collo and Silvia Benso, *Sogno: Bamba, Pemba, Ovando e altre contrade dei regni di Congo, Angola e adiacenti*, Guide Impossibili (Milano: F.M. Ricci, 1986).

4. See the description of the life and death of Georges de Gheel in Graziano M. da Leguzzano Saccardo, *Congo e Angola: Con la storia dell'antica missione dei cappuccini*, 3 vols. (Venezia-Mestre: Curia Povinciale dei Cappuccini, 1982–83), 1: 489–90. For an account of the reign of Queen Njinga, see Linda Marinda Heywood and John Kelly Thornton, *Central Africans, Atlantic Creoles, and the Foundation of the Americas, 1585–1660* (Cambridge: Cambridge University Press, 2007). Capuchin missionaries obtained the reconversion of Queen Njinga to Catholicism on her deathbed, a feat that the celebratory drawing would surely not have left aside, had it happened before its composition.

5. My translation. The Sacred Congregation for the Propagation of the Faith or Propaganda Fide was the papal administration that sponsored the Capuchin Central African mission. The mission, although first approved by the pope in 1618 before the constitution of the congregation, was reinstated in 1622 under its auspices. The friars, however, only effectively arrived in the Kongo in the 1640s because of the long and bitter diplomatic conflict between Spain and Portugal, which reverberated in Rome in a clash between Portugal and the papacy, the latter having strongly sided with Spain in the dispute. A useful history of the peripeties surrounding the planning of the Capuchin Kongo mission during these two decades can be found in Francisco Leite de Faria, *A primeira tentativa para os Capuchinhos Missionarem no Congo*, Separata from Itinerarium, ano II, no. 8 ed. (Braga: Montariol, 1956).

6. A description of the regalia of the king of Kongo can be found in André Cordeiro, "Descrição da eleição e coroação dos Reis do Congo—Segunda Relação," in *General Archives of the Society of Jesus* (Rome, 1622), Goa tome 39, vol. 1, ff. 170v–76.

7. See the description of Central African musical instruments in early modern illustrations in Bassani and Cavazzi, *Un cappuccino nell'Africa*.

8. The text of folio 101 sets the lower date by referring to Queen Njinga of Matamba. It describes an actual historical event in which two missionaries, Bonaventura da Corella and Francisco de Veas, were taken prisoners and brought to the Angolan queen to be executed. The event is reported in various sources such as Antonio Teruel, "Descripcion narrativa de la mission serafica de los padres capuchinos y sus progressos en el Reyno de Congo," in

Biblioteca Nacional de Madrid (Madrid, ca. 1640), 89. Also in Antonio da Gaeta and Francesco Maria Gioia, *La Maravigliosa conversione alla santa fede di Cristo della Regina Singa e del svo Regno di Matamba mell'africa meridionale, descritta con historico stile* (Napoli: G. Passaro, 1669), 298. "By divine intervention," reports the text of the image, "in a sudden change, [Queen Njinga] received them with benevolence and got baptized, and died a true Christian, marvelous strike of the divine providence." It then continues: "but as soon as the Queen died, faith failed in this kingdom and today we are working to bring it back, but as of now, God our Lord has not yet permitted it." Njinga died in December 1663 and was succeeded on the throne by her sister Dona Barbara under whose rule Christianity unraveled rapidly in the Matamba kingdom. As John Thornton kindly pointed to me, the assessment of the state of the mission by the author of the watercolors, therefore, places the redaction of the corpus at the earliest in the mid-1660s. At the other end of the chronological spectrum, the upper limit date is established by the publication of a number of the images from the *Parma Watercolors* in the form of prints, as illustrations for the first edition of another book, Giovanni Antonio Cavazzi and Fortunato Alamandini, *Istorica descrizione de' tre regni Congo, Matamba et Angola sitvati nell' Etiopia inferiore occidentale e delle missioni apostoliche esercitateui da religiosi capuccini* (Bologna: Giacomo Monti, 1687). Cavazzi was a Capuchin missionary who worked in Kongo and Angola between the 1650s and the 1680s.

9. The purple mombin is a small fruit of reddish color that the author describes very accurately as "frutto detto chingero [che] fa i suoi pomi come le nostre susine ma con un osso molto grosso" or "fruit called *chingero* which apples are like our prunes but with a very large pit." The image presents the small tree with its caracteristic reddish-purple fruits and small oval leaves connected directly to the main branches. For a scientific description of the fruit, see Julia Frances Morton, "Purple Mombin," in Morton, ed., *Fruits of Warm Climates* (Miami: Morton, 1987).

10. The author of the Museo Francescano drawing also declares recognizing sometimes the images of the Immaculate Conception in the transversal cut of the bananas. The crucifix and the Immaculate Conception are two of the principal devotions of the Capuchin order. This shared detail between the two works suggests the possibility that the author of the second was aware of the first. Another very close similarity between the two works is in the representation of the potatoes on the fourth row of the Museo Francescano drawing and folio 29 of the *Parma Watercolors*. This particular representation of the American root imported to Africa was also used as the basis for a print in Cavazzi's *Istorica descrizione*, in plate 10.

11. Respectively Biblioteca Nacional de Lisboa, MS 1432 FG; Biblioteca Vaticana, MS Borgiano Latino 316; and Bibioteca Civica Centrale di Torino, MS 457. The Lisbon and Vatican versions are not published. Partial reproductions of the Turin manuscript can be found in Guattini, Carli, and Surdich, *Viaggio nel Regno del Congo*, also in Collo and Benso, *Sogno: Bamba, Pemba, Ovando e altre contrad*. The entire manuscript is also available in a full online version at http://www.comune.torino.it/cultura/biblioteche/iniziative_mostre/mostre/missione/frontespizio.html/: Luca Vittonetto et al., "*Missione in Prattica*: Padri Cappuccini ne regni di Congo, Angola, et . . ." (Turin: Settore Sistema bibliotecario urbano della Città di Torino, 2003). The text and images of the three versions clearly demonstrate that they constitute a single opus. I believe that the Turin manuscript is the first version of the work, later reworked in a fuller text in the Vatican exemplar, probably in view of publication, with images presented outside the text as plates, but referring directly to the body of the text. The Lisbon codex is a direct copy of the Vatican version. Regarding authorship, although not signed, the manuscripts have been attributed convincingly to d'Asti by various authors. I am able to confirm this attribution from my own research by comparing paragraph 5 of page 3 of the Vatican manuscript to the similar relation given by d'Asti in the Propaganda Fide's SRCG

Africa-Angola, vol. 5, 1736–80, ff. 180ff. See Carlo Toso, "Relazioni inedite di P. Cherubino Cassinis da Savona sul 'Regno del Congo e sue missioni'," *Italia Francescana* 45 (1974): 138 n. 18; Louis Jadin, "Les Survivances chrétiennes au Congo au XIXème siècle," *Études d'Histoire Africaine* 1 (1970): 139 n. 4. and J. Cuvelier, "Le Vénérable André de Burgio et la situation religieuse au Congo et dans l'Angola au temps de son apostolat (1745–1761)," *Collectanea Franciscana* 32 (1962): 98 n. 53.

12. The stamp of the Sacred Congregation of the Propagation of the Faith is on the first page numbered "I" of the front matter of the manuscript.

13. Illustrated catechisms were used, for example, in colonial Latin America; see Pedro de Gante's manuscript catechisms produced in the mid-sixteenth century discussed in Pauline Watts, "Hieroglyphs of Conversion: Alien Discourses in Diego Valades's Rhetorica Christiana," *Memoriae Domenicanae* 22 (1991): 405–33.

14. The Capuchin missionaries to Central Africa came almost exclusively from Italy, except for an early Spanish mission. For a complete list of missionaries including their geographical origin, see the third volume of Saccardo, *Congo e Angola con la storia dell'antica missione dei cappuccini*.

15. See "*Parma Watercolors*," in *Private Collection* (Parma, 1663–87), 29, 35, 53.

16. Paul Hulton, "Realism and Tradition in Ethnological and Natural Imagery in the Sixteenth Century," in Allan Ellenius, ed., *The Natural Sciences and the Arts: Aspects of Interaction from the Renaissance to the 20th Century: An International Symposium* (Uppsala: Almqvist & Wiksell, 1985), 19.

17. Other similar examples of the same process are present in the *Parma Watercolors* in the depiction of the *peixe-mulher* or manatee on fols. 19 and 20 or the flamingo on fols. 47 and 53 or in the Turin *Missione in prattica* in the representation of a formidably large snake in table 20.

18. See Odell Shepard, *The Lore of the Unicorn* (New York: Barnes & Noble, 1967).

19. See T. H. Clarke, *The Rhinoceros from Dürer to Stubbs, 1515–1799* (London: Sotheby's, 1986).

20. The same simile is used in 1654 by another Serafino da Cortona in a letter: "he is also sending the horn of a unicorn that the one who gave it to me said to be real, in this language it is called abada and it is a ferocious animal that has a horn in the front"; Filippo da Firenze, "Ragguagli del Congo," in *Archivio provinziale dei Cappuccini* (Firenze, 1711), 157. See also the explanation from a Portuguese text in Biblioteca Nacional de Lisboa, Caixa 29, doc 25, "E acerca do corno do Unicorne q[u]e em Benguela dizẽ auer m[ui]tos E eu creio são Abadas, mas tẽ a mesma uirtude q[ue] o Unicorne" from Adriano Parreira, *Dicionário glossográfico e toponímico da documentação sobre Angola, séculos XV–XVII*, Imprensa Universitária 79 (Lisboa: Editorial Estampa, 1990). The description of the rhinoceros as a horse with a horn also calls to mind the parallel name given in Italian to the hippopotamus, "cavallo marino," included in the Museo Francescano drawing, that follows the same idea.

21. Bernardino Ignazio da Vezza d' Asti, "*Missione in prattica* de Rp cappuccini italiani ne regni di Congo, Angola, et Adiacenti," in *Biblioteca Vaticana* (Vatican, ca. 1750), 41.

22. "Mucha falta nos hacia el no saber hablar en su lengua pero ya con acciones esteriores, ya con lagrimas y otras demonstraciones que N. S. inspiraba procuraba cada uno significar como podia la fuerza de la divina palabra, y de la doctrina que sin entenderle ellos predicaban porque en la boca del interprete perdia la mayor p.te del ser en la substancia y modo, si bien experimentamos muchas vezes estar ya movidos los oyentes antes que el interprete les explicasse las palabras en su lengua Mosiconga, y a mi me sucedido en Pinda que sacando un devoto crucifixo con palabras mui sencillas moverse en un pequeño auditorio mas de doce hidalgos"; Juan de Santiago, "Breve relacion de lo sucedido a doce religiosos

cappuchinos de la santa sede apostolica enbio por missionarios apostolicos al Reyno de Congo. Recopilada por uno y el mas minimo indigno totalmente de tan sublime ministerio. Dedicada a nr. rm. pe. fr. Inocencio de Catalagirona, ministro general de los frailes menores capuchinos de nr. serafico se. S. Francisco," in *Real Biblioteca del Palacio* (Madrid, ca. 1650), 160–61.

23. Santiago, "Breve relacion."

24. Bernardino Ignazio da Vezza d'Asti, "*Missione in Prattica*: Padri cappuccini ne' regni di Congo, Angola, et Adiacenti," in *Biblioteca civica centrale di Torino* (Turin, ca. 1750), 2; my translation.

25. A discussion of the linguistic competence of the Capuchins can be found in Adalberto da Postioma, "Méthodologie missionaire des capucins au Congo-Matamba-Angola [1645–1834]," *Revue du Clergé Africain* 19 (1964): 368–71. For example, Girolamo de Montesarchio described his industrious efforts to learn the language: "I had copied a vocabulary, the rules of the language, the elements of catechism to prepare adults to baptism and a method to hear confession." Yet nothing would help him learn the language in spite of his efforts. He reported that it was finally a divine intervention that gave him the gift of the language. See J. Cuvelier, O. de Bouveignes, and Geronimo da Montesarchio, *Jérôme de Montesarchio, apôtre du vieux Congo*, vol. 39, Collection Lavigerie (Namur: Grands Lacs, 1951), 52.

26. Giovanni da Romano Belotti, "Avvertimenti salutevoli agli apostolici missionari, specialmente nei regni del Congo, Angola e Circonvicini," in *Biblioteca del clero* (Bergamo, 1680), 73.

27. Asti, "*Missione in Prattica* de rp cappuccini italiani," pl. II.

28. Asti, "*Missione in Prattica*," 43.

29. Asti, "*Missione in Prattica*," 44.

30. See Michel de Certeau and Luce Giard, *L'Invention du quotidien*, Collection Folio/Essais (Paris: Gallimard, 1990).

31. In the face of the cultural differences they encountered in Central Africa, the Capuchins frequently inquired to the papacy about the limits of acceptable Christian behavior and the ways in which they could or could not adapt the doctrine to the reality of their mission field. For example, in a 1650 document, the *Propaganda Fide* answered to the doubts expressed by the Capuchin friar Bonaventura da Sorrento about the administration of the sacraments in the Kongo. See Manso Paiva and Academia real das ciencias de Lisboa, *Historia do Congo* (Lisboa: Typ. da Academia, 1877), 217–24.

32. See Cécile Fromont, "Icônes chrétiennes ou symboles Kongo? L'art et la religion en Afrique centrale au temps de la traite, XVIIème–XVIIIème siècles," *Cahiers des Anneaux de la Mémoire* 12 (2008): 48–59.

33. Giuseppe Monari da Modena, "Viaggio al Congo, fatto da me fra Giuseppe da Modena missionario apostolico e predicatore capuccino, incomentato alli 11 del mese di novembre del anno 1711, e terminato alli 22 di febraro del anno 1713 etc. . . ." in *Biblioteca estense* (Modena: 1723), f. 172.

34. "De Costumi mali de Conghesi"; Asti, "*Missione in Prattica*," 58. From the index of the manuscript, 132.

35. Asti, "*Missione in Prattica*," 67, 132.

36. Asti, "*Missione in Prattica*," 76.

37. Asti, "*Missione in Prattica*."

38. The word "Religion" with a capital R here refers, of course, to the Catholic faith. In the same paragraph, the generally pessimistic Cavazzi gives a partial positive assessment of Catholicism in the Kongo: "After all, Congolese Christianity even if it had not abandoned

entirely the vain rites and heathenry (being impossible to reform these corruptions, that do not prejudice the essence of the Religion) merit the praise of very pious and zealous with regards to its dead." See Cavazzi and Alamandini, *Istorica descrizione*, 117.

39. *Parma Watercolors*, f. 83. This attitude is close to that described by William Pietz as the origin of the concept of fetishism, yet the Capuchin friars do not use this concept. See William Pietz, "The Problem of the Fetish," *Res* 9 (1985): 5–17.

40. Luca da Caltanisetta, *Diaire congolais. 1690–1701*, trans. François Bontinck, vol. 27, Publications de l'Université Lovanium de Kinshasa (Louvain: Éditions Nauwelaerts; Paris: Béatrice-Nauwelaerts, 1970), 107; Girolamo Merolla da Sorrento, "A Voyage to Congo and Several Other Countries Chiefly in Southern-Africk," in *A Collection of Voyages and Travels, Some Now First Printed from Original Manuscripts, Others Now First Published in English. In Six Volumes. With a General Preface, Giving an Account of the Progress of Navigation, from Its First Beginning. Illustrated with a Great Number of Useful Maps and Cuts, Curiously Engraven*, ed. Awnsham Churchill and John Churchill (London: Messrs. Churchill. For John Walthoe; Tho. Wotton; Samuel Birt; Daniel Browne and 3 others in London, 1732), 653.

41. Marcellino Canzani d'Atri, "Giornate apostoliche fatte a me fra Marcellino d'Atri predicatore cappucino nelle missioni de Regno d'Angola e Congo, nella Etiopia inferiore parte occidentale nell'Africa 1690" (L'Aquila, 1690–1708), 118.

42. Giovanni Antonio Cavazzi, "Missione evangelica al Regno del Congo: Araldi Manuscript," in *Araldi Collection* (Modena, 1665–68), vol. A, bk. 2, chap. 11, 171. Trans. John K. Thornton; see the translation on Thornton's blog "Central African History," at http://cen tralafricanhistory.blogspot.com/2008/08/giovanni-antoni o-cavazzi-da.html

43. Bontinck, *Diaire congolais*, 104.

44. The problem of representation was key to the definition of the idol as the locus where worship was mistakenly directed to the wrong recipient.

45. *Parma Watercolors*, f. 83.

46. Historiography on the Jaga is long and contentious. John Thornton and Linda Heywood justly recommend the summary and synthesis of the debate in the long footnote by Michel de Chandeigne in his updated translation of Pigafetta; see Filippo Pigafetta and Duarte Lopes, *Le Royaume de Congo & les contrées environnantes, 1591*, trans. Willy Bal, rev. and updated by Michel de Chandeigne and John Thornton, Collection Magellane (Paris: UNESCO, 2002), 291–95.

47. See Ezio Bassani and M. D. McLeod, *African Art and Artefacts in European Collections: 1400–1800* (London: British Museum, 2000), object number 451.

48. The basis for the image is, of course, the biblical story of the adoration of the Golden Calf. However, here the friar makes clear visually that the idol is the live animal itself rather than an image of the animal. This difference is all important for understanding and recognizing this particular setting as idolatrous.

49. Some of the images from the *Parma Watercolors* were used in Cavazzi's *Istorica descrizione* but in an illustrative manner radically different from their original intent.

CHAPTER 8. EUROPEAN WONDERS AT THE COURT OF SIAM

I thank Her Royal Highness Princess Maha Chakri Sirindorn for her comments on an early proposal for this project. I also thank William J. Klausner, president of the James H. W. Thompson Foundation in Bangkok, and Professor Thak Chaloemtiarana and the Southeast Asia Program at Cornell University, where I carried out the research for this project as a Visiting Fellow in 2006–2007.

Epigraph: *The Diary of Kosa Pan: Thai Ambassador to France, June-July 1686*, trans. Visudh Busyakul, intro. Dirk van der Cruysse, ed. Michael Smithies (Chiang Mai: Silkworm Books, 2002), 31.

1. Although the Siamese already referred to themselves in this period as Thai, I retain the terms Siam and Siamese here to distinguish between the premodern kingdom administered from Ayutthaya and the other ethnically Tai polities in parts of what are now Laos, northern Thailand, and Burma.

2. See Dhiravat Na Pombejra, *Siamese Court Life in the Seventeenth Century as Depicted in European Sources* (Bangkok: Faculty of Arts, Chulalongkorn University, 2001); Bhawan Ruangsilp, *Dutch East India Company Merchants at the Court of Ayutthaya: Dutch Perceptions of the Thai Kingdom, ca. 1604–1765* (Leiden: Brill, 2007).

3. See Dhiravat, "Curiosities and Luxuries for King and Court," in *Siamese Court Life in the Seventeenth Century*, 146–67.

4. Timon Screech, *The Lens Within the Heart: The Western Scientific Gaze and Popular Imagery in Later Edo Japan* (Honolulu: University of Hawaiʻi Press, 2002); Catherine Pagani, *Eastern Magnificence and European Ingenuity: Clocks of Late Imperial China* (Ann Arbor: University of Michigan Press, 2001).

5. Examples of the kind of mathematical and scientific apparatuses sent from France to Siam as diplomatic gifts can be seen in Michel Jacq-Hergoualc'h, *Phra Narai, Roi de Siam, et Louis XIV* (Paris: Musée de l'Orangerie, 1986).

6. Rumphius died in 1702, and his work was published posthumously as *D'Amboinsche rariteitenkamer* (Amsterdam: François Halma, 1705) and *Herbarium Amboinense* (Amsterdam, 1741–55).

7. Alexandre Chaumont, Chevalier de, *Relation de l'ambassade de Mr le Chevalier de Chaumont à la cour du Roy de Siam* (Paris: Arnoul Seneuze and Daniel Horthemels, 1686); English translation from the 1687 edition published in London and reprinted in *The Chevalier de Chaumont and the Abbé de Choisy: Aspects of the Embassy to Siam*, ed. Michael Smithies (Chiang Mai: Silkworm Books, 1997), 104.

8. For a history of Siamese relations with Europe, see Dirk van der Cruysse, *Siam and the West, 1500–1700*, trans. Michael Smithies (Chiang Mai: Silkworm Books, 1991); originally published as *Louis XIV et le Siam* (Paris: Fayard, 1991).

9. Chaumont, *Aspects of the Embassy to Siam*, 94–95.

10. Chaumont, *Aspects of the Embassy to Siam*, 97.

11. See, for example, Kenneth R. Hall, *Maritime Trade and State Development in Early Southeast Asia* (Honolulu: University of Hawaiʻi Press, 1985).

12. Chaumont, *Aspects of the Embassy to Siam*, 14, 137.

13. Jacq-Hergoualc'h, *Phra Narai, Roi de Siam, et Louis XIV*, catalogue entry 110.

14. A. D. Howell Smith, "Eastern Embroideries for the Western Market—The Victoria and Albert Museum," *Burlington Magazine for Connoisseurs* 34 (February 1919): 56–57, 59.

15. Guy Tachard, *Voyage de Siam, des Pères Jésuites, envoyez par le Roy aux Indes & à la Chine. Avec leurs observations astronomiques, et leurs remarques de physique, de géographie, d'hydrographie, & d'histoire* (Paris: Chez A. Seneuze, D. Horthemels, 1686); English translation from *A Relation of the Voyage to Siam Performed by Six Jesuits, sent by the French King, to the Indies and China, in the Year, 1685, with their Astrological Observations, and their Remarks of Natural Philosophy, Geography, Hydrography, and History* (London: T.B. for A. Churchil, 1688; Bangkok: White Lotus Press, 1999), 5–6.

16. *The Discourse at Versailles of the First Siamese Ambassadors to France, 1686–7*, trans. Michael Smithies (Bangkok: Siam Society, 1986), 52–54; cited in van der Cruysse, "Introduction" to *The Diary of Kosa Pan*, 13–14.

17. Adrien Launay, *Histoire de la mission de Siam, 1662–1811*, Archives des Missions Étrangères (Paris: Anciennes Maisons Charles Douniol et Retaux, 1920; Missions Étrangères de Paris, 2000), 1: 51; translation mine.

18. Bhawan, *Dutch East India Company Merchants at the Court of Ayutthaya*, 85.

19. Jeremias van Vliet, *Description of the Kingdom of Siam*, trans. L. F. van Ravenswaay in *Van Vliet's Siam*, ed. Chris Baker, Dhiravat Na Pombejra, Alfons van der Kraan, and David K. Wyatt (Chiang Mai: Silkworm Books, 2005), 119. Composed in 1638, the account was first published as *Beschrijving van het Koningrijk Siam* (Leyden: Frederik Haaring, 1692).

20. Simon de la Loubère, *A New Historical Relation of the Kingdom of Siam* (London: F.L for Tho. Horne, Francis Saunders, and Tho. Bennet, 1693), 30. A French edition was originally published in Amsterdam in 1691.

21. La Loubère, *A New Historical Relation of the Kingdom of Siam*, 36.

22. La Loubère, *A New Historical Relation of the Kingdom of Siam*, 37.

23. La Loubère, *A New Historical Relation of the Kingdom of Siam*, 16.

24. See Mary Baine Campbell, *Wonder and Science: Imagining Worlds in Early Modern Europe* (Ithaca, N.Y.: Cornell University Press, 1999), 5: "wonder is a form of perception now mostly associated with innocence: with children, the uneducated (that is, the poor), women, lunatics, and non-Western cultures"; Lorraine Daston and Katherine Park, *Wonders and the Order of Nature, 1150–1750* (New York: Zone Books, 1998); Joy Kenseth, ed., *The Age of the Marvelous* (Hanover, N.H.: Hood Museum of Art, Dartmouth College, 1991).

25. John Locke, *Essay Concerning Human Understanding* (London: Eliz. Holt, for Thomas Basset, 1690), 333. I am grateful to Juan Pimentel for reminding me of this anecdote.

26. Locke, *Essay Concerning Humane Understanding* (London: Printed for Awnsham and John Churchill and Samuel Manship, 1700), 29.

27. Tachard, *A Relation of the Voyage to Siam,* 171.

28. Ian Hodges, "Western Science in Siam: A Tale of Two Kings," *Osiris* 13 (1991): 80–95.

29. Engelbert Kaempfer, *A Description of the Kingdom of Siam 1690*, trans. Johann Kaspar Scheuchzer (London, 1727; Bangkok: White Orchid Press, 1987), 38.

30. On the history of indigenous and European mapping techniques in Siam, see Thongchai Winichakul, *Siam Mapped: A History of the Geo-Body of a Nation* (Honolulu: University of Hawai'i Press, 1994).

31. Jean Donneau de Visé, *Suite de voyage des ambassadeurs de Siam en France* (Paris: G. de Luyne, 1686), 55–58. This volume appeared as part 2 of the November issue of the *Mercure Galant*.

32. Chaumont, *Aspects of the Embassy to Siam*, 144.

33. Chaumont, *Aspects of the Embassy to Siam*, 138, 139, 141, 143, 145.

34. Joseph Needham, *Science and Civilization in China*, vol. 4, pt. 2 (Cambridge: Cambridge University Press, 1965), 156–65.

35. Bhawan, *Dutch East India Company Merchants at the Court of Ayutthaya*, 83–85.

36. On traditional sources of power among Tai peoples, see David K. Wyatt, *Thailand: A Short History* (New Haven, Conn.: Yale University Press, 1984).

37. Barbara Watson Andaya, "Historicising 'Modernity' in Southeast Asia," *Journal of the Economic and Social History of the Orient* 40 (1997): 391–409. The story of the Siamese monarchy's creation of a Western and modern self-image in the nineteenth and twentieth centuries has been told by Maurizio Peleggi, *Lords of Things: The Fashioning of the Siamese Monarchy's Modern Image* (Honolulu: University of Hawai'i Press, 2002).

CHAPTER 9. COLLECTING AND ACCOUNTING: REPRESENTING
SLAVES AS COMMODITIES IN JAMAICA, 1674–1784

1. *Supplement to the Cornwall Chronicle*, No. 704 [Supp. No. 625], December 16, 1786.

2. Trevor Burnard, *Mastery, Tyranny, and Desire: Thomas Thistlewood and His Slaves in the Anglo-Jamaican World* (Chapel Hill: University of North Carolina Press, 2004).

3. David Brion Davis, *Inhuman Bondage: The Rise and Fall of Slavery in the New World* (New York: Oxford University Press, 2006), 141–56.

4. James Delbourgo, "Slavery in the Cabinet of Curiosities: Hans Sloane's Atlantic World," http://www.britishmuseum.org/PDF/Delbourgo%20essay.pdf.

5. For an intriguing attempt to make slaves central to the intellectual history of the French Enlightenment, see Laurent Dubois, "An Enslaved Enlightenment: Rethinking the Intellectual History of the French Atlantic," *Social History* 31 (2006): 1–14.

6. For attempts to recreate the worlds of individual slaves, see Jon F. Sensbach, *Rebecca's Revival: Creating Black Christianity in the Atlantic World* (Cambridge, Mass.: Harvard University Press, 2005) and John Lean and Trevor Burnard, "Hearing Slave Voices: The Fiscal's Reports of Berbice and Demerara-Essequebo," *Archives* 27, 106 (2002): 37–50. For attempts to examine the material culture of slaves, see Ann Smart Martin, *Buying into the World of Goods: Early Consumers in Backcountry Virginia* (Baltimore: Johns Hopkins University Press, 2008); and Jerome S. Handler, "The Middle Passage and the Material Culture of Africans," *Slavery & Abolition* 30 (2009): 1–26.

7. Diaries of Thomas Thistlewood, June 19, July 17–18, 29, August 3, September 2, December 31, 1760; August 3, 1761; May 24, 1768, Monson 31/11–12, 19, Monson Deposit, Lincolnshire Archives, Lincoln.

8. James Ramsay, *An Essay on the Treatment and Conversion of African Slaves in the British Sugar Colonies* (London, 1784).

9. For Franklin as a scientist, see Joyce E. Chaplin, *The First Scientific American: Benjamin Franklin and the Pursuit of Genius* (New York: Basic Books, 2006).

10. Michael Chenoweth, *The 18th Century Climate of Jamaica, Derived from the Journals of Thomas Thistlewood, 1750–1786* (Philadelphia: American Philosophical Society, 2003), 8; J. R. Fleming, *Meteorology in America, 1800–1870* (Baltimore: Johns Hopkins University Press, 1990).

11. Andrew Jackson O'Shaughnessy, *An Empire Divided: The American Revolution and the British Caribbean* (Philadelphia: University of Pennsylvania Press, 2000), 21; Delbourgo, "Slavery in the Cabinet of Curiosities"; and Kay Dian Kriz, "Curiosities, Commodities and Transplanted Bodies in Hans Sloane's *Natural History of Jamaica*," *William and Mary Quarterly* 56 (2000): 35–78.

12. Marcus Wood argues that "the experience of millions of individuals who were the victims of slavery is not collectable; it is unrecoverable as a set of relics." Wood, *Blind Memory: Visual Representations of Slavery in England and America 1780–1865* (New York: Oxford University Press, 2002), 7.

13. Elizabeth Kowaleski Wallace, *The British Slave Trade and Public Memory* (New York: Columbia University Press, 2006), 38–39; Wood, *Blind Memory*, 216.

14. Michael Graham Stewart Slavery Collection, 214 items, National Maritime Museum, Greenwich, London. For excellent works on pictorial descriptions of blacks in the West Indies, see Beth Fowkes Tobin, *Picturing Imperial Power: Colonial Subjects in Eighteenth-Century British Painting* (Durham, N.C.: Duke University Press, 1999); and Kay Dian Kriz, *Slavery, Sugar and the Culture of Refinement: Picturing the British West Indies, 1700–1840* (New Haven, Conn.: Yale University Press, 2008).

15. MGS/19, Mss 1785, Michael Graham Stewart Slavery Collection.

16. The Atlantic Worlds collection at the National Maritime Museum can be accessed at http://www.nmm.ac.uk/collections/explore/index.cfm/category/90571.

17. The best guide to the public records of Jamaica is K. E. Ingram, *Sources of Jamaican History 1655–1838* (Zug, Switz.: Inter-Documentation, 1976).

18. David Eltis, *The Rise of African Slavery in the Americas* (Cambridge: Cambridge University Press, 2000), 1–84.

19. J. R. Ward, *British West Indian Slavery, 1750–1834: The Process of Amelioration* (Oxford: Oxford University Press, 1984), 265. Ward lists in his bibliography an extensive guide to West Indian estate accounts in Britain.

20. Christopher Napier, "Aristocratic Accounting: The Bute Estate in Glamorgan, 1814–1880," *Accounting and Business Research* 21 (1991): 163–74.

21. B. W. Higman, *Plantation Jamaica 1750–1850: Capital and Control in a Colonial Economy* (Kingston: University of the West Indies Press, 2005), 95–96.

22. P. J. Laborie, *The Coffee Planter of Saint Domingo* (London: T. Cadell and W. Davies, 1798), cited in Higman, *Plantation Jamaica*, 98.

23. "List of Slaves on York Estate, Jamaica, 1 Jan. 1778," Gale-Morant Papers, 3/c, University of Exeter Library, Exeter. The Old Montpelier records are explored in B. W. Higman, *Montpelier Jamaica: A Plantation Community in Slavery and Freedom 1739–1912* (Kingston: University of the West Indies Press, 1998).

24. See, inter alia, Richard K. Fleischman and Thomas N. Tyson, "Accounting in Service to Racism: Monetizing Slave Property in the Antebellum South," *Critical Perspectives on Accounting* 15 (2004): 376–99; and Fleischman, David Oldroyd, and Tyson, "Monetizing Human Life: Slave Valuations in United States and West Indian Plantations," *Accounting History* 9 (2004): 35–62.

25. Heather Cateau, "The New 'Negro' Business: Hiring in the British West Indies, 1750–1810," in Alvin O. Thompson, ed., *In the Shadow of the Plantation: Caribbean History and Legacy* (Oxford: James Currey, 2003), 100–120.

26. W. T. Baxter, "Accounting in Colonial America," in A. C. Littleton and B. S. Young, eds., *Studies in the History of Accounting* (London: Sweet and Maxwell, 1956), 272–87; Arthur Young, *Arthur Young and His Times*, ed. G. E. Mingay (London: Macmillan, 1975).

27. This analysis is drawn from a survey of over 5,000 inventories listed in Inventories IB1/11/1–64, Jamaica Archives, Spanishtown, Jamaica. The individual inventories examined here are those of: John James (1674), John Stephenson (1674), Alexander Pitt (1674), Benjamin Whatcomb (1675), Robert Freeman (1675), John Blair (1675), John Guy (1703), Robert Phillips (1703), Nicholas Richardson (1703), Benjamin Douce (1723), Edward Harris (1723), George Pattinson (1724), Mathew Hughes (1746), William Vassall (1746), Gilbert Mathison (1775), William Leacock (1775), John Nelson Kentish (1775), Francis Darcy (1778), and Edward Clarke (1779). The inventories from 1775 come from IB11/1/56.

28. Fleischman, Olroyd and Tyson, "Monetizing Human Life."

29. Michael Craton, *Searching for the Invisible Man: Slaves and Plantation Life in Jamaica* (Cambridge, Mass.: Harvard University Press, 1978); Richard D. E. Burton, *Afro-Creole: Power, Opposition, and Play in the Caribbean* (Ithaca, N.Y.: Cornell University Press, 1997).

30. For the prices of slaves in Jamaica, see Trevor Burnard, "Evaluating Gender in Early Jamaica, 1674–1784," *History of the Family* 12, 2 (2007): 81–91. For the prices of slaves elsewhere in British America, see Peter C. Mancall, Joshua L. Rosenbloom, and Thomas Weiss, "Slave Prices and the South Carolina Economy, 1722–1809," *Journal of Economic History* 61 (2001): 616–39; David Eltis, Frank D. Lewis, and David Richardson, "Slave Prices, the African Slave Trade and Productivity in Eighteenth-Century South Carolina: A Reassessment," *Journal of Economic History* 66 (2006): 1054–65; and Mancall, Rosenbloom, and Weiss, "Rejoinder," *Journal of Economic History* 66 (2006): 1066–71.

31. Burnard, "Evaluating Gender."

32. Philip D. Morgan, "Slaves and Livestock in Eighteenth-Century Jamaica: Vineyard Pen, 1750–1751," *William and Mary Quarterly* 52 (1995): 47–76.

33. For an interesting analysis of the relationship between slaves and animals, see Karl Jacoby, "Slaves by Nature? Domestic Animals and Human Slaves," *Slavery & Abolition* 15 (1994): 89–99.

1. See, e.g., Kirkpatrick Sale, *The Conquest of Paradise: Christopher Columbus and the Columbian Legacy* (New York: Knopf, 1990) (slave trade); David E. Stannard, *American Holocaust: The Conquest of the New World* (New York: Oxford University Press, 1992), 66–67 (slavery); Alden Vaughan, "Sir Walter Ralegh's Indian Interpreters, 1584–1618, *William and Mary Quarterly* 3rd ser. 59 (2002): 341–76 (diplomacy); Vaughan, *Transatlantic Encounters: American Indians in Britain, 1500–1776* (Cambridge: Cambridge University Press, 2006) (the other); and Margaret T. Hodgen, *Early Anthropology in the Sixteenth and Seventeenth Centuries* (Philadelphia: University of Pennsylvania Press, 1964) (the other).

2. William Bradford, *Of Plymouth Plantation, 1620–1647*, ed. Samuel Eliot Morison (New York: Knopf, 1952), 271.

3. See Thomas Harriot, *A Briefe and true report of the new founde lande of Virginia* (orig. pub. London, 1588; illustrated ed. Frankfurt, 1590), 27–29. See also Joyce Chaplin, *Subject Matter: Technology, the Body, and Science on the Anglo-American Frontier, 1500–1676* (Cambridge, Mass.: Harvard University Press, 2001).

4. See David S. Jones, "The Persistence of Health Disparities," *American Journal of Public Health* 96 (2006): 2122–34.

5. Jared Diamond, *Guns, Germs, and Steel: The Fates of Human Societies* (New York: Norton, 1997); Alfred Crosby, *The Columbian Exchange: The Biological Consequences of 1492* (Westport, Conn.: Greenwood Press, 1969); Crosby, *Ecological Imperialism: The Biological Expansion of Europe, 900–1900* (Cambridge: Cambridge University Press, 1986).

6. David S. Jones, "Virgins Soils Revisited," *William and Mary Quarterly* 3rd ser. 60 (2003): 703–42; Jones, *Rationalizing Epidemics: Meanings and Uses of American Indian Mortality Since 1600* (Cambridge, Mass.: Harvard University Press, 2004).

7. See Richard H. Steckel and Jerome C. Rose, eds., *The Backbone of History: Health and Nutrition in the Western Hemisphere* (Cambridge: Cambridge University Press, 2002). For the scale of mortality over time, see Russell Thornton, *American Indian Holocaust and Survival: A Population History Since 1492* (Norman: University of Oklahoma Press, 1987).

8. For the link between alcohol and Americans' health, see Peter C. Mancall, *Deadly Medicine: Indians and Alcohol in Early America* (Ithaca, N.Y.: Cornell University Press, 1995), esp. 91–96.

9. For the depiction of one mummified body, see Christian F. Feest, "The Collecting of American Indian Artifacts in Europe, 1493–1750," in Karen Ordahl Kupperman, ed., *America in European Consciousness, 1493–1750* (Chapel Hill: University of North Carolina Press, 1995), 345.

10. "The Barcelona Letter of 1493," trans. Lucia Graves, in Mauricio Obregón, ed., *The Columbus Papers: The Barcelona Letter of 1493, the Landfall Controversy, and the Indian Guides* (New York: Macmillan, 1991), 66–68.

11. Richard Hakluyt, *The Principall Navigations, Voiages, and Discoveries of the English Nation* (London, 1589), 515.

12. Alden T. Vaughan, "People of Wonder: England Encounters the New World's Natives," in Rachel Doggett et al., eds., *New World of Wonders: European Images of the Americas, 1492–1700* (Seattle: University of Washington Press, 1992), 16–17 (limited early English interest); Michael Harbsmeier, "Bodies and Voices from Ultima Thule: Inuit Explorations of the Kablunat from Christian IV to Knud Rasmussen," in Michael Bravo and Sverker Sörlin, eds., *Narrating the Arctic: A Cultural History of Nordic Scientific Practices* (Canton, Mass.: Science History Publications/USA, 2002), 37–39. Europeans had interest in other bodies too, including individuals who resembled monsters, whether they were born in Europe or abroad,

including a family from the Canary Islands whose members were covered in hair; see Merry Wiesner-Hanks, *The Marvelous Hairy Girls: The Gonzales Sisters and Their World* (New Haven, Conn.: Yale University Press, 2009).

13. *Cest la Deduction du sumpeux ordre plaisatz spectacles et magnifiques theatres dresses, et exhibes parles citoiens de Rouen* [1551; facs. titled *L'Entrée de Henri II à Rouen 1550* [Amsterdam, 1977], sig. [Ki^v–Kii^r]. For an analysis of this event, see Michael Wintroub, "Civilizing the Savage and Making a King: The Royal Entry Festival of Henri II (Rouen, 1550)," *Sixteenth-Century Journal* 29 (1998): 465–94, and Wintroub, *A Savage Mirror: Power, Identity, and Knowledge in Early Modern France* (Stanford, Calif.: Stanford University Press, 2006).

14. Harald E. L. Prins, "To the Land of the Mistigoches: American Indians Traveling to Europe in the Age of Exploration," *American Indian Culture and Research Journal* 17, 1 (1993): 175–95.

15. Dionyse Settle, *A true reporte of the laste voyage into the West and Northwest regions, & c. 1577, worthily achieved by Capteine Frobisher of the sayde voyage the first finder and Generall. With a description of the people there inhabiting, and other circumstances notable* (London, 1577), sig. [Bviii^v], C^v–Cij^r.

16. Settle, *A true reporte*, sig. Ciiij^r–Cv^r.

17. Settle, *A true reporte*, sig. Cv^r–[Diii^r].

18. Paul Hulton, *America 1585: The Complete Drawings of John White* (Chapel Hill: University of North Carolina Press, 1984), 35, drawing on "Corte beschryvinghe van England, Scotland ende Irland," in Add. Mss. 28330, British Library; see also Kim Sloan, *A New World: England's First View of America* (Chapel Hill: University of North Carolina Press, 2007), 164–69.

19. "Postmortem Report by Dr. Edward Dodding, at Bristol, on the Thule Eskimo Man Brought by Frobisher" in David B. Quinn, ed., *New American World*, 5 vols. (New York: Arno Press, 1979), 4: 216–18; see also Sir James Watt and Ann Savours, "The Captured 'Countrey People': Their Depiction and Medical History," in Thomas H. B. Symons, ed., *Meta Incognita: A Discourse of Discovery: Martin Frobisher's Arctic Expeditions, 1576–1578*, 2 vols. (Hull, Quebec: Canadian Museum of Civilization, 1999), 2: 553–62.

20. For the engravings, see *La Navigation du capitaine Martin Forbisher* (La Rochelle, 1578) and *Beschreibung der schiffart des haubtmans Martine Forbissher* (Nürnberg, 1580).

21. "Instructions to Be Observed by Thomas Bavin," in Quinn, ed., *New American World*, 3: 242–44, at 244; Karen Ordahl Kupperman, *Indians and English: Facing Off in Early America* (Ithaca, N.Y.: Cornell University Press, 2000), 43.

22. "The Marckes of sundreye of the Cheif mene of Virginia" (plate XXIII) in Thomas Harriot, *A briefe and true report of the new found land of Virginia* (Frankfurt-am-Main, 1590).

23. See Carville V. Earle, "Environment, Disease, and Mortality in Early Virginia," in Thad W. Tate and David L. Ammerman, eds., *The Chesapeake in the Seventeenth Century* (Chapel Hill: University of North Carolina Press, 1979), 96–125.

24. William Crashaw, *A Sermon Preached in London Before the Right Honourable the Lord Lawarre* [London, 1610], sig. [D4^r]; Kupperman, *Indians and English*, 75–76.

25. Kupperman, *Indians and English*, 76.

26. Cotton Mather, "A Narrative of Hannah Dustan's Notable Deliverance from Captivity," in Alden T. Vaughan and Edward W. Clark, eds., *Puritans Among the Indians: Accounts of Captivity and Redemption, 1676–1724* (Cambridge, Mass.: Belknap Press of Harvard University Press, 1981), 161–64. On scalping see, among other sources, James Axtell and William Sturtevant, "The Unkindest Cut, or Who Invented Scalping? A Case Study," in James Axtell, *The European and the Indian: Essays in the Ethnohistory of the Colonial North America* (New York: Oxford University Press, 1981), 16–35.

27. For their mission, see Eric Hinderaker, "The 'Four Indian Kings' and the Imaginative Construction of the First British Empire," *William and Mary Quarterly* 3rd ser. 53 (1996): 487–526.

28. This image is reprinted in Eric Hinderaker and Peter C. Mancall, *At the Edge of Empire: The Backcountry in British North America* (Baltimore: Johns Hopkins University Press, 2003), 83.

29. See Kupperman, *Indians and English*, 42; John Peacock, "The Politics of Portraiture," in Kevin Sharpe and Peter Lake, eds., *Culture and Politics in Early Stuart England* (London, 1994), 199–228.

30. See Hodgen, *Early Anthropology in the Sixteenth and Seventeenth Centuries*.

31. The literature on Indian slavery in North America suggests, so far, the limited use of indigenous slaves in eastern North America, though deep into the seventeenth century English colonists captured political enemies in Massachusetts and sent them into slavery. Further, there is some evidence that the English manipulated their courts to take advantage of Natives sentenced to temporary captivity or who were taken in as orphans. Finally, it should be noted that Indian slavery existed in other parts of the Americas, as recent scholarship has suggested. See, among other sources, Alan Gallay, *The Indian Slave Trade: The Rise of the English Empire in the American South, 1670–1717* (New Haven, Conn.: Yale University Press, 2002); Margaret Ellen Newell, "The Changing Nature of Indian Slavery in New England, 1670–1720" and Ruth Wallis Herndon and Ella Wilcox Sekatau, "Colonizing the Children: Indian Youngsters in Servitude in Early Rhode Island," in Colin G. Calloway and Neal Salisbury, eds., *Reinterpreting New England Indians and the Colonial Experience* (Boston: Colonial Society of Massachusetts, 2003), 106–73. For the enslavement of Natives in other parts of North America, see Brett Rushforth, "'A Little Flesh We Offer You': The Origins of Indian Slavery in New France," *William and Mary Quarterly* 3rd ser. 60 (2003): 777–808; and James Brooks, *Captives and Cousins: Slavery, Kinship, and Community in the Southwest Borderlands* (Chapel Hill: University of North Carolina Press, 2002).

32. John Lawson, *A New Voyage to Carolina*, ed. Hugh T. Lefler (Chapel Hill: University of North Carolina Press, 1967), 232 (depopulation), 244–46 (intermarriage).

33. Thomas Jefferson, *Notes on the State of Virginia* (1787), ed. William Peden (Chapel Hill: University of North Carolina Press, 1954), 97–98.

34. Jefferson, *Notes on the State of Virginia*, 98.

35. Jefferson, *Notes on the States of Virginia*, 98–99.

36. Jefferson, *Notes on the State of Virginia*, 99–100.

37. Jefferson, *Notes on the State of Virginia*, 100–102.

38. Historian John Farragher has called for the elimination of this term and proposed that this era be referred to as the period of American "ethnic cleansing"; see Farragher, "'More Motley than Mackinaw': From Ethnic Mixing to Ethnic Cleansing on the Frontier of the Lower Missouri, 1783–1833," in Andrew R. L. Cayton and Fredrika Teute, eds., *Contact Points: American Frontiers from the Mohawk Valley to the Mississippi, 1750–1830* (Chapel Hill: University of North Carolina Press, 1998), 305. See Ann Fabian, *Headhunting: Flatheads, Fijians, and America's Skull-Collecting Naturalists* (Chicago: University of Chicago Press, 2010), chap. 1.

39. George Catlin, *Letters and Notes on the Manners, Customs, and Conditions of the North American Indians*, 2 vols. (London, 1844; rpt. New York: Dover, 1973), 2: 10.

40. [Samuel George Morton], *Notice of the Academy of Natural Sciences of Philadelphia* (Philadelphia, 1930), 3.

41. Ann Fabian, "Bones of Contention," *Common-Place* 1, 2 (January 2001), part three.

42. Fabian, "Bones of Contention," part three.

43. Samuel George Morton, *An Inquiry into the Distinctive Characteristics of the Aboriginal Race of America*, 2nd ed. (Philadelphia: John Penington, 1844), 23.

44. Morton, *Distinctive Characteristics of the Aboriginal Race*, 5.

45. Morton, *Distinctive Characteristics of the Aboriginal Race*, 12–14.

46. Samuel George Morton, *Crania Americana; Or, A Comparative View of the Skulls of Various Aboriginal Nations of North and South America* (Philadelphia, 1839). Morton notes that he was in a position to conduct this study because the "author's materials in this department are ample, and have enabled him to give a full exposition of a subject which was long involved in doubt and controversy." In other words, it was the extent of his collection—or his access to an extensive collection—which allowed him to approach the subject more comprehensively than others had to that point. See Morton, *Crania Americana*, iii, and cf. Fabian, *Headhunting*, chap. 1.

47. Morton, *Crania Americana*, 62–83, at 63.

48. Fabian, "Bones of Contention," part three.

49. The standard study, highly sympathetic to Kroeber (no surprise since it was written by his widow) is Theodora Kroeber, *Ishi in Two Worlds: A Biography of the Last Wild Indian in North America* (Berkeley: University of California Press, 1961); the estimate on museum attendance is from Nancy Rockafellar, "The Story of Ishi, a Chronology," in "A History of the UCSF Medical School," http://history.library.ucsf.edu/ishi.html, accessed July 11, 2010.

50. Fabian, "Bones of Contention," part three.

51. For examples of the kinds of conclusions that can be obtained from analysis of such remains, see John W. Verano and Douglas H. Ubelaker, eds., *Disease and Demography in the Americas* (Washington, D.C.: Smithsonian Institution Press, 1992), 5–166.

52. Steckel and Rose, *The Backbone of History*.

CHAPTER 11. SPANISH COLLECTIONS OF AMERICANA
IN THE LATE EIGHTEENTH CENTURY

1. On Spanish Enlightenment investigations of American archaeology see Paz Cabello Carro, "La arqueología en América en el siglo XVIII," in *La Corona y la arqueología en el siglo de las luces* (Madrid: Patrimonio Nacional, 2010), 374–86 and "Colecciones españolas del Caribe, viajes científicos e inicios de la arqueología en las Antillas (siglos XVIII y XIX)," in *El Caribe precolombino. Fray Ramón Pané y el universo taino* (Madrid-Barcelona: Ministerio de Cultura, 2008), 203–21.

2. Due to the scarcity of documentation on the Royal Cabinet collections, reconstructing the collections has required recourse to a variety of Spanish archives (the Archive of the Indies, in Seville; the National Historical Archive; the Museum of Science; and the National Archaeological Museum) and recent editions of ancient chronicles and expedition logs. However, not all objects in the collections can be identified because some objects were renumbered, others moved, and yet others destroyed during wartime. See Paz Cabello Carro, *Coleccionismo americano indígena en la España del siglo XVIII* (Madrid: Ediciones de Cultura Hispánica, 1989).

3. Paz Cabello Carro, "Pervivencias funerarias prehispánicas en época colonial en Trujillo del Perú: Nueva interpretación de los dibujos arqueológicos de Martínez Compañón," *Anales del Museo de América* (Madrid) 11 (2003): 9–56.

4. Paz Cabello Carro, "Las colecciones peruanas en España y los inicios de la arqueología andina en el siglo XVIII," in *Los Incas y el antiguo Perú: 3000 años de historia* (Madrid: Sociedad Estatal Quinto Centenario, Lunwerg Editores, 1991), 466–85.

5. Miguel Feyjoo, *Relación descriptiva de la ciudad, y provincia de Truxillo del Peru* (Madrid, 1763).

6. Baltasar Jaime Martínez Compañón, *Trujillo del Perú en el siglo XVIII* [ca. 1779–89], facs. ed., 9 vols. + 3 vols. appendix (Madrid: Ediciones Cultura Hispánica del Centro Iberoamericano de Cooperación, 1978–94). All nine volumes are available through the online collection "Manuscritos de América en las colecciones reales," http://www.cervantesvirtual.com/portal/patrimonio/catalogo.shtml. See also [José Ignacio Lecuanda], "Descripciones corográficas y geográficas de la provincia de Chachapoyas y de los partidos de Trujillo (y ciudad), Piura, Saña o Lambayeque y Cajamarca," *Mercurio Peruano* [1792–94], reprinted in *Trujillo del Perú* (Madrid: Ediciones de Cultura Hispánica, 1994), appendix 3.

7. The dossier on the Palenque excavations at the Archive of the Indies in Seville was published by Ricardo Castañeda Paganini, *Las ruinas de Palenque: su descubrimiento y primeras exploraciones en el siglo XVIII* (Guatemala: Publicaciones del Ministerio de Educación Pública, 1946). I published the same texts, reconstructing the excavations and identifying the pieces, in Paz Cabello Carro, *Política investigadora de la época de Carlos III en el área maya* (Madrid: Ediciones de la Torre, 1992).

8. Various copies of the report are housed in the Museo Nacional de Ciencias Naturales, Madrid; Real Academia de la Historia, Madrid; and the Archive of the Indies, Seville. There are original drawings in the Archive of the Indies and copies in the British Library, although the latter are incomplete. The Biblioteca de Palacio in Madrid has a period copy that is complete but of inferior quality. There is a facsimile edition, *Estampas de Palenque* (Madrid, Testimonio, 1993).

9. Paz Cabello Carro, "La Estela de Madrid," *Descubrir el arte* (Madrid) 7, 77 (July 2005).

10. Hipólito Ruiz, *Relación del viaje hecho a los reynos del Perú y Chile . . . extractado de los diarios . . . Don Hipólito Ruiz*, ed. Agustín Barreiro (Madrid: Huelves y Compañía, 1931); Ruiz, *Relación histórica del viage, que hizo a los reinos* del Perú y Chile el botánico D. Hipólito Ruiz en el año 1777 hasta el de 1788, en cuya época regresó a Madrid, ed. Jaime Jaramillo Arango, 2 vols., 2nd ed. (Madrid: Real Academica de Ciencias Exactas Físicas y Naturales, 1952).

11. Abel Romero Castillo, *Copia de documentos referentes a Pedro Franco Dávila, fundador del Gabinete de Historia Natural de Madrid, de varios archivos españoles*, 2 vols., typewritten, Lib. 1030–31, Archivo Histórico Nacional, Madrid. This text contains copies of documents that disappeared during the Spanish Civil War in the 1936 fire at the Administration Archive (Archivo de la Administración) in Alcalá de Henares.

12. José Andía y Varela, *Relación del viaje hecho a la isla de Amat, por otro nombre Otahiti y descubrimiento de otras adyacentes en los años 1774 y 1775*, ed. Joaquín de Sarriera (Barcelona: José Porter, 1947).

13. "Relación de la entrada de San Lorenzo de Nutka, formada por individuos de la expedición que . . . salió el año de 1788 del Puerto de San Blas en la Fragata llamada Princesa," 1788, Biblioteca de Palacio, Madrid, ms. 2866. *Apéndice a la Relación del viaje al Magallanes de la fragata de guerra Santa María de la Cabeza . . . de los paquebotes Santa Casilda y Santa Eulalia para completar el reconocimiento del estrecho en los años 1788 y 1789* (Madrid, 1793). *Relación del viaje hecho por las goletas Sutil y Mexicana en el año de 1782 para reconocer el Estrecho de Fuca, con una introducción en que se dá noticia de las expediciones executadas anteriormente por los españoles en busca del paso del noroeste de la América* (Madrid, 1802).

14. Paz Cabello Carro, "The Ethnographic Collections: A Special Legacy of the Spanish Presence on the Northwest Coast, 1774–1792," in Robin Inglis, ed., *Essays in Recognition of the Bicentennial of the Malaspina Expedition, 1791–1792* (Vancouver: Vancouver Maritime Museum, 1992); Cabello Carro, "Ancient Spanish Collections from North America," *European Review of Native American Studies* 6, 2 (1992): 13–20; Cabello Carro, "Eighteenth-Century Spanish Expeditions, Discoveries, and Collections in the Northwest Coast," in Steven

Clay Brown et al., eds., *Spirits of the Water: Native Art Collected on Expeditions to Alaska and British Columbia, 1774–1910* (Seattle: University of Washington Press, 2000).

15. Spanish texts transcribe the name as "Nutka," and English texts as "Nootka." *Nuu-chah-nulth* is the indigenous group. James Cook, who arrived after Pérez, called this "Friendly Cove."

16. Juan Francisco de la Bodega y Quadra, *El descubrimiento del fin del mundo (1775–1792)*, ed. Salvador Bernabeu Albert (Madrid: Alianza, 1990); Mourelle's logs are reproduced in Amancio Landin Carrasco, *Mourelle de la Rua, explorador del Pacífico* (Madrid: Cultura Hispánica, 1978).

17. The original is in the Archive of the Indies, and a copy is in the National Archaeological Museum in Madrid.

18. Álvaro del Portillo, *Descubrimientos y exploraciones en las costas de California 1532–1650* (Madrid: Rialp, 1982), 91.

19. "Relación de la entrada de San Lorenzo de Nutka."

20. "Relación de la entrada de San Lorenzo de Nutka."

21. This Hawaiian stayed at the Franciscan school at Mexico until Colnett was freed, whereupon he traveled to England with Colnett. He was the source of the information that Father Lorenzo Socies used to create a Sandwich Island vocabulary, which was appended to the manuscript "Relación de la entrada de San Lorenzo de Nutka," along with another vocabulary in "Nootka tongue."

22. "Relación de la entrada de San Lorenzo de Nutka."

CHAPTER 12. MARTÍNEZ COMPAÑÓN AND HIS ILLUSTRATED "MUSEUM"

The authors would like to thank Daniela Bleichmar, Paz Cabello Carro, Thomas B. F. Cummins, Swift Edgar, Emily Gulick, David Guss, Edward S. Harwood, John Hanson, Leonardo López Luján, Megan O'Neil, Daniel Restrepo, Jennifer L. Roberts, Gary Urton, and Sasha Wachtel for invaluable conversation and assistance in the production of this essay. All errors remain our own.

1. On Martínez Compañón's life and work, see José Manuel Pérez Ayala, *Baltasar Jaime Martínez Compañón y Bujanda: Prelado español de Colombia y Perú* (Bogota: Imprenta Nacional, 1955); Daniel Restrepo Manrique, *Sociedad y religión en Trujillo (Perú), 1780–1790: La iglesia de Trujillo (Perú) bajo el episcopado de Baltasar Jaime Martínez Compañón, 1780–1790*, 2 vols. (Vitoria-Gasteiz: Eusko Jaurlaritzaren Argitalpen Zerbitzu Nagusia, Servicio Central de Publicaciones, Gobierno Vasco, 1992); and Restrepo, "Acción de Martínez Compañón en Perú y Nueva Granada," in Ignacio Arana Pérez, ed., *Los Vascos y América: Ideas, hechos, hombres* (Madrid: Espasa-Calpe, 1990), 333–41. See also Manuel Ballesteros Gaibrois: "Estudio de la obra de Martínez Compañón enviada al Rey de España," in *Trujillo del Perú* (Madrid: Ediciones Cultura Hispánica, 1994), app. 3, 13–48; "Un manuscrito colonial del siglo XVIII: Su interés etnográfico," *Journal de la Société des Américanistes* (Paris) n.s. 27 (1935): 145–74; and "El obispo Martínez Compañón: El último ilustrado en América," in Rafael Varón Gabai and Javier Flores Espinoza, eds., *Arqueología, antropología e historia en los Andes: Homenaje a María Rostworowski* (Lima: Instituto de Estudios Peruanos, Banco Central de Reserva del Perú, 1997), 133–50. See also José Navarro Pascual, ed., *Vida y obra del Obispo Martínez Compañón* (Piura: Universidad de Piura, Facultad de Ciencias y Humanidades, 1991); and Emily Berquist, "The Science of Empire: Bishop Martínez Compañón and the Enlightenment in Peru" (Ph.D. dissertation, University of Texas, Austin, 2007).

2. Detailed inventories of these two shipments survive in the Archivo General de Indias in Seville, Spain, and have been published. The inventory of the 1788 shipment of twenty-four boxes of botanical, zoological, mineralogical, archaeological, and ethnographic objects

(Audiencia de Lima 798) is reproduced as Baltasar Jaime Martínez Compañón y Bujanda, *Razón de las especies de la naturaleza y del arte del obispado de Trujillo del Perú: Del D. Baltasar Martinez Compañon, 1788–89*, transcribed and ed. Inge Schjellerup (Trujillo: Museo de Arqueología, Universidad Nacional de Trujillo, 1991). The inventory of the 1790 shipment of six boxes of ceramics (Indiferente general, 1.545) is published in Pérez Ayala, *Baltasar Jaime Martínez Compañón*, app. 42, pt. 6, 406–11; and in Paz Cabello Carro, *Coleccionismo americano indígena en la España del siglo XVIII* (Madrid: Ediciones de Cultura Hispánica, 1989), app., 169–77.

3. Cabello Carro, *Coleccionismo americano*; "Las colecciones peruanas en España y los inicios de la arqueología andina en el siglo XVIII," in *Los Incas y el antiguo Perú: 3000 años de historia* (Madrid: Sociedad Estatal Quinto Centenario, Lunwerg Editores, 1991), 466–85; *Política investigadora de la época de Carlos III en el área Maya: Descubrimiento de Palenque y primeras excavaciones de carácter científico; según documentación de Calderón, Bernasconi, Del Río y otros* (Madrid: Ediciones de la Torre, 1992); "Mestizaje y ritos funerarios en Trujillo, Perú: Según las antiguas colecciones reales españolas," in *Iberoamérica mestiza: Encuentro de pueblos y culturas* (Madrid: Fundación Santillana y Sociedad Estatal Acción Cultural Exterior, 2003), 85–102; and "Pervivencias funerarias prehispánicas en época colonial en Trujillo del Perú: Nueva interpretación de los dibujos arqueológicos de Martínez Compañón," *Anales del Museo de América* 11 (2003): 9–56.

4. Berquist, "Science of Empire"; Pérez Ayala, *Baltasar Jaime Martínez Compañón*; and Restrepo, *Sociedad y religión*.

5. The nine volumes of watercolors date to 1781–89 and are catalogued as MS 343 in the Biblioteca del Palacio Real, Madrid. A facsimile edition was published in Madrid in 1978–94. Martínez Compañón, *Trujillo del Perú*. A partial facsimile edition had been published in 1936 by Jesús Domínguez Bordona. Martínez Compañón, *Trujillo del Perú a fines del siglo XVIII*. An eighteenth-century copy of vol. 1 is in the Biblioteca Nacional de Colombia, Bogotá (MS 216) and has been reproduced as app. 1 of the Madrid facsimile. Other watercolors created as part of the bishop's project have come to light since the creation of the Madrid facsimile. One hundred and twenty watercolors corresponding to portions of vol. 2 (native customs), vol. 7 (illustrating birds, a bat, and a flying insect), and vol. 9 (an image of an archaeological textile), which might have been studies for the final Madrid version, are now in the collection of the Banco Continental in Lima, Peru. A volume dedicated to these illustrations appeared in 1997: Pablo Macera, ed., *Trujillo del Perú: Baltazar Jaime Martínez Compañón; Acuarelas; siglo XVIII* (Lima: Fundación del Banco Continental, 1997). In that volume, Macera (42–43) reports that there are also five illustrations of birds and two illustrations of rural industry from the bishop's project in a collection in Cajatambo.

6. Ballesteros Gaibrois, "Estudio de la obra de Martínez Compañón"; and Daniel Restrepo Manrique, "Las fuentes: Notas preliminares," in *Trujillo del Perú* (Madrid: Ediciones Cultural Hispánica, 1993), app. 2, 31–39.

7. The contents of the sixth volume, according to its index, are "Animales quadrupedos, Reptiles, y Sabandijas." Martínez Compañón, *Trujillo del Perú*, vol. 6, f. 105.

8. On the drawings of burials in particular, see Lisa Trever, "The Uncanny Tombs in Martínez Compañón's *Trujillo del Perú*," in Joanne Pillsbury, ed., *Past Presented: Archaeological Illustration in the Americas* (Washington, D.C.: Dumbarton Oaks Research Library and Collection, forthcoming).

9. Ballesteros Gaibrois, "Estudio de la obra de Martínez Compañón," 21–22.

10. "También he procurado acoger quantas producciones de naturaleza, o curiosidades del Arte de la gentilidad, he podido, con el designio de formar aunque no sea más que con Disposición de Múseo, que tal vez sea el primero, que haya formado ninguno de los Obispos

de las Americas, y acaso ni los de esa Provincia . . . se pueda formar una Historia completa de esta Diócesis intitulandola así: Múseo Histórico, Fícico, Político y Moral del Obpdo. de Truxillo de Peru." Letter from Martínez Compañón to Viceroy Croix, July 1785, cited in Ballesteros Gaibrois, "El obispo Martínez Compañón," 139.

11. Rogger Ravines, *Los museos del Perú: Breve historia y guía* (Lima: Dirección General de Museos, Instituto Nacional de Cultura, 1989), 15. José Alcina Franch indicates that the earliest museum of antiquities in the Americas was the short-lived university museum established by Viceroy Bucareli (1771–79) in Mexico City. *Arqueólogos o anticuarios: Historia antigua de la arqueología en la América española* (Barcelona: Ediciones del Serbal, 1995), 24.

12. Ballesteros Gaibrois, "Estudio de la obra de Martínez Compañón," 25.

13. David Freedberg, *The Eye of the Lynx: Galileo, His Friends, and the Beginnings of Modern Natural History* (Chicago: University of Chicago Press, 2002).

14. Freedberg, *The Eye of the Lynx*.

15. Lorenzo Boturini Benaduci, *Idea de una nueva historia general de la América Septentrional*, 1746, facs. ed. (México: Instituto Nacional de Antropología e Historia, Consejo Nacional para la Cultura y las Artes, 1999).

16. Martínez Compañón took a special interest in the itineraries of religious writers. See Miguel Arturo Seminario Ojeda, "Itinerario de la visita pastoral del obispo Martínez Compañón, 1782–1785," *Revista del Archivo General de la Nación* (Lima) 15 (1997): 211–20.

17. John H. Rowe, "What Kind of Settlement Was Inca Cuzco?" *Ñawpa Pacha* 5 (1967): 59–76.

18. Martín de Murúa, *Códice Murúa: Historia y genealogía de los reyes incas del Perú del padre mercedario Fray Martín de Murúa*, ca.1590, facsimile edition and transcription by Juan Ossio (Madrid: Testimonio, 2004), bk. 3, chap. 45, f. 97r. For the practice of "huaca hostage" in earlier times, see Michael E. Moseley, "Structure and History in the Dynastic Lore of Chimor," in Michael E. Moseley and Alana Cordy-Collins, eds., *The Northern Dynasties: Kingship and Statecraft in Chimor: A Symposium at Dumbarton Oaks, 12th and 13th October 1985* (Washington, D.C.: Dumbarton Oaks Research Library and Collection, 1990), 1–41.

19. Brian S. Bauer, *Ancient Cuzco: Heartland of the Inca* (Austin: University of Texas Press, 2004), especially "The Mummies of the Royal Inca," 159–84.

20. Bauer, *Ancient Cuzco*, 183.

21. Polo Ondegardo's own account of the collection of Inca royal mummies and effigies is lost, but his work and the mummies he found are described in Bernabé Cobo, *History of the Inca Empire: An Account of the Indians' Customs and Their Origin, Together With a Treatise on Inca Legends, History, and Social Institutions by Father Bernabé Cobo*, 1653, trans. and ed. Roland Hamilton (Austin: University of Texas Press, 1979); and in Pedro Sarmiento de Gamboa, *The History of the Incas*, 1572, trans. and ed. Brian S. Bauer and Vania Smith (Austin: University of Texas Press, 2007). For a full discussion of these sources on the Inca mummies, see Bauer, *Ancient Cuzco*, 159–84.

22. On the destruction of Andean temples and "idols," see, for example, Cristóbal de Albornoz, "Instrucción para descubrir todas las guacas del Piro y sus camayos y haziendas," 1581–85, in Henrique Urbano and Pierre Duviols, eds., *Fábulas y mitos de los Incas* (Madrid: Historia 16, 1989), 135–98; and Pablo José Arriaga, *The Extirpation of Idolatry in Peru*, 1621, trans. and ed. L. Clark Keating. (Lexington: University Press of Kentucky, 1968).

23. It should be noted that collecting practices operated in a reverse direction as well, with Europeans bringing to the Andes items of European manufacture. For example, artists such as Mateo Pérez de Alesio brought prints by Albrecht Dürer and other Old Masters with them to South America to use as models. Teresa Gisbert, "Textual Sources for the Study of Art and Architecture," in Joanne Pillsbury, ed., *Guide to Documentary Sources for Andean*

Studies, 1530–1900 (Norman: University of Oklahoma Press, with Center for Advanced Study in the Visual Arts, National Gallery of Art, 2008), 1: 353–77.

24. Catherine Julien, "History and Art in Translation: The *Paños* and Other Objects Collected by Francisco de Toledo," *Colonial Latin American Review* 8, 1 (1999): 61–89.

25. See, for example, Susan E. Ramírez, "Rich Man, Poor Man, Beggar Man, or Chief: Material Wealth as a Basis of Power in Sixteenth-Century Peru," in Susan Kellogg and Matthew Restall, eds., *Dead Giveaways: Indigenous Testaments of Colonial Mesoamerica and the Andes* (Salt Lake City: University of Utah Press, 1998), 215–48; and Carolyn Dean, *Inka Bodies and the Body of Christ: Corpus Christi in Colonial Cuzco, Peru* (Durham, N.C.: Duke University Press, 1999).

26. Ravines, *Los museos del Perú,* 15; and Luis Eduardo Wuffarden, "Las escuelas pictóricas virreinales," in Rafael López Guzmán, ed., *Perú indígena y virreinal* (Madrid: Sociedad Estatal para la Acción Cultural Exterior, SEACEX, 2004): 80–87, 296–99.

27. Note that bishop Martínez Compañón's nephew José Lecuanda was also a member of the society and submitted detailed, geographic descriptions of northern Peru to the *Mercurio peruano* during its print run. Several of these accounts contain descriptions of the natural resources and antiquities discovered in his uncle's bishopric that loosely correspond to the bishop's collections and illustrations. Joseph Ignacio Lequanda [José Ignacio Lecuanda], "Descripción geográfica de la ciudad y partido de Truxillo," *Mercurio peruano,* May 16–June 9, 1793, 247–54, facs. ed., vol. 8. (Lima: Biblioteca Nacional del Perú, 1965); Lequanda, "Descripción geográfica del partido de Cajamarca," *Mercurio peruano,* March 13–30, 1793, 333–38, facs. ed., vol. 9. (Lima: Biblioteca Nacional del Perú, 1966); and Lequanda, "Descripción geográfica del partido de Piura," *Mercurio peruano,* July 11–August 4, 1793, 263–70, facs. ed., vol. 8.

28. Hesperiophylo [José Rossi y Rubí]. "Descripción de un ternero bicípite seguida de algunas reflexiones sobre los monstruos," *Mercurio peruano,* March 18, 1792, 126, facs. ed., vol. 4 (Lima: Biblioteca Nacional del Perú, 1964). See also Rosa Zeta Quinde, *El pensamiento ilustrado en el Mercurio peruano, 1791–1794* (Piura, Peru: Universidad de Piura, 2000), 55, 179. Discourse surrounding natural history played an important role in the construction of creole political identities in late colonial Spanish America. See Jorge Cañizares-Esguerra, *How to Write the History of the New World: Histories, Epistemologies, and Identities in the Eighteenth-Century Atlantic World* (Stanford, Calif.: Stanford University Press, 2001); Charles Walker, "Voces discordantes: Discursos alternativos sobre el indio a fines de la colonia," in Walker, ed., *Entre la retórica y la insurgencia: Las ideas y los movimientos sociales en los Andes, siglo XVIII* (Cusco: Centro de Estudios Regionales Andinos "Bartolomé de Las Casas," 1996), 91–95; and Alcina Franch, *Arqueólogos o anticuarios,* 58–62.

29. Julien, "History and Art in Translation."

30. Acosta wrote his *Historia natural y moral de las Indias* in 1590; Cobo's *Historia del Nuevo Mundo* was completed by 1653 but not published until the end of the nineteenth century. Despite their remarkable achievements, these were still part of an intellectual world based on textual verification rather than the collection of specimens and scientific observation. For an eloquent discussion of these issues, see Anthony Grafton, with April Shelford and Nancy Siraisi, *New Worlds, Ancient Texts: The Power of Tradition and the Shock of Discovery* (Cambridge, Mass.: Belknap Press of Harvard University Press, 1992).

31. Louis Feuillée, *Journal des observations physiques, mathématiques et botaniques, faites par l'ordre du roy sur les côtes orientales de l'Amérique méridionale, & dans les Indes occidentales, depuis l'année 1707, jusques en 1712,* 3 vols. in 2 (Paris: Pierre Giffart; Jean Mariette, 1714–25); Amédée François Frézier, *Relation du voyage de la Mer du Sud aux côtes du Chily et du Pérou: fait pendant les années 1712, 1713 & 1714* (Paris: Chez Jean-Geoffroy Nyon, Étienne

Ganeau, Jacques Quillau, 1716); and Charles-Marie de La Condamine, *Relation abrégée d'un voyage fait dans l'intérieur de l'Amérique méridionale* (Paris: Chez la Veuve Pissot, 1745). On Ruiz, Pavón, and Dombey, see Hipólito Ruiz, *The Journals of Hipólito Ruiz, Spanish Botanist in Peru and Chile, 1777–1788*, trans. Richard Evans Schultes and María José Nemry von Thenen de Jaramillo-Arango, transcribed from the original manuscripts by Jaime Jaramillo-Arango (Portland, Ore.: Timber Press, 1998); and Ernst-Théodore Hamy, ed., *Joseph Dombey: médecin, naturaliste, archéologue, explorateur du Pérou, du Chili et du Brésil (1778–1785); Sa vie, son oeuvre, sa correspondance; Avec un choix de pièces relatives à sa mission* (Paris: Guilmoto, 1905). On Malaspina, see Alessandro Malaspina, *La expedición Malaspina, 1789–1794*, study by Ricardo Cerezo Martínez, transcription Carmen Sanz Alvarez, 2 vols. (Madrid: Ministerio de Defensa, Museo Naval; Barcelona: Lunwerg, 1990); and *The Malaspina Expedition, 1789–1794: Journal of the Voyage by Alejandro Malaspina*, ed. Andrew David et al., Hakluyt Society 3rd ser. 8, 3 vols. (London: Hakluyt Society with Museo Naval de Madrid, 2001–4). Martínez Compañón also had an interest in Nicolás Monardes (1493–1588), a Spanish physician and botanist who studied medicinal plants of the New World. Seminario Ojeda, "Itinerario de la visita pastoral."

32. For recent studies, see Daniela Bleichmar, "Atlantic Competitions: Botanical Trajectories in the Eighteenth-Century Spanish Empire," in James Delbourgo and Nicholas Dew, eds., *Science and Empire in the Atlantic World* (London: Routledge, 2007), 225–52; Bleichmar, "Painting as Exploration: Visualizing Nature in Eighteenth-Century Colonial Science," *Colonial Latin American Review* 15, 1 (2006): 81–104; and Cabello Carro, *Coleccionismo americano*.

33. Pérez Ayala, *Baltasar Jaime Martínez Compañón*, 83–86.

34. On these two questionnaires, see Daniel Restrepo Manrique, "La visita pastoral de d. Baltasar Jaime Martínez Compañón a la diocesis de Trujillo (1780–1785)," in José Navarro Pascual, ed., *Vida y obra del obispo Martínez Compañón* (Piura, Peru: Universidad de Piura, 1991): 100–117.

35. See Barbara E. Mundy, *The Mapping of New Spain: Indigenous Cartography and the Maps of the* Relaciones Geográficas (Chicago: University of Chicago Press, 1996); and "Relaciones Geográficas," in Pillsbury, ed., *Guide to Documentary Sources for Andean Studies, 1530–1900*, 1: 144–59.

36. Emily Berquist, "Bishop Martínez Compañón's Practical Utopia in Enlightenment Peru," *The Americas* 64, 3 (January 2008): 377–408; and "The Science of Empire."

37. Martínez Compañón, *Trujillo del Perú*, vol. 3, f. 9; *Razón de las especies*, 63–64 (box 14).

38. Fiametta Rocco, *The Miraculous Fever-Tree: Malaria and the Quest for a Cure that Changed the World* (New York: HarperCollins, 2003).

39. Martínez Compañón, *Razón de las especies*, 28–38 (boxes 8–9).

40. Martínez Compañón, *Trujillo del Perú*, vol. 1, f. 101r; vol. 2, estampa 106.

41. Joanne Pillsbury and Lisa Trever, "The King, the Bishop, and the Creation of an American Antiquity," *Ñawpa Pacha* 29 (2008): 191–219.

42. Alcina Franch, *Arqueólogos o anticuarios*, 182; Cabello Carro, *Coleccionismo americano*, 60–61; Cabello Carro, *Política investigadora*, 17–18.; Cabello Carro, "Las colecciones peruanas," 469; and Restrepo, *Sociedad y religión*, 34.

43. Jorge Juan and Antonio de Ulloa, *Relación histórica del viage a la América Meridional, hecho de orden de S. Mag. para medir algunos grados de meridiano terrestre, y venir por ellos en conocimiento de la verdadera figura, y magnitud de la tierra, con otras varias observaciones astronómicas, y phísicas*, 4 vols. in 2 (Madrid: Antonio Marin, 1748). Martínez Compañón also owned a copy of Miguel de Feyjoo de Sosa's *Relación descriptiva de la ciudad y provincia de Trujillo*. Feyjoo was born in Arequipa and preceded Martínez Compañón in Trujillo as a

royal magistrate. Feyjoo's work is closer in geographical coverage, but as with Ulloa, Feyjoo's work is in the spirit of the bureaucratic report, with scant attention to illustrations. Antón Pazos, "Presentación," in Daniel Restrepo Manrique, *Sociedad y religión en Trujillo (Perú), 1780–1790: La iglesia de Trujillo (Perú) bajo el episcopado de Baltasar Jaime Martínez Compañón, 1780–1790,* (Vitoria-Gasteiz: Eusko Jaurlaritzaren Argitalpen Zerbitzu Nagusia, Servicio Central de Publicaciones, Gobierno Vasco, 1992); 1: 30, n. 12. Feyjoo's work was written in response to the Bourbon mandates of 1741 and 1751 "to know the country well" in order to govern well. Guillermo Lohmann Villena, "Miguel Feijoo de Sosa: El hombre y su obra," in Feijoo de Sosa, *Relación descriptiva de la ciudad y provincia de Trujillo del Perú* (Lima: Fondo del Libro, Banco Industrial del Perú, 1984), 34. Part of the mandate was to understand native traditions, and it is possible that Feyjoo sent back one of the earliest collections of antiquities to Spain, responding to specific requests for specimens for the Royal Cabinet. Cabello Carro, *Política investigadora,* 19–20; and "Las colecciones peruanas," 469–70.

44. Frézier, *Relation du voyage,* pl. 30, opp. 247.

45. Documentation of Martínez Compañón's interest in the intellectual debates current in Europe and the Americas is relatively abundant. From his correspondence and inventories, we can gain a glimpse of the interests of this erudite bishop. He knew, for example, of the illustrated books of Athanasius Kircher (ca. 1602–80), as well as the collections of Pope Clement XIV. Seminario Ojeda, "Itinerario de la visita pastoral," 219. Pope Clement XIV founded the Museo Pio-Clementino (now part of the Vatican) in 1771.

46. Denis Diderot and Jean Le Rond d'Alembert, *Encyclopédie, ou Dictionnaire raisonné des sciences, des arts et des métiers, par une société de gens de lettres. Mis en ordre & publié par M. Diderot . . . & quant a la partie mathématique, par M. d'Alembert,* 28 vols. (Geneva, 1754–72). The plates were published in volumes 18–28 with the title *Recueil de planches, sur les sciences, les arts liberaux, et les arts méchaniques, avec leur explication.*

47. Compare, for example, two illustrations of weaving in the French and Peruvian volumes: "Cotton weaving," *Encyclopédie (Recueil de planches),* vol. 18, pl. 60, and Indians weaving cloth, Martínez Compañón, *Trujillo del Perú,* vol. 2, estampa 91.

48. Martínez Compañón, *Trujillo del Perú,* vol. 6, estampa 83.

49. Albornoz, "Instrucción," 174–75; Frank Salomon and George L. Urioste, trans., *The Huarochirí Manuscript: A Testament of Ancient and Colonial Andean Religion,* annotations and introductory essay by Frank Salomon, transcription by George L. Urioste (Austin: University of Texas Press, 1991): chap. 16, 92–93; and Gary Urton, *At the Crossroads of the Earth and the Sky: An Andean Cosmology* (Austin: University of Texas Press, 1981), 177–80.

50. Deniss J. McKenna, L. E. Luna, and G. N. Towers, "Biodynamic Constituents in Ayahuasca Admixture Plants: An Uninvestigated Folk Pharmacopeia," in Richard Evans Schultes and Siri Von Reis, eds., *Ethnobotany: Evolution of a Discipline* (Portland, Ore.: Dioscorides Press, 1995), 353.

51. James A. Duke, with contributions from Mary Jo Bogenschutz-Godwin and Andrea R. Ottesen, *Duke's Handbook of Medicinal Plants of Latin America* (Boca Raton, Fla.: CRC, Taylor & Francis, 2008), 360–62.

52. Martínez Compañón, *Razón de las especies,* 55, box 12, no. 16. The catahua tree is illustrated elsewhere, without the omeco-machacuai, in the bishop's botanical illustrations. Martínez Compañón, *Trujillo del Perú,* vol. 3, estampa 10.

53. "Pollo monstruoso," Martínez Compañón, *Trujillo del Perú,* vol. 7, f. 158.

54. Lorenzo Legati, *Mvseo Cospiano annesso a quello del famoso Vlisse Aldrovandi e donato alla sua patria dall'illustrissimo Signor Ferdinando Cospi* (Bologna: G. Monti, 1677), bk. 1, chap. 7, no. 9, p. 28.

55. "Figura de un crucifixo naturalmente formada" and "Cruzes naturalmente formadas." Martínez Compañón, *Trujillo del Perú,* vol. 4, ff. 92, 93.

56. Joy Kenseth et al., "Nature's Wonders and Wonders of New Worlds," in Joy Kenseth, ed., *The Age of the Marvelous* (Hanover, N.H.: Hood Museum of Art, Dartmouth College, 1991), 358–60, cat. nos. 136, 137; and William Royall Newman, *Promethean Ambitions: Alchemy and the Quest to Perfect Nature* (Chicago: University of Chicago Press, 2004).

57. Legati, *Mvseo Cospiano*, bk. 2, chap. 26, no. 12, p. 145; and bk. 2, chap. 30, no. 5, pp. 173–74.

58. Lorraine Daston and Katharine Park, *Wonders and the Order of Nature, 1150–1750* (New York: Zone Books, 1998).

59. It seems that miraculous and monstrous objects were not sent to Spain with the bishop's other collections. The examples discussed here are found in the bishop's collection of illustrations but not in the inventories of the 1788 or 1790 shipments (see n. 2).

60. Alonso de Ovalle, *Histórica relación del reyno de Chile; Y de las misiones, y ministerios que exercita en el la Compañia de Iesus* (Rome: Por Francisco Cauallo, 1646), chap. 23, 58–60.

61. ". . . y quedó admirado, y confolado de ver vn tan grande, y nueuo argumento de nueftra fee, que como comiença en aquel nueuo mundo a hechar fus raizes quiere el autor dela naturaleza, que las delos mefmos arboles broten y den teftimonios de ella" (Ovalle, *Histórica relación del reyno de Chile*, 59). English translation from Jorge Cañizares-Esguerra, *Puritan Conquistadors: Iberianizing the Atlantic, 1550–1700* (Stanford, Calif.: Stanford University Press, 2006), 152.

62. As discussed in Lorraine Daston, "Marvelous Facts and Miraculous Evidence in Early Modern Europe," *Critical Inquiry* 18, 1 (Autumn 1991): 97.

63. This is somewhat unexpected because, since the Orinoco Expedition of 1752, the Spanish crown dictated that the Linnaean binomial system was to be the official taxonomic classification used by royal expeditions to the New World and elsewhere. Antonio Lafuente and Nuria Valverde, "Linnaean Botany and Spanish Imperial Biopolitics," in Londa Schiebinger and Claudia Swan, eds., *Colonial Botany: Science, Commerce, and Politics in the Early Modern World* (Philadelphia: University of Pennsylvania Press, 2004), 136.

64. Martínez Compañón, *Trujillo del Perú*, vol. 3, estampa 153.

65. "Ampihuasca, en castellano Bejuco del Veneno, de este le hacen los Yndios para cazar." Martínez Compañón, *Razón de las especies*, 59 (box 12, no. 84). Ampihuasca (*Chondrodendron tomentosum*) is one of the primary ingredients in curare, used by lowland South American peoples as a poison (muscle relaxant) applied to the tips of hunting arrows and spears. *Duke's Handbook*, 205–6; and Norman G. Bisset, "Arrow Poisons and Their Role in the Development of Medicinal Agents," in Schultes and Von Reis, eds., *Ethnobotany*, 289–302.

66. Susan Scott Parrish, *American Curiosity: Cultures of Natural History in the Colonial British Atlantic World* (Chapel Hill: University of North Carolina Press for Omohundro Institute of Early American History and Culture, 2006) esp. chap. 6, "Indian Sagacity," 215–48.

67. Martínez Compañón, *Trujillo del Perú*, vol. 8, ff. 176, 177; vol. 2, ff. 125, 126. At least one other pair of these images was made and exists in the Banco Continental collection in Lima. Macera, *Trujillo del Perú*, cat. nos. 170, 171 (ff. 131, 132). Although some other drawings in the Continental collection seem to be drafts of the Madrid drawings, the relationship between this pair of drawings of Indians fishing and those in the Madrid volumes remains unclear.

68. Both illustrations are captioned "Red de pescar," but the index on f. 181v lists these as "Red de pescar" (vol. 8, f. 176) and "Otra red diferente" (vol. 8, f. 177).

69. According to the volume index on f. 206v, these illustrations are "Yndios pescando con chinchorro" (vol. 2, f. 125) and "Ydem pescando con red" (vol. 2, f. 126). *Chinchorro* is a kind of net (*red*).

70. On his contemporaries in Mexico, such as Antonio Bernasconi and Antonio del Río, see Cabello Carro, *Coleccionismo americano*; *Política investigadora*; and "Las colecciones peruanas."

CHAPTER 13. EUROPE REDISCOVERS LATIN AMERICA: COLLECTING ARTIFACTS AND VIEWS IN THE FIRST DECADES OF THE NINETEENTH CENTURY

1. While the Spanish colonies were the subject of intensive scientific investigation in the second part of the eighteenth century, very little information made its way outside Spain. The main exception is the account of a Spanish expedition conducted with French academicians published by Jorge Juan y Antonio Ulloa and translated into French and English: *Relación del viaje hecho a la América meridional por orden de su Majestad . . .* (Madrid: Antonio Marin and Juan de Zuniga, 1748). For a global view of Spanish expeditions, see María Angeles Catalayud Arinero, *Catalogo de las expediciones y viajes científicos españoles a América y Filipinas, siglos XVIII y XIX* (Madrid: CSIC, 1984). For a study of archaeological research during the colonial period, see José Alcina Franch, *Arqueologos o anticuarios: Historia antigua de la arqueología en la América española* (Barcelona: Ediciones del Serbal, 1995).

2. Jacqueline Duvernay-Bolens, "L'Homme zoologique: Races et racisme chez les naturalistes de la première moitié du XIXe siècle," *L'Homme* 133 (January–March 1995): 9–32.

3. Samuel George Morton, *Crania Americana* (Philadelphia: J. Dobson, 1839). For a complete study of this work and more on the American school of anthropology, see William Stanton, *The Leopard's Spots* (Chicago: University of Chicago Press, 1960). A major defender of the unity of humankind was James Cowles Prichard, *Researches in the Physical History of Man* (London, 1813); this work was later extended into five volumes as *Researches in the Physical History of Mankind* (London: Houlston and Stoneman, 1836); and *The Natural History of Man* (London, 1843), also published in German (Leipzig, 1840–1848) and in French (Paris: J.B. Baillière, 1843–1845).

4. Joseph Barclay Pentland, "On the Inhabitants of the Andes," in *Report of the Fourth Meeting of the British Association for the Advancement of Sciences* (London: J. Murray, 1835), 264.

5. "Lettre du Dr Lund, datée de Lagoa Santa (Minas Gerais) du 21 avril 1844," *Bulletin de la Société de Géographie de Paris* 3, 2 (1845): 250–60.

6. Pedro Correa do Lago and Louis Franck, *Le Comte de Clarac et la forêt vierge du Brésil* (Paris: Louvre-Chandeigne, 2005). The use of scenes from the New World to illustrate the Earth's infancy can also be found in the works of later artists, such as Edwin Church.

7. [Claude Antoine?] Rozet, "Résumé des travaux de la Société Géologique de France et des progrès de la géologie," *Bulletin de la Société Géologique de France* 6 (1835): 10.

8. *Mémoires de la Société Ethnologique* 1 (1841): 3.

9. The proposal for this museum, written by Jules de Blosseville in 1829, was published by his brother in 1832. "Lettre au Directeur de la *Revue des Deux Mondes* sur un projet de création d'un musée ethnographique," *Revue des Deux Mondes* 1 (1832): 135. Various contemporary projects of ethnographical museums were proposed in those years in France by the likes of the Comte de Férussac and Edmé Jomard; see Pascal Riviale, *Un siècle d'archéologie française au Pérou (1821–1914)* (Paris: L'Harmattan, 1996), 265–66.

10. This museum contained many ethnographical artifacts from all over Latin America. See "Inventaire Duhamel du Monceau" (1830), "Inventaire Louis-Philippe" (1830–55), and "Inventaire Morel Fatio" (1856) in the archives of the Musée National de la Marine, Paris.

11. Robert D. Aguirre, *Informal Empire: Mexico and Central America in Victorian Culture* (Minneapolis and London: University of Minnesota Press, 2005), 4–33.

12. *Lettre à M. Dacier . . . relative à l'alphabet des hiéroglyphes* (Paris: Firmin Didot, 1822).

13. Adrian Locke, "Exhibitions and Collections of Pre-Hispanic Mexican Artifacts in Britain," *Aztec: Catalog of the Exhibition in the Royal Academy of Arts* (London: Royal Academy of Arts, 2003), 82.

14. For instance, among the first Peruvian collections in the National Museum of Denmark in Copenhagen were ceramics collected by the frigate *Bellona* (1840–41) and during the expeditions of the *Galathea* (1845–47). Inge Schjepellerup, "Information about Pre-Columbian Objects from the Andean Countries in the Ethnographic Department of the National Museum of Denmark," in A. M. Hocquenghem, P. Tamasi, and Ch. Villlain-Gandossi, eds., *Pre-Columbian Collections in European Museums* (Budapest: European Coordination Center for Research and Documentation in Social Sciences, Akadémai Kiadó, 1987), 92. For an analysis of individual contributions in Peru, see Riviale, *Un siècle d'archéologie française*.

15. *Instructions pour les voyageurs et pour les employés des colonies sur la manière de recueillir, de conserver et d'envoyer des objets d'histoire naturelle*, 3rd ed. (Paris: A. Belin, 1839). In English, see James Cowles Prichard, *Queries Respecting the Human Race, to be Addressed to Travellers and Others, Drawn up by a Committee of the British Association for the Advancement of Science . . .* (London, 1839).

16. Letter from Brongniart to Montalivet (Sèvres, March 28, 1834), in the archives of the Musée national de la Céramique, Sèvres.

17. Pascal Riviale, "L'oeuvre archéologique d'Alcide d'Orbigny," in Philippe de Laborde Pédelahore, *Alcide d'Orbigny: À la découverte de nouvelles républiques sud-américaines* (Biarritz: Atlantica, 2000), 363–86.

18. Antonio del Rio, *Description of the Ruins of an Ancient City Discovered near Palenque* (London: Henry Berthoud, 1822).

19. William Bullock, *Six Months' Residence and Travels in Mexico* (London, 1824); part of the report was also published in France, D. B. Warden, *Recueil des voyages et des mémoires publiés par la Société de géographie* 2 (1825): 170–93.

20. Between 1825 and 1840, an impressive number of letters were received by the Geographical Society of Paris, which published extensive extracts of this correspondence in its bulletin. About this contest see also Nadia Prévost Urkidi, "Historiographie de l'américanisme scientifique français au XIXe siècle: Le 'Prix Palenque' (1826–1839) ou le choix *archæologique* de Jomard," *Journal de la Société des Américanistes* 95, 2 (2009): 117–49.

21. Carl Nebel, *Voyage pittoresque et archéologique dans la partie la plus intéressante du Mexique* (Paris: M. Moench, 1836); Leonardo López-Luján, "La arqueología mesoamericana en la obra de Nebel," *Artes de México* 80 (2006): 20–33; Jean Frédéric Waldeck, *Voyage pittoresque et archéologique dans la province d'Yucatan (Amérique centrale), pendant les années 1834 et 1836* (Paris: Bellizard, Dufour et Cie, 1838); Claude-François Baudez, *Jean Frédéric Waldeck, peintre: Le premier explorateur des ruines mayas* (Paris: Hazan, 1993).

22. M. Bonnetty, "Description des antiquités mexicaines d'après la première expédition du capitaine Dupaix," *Annales de philosophie chrétienne* 6, 11 (1835): 277.

23. Letter from the Count Ange de Saint-Priest [to an unknown correspondent], London, May 27, 1843, British Library, Manuscripts Department, Add 40529.

24. Cited in David M. Pendergast, *Palenque: The Walker-Caddy Expedition to the Ancient Maya City, 1839–1840* (Norman: University of Oklahoma Press, 1967), 31.

25. John Lloyd Stephens, *Incidents of Travel in Central America, Chiapas and Yucatan* (London: J. Murray, 1841).

26. Benjamin Moore Norman, *Rambles in Yucatan or Notes of Travel Through the Peninsula* (New York: J. and H.G. Langley, 1843).

27. Marie-France Fauvet-Berthelot, Leonardo López-Luján, and Susana Guimaraes, "Six personnages en quête d'objets: Histoire de la collection archéologique de la Real Expedición Anticuaria en Nouvelle Espagne," *Gradhiva* 6 (2007): 105–26.

28. Regarding these first collections and the Musée Américain, see Leonardo López-Luján and Marie-France Fauvet-Berthelot, *Aztèques: La collection des sculptures du musée du quai Branly* (Paris: Musée du quai Branly, 2005), 28–39; Fauvet-Berthelot et al., "Six personnages en quête d'objets"; Riviale, *Un siècle d'archéologie française*, 270–72; Pascal Riviale, "Léonce Angrand: Le charme discret d'un collectionneur américaniste," *Alma* 2 (2001): 28–34.

29. Pendergast, *Palenque*, 32.

30. Drawings by the Peruvian Pancho Fierro and the Brazilian Joaquin Guillobel are examples of the commercial diffusion of and influence on local artistic production. Gilberto Ferrez, *O velho Rio de Janeiro a traves de gravuras de Thomas Ender* (Sao Paulo: Edições Malhoramentos, n.d.), 155–69; Pascal Riviale, "La etnografía pintoresca de los viajeros a las Américas, durante la primera mitad del siglo XIX," in Fermín del Pino, Pascal Riviale, and Juan José Villarías, coord., *Entre textos e imágenes: Representación antropológica del Indio americano* (Madrid: Consejo Superior de Investigaciones Científicas, colección "De aca y de alla," 2009): 181–91.

31. *América exotica: Panorámicas, tipos y costumbres del siglo XIX; Obras sobre papel; Colecciones de la Banca Central; Colombia, Ecuador, México, Perú y Venezuela* (Bogotá: Banco de la República, Biblioteca Luis Angel Arango, 2004); Riviale, "La etnografía pintoresca."

32. Louis Choris, *Voyage pittoresque autour du monde avec des portraits de sauvages d'Amérique, d'Asie, d'Afrique et des îles du Grand océan, des paysages, des vues maritimes et plusieurs objets d'histoire naturelle* (Paris, 1822).

33. Jean-Baptiste Debret, *Voyage pittoresque et historique au Brésil ou séjour d'un artiste français au Brésil depuis 1816 jusqu'en 1831, inclusivement . . .* , vol. 3 (Paris: Firmin-Didot, 1834–39); Johann Moritz Rugendas, *Voyage pittoresque dans le Brésil*, trans. M. de Golbéry (Paris: Engelmann et cie, 1835); Maximilian Prinz zu Wied Neuwied, *Reise nach Brasilien in den Jahren 1815 bis 1817* (Frankfurt, 1820–21). For a survey of the French artistic mission, see *Missão artística francesa e pintores viajantes/La mission artistique française et les peintres voyageur* (Rio de Janeiro: Instituto Cultural Brasil-Francia, 1990).

34. Carl Nebel, *Voyage pittoresque et archéologique*, 1836; Jean Frédéric Waldeck, *Voyage pittoresque et archéologique*, 1838; Claudio Linati, *Costumes civils, militaires et religieux du Mexique: Dessinés d'après nature par C. Linati* (Bruxelles: Lithographie Royale de Jobard, 1828); Alcide Dessalines d'Orbigny, *Voyage dans l'Amérique méridionale* (Paris: P. Bertrand, 1835–45); Emeric Essex Vidal, *Picturesque Illustrations of Buenos Ayres and Montevideo: Consisting of Twenty-Four Views, Accompanied with Descriptions of the Scenery, and of the Costumes and Manners, etc. of the Inhabitants of Those Cities and Their Environs* (London: R. Ackermann, 1820); Claude Gay, *Historia física y política de Chile* (Paris, 1844–54); Louis Choris, *Voyage pittoresque autour du monde, avec des portraits de sauvages d'Amérique, d'Asie, d'Afrique et des îles du grand Océan, des paysages, des vues maritimes* (Paris: Firmin-Didot, 1822).

35. For instance, see the volumes dedicated to the New World in the series *L'Univers pittoresque: Histoire et description de tous les peuples, de leurs religions, de leurs moeurs, coutumes, industries* (Paris: Firmin Didot, 1836–43); *Cosmorama: A View of the Costumes and Particuliarities of All Nations* (London: J. Harris, 1827); and *Völkständinge Volkergallerie in getreuen Abbildungen aller nationene der Welt mit ausführrbucher Beschreibung* (Meissen: F.W. Goedsche, Löwenberg, bei Eschrich und Camp, Pesth, in der Migandsche Buchhandlung, 1850).

36. Aguirre, *Informal Empire*, 21, 42.

37. *Brésil panoramique: Papiers peints du XIXe siècle* (Boulogne-Billancourt: Ville de Boulogne-Billancourt/Bibliothèque Marmottan, Éditions Monelle Hayot, 2005).

38. The iconographical production dedicated to Pacific islands and their inhabitants in that period were surely even more significant.

39. Pascal Riviale, "Johan Moritz Rugendas, un artiste voyageur à la rencontre d'une Amérique méconnue . . . et pittoresque," in Yves Le Fur, coord., *D'un regard l'autre: Histoire des regards européens sur l'Afrique, l'Amérique et l'Océanie* (Paris: Réunion des Musées Nationaux, 2006), 164–66.

40. Deborah Poole, *Vision, Race, and Modernity: A Visual Economy of the Andean Image World* (Princeton, N.J.: Princeton University Press, 1997). The first images brought by travelers had a noteworthy influence on the iconographical production of Latin Americans themselves. For the Mexican case in the mid-nineteenth century, see María Esther Pérez Salas, *Costumbrismo y litografía en México: Un nuevo modo de ver* (México: Universidad Nacional Autónoma de México, Instituto de Investigaciones Estéticas, 2005).

41. Alexandre Brongniart, *Traité des arts céramiques ou des poteries* (Paris: Fain et Thunot, 1844), 1: 529.

CHAPTER 14. IMAGE AND EXPERIENCE IN THE LAND OF NOPAL AND MAGUEY: COLLECTING AND PORTRAYING MEXICO IN TWO NINETEENTH-CENTURY FRENCH ALBUMS

Epigraph: Louis Falconnet, *Mexique, 1865,* unpublished leather-bound album, Research Library, The Getty Research Institute (93.R.20).

1. Maximilian and his wife Carlotta arrived in Mexico in May 1864, and Maximilian was executed in June 1867. Arturo Aguilar Ochoa, *La fotografía durante el Imperio de Maximiliano* (México: Universidad Nacional Autónoma de México, Instituto de Investigaciones Estéticas, 1996), 16–17. Louis Falconnet arrived in Mexico in June 1865 and left in February 1867, returning to France on April 8, 1867, two months before Maximilian's execution. See Louis Falconnet, unpublished leather-bound album, Research Library, The Getty Research Institute (93.R.20), 4r.

2. It is unclear how many artists were involved in the production of the paintings and drawings in this album. One image is signed "L.F.," for Louis Falconnet, and the same hand is apparent on a number of other images in the album, whereas other paintings are clearly by other artists. A focused study of every image in the album, in addition to more information about Falconnet and his entourage, which may be available through further archival research, could shed light on the number of artists' hands involved in the production of this album's images.

3. *Album of Mexican and French Cartes-de-Visite* (title devised), unpublished leather-bound album, Research Library, The Getty Research Institute (2000.R.25).

4. See Elizabeth Anne McCauley, *A. A. Disdéri and the Carte de Visite Portrait Photograph* (New Haven, Conn.: Yale University Press, 1985), for more information on *cartes de visite* in France, and William C. Darrah, *Cartes de Visite in Nineteenth-Century Photography* (Gettysburg, Pa.: W.C. Darrah, 1981), 8, for more information on *cartes de visite* albums.

5. At this time, I cannot determine whether the person who made this album was in Mexico and recording personal experience through the collection and assemblage of *cartes de visite* or in Europe and collecting and assembling these cards to create a narration of what Mexico seemed to be—from afar. Although I suspect the former, additional research is necessary to make a determination. Regardless, we can still make productive comparisons between Falconnet's album and this one.

6. At this time, this is all the information I have on Louis Falconnet, though more could be obtained through research in French archives, planned for the future.

7. "Coupe géologique de la route de Vera-Cruz à Mexico suivant le développement de la ligne brisée passant par Mexico Puebla Orizaba et Vera-Cruz: Travail exécuté en février 1865 par M. M. A. Dollfus et E. de Monserrat," digital image, http://archives.getty.edu: 30008/getty_images/digitalresources/mexico/jpegs/m exo74.jpg.

8. See, for example, François Aubert, *Anciana Mexicana cargando leña*, illustrated in Aguilar Ochoa, *Fotografía durante el Imperio*, 126.

9. For an illustration of Pingret's *Boceto de la Aduana de Vera Cruz*, see Luis Ortiz Macedo, *Edouard Pingret: un pintor romántico francés que retrató el México del mediar del siglo XIX* (México: Fomento Cultural Banamex, A.C., 1989), 93.

10. See Olivier Debroise, *Fuga mexicana: un recorrido por la fotografía en México* (México: Consejo Nacional para la Cultura y las Artes, 1994); trans. Stella de Sá Rego, *Mexican Suite: A History of Photography in Mexico* (Austin: University of Texas Press, 2001), 120, regarding the popularity of pulque and the *Tlachiquero* images among artists and foreigners. For an illustration of Edouard Pingret's *Tlachiquero*, see Ortiz Macedo, *Edouard Pingret*, 97.

11. See Debroise, *Mexican Suite*, 116–20, regarding the *tipos populares* and their origins and inspirations, which included oil paintings from the 1840s by Edouard Pingret. See also Aguilar Ochoa, *Fotografía durante el Imperio*, 115–17.

12. For an illustration of Edouard Pingret's *El Aguador*, see Ortiz Macedo, *Eduoard Pingret*, 97.

13. See, for example, Aguilar Ochoa, *Fotografía durante el Imperio*, 33, for a discussion of *tarjetas de visita* in Mexico during the French Intervention.

14. What is interesting is that, after the identification of the "Porte-faix" and the "Femme indienne," a caption in the same ink says "Envoyé à mere dans une lettre." This caption suggests that the album—all or part—was compiled on Falconnet's return to France with drawings and paintings made in Mexico and photographs acquired in Mexico and France.

15. The Museo Nacional was founded in 1825 to house the new nation's antiquities; it was located in the University. In 1865, Maximilian founded the Museo Público de Historia Natural, Arqueología e Historia, although it was still often called the "National Museum." This museum was located in the Casa de Moneda (formerly the National Mint from the Colonial Period), which was next to the National Palace. With the foundation of this museum, Maximilian moved the nation's archaeological collection (in addition to collections of books and natural history specimens) to the Casa de Moneda location. The archaeological materials later became part of the National Museum of Anthropology, which is in Chapultepec Park. Luis Castillo Ledon, *Arqueología, historia y etnografía 1825–1925: reseña histórica escrita para la celebración de su primer centenario* (México: Talleres Gráficos del Museo Nacional de Arqueología, Historia y Etnografía, 1924), 21–22; Jesús Bustamante García, "La conformación de la antropología como disciplina científica, el Museo Nacional de México y los Congresos Internacionales de Americanistas," *Revista de Indias* 65, 234 (2005): 303–18, 304–6.

16. The first publication of the Calendar Stone and the Coatlicue sculpture was in Antonio de León y Gama's *Descripción histórica y cronológica de las dos piedras que con ocasión del nuevo empedrado que se está formando en la plaza principal de México, se hallaron en ella el año de 1790* (México: F. Zuniga y Ontiveros, 1792).

17. The likely source of this drawing is *Antigüedades*, an image that accompanied a document entitled *Breve noticia sobre las antigüedades de Jonuta (Carmen) Cerros o monticulos artificiales existentes en dicha villa*, written by Pedro C. Paz and dated November 21, 1865. The text and two images (a map and the figurine collection) were published in the Mexican literary newspaper *El Renacimiento* in 1869 (vol. 1) (Carlos Alvarez, personal communication, 2009). They are reproduced in Carlos Alvarez A. and Luis Casasola, *Las figurillas de Jonuta,*

Tabasco (México: Instituto de Investigaciones Filológicas, Centro de Estudios Mayas, Universidad Nacional Autónoma de México, 1985), 103–11. Alvarez and Casasola (*Las figurillas de Jonuta*, 11) note that this is the first documentation of which they are aware of the Jonuta figurine complex.

18. See Alvarez and Casasola *Las figurillas de Jonuta*, 104–5. See 111 for the image of the figurine collection; the numbering and labels of the figurines are different in the drawing in Falconnet's album.

19. For example, in the introduction to Alfredo Chavero and Joaquín Baranda, *Homenaje á Cristóbal Colón, Antigüedades Mexicanas publicadas en homenaje a la memoria de Cristóbal Colón, por la Junta Colombina de México en el cuarto centenario del descubrimiento de América* (México: Oficina tipográfica de la Secretaría de fomento, 1892), published in relation to the exposition in Madrid of that year, Chavero wrote that "se acordó formar una importante colección de antigüedades . . . que en ella estuviesen representadas todos nuestras principales razas y nacionalidades antiguas, así como todos los objetos á ellas pertenecientes, en cuanto fuese posible adquirirlos y coleccionarlos" (iii). This collection included objects and manuscripts that the text identified as Nahua, Mixtec, Zapotec, Maya, and Cuicatec.

20. For more on this battle, see James W. Ryan, *Camerone: The French Foreign Legion's Greatest Battle* (Westport, Conn.: Praeger, 1996).

21. See Aguilar Ochoa, *Fotografía durante el Imperio*, 17, 40–50, concerning the photographs and *cartes de visite* that documented Maximilian's execution, many of which were censored in France by Napoleon III.

22. *Cartes de visite* of Benito Juárez were extremely popular among Mexicans and foreigners and were distributed in massive quantities, particularly on Juárez's death (in 1872), when 20,000 copies of his portrait were sold (Aguilar Ochoa, *Fotografía durante el Imperio*, 25, citing Olivier Debroise).

23. Debroise, *Mexican Suite*, 116–18, notes that wax figurines of Mexican types were created and collected in Mexico in the nineteenth century, especially during the reign of Maximilian, in the early 1860s. He states that, like the *cartes de visite* photographs of types, these figurines were of people carrying out trades such as men harvesting pulque, women making or selling tortillas, and other street vendors. As seen here in this album's *cartes de visite*, also manufactured were wax figurines of indigenous figures; some of these remain intact in collections such as those at the Museo de América in Madrid and the Museo Goya de Castres. María José Esparza Liberal, "Las figuras de cera en el Museo de América de Madrid" (38–71, 70); Elisa García Barragán, "Las figuras de cera en el Museo Goya de Castres" 72–79, 77–79), both in *México Moderno*, vol. 7 of *México en el mundo de las colecciones de arte*, general ed. María Luisa Sabau García (México: Gobierno de la República, 1994).

24. Other Mexican historical figures—those in alliance with and those who resisted the French occupation—included in the album are Ignacio Comonfort, Benito Juárez (captioned "Ex-Président"), General Ignacio S. Saragoza/Zaragoza, General Jesús Gonzalez Ortega, General Tomás Mejía, and Manuel Doblado.

25. In *Mexican Suite*, Olivier Debroise discusses the late nineteenth-century genre of the family album: "Bound in embossed leather or cloth, the family album was an indispensable object in homes after 1865, when the carte-de-visite facilitated circulation, in multiple copies, of photographic images. The album became the repository of family memory and had its place of honor in the parlor. . . . It served as a mnemonic device that was exhibited from time to time, unleashing personal stories and family anecdotes. Recognized faces paraded past: the country uncle, the married cousin, the deceased grandfather," in addition to images of travel and tourism and public figures (38–39).

Malcolm Baker is Distinguished Professor of the History of Art at the University of California, Riverside and Honorary Senior Research Fellow of the Victoria and Albert Museum. He is author of *Roubiliac and the Eighteenth-Century Monument: Sculpture as Theatre* (with David Bindman), which received the Mitchell Prize for the History of Art and best book prize of the American Historians of British Art, and *Figured in Marble: The Making and Viewing of Eighteenth-Century Sculpture*. He is currently writing *The Marble Index: Sculptural Portraiture in Eighteenth Century Britain*, a study of the portrait bust and its roles in eighteenth-century Britain.

Robert Batchelor is Associate Professor of History at Georgia Southern University. He is author of several articles about relations between Europe and East Asia during the early modern period. He has a forthcoming book about the emergence of London as global city in the sixteenth and seventeenth centuries.

Sarah Benson is an art historian whose research has focused on Renaissance print culture, early modern tourism to Italy, and the intersections between scientific and artistic image making. Her current book project examines how Roman monuments and antiquities were packaged for virtual collection in media such as painting, print, and reproducible models and casts. Her contribution to this volume is based on research as a Visiting Researcher at the Faculty of Architecture, Chiang Mai University, Thailand, and Cornell University's George McT. Kahin Center for Advanced Research on Southeast Asia.

Daniela Bleichmar teaches in the Departments of Art History and History at the University of Southern California. She was the recipient of a Mellon Post-Doctoral Fellowship at the USC-Huntington Early Modern Studies Institute (2004–6) and a Getty Foundation Post-Doctoral Fellowship (2008–9). She is author of numerous essays on the history of science, visual culture, and print in the Spanish Empire and coeditor of *Science in the Spanish and Portuguese Empires, 1500–1800*. Her book *Visible Empire: Colonial Botany and Visual Culture in the Hispanic Enlightenment* is forthcoming.

TREVOR BURNARD is Professor of History at the University of Warwick. He is author of *Creole Gentlemen: The Maryland Elite, 1691–1776* and *Mastery, Tyranny, and Desire: Thomas Thistlewood and His Slaves in the Anglo-Jamaican World*; he is currently completing *Expanding the Boundaries: The Practice and Politics of Writing Early American History* and (with John Garrigus), *Tropical Transformations: St. Domingue, Jamaica, and the Making of Racial Order, 1748–1791*.

PAZ CABELLO CARRO is Chief Curator of the Royal Collections at the Patrimonio Nacional in Madrid. From 1992 to 2008 she was Director of the Museo de América in Madrid and previously worked as its Curator of pre-Columbian and indigenous collections. She has published widely on Spanish pre-Columbian collections, Enlightenment collectors and voyagers, scientific expeditions, early archaeology in the Spanish Americas and museology.

CÉCILE FROMONT teaches in the department of Art History at the University of Chicago. She was a postdoctoral scholar at the Michigan Society of Fellows and is currently working on a book analyzing the reciprocal influence of artistic form and religious thought in the encounter between Christianity and African cosmology in the early modern Kingdom of Kongo, in Central Africa.

CARINA L. JOHNSON is Associate Professor of history at Pitzer College. Her book examining political authority, religious orthodoxy, and the reception of Mexican and Ottoman cultures in the sixteenth-century Habsburg Empire is forthcoming in 2011.

PETER C. MANCALL is Professor of History and Anthropology at the University of Southern California and Director of the USC-Huntington Early Modern Studies Institute. He is author or editor of fifteen books, including *Hakluyt's Promise: An Elizabethan's Obsession for an English America* and *Fatal Journey: The Final Expedition of Henry Hudson—A Tale of Mutiny and Murder in the Arctic*.

JOSÉ RAMÓN MARCAIDA is working on a doctoral dissertation at the Institute of History of the Spanish Consejo Superior de Investigaciones Científicas on the relation between early modern science and baroque visual and material culture in seventeenth-century Spain.

MEGAN E. O'NEIL has taught art history at USC. From 2009 to 2011 she was A. W. Mellon Postdoctoral Fellow at the Center for the Advanced Study in the Visual Arts at the National Gallery of Art. She is author of two forthcoming books: *Engaging Ancient Maya Sculpture at Piedras Negras, Guatemala* and *The Lives of Ancient Maya Sculptures*.

JOANNE PILLSBURY is Director of Pre-Columbian Studies at Dumbarton Oaks, a research institute of Harvard University located in Washington, D.C. She was previously Dumbarton Oaks Professor of Pre-Columbian Studies at the University of Maryland, and before that, assistant dean at the Center for Advanced Study in the Visual Arts, The National Gallery of Art, and lecturer at the Sainsbury Research Unit for the Arts of Africa, Oceania, and the Americas, University of East Anglia. She is editor of the three-volume *Guide to Documentary Sources for Andean Studies, 1530–1900*; *Moche Art and Archaeology in Ancient Peru*; and coeditor (with Susan Toby Evans) of *Palaces of the Ancient New World*.

JUAN PIMENTEL is Tenure Researcher at the Institute of History of the Spanish Consejo Superior de Investigaciones Científicas and has been Visiting Scholar at the HPS, University of Cambridge. His books include *La física de la Monarquía: Alejandro Malaspina, 1754–1810*; *Testigos del mundo: Ciencia, literatura y viajes en la Ilustración*; and *El Rinoceronte y el Megaterio* (2010). His research focuses on early modern scientific explorations, travel literature, court culture, and imperial science.

PASCAL RIVIALE is the author of *Un siècle d'archéologie française au Pérou (1821–1914)*; *Los viajeros franceses en busca del Perú antiquo (1821–1914)*; *Una historia de la presencia francesa en el Perú, de las Luces a los años locos*, and coauthor (with Fermín del Pino-Diaz and Juan J. R. Villarías-Robles) of *Entre textos e imágenes: Representaciones antropológicas de la América indígena*. He is currently preparing a critical edition of Charles Wieners's travel account *Pérou et Bolivie* (originally published in Paris in 1880). He is in charge of the printed archives at the Archives Nationales in Paris and is an associated researcher in the Équipe Recherche et Enseignement Américaniste (CNRS).

BENJAMIN SCHMIDT is Professor of History at the University of Washington. His recent books include *Making Knowledge in Early Modern Europe: Practices, Objects, and Texts, 1400–1800* (with Pamela H. Smith); *Going Dutch: The Dutch

Presence in America, 1609–2009 (with Joyce D. Goodfriend and Annette Stott); and *The Discovery of Guiana by Sir Walter Ralegh*. His first book, *Innocence Abroad: The Dutch Imagination and the New World, 1570–1670*, won the Renaissance Society of America Gordan Prize for best book in Renaissance studies and the Holland Society Hendricks Prize for best book in colonial Dutch studies. His current research explores the culture and politics of "globalism" and colonial expansion in Europe circa 1700.

ALAIN SCHNAPP is Professor of Classical Archaeology at Université Paris I (Panthéon-Sorbonne). His main interests are Greek iconography and cultural history of antiquity. He has been visiting scholar or visiting professor at Princeton University, Stanford University, the Getty Research Institute, Universität Heidelberg, Universität Basel, Wissenschaftskolleg Berlin, Instituto Orientale Napoli, Universita di Perugia, and Collegium Budapest. He was also the first director of the Institut National d'Histoire l'Art and coordinator of the European cultural project "Archives of European Archaeology."

LISA TREVER is a doctoral candidate in History of Art and Architecture at Harvard University whose dissertation investigates the ancient Moche (200–850 C.E.) mural paintings of Pañamarca, Peru. She is author of a forthcoming study of Felipe Guaman Poma de Ayala's illustrations of native Andean religion in Martín de Murúa's *Historia del origen y genealogía real de los reyes ingas del Piru* (ca. 1590) and in the artist's own *El primer nueva corónica y buen gobierno* (ca. 1615).

INDEX

—ɯ—

Italicized page numbers refer to illustrations.

Anglerius, Peter Martyr, 88, 90

Angola, 7, 134, 136–37, 139, 145, 147, 150, 153, 311n4, 311–12n8

Annales de Philosophie Chrétienne, 262

Anne, queen of England, 203

Anom, Pangéran, 129–31

anomie, 132

anthropology, 10, 39, 205, 212, 254–58, 332n3; and classification of humans, 8, 209–12, *211*, 255–56, *257*, 261–62, 323n46, 332n3; physical anthropology, 258

Anthropology Museum (San Francisco), 212

antiquarianism, 9, 58–79; comparison of Old and New Worlds, 9, 61–79, *65*, *67*, *68*, *79*, 298n22; criticism of, 58–60; distance between past and present, 69, 77; English, 9, 62–67, *65*, 68–69, 72; and Florida, 62, 64, 66; and global collecting gone "muck," 123; Italian, 58–59, 61, 66, 72, 77; and Lastanosa, 15–17, 19–20, 30; and Mexico, 69–78, *73*, *74*; and parasols, 42; and Peru, 9, 62, 69–70, 76–77; southern versus northern European traditions, 60–66, *65*, 76–77; Spanish, 9, 62, 64, 69–79, *73*, *74*; and Virginia, 9, 61–62, 64, 66–67, 69

Antiquités mexicaines, 262

Antiquity Explained (Montfaucon), 60

Antiquity Revealed (Boulanger), 60

Appadurai, Arjun, 39, 87, 299n5

aquarelles, 62, 64, 66

Araldi Manuscript, 136–37

Aránzazu (ship), 231, 234

archaeology, 58–59, 69, 298n22; and collecting American bodies, 206, 212; and Martínez Compañón's "museum," 237, 244, 325–26n2, 326n5; and rediscovery of Latin America, 10, 254–55, 259–62, 264, 267; and Siamese court, 159; and Spanish Americana, 9, *plates 9, 10*, 217–23, 324n7. *See also* excavations, and antiquarianism

architecture: and antiquarianism, 61, 70, 72; in Central Africa, 139, 146; in French albums of Mexico, 276–77; of Native Americans, 206, 210; and Siamese court, 159–60; and Spanish baroque culture, 5, 99

Archive of the Indies (Seville), 220, 225, 323n2, 324n7, 325–26n2, 327n17

Arenberg, duke of, 50

Argonaut (ship), 229

arma christi, 118

Ars Amatoria (Ovid), 43, 295n28

Arteaga, Ignacio de, 226

art historians, 3, 47, 100, 103–4, 114, 305n19

artificialia, 15, 20; and Capuchin missionaries in Central Africa, 135, 151; and Siamese court, 157;

and Spanish baroque culture, 103–4, 106, 110–11, 113, 306n46

Ascension of Sri Ajnyana, The (Teeuw), 127

Asti, Bernardino Ignazio da Vezza d', 137, 142, 145–51, *148*, *plate 6*, 312–13n11

astronomy, 102, 160–62, 169, *171*, 234

Atahualpa, 42, 96, 241

Atlantic World, 4, 7, 117, 121, 130, 133, 135–36

Atrevida (ship), 232

Aubrey, John, 61, 69

Augustine, 248

Augustinians, 76

authority, 77, 130, 136; and royal regalia, 85–86, 88, 93–95; and Siamese court, 162, 164

autopsy, 198

ayahuasca, 246

Aymara ethnic group, 261

Ayutthaya, 157–58, 160, 170, 173, 316n1; Burmese sack of (1767), 164

Aztecs, 19, 42; accompanying regalia to Spain, 88; and antiquarianism, 69–72, 78; Calendar Stone, 270, 280–81, 286–88, *287*, 336n16; Coatlicue sculpture, 280–81, 283, 336n16; and French albums of Mexico, 270, 274, 280–81, 283, 285–88, *287*, 336n16; royal regalia of, 1, 6–7, 83–84, 86–92, 94–98, 301–2n31

Bacon, Francis, 59–60, 77

Bacon's Rebellion (1676), 40

Bada, 144–45

Bailyn, Bernard, 117

bananas, *140*, *141*, 143–44, 312n10

Banks, Thomas, 118

Banten, 117–22, *119*, 129–33

Baradère, Henri, 262

baroque culture, 27–28, 39–40, 43, 54, 173; and Spanish still life painting, 5–6, 99–115, *107*, *109*, *112*, *plates 3, 4b*

barrows, 206–8

Baudrillard, Jean, 104

Baumgartner, Johann Wolfgang, 47, 50, *plate 2*

Baxandall, Michael, 291n20

Baxter, W. T., 184

Bayly, C. A., 120

beavers, 45

Beckford, William, III, 179

beds, 15, 290n2

Behn, Aphra, 40, 43, 49, 294n22

Belotti, Giovanni da Romano, 147

Berchem, Nicolaes, 43–45, 47, 50, 53, 295nn30,31,34

Bernasconi, Antonio, 220–21

Bernini, 109

Berquist, Emily, 243

Betanzos, Juan de, 76
Betterton, Thomas, 39, 49
Bible, polyglot, 127
Biblioteca del Palacio Real (Madrid), 237, 326n5
bicephalic serpent, 246
Bidloo, Govard, 108
bird sculpture, 225, *225*
Blaeu, Joan, 295n30
Blaeu, Willem, 43, 295n30
Blair, John, 186, 319n27
Bleichmar, Daniela, 242, 283
Blosseville, Jules de, 332n9
Blubber Valley Plantation (Antigua), 184
Boban, Eugène, 285
Boceto de la Aduana de Vera Cruz (Pingret painting), 276
Bodega y Quadra, Juan Francisco de la, 226–27, 230–32, 234
Bodenstein von Karlstadt, Andreas, 93, 303n44
Bodleian Library, 122–23, *124*, *125*, 127, *128*
Bolivia, 243, 256, 266–67
bones: of Native Americans, 194, 206–12, *211*; in still life paintings, 5–6, 106–9, *107*, *109*, 113–14, *plate 4*
Book of Common Prayer, 130
Borbón, Cardinal, 223
borlas (head ornaments), 242
botanical gardens, 6, 102, 111, 238
botanists. *See* naturalists
Boturini Benaduci, Lorenzo, 240
Bougainville, Louis-Antoine de, 255
Boulanger, Nicolas Antoine, 60
Le Bourgeois gentilhomme (Molière), 38
bow and arrow, 32, *32*, 37, 47, *plate 1*
Boy Bitten by Lizard (Caravaggio painting), 109
Bracegirdle, Anne, 40, 49–50
Bradford, William, 192–93
Bravo de Lagunas y Castillo, Pedro, 242
Brazil, 2, 67, 135; and collecting American bodies, 195–96, *197*; rediscovery of, 255–56, 259, 264–65, *266*, 267, 334n30
Brevíssima relación (Las Casas), 54
Briefe and True Report of the New Found Land of Virginia (Harriot), 9, 199–200, *200*, 203
Bristol Slave Trade Trail, 180
Britannia (Camden), 67–68, *68*, 77
British Honduras, 263
British Museum, 261, 263
Brongniart, Alexandre, 261, 267–68
Brosses, Charles de, 59
Brown, Jonathan, 101–2
Browne, Thomas, Sir, 132, 310n42
Bry, Theodor de, 9

Bryson, Norman, 115
Bucareli, Antonio María de, 224, 238
Bucareli Bay, 226–27
Buddhas, 159
Buddhism, 127, 158–59, 168
Buen Retiro Palace (Madrid), 101–2, 113
Bujangga Manik, 122–23, *125*, 126–27
Bullock, William, 259, 262, 266, 280
Burford, Robert, 266
Burke Museum (University of Washington, Seattle), 212
Burma, 156, 158, 164, 316n1
Bustamante, José, 232

Caamaño, Jacinto, 231, 234
Cabello Carro, Paz, 236, 242
cabinets of curiosities, 1–4, 10, 15–30, 291nn17,20, 292n26; and Aztec regalia, 83–84; of Calzolari, 4, 27–28, *28*; and collecting American bodies, 194; of Cospi, 4, 19, 24–26, *25*, 30; of Imperato, 4, 22, *23*, 30; *Kunstkammern*, 84, 97, 101; of Lastanosa, 4, 15–21, *18*, 22, 26–28, 30, 290nn2,4; and Martínez Compañón's "museum," 248; of Settala, 4, 27–28, *29*; and Siamese court, 157, 171–74; and Spanish baroque culture, 101–3, 106–8, 110–11, 113–15; of Worm, 4, 22, 26, *26*, 78; *Wunderkammer*, 2, 8, 32–33, 38, 101–3, 106–7, 113, 135
Cabot, Sebastian, 192, 195
Caddy, John, 263–64
Cadornega, António Oliveira de, 137
caducity, 106, 108–10
caimans, 268
Cajamarca, 218, 244
Calderón, José Antonio, 220
Calderón de la Barca, 104
Calendar Stone, Aztec, 270, 280–81, 286, *287*, 288, 336n16
Caltanisetta, Luca da, 152
calvarium, 68, *68*
Calvo, Fabio, 72
Calzolari, Francesco, 4, 27–28, *28*
Camden, William, 67–68, *68*, 77
camels, 160, *161*
Camerone, Battle of, 283
Camilo, Giulio, 24
Campeggio, Lorenzo, 93
caning vignettes, 54, *55*, *56*
Cañizares-Esguerra, Jorge, 71, 295n31
cannibalism, 37, 194, 198
Capuchin missionaries, 7, 134–54, 311–12nn4,5, 311–12n8, 312n10, 313n14, 314nn25,31; and culturally constructed representations, *141*, 142–45, 151–54, *plate 6*; didactic manuscripts of, 134–35,

Codrington, Christopher, 179

Colegio de Santa Cruz de Tlatelolco, 72, 74–75

Coligny, Gaspard de, 62

Collichang, 198, *199*

Colnett, James, 229–31, 325n21

colonialism, 2; and antiquarianism, 61–62, 69–71, 75–76; and Capuchin missionaries in Central Africa, 7, 134–37, 145, 147, 150, 153, 311n5; and collecting American bodies, 192–93, 195, 200–203, *200*, *202*, 205, 322n31; and exotica, 16, 33; and global collecting gone "muck," 117, 130, 133; and Martínez Compañón's "museum," 236, 241, 252–53, 328n28; and parasols, 43, 45, 53; and rediscovery of Latin America, 254–55, 262, 332n1; and Spanish Americana, 222–24; and tyranny as exotic motif, 54

Columbian Exchange, 193

Columbus, Christopher, 1, 7, 192, 194–96; 400th anniversary of voyage, 211–12, 235

commerce: and Capuchin missionaries in Central Africa, 135; and exotica, 31, 33–34; and global collecting gone "muck," 121–23, 127, 129–33; and parasols, 43–45, *44*, 53, 295n31; and rediscovery of Latin America, 255, 260, 334n30; and Spanish baroque culture, 101–2, 112–15. *See also* global collecting/trade

commodities, slaves as, 8, 181, 183–91

Comonfort, Ignacio, 284, 337n24

Concepción (ship), 230

La Condamine, Charles-Marie de, 242, 244, 254

conquistadores, 62, 69–79, 88, 96–97. *See also names of conquistadores*

conspiracy, 132–33

Contarini, Gasparo, 97–98

continents, 35–37, *36*. *See also names of continents*

Cook, James, 59, 226, 232, 255, 325n15

Cope, Walter, Sir, 22–24, 26–27, 120

Copernicus, 170

Córdoba, Antonio de, 222

Corella, Bonaventura da, 311–12n8

cornucopias, 37, *plate 1*, 293n10

Cornwall Gazette, 177

coronations, 86–87, 90, 94, 96

Cortés, Hernán: and antiquarianism, 69–70; and Aztec regalia, 6, 83–84, 87–92, 94–96; letters of, 1, 88–90, 94–95, 301–2n31

Cortona, Serafino da, 313n20

Cospi, Ferdinando, 4, 19, 24–26, *25*, 30

Coster (ship), 117–18, *119*, 131–33

Cotton, Robert, Sir, 123

Council of the Indies, 74–75

Council of Trent, 76

counterfeiters, 121

Counter-Reformation, 99, 101, 107

Crania Americana (Morton), 210–11, *211*, 323n46

Crashaw, William, 201

Crespi, Juan, 224–25

Croix, Teodoro de, 237

crowns, 85–86, 88, 91, 97, 139

crucifix: and Capuchin missionaries in Central Africa, 141, 143, 146, 312n10; and Martínez Compañón's "museum," 247–48, *249*, *250*, *251*; and rediscovery of Latin America, 260, *260*; and royal regalia, 84

Cuauhtlehuanitzin, Francisco de San Anton Munon Chimalpahin, 75

Cuba, 273, 283–84

Cuéllar, Juan de, 221

curiosity, culture of, 4, 21–22, 24; and antiquarianism, 58, 60, 66, 71–72, 75; and Capuchin missionaries' illustrations, 143; and global collecting gone "muck," 120; and Martínez Compañón's "museum," 241–42, 246–48, *247*; and Siamese court, 155–56; and Spanish baroque culture, 101, 103, 113. *See also* cabinets of curiosities

Cuzco, 70, 76, 222, 240–41

Cyrillic type, 45

Dale, Thomas, Sir, 117

dal Pozzo, Cassiano, 244

D'Alembert, Jean Le Rond, 244

D'Amboinsche rariteitenkamer (Rumphius), 316n6

Danckerts, Justus, 45, 295n34

Danicorum Monumentorum libri sex (Worm), 78

"dance of the Puris," 265, *266*

Dapper, Olfert, 48, 55, 296n43

Darcy, Francis, 189, 319n27

Daston, Lorraine, 21, 305n21

Dávila, Pedro Franco, 217–18

Debret, Jean-Baptiste, 256, 264, *265*

Debroise, Olivier, 337n25

de Bry, Theodor, 9, 42, 61–62, 66, *67*, 199, *200*, 203, 209

decorative arts: and exotica, 33, 37, 49–50, 53–55, *56*, 296n43; and rediscovery of Latin America, 266–67; and Spanish baroque culture, 100, 103, 111, 113, 306n46

Defoe, Daniel, 50

de Heere, Lucas, 64–66, *65*, 78, 198

De humani corporis fabrica (Vesalius), 107

de la Cruz, Ines, 78

de Landa, Diego, 72, *73*, *74*, 298n34

Delbourgo, James, 178

delftware, 33–34, 296n41

del Río, Antonio, 219–21, 262

Denmark, 195, 262

German language, 11, 103
Germany, 63, 66, 87–88, 90, 198
Gesamtkunstwerk, 27
Gesner, Conrad, 10–11
al-Ghazali, 130
Gheel, George de, *138*, 139, 311n4
Gibraltar, 273, 284
gift exchanges: and Aztec regalia, 84, 87–92,
    97–98; and cabinets of curiosities, 19, 21; and
    global collecting gone "muck," 118, 123, 127,
    129–32, 310n30; and Siamese court, 159–60,
    172–73; and Spanish Americana, 231; and
    Spanish baroque culture, 113
Ginzburg, Carlo, 295–96n36
global collecting/trade, 2, 4, 7–8, 16; and exotica,
    31–39, 41, 55, 57, 293n5; gone "muck," 116–33,
    119; and Japan, 156; and Siamese court, 156–60,
    169, 171–74; and Spanish Americana, 217–35,
    225, 325n17; and Spanish baroque culture,
    101–2, 105, 111–15. *See also* commerce
glyphs, Mayan, 72, 221, 260
goats, 153–54, *plate 7*, 315n48
God's creation, 3, 170, 248
Goetz, Gottfried Bernhard, 37, *plate 1*, 293–94n10,
    294n11
gold: and collecting American bodies, 196; and
    global collecting gone "muck," 129, 131–32; and
    Martínez Compañón's "museum," 241;
    melting of, 6, 83, 89, 96–98, 241; and parasols,
    44–45, 47, 53; and royal regalia, 1, 6, 83, 85,
    88–89, 93, 96–97; and Spanish Americana, 218,
    222; and Spanish baroque culture, 106
Gombrich, Ernst, 103
Gonzalez Ortega, Jesús, 337n24
Gordon, William, 182
Gracián, Baltazar, 15
Graham-Stewart, Michael, 180–81
Greek antiquities: and antiquarianism, 58–61, 63,
    69–71, 77; Greek vases, 43, 59; and Kircher, 17;
    and Oriental "tyranny," 54
Greek language, 11, 76, 239–40
"grotesques," 100
Guadalupe, shrine of, 89
Gualdi, Pedro, 276
Guillobel, Joaquin, 334n30
Guinea (Donker), 47
Guy, John, 186, 319n27

"Habit of a Floridian King" (van Meurs), *48*
Habsburgs, 93; Habsburg Imperial Library, 19;
    and royal regalia, 6, 84, 88–97; tyranny of, 54
Hacienda San Bartolo, 276–77
Haida people, 231
Hakluyt, Richard, 63, 195, 199–200, *200*, 209

Hamilton, William, Sir, 59
Hamzah, Amir, 122
Hannart, Jean, 92
Harriot, Thomas, 9, 61–62, 199, *200*, 203, 209
Harris, Edward, 319n27
Hawaii, 222, 230, 325n21
Hebrew language, 76, 78
Henri II, king of France, 195
Henry II, Holy Roman Emperor, 85
herbaria, 104, 110–11, 248
Herculaneum, 58–59, 244
herders, 64, 66
Herodotus, 71
Hesperiophylo, 242
Heuland, Christian and Conrad, 223
Heywood, Linda, 315n46
Hezeta, Bruno de, 226
Hidalgo y Costilla, Miguel, 287
Hiepes, Tomás, 111, *112*
hieroglyphs, 9, 78, 259–60
Higman, Barry, 182–83
Hijosa, Francisco, 227
Hinduism, 159
Historia chichimeca (Ixtlilxochitl), 76
Histórica relación del reyno de Chile (Ovalle), 248,
    251
Historie of Foure-Footed Beastes, The (Topsell),
    10–11
Holy Roman Empire: emperors of, 1, 6, 83–87,
    89–92, 96, 301n17; and royal regalia, 6–7, 83–98
Hooke, Robert, 105
Horathibodi, Phra, 170
horror vacui, 27
Hospital de San Andrés, 241
house society, 122, 126–27, 129, 309n24
Howard, Thomas, 123
Huaca de Tantalluc (Cajamarca), 218–19
Hualgayoc mines, 244
Hübner, Johann, *46*, 295n34
Hudson, Thomas, 229, 231
Hughes, Mathew, 186, 319n27
Huguenots, 62
Huitzilopochtli, 78
Huitzimengari, Antonio, 76
hukuman, 132
Hulton, Paul, 144
humans, classification of, 8, 209–12, *211*, 255–56,
    257, 261–62, 323n46, 332n3
human sacrifices, 6, 91, 94–95, 280
hunter-gatherer tribes, 63, 69
Hurtado de Mendoza, Andrés, 241
hybridizations, 111

malaria, 243

Malaspina, Alessandro, 232, 242

Malaspina expedition (1789–94), 222, 225, 231–35, *233*

Malays, 7, 122, 126–27, 158

Maldonado, José, 231

Malinche, 272–73

manatee (*peixe-mulher*), 313n17

Mandeville, John, 8

mandrake, 248

Manet, Edouard, 284

manuscripts: of Capuchin missionaries in Central Africa, 7, 134–54, *138, 140, 141*, plates 6, 7, 315n49; Javanese palm-leaf, 7, 117, 122–27, *124, 125, 128*, 131, plate 5. *See also* illustrated texts; *titles of manuscripts*

Many and infinite are the idols of these deserts (anon. watercolor), 153–54, plate 7

Maquinna, Chief, 229, 232–34, *233*

Margaret of Austria, 90–91

Martínez, Crisóstomo, 105

Martínez, Esteban, 224, 226, 228–30

Martínez Compañón, Baltasar Jaime, 9, *plates 9, 10*, 218–19, 236–53, *238, 239, 247, 249, 250*, 325–26n2, 326n5, 327n16, 329–30n43, 330n45, 331nn59,67–69

Martinique women, 273–74, *275*

Martius, Carl Friedrich Philipp, 265

Marvelous Theater [wondertooneel] *of Nature* (Vincent), 38

Mary (sister of Charles V), 97

Masulipatam, 117

Mathison, Gilbert, 189, 319n27

al-Mawahib al-Rabbaniyyah (Alan), 130

Maximilian, emperor of Mexico, 269–73, 280, 284–85, 335n1, 336n15, 337n23; execution of, 270–71, 273, 284–85, 335n1

Maximilian I, Holy Roman Emperor, 84–86, 96

Maxwell, James, 63

Mayas, 9, 70, 72, *73, 74*, 219–21, 260, 262–63, 281, *282*, 324n7

Mbuti people, 139

McLeod, John, 189

media transfers, 33, 37, 39, 53

meditatio mortis, 107

Meeting of Cortés and Montezuma, The (painting), 42

megaliths, 66, 77

megalography, 104

Mehmet, 69

Meisterlin, Sigismond, 63–64

Mejía, Tomás, 337n24

Meléndez, Luis, 306n46

memento mori, 78, 104, 118

memory: and antiquarianism, 61, 66, 77; and forgetfulness, 61, 77; and French albums of Mexico, 269–73, 277, 285, 288, 337n25; theater of, 24

Ménak stories, 122

Menéndez de Avilés, Pedro, 62

Las Meninas (Velázquez painting), 113

Mercure Galant, 155, 172

Mercurio peruano, 242, 328n27

Mercurius Britanicus (1648), 118

Mérida, 70, 72, *74*

Merseyside Maritime Museum, 180

mestizaje, 223

mestizos, 76

mestre, 148–49, *148*

Mexicana (ship), 222, 231, 234–35

Mexican Antiquities, 262

Mexico: and antiquarianism, 69–78, *73, 74*; and Aztec regalia, 6–7, 83–84, 86–92, 95–98; conquest of, 1, 6, 62, 276; French albums of, 10, *plate 12*, 269–88, *271, 272, 275, 279, 282, 287*, 335nn1,2,5, 336n15, 337nn23–25; French occupation of, 269, 286, 335n1, 337n24; independence from Spain, 219, 262, 287; and Martínez Compañón's "museum," 240, 252; rediscovery of, 255, 259–62, *260, 263*, 266; and Spanish Americana, 219–21, 223, 225–26, 230–31, 235, 325n21; and still life painting, 105

Mexico City, 224–25, 262, 266, 273–74, 277, 280, 283, 285

Mexique, 1865 (Falconnet), plate 12, 269–85, *271, 275, 279, 282*

Michoacan, 76

Micrographia (Hooke), 105

microscopes, 105, 111, 170

mimesis, 110, 114, 151–52. *See also* realism

mining industry, 53, 243–44, 255

Ministry of Foreign Affairs (Spain), 231–32

Minor, William, *119*

missionaries, 2, 71, 113; Capuchin, 7, 134–54, *138, 140, 141*, plates 6, 7, 311nn4,5, 8, 311–12n11, 312n10, 313n14, 314nn25,31; French, 156. *See also names of religious orders*

Missionary in Open Land, The (Asti watercolor), plate 6

Missione in prattica (Asti), 137, 142, 145–51, *148*, plate 6 313n17

Mixtec manuscript, 19

Moche culture, 237, *238*

mochica ceramics, 267

Mociño, José Mariano, 231–32, 234

Moctezuma, 1, 6, 42, 69–71, 84, 88–90, 92, 94–95, 272–73

quipus, Incan, 70, 76

Quirós, Fernando de, 226

Quito, 222–23

Rafn, Charles, 259

Raleigh, Walter, 61–62

Ramsay, James, 179

Rasa Carita mwang Kalpa rakwa manawatsa, 122, *124*

Rattanarithikul, Manop and Rampa, 173–74

Ratu, Pangéran, 130–31, 310n30

Reales Alcázares fire (1734), 217

realism: and Capuchin missionaries in Central Africa, 135, 143–44, 151–52; and Spanish baroque culture, 100, 103, 105, 110, 114–15

Reconquista, 70

Reformation. *See* Protestant Reformation

"regime of value," 87

Relación (1662), 16–17, 22

Relación (1802), 234

Relación de la entrada de San Lorenzo de Nutka" (Socies), 325n21

Relación de las cosas de Yucatán (de Landa), 72, *73*, *74*

Relación de los hechos acaecidos en Nutka en 1788 (anon.), 230

Relación histórica (Juan and Ulloa), 244

Relación histórica de la nación tulteca (Ixtlilxochitl), 76

Relation du voyage (Frézier), 244, *245*

relics, 84–87, 92–96; bones as, 106–7, 113; of Christ's Passion, 86, 94, 96; imperial (*Reichskleinodien*), 86, 93–96, 301n17; and Spanish baroque culture, 101, 106–7, 113, 120; viewings of (*Heiltumweisungen*), 85–86, 93–96

religious significance, 3, 10–11.; and antiquarianism, 62–63, 71–72, 74–75; of Capuchin missionaries' manuscripts, 7, 134–54, *138*, *plates 6, 7*; and exotica, 34, 43–45, *44*; and global collecting gone "muck," 118, 123, 126–27, 129–30, 133; and Martínez Compañón's "museum," 241, 243, 248, *249*, *250*, *251*, 253; and rediscovery of Latin America, 260, *260*, 262; and royal regalia, 6–7, 84–96, 98; of "seat of the soul" problem, 108; and Siamese court, 168–70; and Spanish baroque culture, 101, 106, 108, 113, 115. *See also names of religions*

Renaissance, European, 2, 35, 54, 291n17; and antiquarianism, 63, 66, 69–70, 72, 76; and Martínez Compañón's "museum," 246, 248; and Spanish baroque culture, 100–103

Restoration, 39, 42, 45

Revillagigedo, Viceroy, 230–31

rhinoceros, 144–45, 313n20

rhopography, 104–6

Richards, John, 120

Richardson, Abraham, 187

Richardson, Nicholas, 186, 319n27

Ripa, Cesare, 35–37, *36*, 44, 293–94n8, 294n11

Roach, Joseph, 38–39

Roanoke, 193, 198–200, *200*, 209

Roberts, Lissa, 110

Robinson, Anthony, 178–79

Robinson Crusoe (Defoe), 50

Rodríguez de la Flor, Fernando, 102, 108

Roland de la Platière, Jean-Marie, 288

Rolfe, John, 201, *202*

Roman antiquities, 17, 100, 209; and antiquarianism, 58–61, 63, 70, 72, 75, 77–78

Roman literature, 43

Rossi y Rubí, José, 242

Roux, Michel, Madame, 288

Royal Academy of History (Spain), 220

Royal Academy of Sciences (France), 162

Royal Cabinet of Natural History (Madrid), 9, 217–18, 222–24, 227, 229–30, 232, 234–35, 237, 244, 306n46, 323n2, 329–30n43

Royal Mary (ship), 118, 131

Royal Museum of Armors, Antiquities and Ethnology (Brussels), 259

royal regalia, 6–7, 83–98; of Aztecs, 6–7, 83–84, 86–92, 94–98, 301–2n31; as inalienable treasures, 7, 85, 87, 93, 96–98; melting of, 6, 83, 89, 96–98; and Siamese court, 173

Royal Society of London for the Improving of Natural Knowledge, 162

Rudolph II, Holy Roman Emperor, 21

Rugendas, Johann Moritz, 256, *258*, 262, 265, *266*, *267*

Ruiz, Hipólito, 221–22, 232, 242–43

Rumphius, Georg Eberhard, 157, 316n6

runic writing, 61, 76–78

Russel, John, 263

Russia, 45, 223–24, 228–30, 295n34

Ruysch, Frederik, 109

Ruysch, Rachel, 109

Sabean, David, 309n24

sacral treasures, 7, 84–87, 90–91, 93–97

Sacred Congregation of the Propagation of the Faith, 142, 311n5, 313n12

Sahagún, Bernardino de, 74

Sajarah Banten, 130

Salamanca, Gabriel, 92

Salinas, Martín de, 83, 96–97

San Blas (Mexico), 224, 226, 229–31

San Carlos (ship), 228, 230

Sánchez Cotán, Juan, 105, *plate 3*

ACKNOWLEDGMENTS

—ɯɯ—

The essays in this book were first presented in a series of workshops and conferences on early modern global collecting organized by the editors together with Malcolm Baker and Megan O'Neil, sponsored by the USC-Huntington Early Modern Studies Institute with generous funding from the Mellon Foundation, the Borchard Foundation, and the College of Letters, Arts, and Sciences of the University of Southern California. The editors wish to thank our superb editor Bob Lockhart as well as the external reader of the manuscript, the production staff at the University of Pennsylvania Press, the participants and audiences at programs in Los Angeles and Missillac, Brittany, the research division of the Henry E. Huntington Library (especially Roy Ritchie, its director), the staff of the Early Modern Studies Institute (particularly Amy Braden), and our editorial assistant Sarah Goodrum.